RAYMOND E. FEIST

MAGICIAN

APPRENTICE

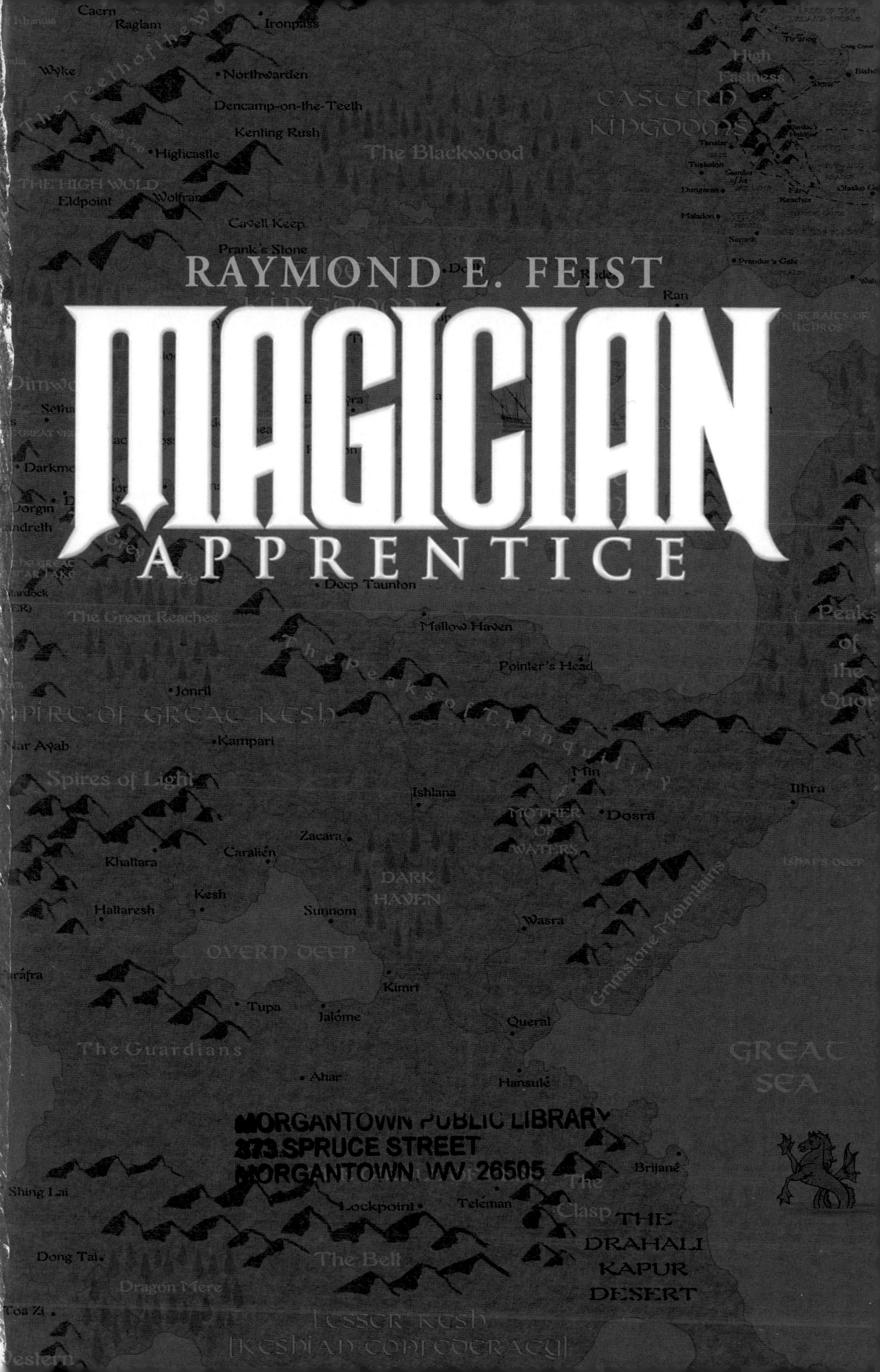
Caern
Raglam
Ironpass
The Teeth of the World
Wyke
Northwarden
Dencamp-on-the-Teeth
Kenting Rush
Highcastle
The Blackwood
EASTERN KINGDOMS
High Fastness
Tiranog
THE HIGH WOLD
Eldpoint
Wolfram
Cavell Keep
Prank's Stone
Tanalar
Tuskalon
Dungaran
Fairy Reaches
Oiasko
Maladon
Semrik
Prandur's Gate
Ran
Darkmoor
Dorgin
Deep Taunton
Mallow Haven
The Green Reaches
Pointer's Head
The Peaks of Tranquility
Peaks of the Quor
Jonril
EMPIRE OF GREAT KESH
Nar Ayab
Kampari
Spires of Light
Min
Ishlana
MOTHER OF WATERS
Dosra
Ithra
Zacara
Khattara
Caralién
DARK HAVEN
Kesh
Hattaresh
Sunnom
Wasra
Grimstone Mountains
OVERN DEEP
Farafra
Kimri
Tupa
Jalóme
Queral
The Guardians
GREAT SEA
Ahar
Hansulé
Brijané
Shing Lai
Lockpoint
Teleman
The Clasp
THE DRAHALI KAPUR DESERT
Dong Tai
The Bell
Dragon Mere
Toa Zi
LESSER KESH
[KESHIAN CONFEDERACY]
Western

Foreword

I've always loved comics. Some of my earliest memories as a child, circa 1951, are of walking down to the corner drug store with a quarter, with which I could buy a candy bar or a soda and two comic books. Ten cents! And for that you got 52 full color pages of all sorts of diverse entertainment. I loved them all. I read Walt Disney Comics and Stories, Captain Marvel, Superman and Action, Batman and Detective, Modern Comics, Rootie Kazootie, and many others.

I also used to root through boxes of old comics my friends' older brothers and sisters had laying around their houses, which is how I discovered back issues of Sub-Mariner, Captain American, and the Invaders. And even more Captain Marvel and Superman.

Then we moved to a community where comics weren't sold, because of the whole ridiculous Seduction of the Innocent nonsense; for those of you too young to remember, Dr. Fredric Wertham published this book in 1954 claiming comics were responsible for all social ills in Western Civilization. And a lot of people bought into the idiocy. So comics more or less vanished from my life for a few years. Then in the late 1950s, I discovered Archie and Friends and other "clean" comics that were charming on their own terms and saw a resurgence of super heroes as the "Silver Age" was born with a new Flash and a new Green Lantern.

Then came Marvel. I was in high school when I discovered a box of comics at a local used bookstore.

I found titles that I had never seen before: Spider-Man, Tales to Astonish, Journey into Mystery, and the Fantastic Four. Once more I was hooked on comics. They were no longer ten cents for 52 pages, but they were still fun. And they were different! Spider-Man was a high school kid like me, and moreover, he was a nerd! He was pushed around by the jocks and ignored by the pretty girls at school and I had a super hero I could identify with!

Despite having "grown up," I still maintain my love of the art form known as comic books (or funny books as we called them when I was a kid). I still head down to the local store a couple of times a month and buy a lot of different things, and now I take my kids.

And now they see a comic with my name on the cover. When I was approached to do a comic book adaptation of my first novel, Magician, by the Dabel Brothers, as soon as they told me how they wished to proceed, I agreed. And to have the entire project published by Marvel is a double joy, for to my way of thinking, Stan Lee, Jack Kirby, Steve Ditko, and a handful of others reinvented the art form in the 1960's.

Seeing my own creation through the eyes of other creators has been a pure joy. You hold in your hands what I hope is but the first of many future volumes which will continue to take my novels and turn them into my first love as a reader, a comic book. Oh, we call them graphic novels now, because they're large and cover a lot of story, but in my heart they will always be "comics!"

Raymond E. Feist
January, 2007

WRITER **RAYMOND E. FEIST**   ADAPTATION **MICHAEL AVON OEMING & BRYAN J. GLASS**

ARTWORK **BRETT BOOTH** (CHAPTERS 1-3) & **RYAN STEGMAN** (CHAPTERS 4-6)

COLORS **VINICIUS ANDRADE** (CHAPTERS 1-3) & **KIERAN OATS** (CHAPTERS 4-6)

LETTERS **SIMON BOWLAND**   EDITOR **SEAN JORDAN**

For Dabel Brothers: **Matt Hansen** *Editor in Chief,* **Mike Raicht** *Managing Editor,* **Bill Tortolini** *Art Director,* **Les Dabel** *Vice President ,* **Ernst Dabel** *President*

For Marvel: **Jeff Youngquist** *Senior Editor, Special Projects ,* **David Gabriel** *Senior Vice President of Sales ,* **Tom Marvelli** *Vice President of Creative ,* **Joe Quesada** *Editor in Chief ,* **Dan Buckley** *Publisher*

CHAPTER ONE

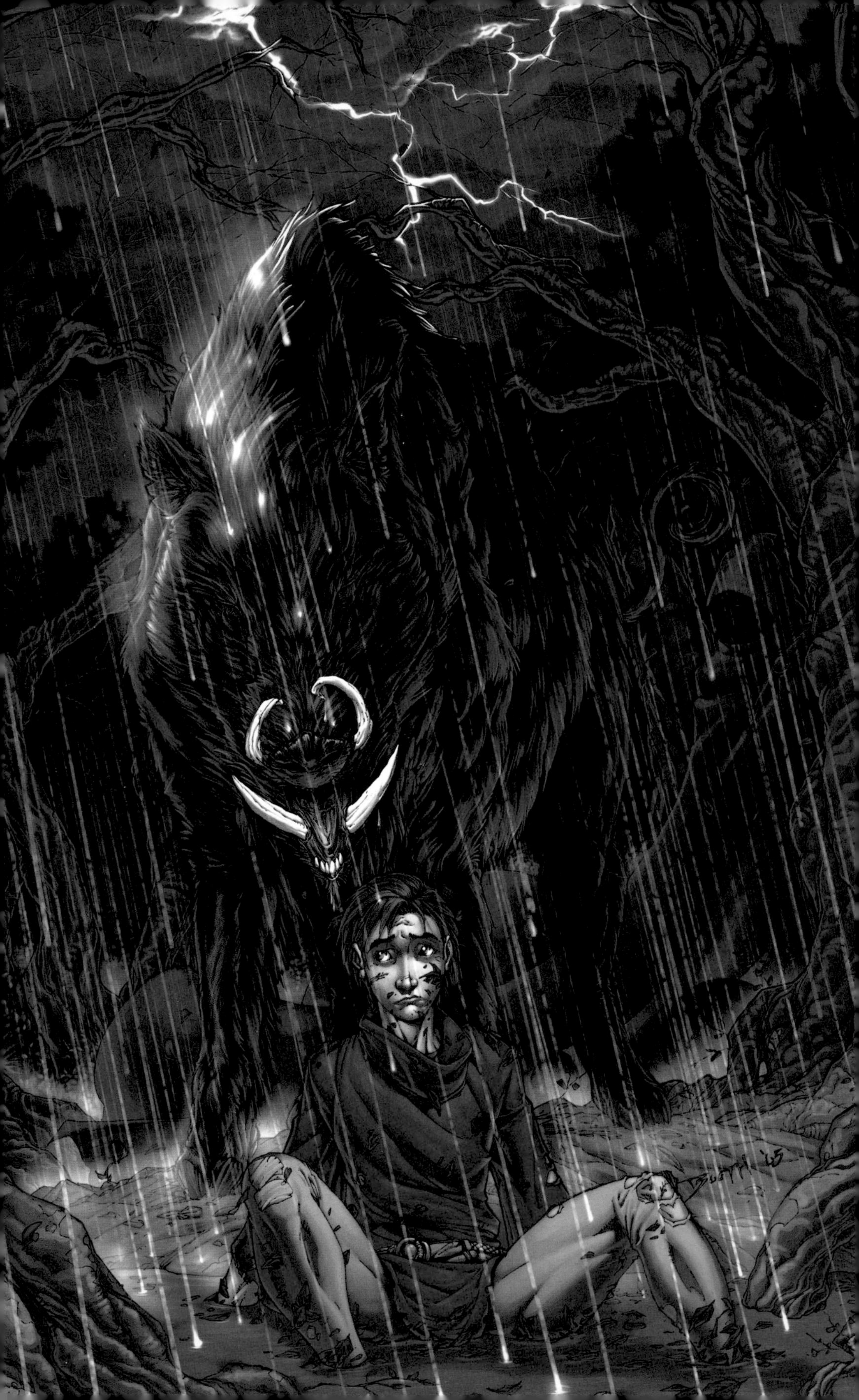

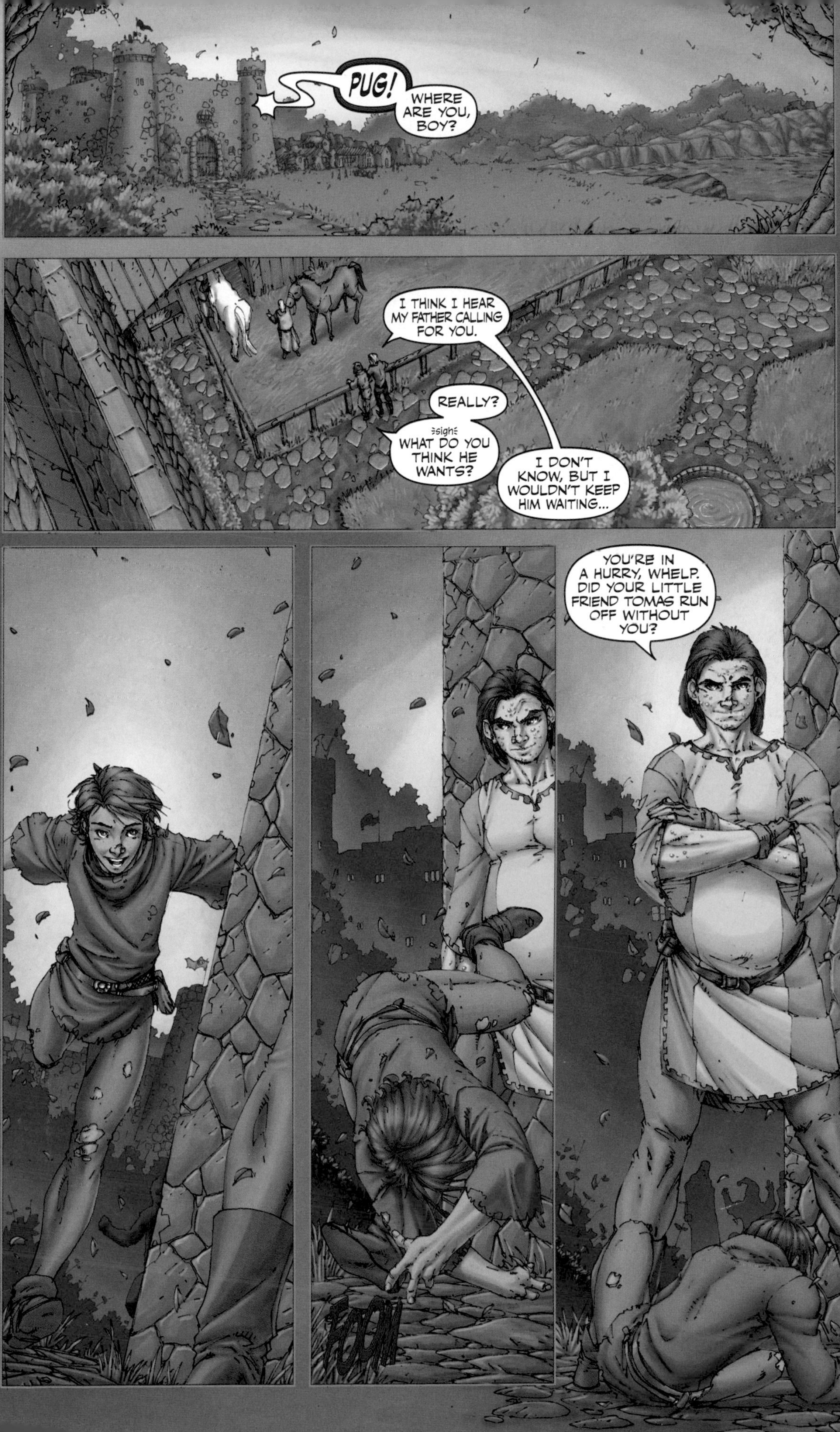
PUG!
WHERE ARE YOU, BOY?
I THINK I HEAR MY FATHER CALLING FOR YOU.
REALLY?
sigh
WHAT DO YOU THINK HE WANTS?
I DON'T KNOW, BUT I WOULDN'T KEEP HIM WAITING...
FOOM!
YOU'RE IN A HURRY, WHELP. DID YOUR LITTLE FRIEND TOMAS RUN OFF WITHOUT YOU?

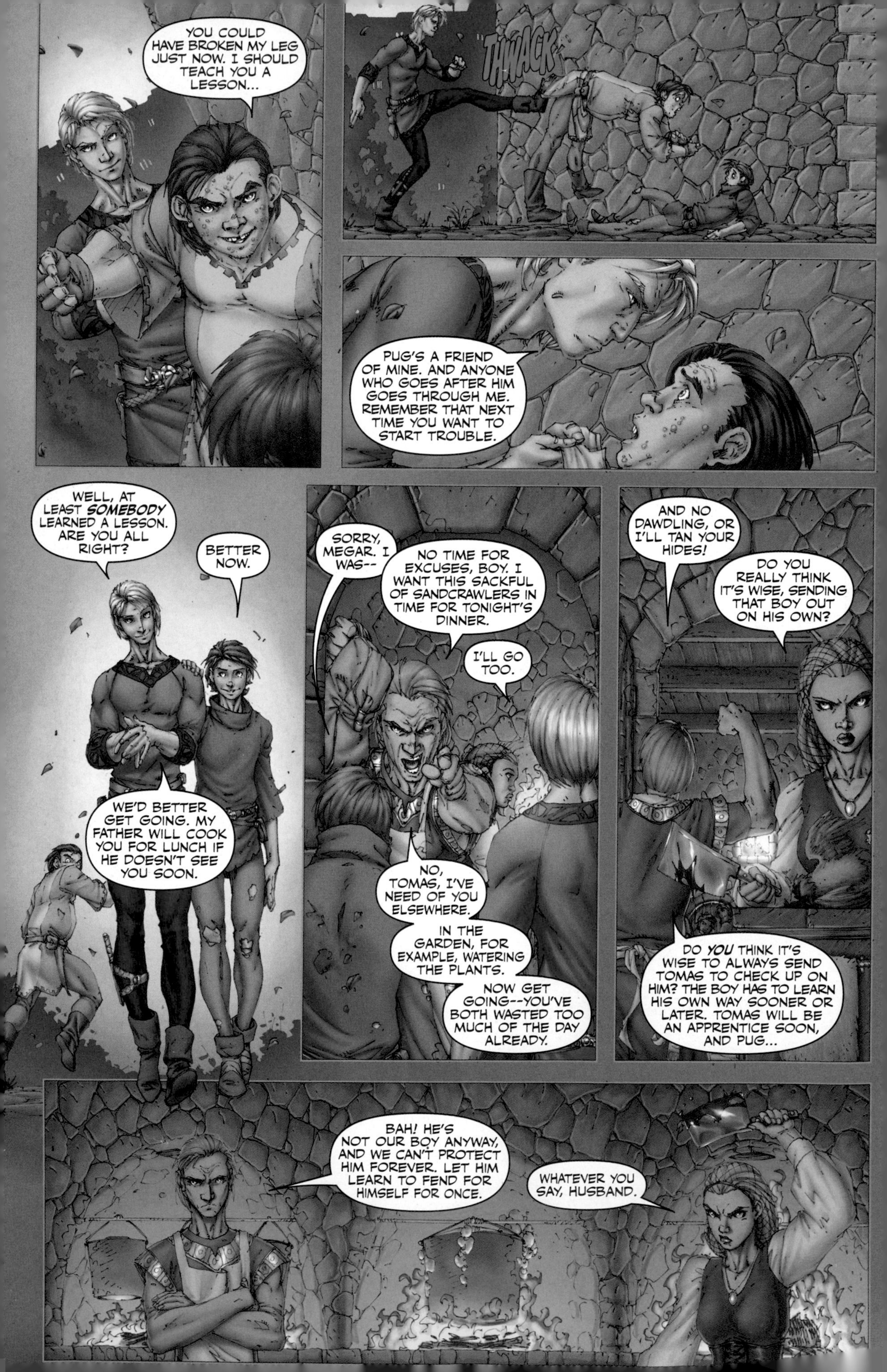
YOU COULD HAVE BROKEN MY LEG JUST NOW. I SHOULD TEACH YOU A LESSON...
THWACK
PUG'S A FRIEND OF MINE. AND ANYONE WHO GOES AFTER HIM GOES THROUGH ME. REMEMBER THAT NEXT TIME YOU WANT TO START TROUBLE.
WELL, AT LEAST SOMEBODY LEARNED A LESSON. ARE YOU ALL RIGHT?
BETTER NOW.
WE'D BETTER GET GOING. MY FATHER WILL COOK YOU FOR LUNCH IF HE DOESN'T SEE YOU SOON.
SORRY, MEGAR. I WAS--
NO TIME FOR EXCUSES, BOY. I WANT THIS SACKFUL OF SANDCRAWLERS IN TIME FOR TONIGHT'S DINNER.
I'LL GO TOO.
NO, TOMAS, I'VE NEED OF YOU ELSEWHERE.
IN THE GARDEN, FOR EXAMPLE, WATERING THE PLANTS.
NOW GET GOING--YOU'VE BOTH WASTED TOO MUCH OF THE DAY ALREADY.
AND NO DAWDLING, OR I'LL TAN YOUR HIDES!
DO YOU REALLY THINK IT'S WISE, SENDING THAT BOY OUT ON HIS OWN?
DO YOU THINK IT'S WISE TO ALWAYS SEND TOMAS TO CHECK UP ON HIM? THE BOY HAS TO LEARN HIS OWN WAY SOONER OR LATER. TOMAS WILL BE AN APPRENTICE SOON, AND PUG...
BAH! HE'S NOT OUR BOY ANYWAY, AND WE CAN'T PROTECT HIM FOREVER. LET HIM LEARN TO FEND FOR HIMSELF FOR ONCE.
WHATEVER YOU SAY, HUSBAND.

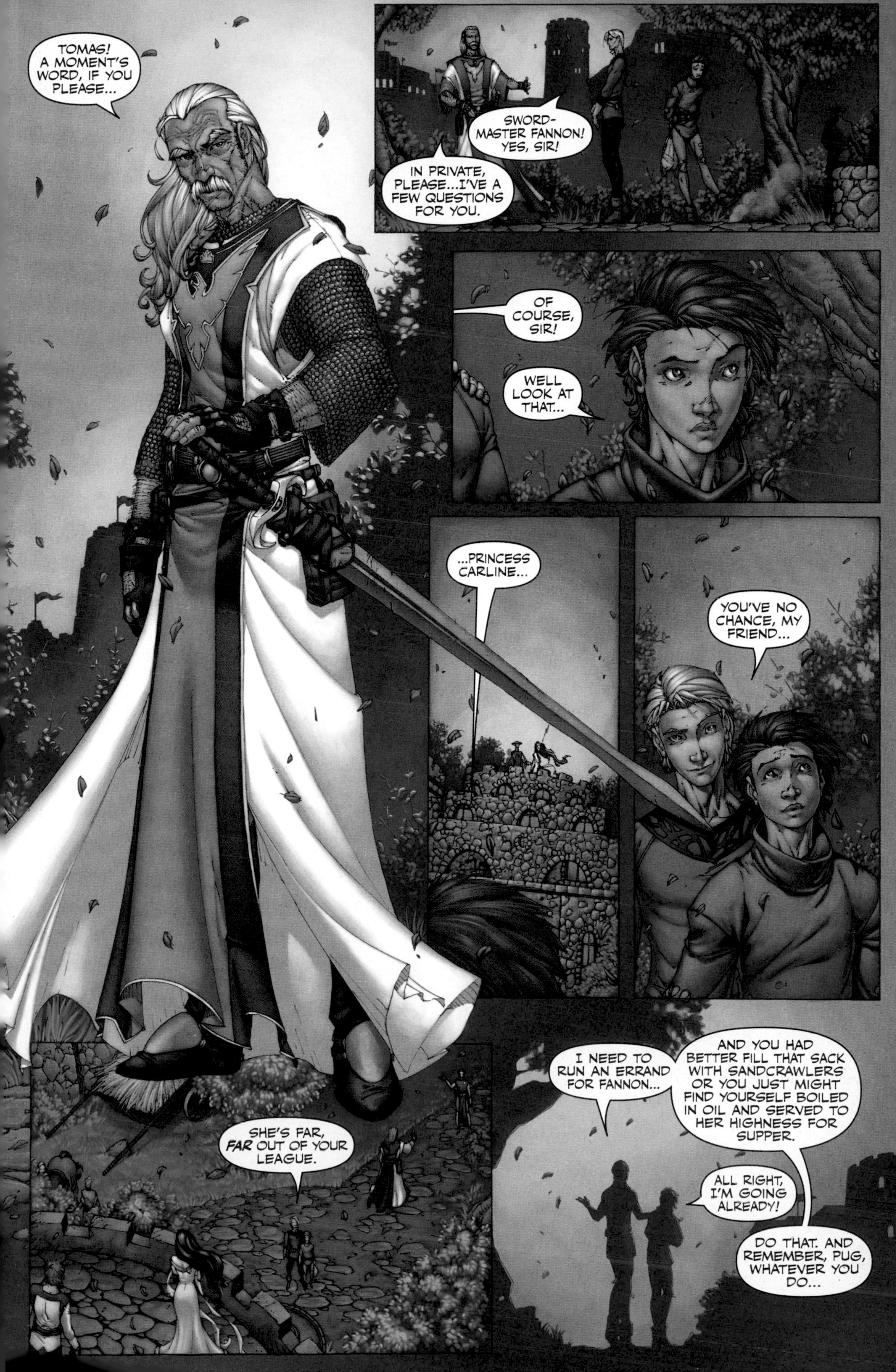
TOMAS! A MOMENT'S WORD, IF YOU PLEASE...
SWORD-MASTER FANNON! YES, SIR!
IN PRIVATE, PLEASE...I'VE A FEW QUESTIONS FOR YOU.
OF COURSE, SIR!
WELL LOOK AT THAT...
...PRINCESS CARLINE...
YOU'VE NO CHANCE, MY FRIEND...
SHE'S FAR, *FAR* OUT OF YOUR LEAGUE.
I NEED TO RUN AN ERRAND FOR FANNON...
AND YOU HAD BETTER FILL THAT SACK WITH SANDCRAWLERS OR YOU JUST MIGHT FIND YOURSELF BOILED IN OIL AND SERVED TO HER HIGHNESS FOR SUPPER.
ALL RIGHT, I'M GOING ALREADY!
DO THAT. AND REMEMBER, PUG, WHATEVER YOU DO...

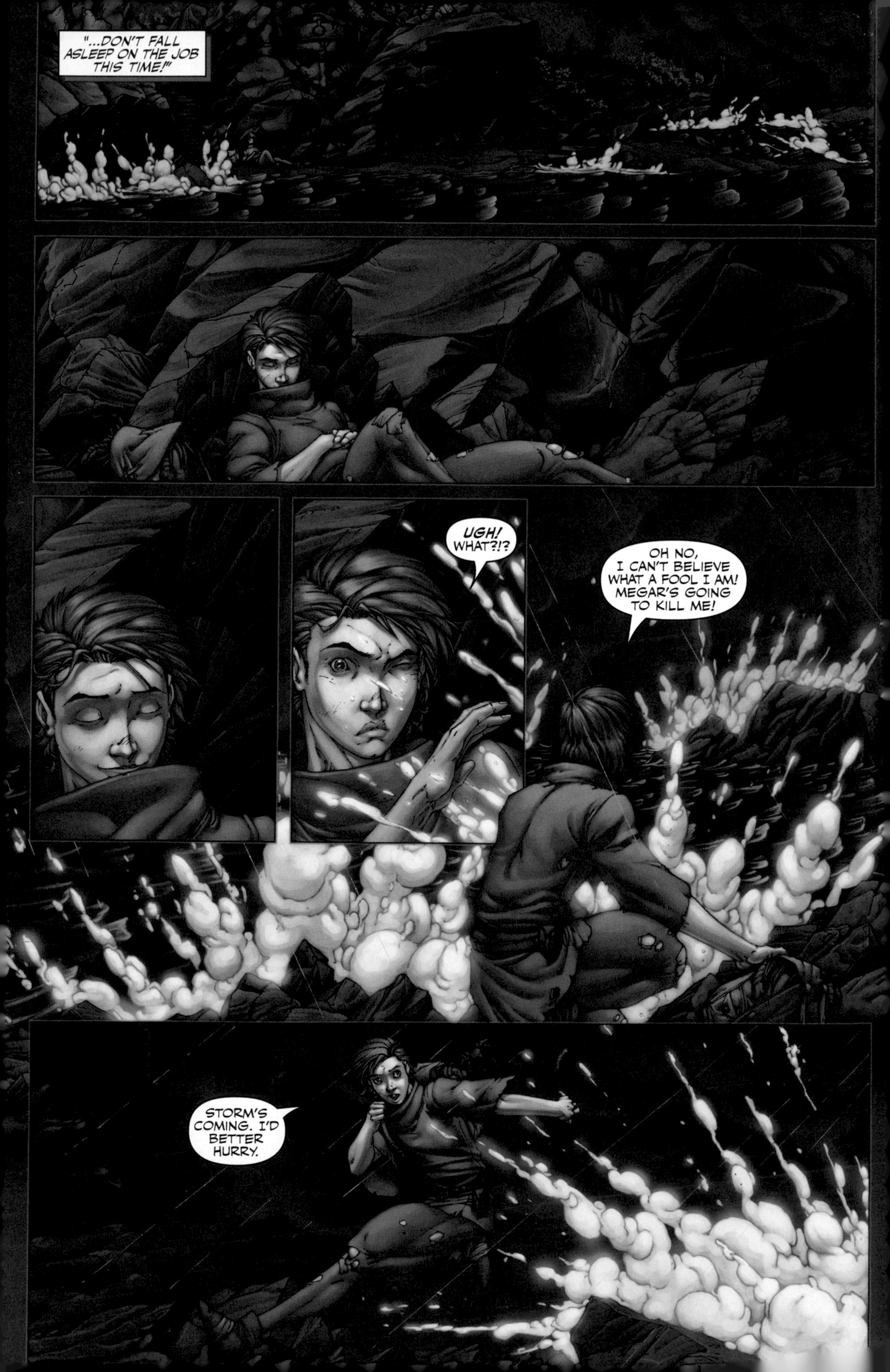
"...DON'T FALL ASLEEP ON THE JOB THIS TIME!"
UGH! WHAT?!?
OH NO, I CAN'T BELIEVE WHAT A FOOL I AM! MEGAR'S GOING TO KILL ME!
STORM'S COMING. I'D BETTER HURRY.

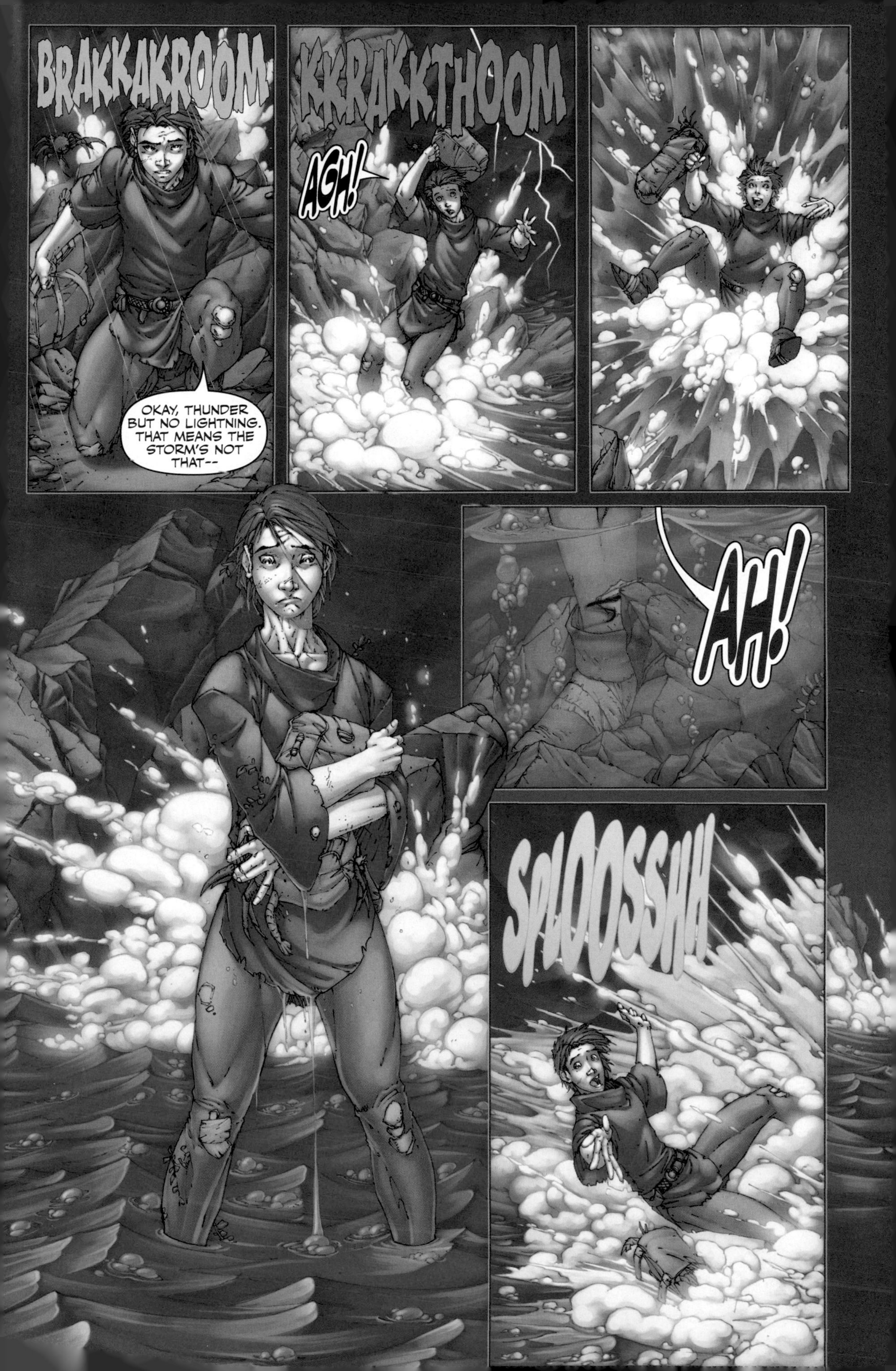
BRAKKAKROOM
OKAY, THUNDER BUT NO LIGHTNING. THAT MEANS THE STORM'S NOT THAT--
KKRAKKTHOOM
AGH!
AH!
SPLOOSSHH

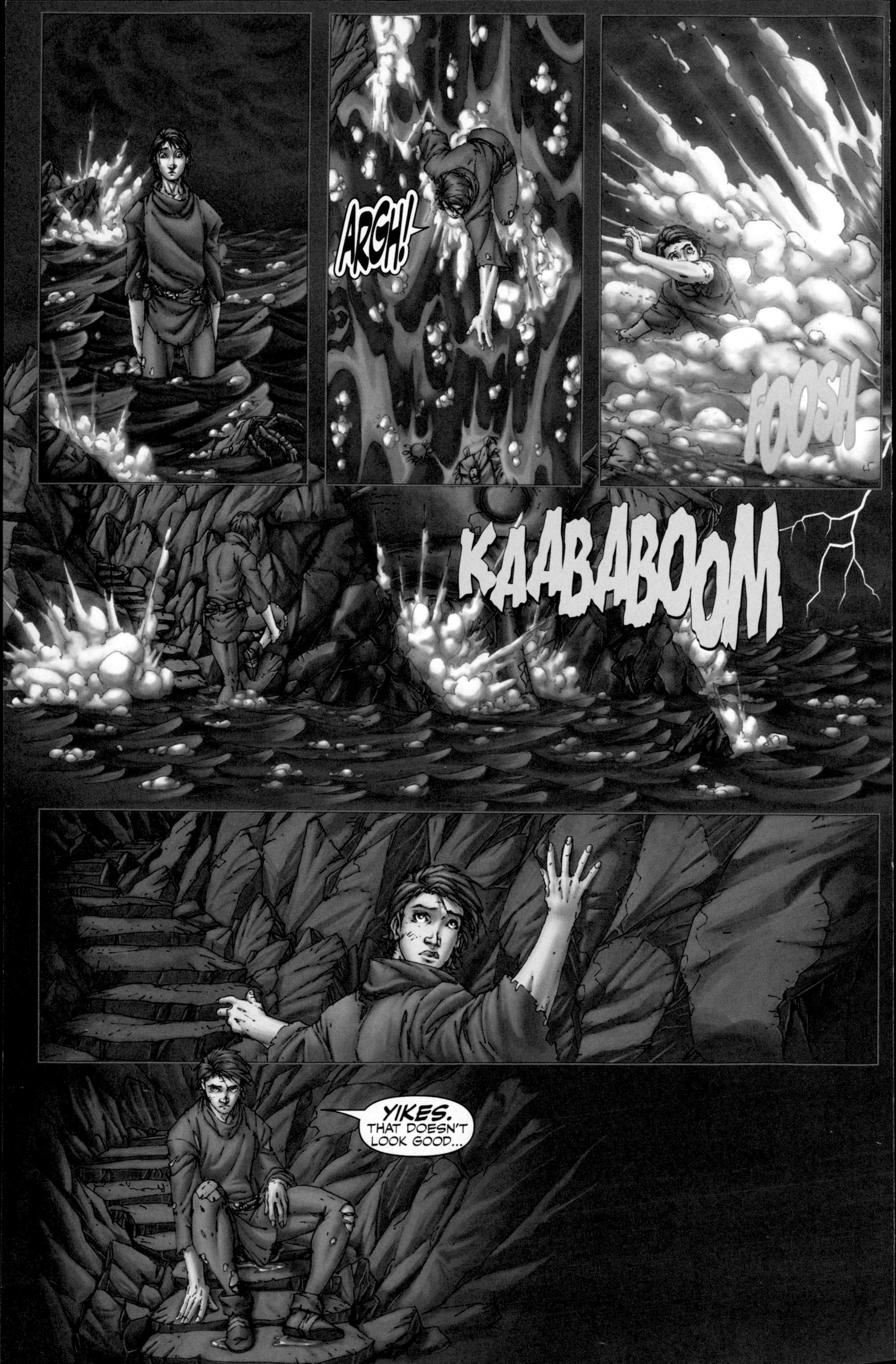
ARGH!
FOOSH
KAABABOOM
YIKES. THAT DOESN'T LOOK GOOD...

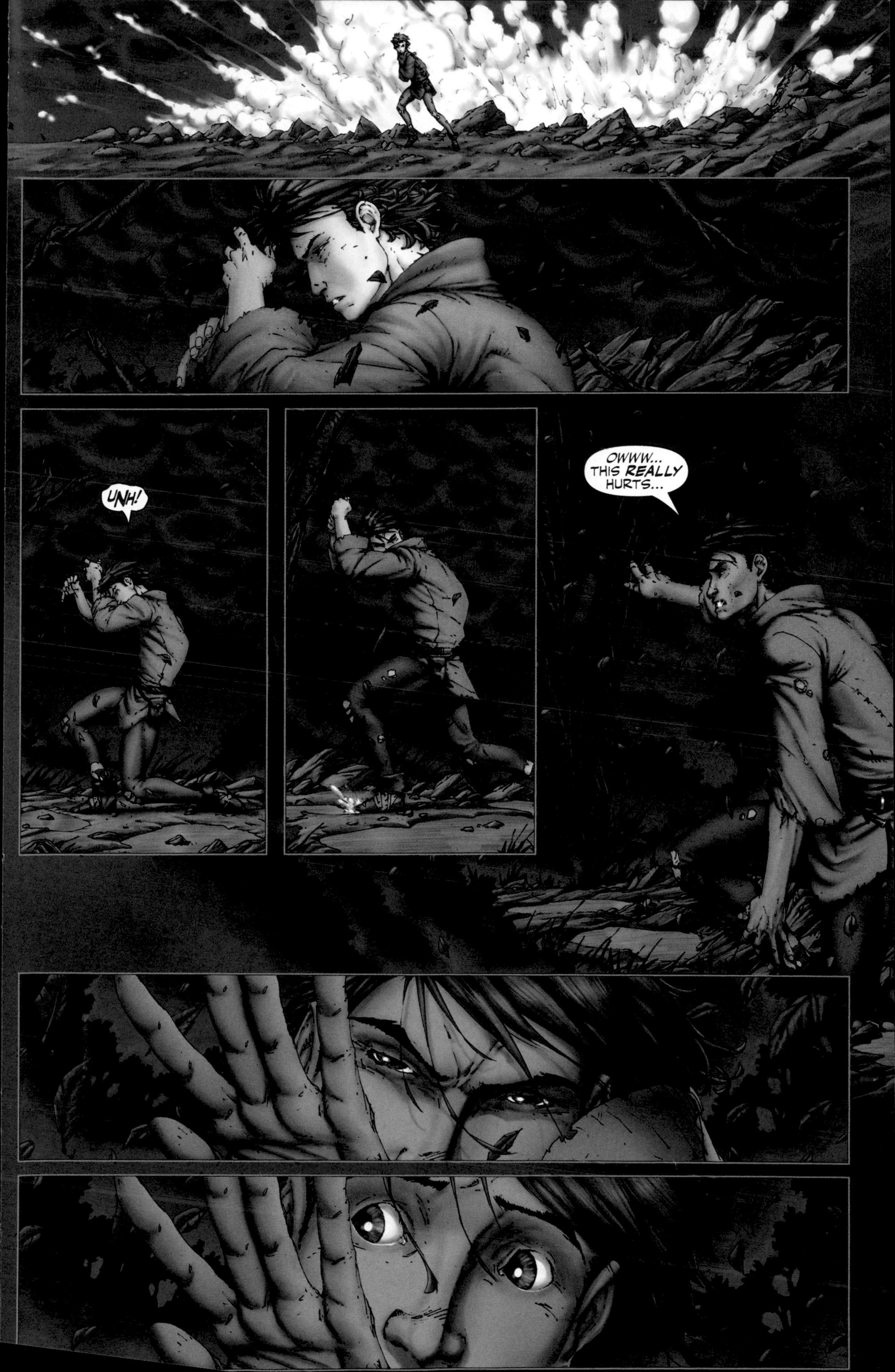
UNH!
OWWW... THIS REALLY HURTS...

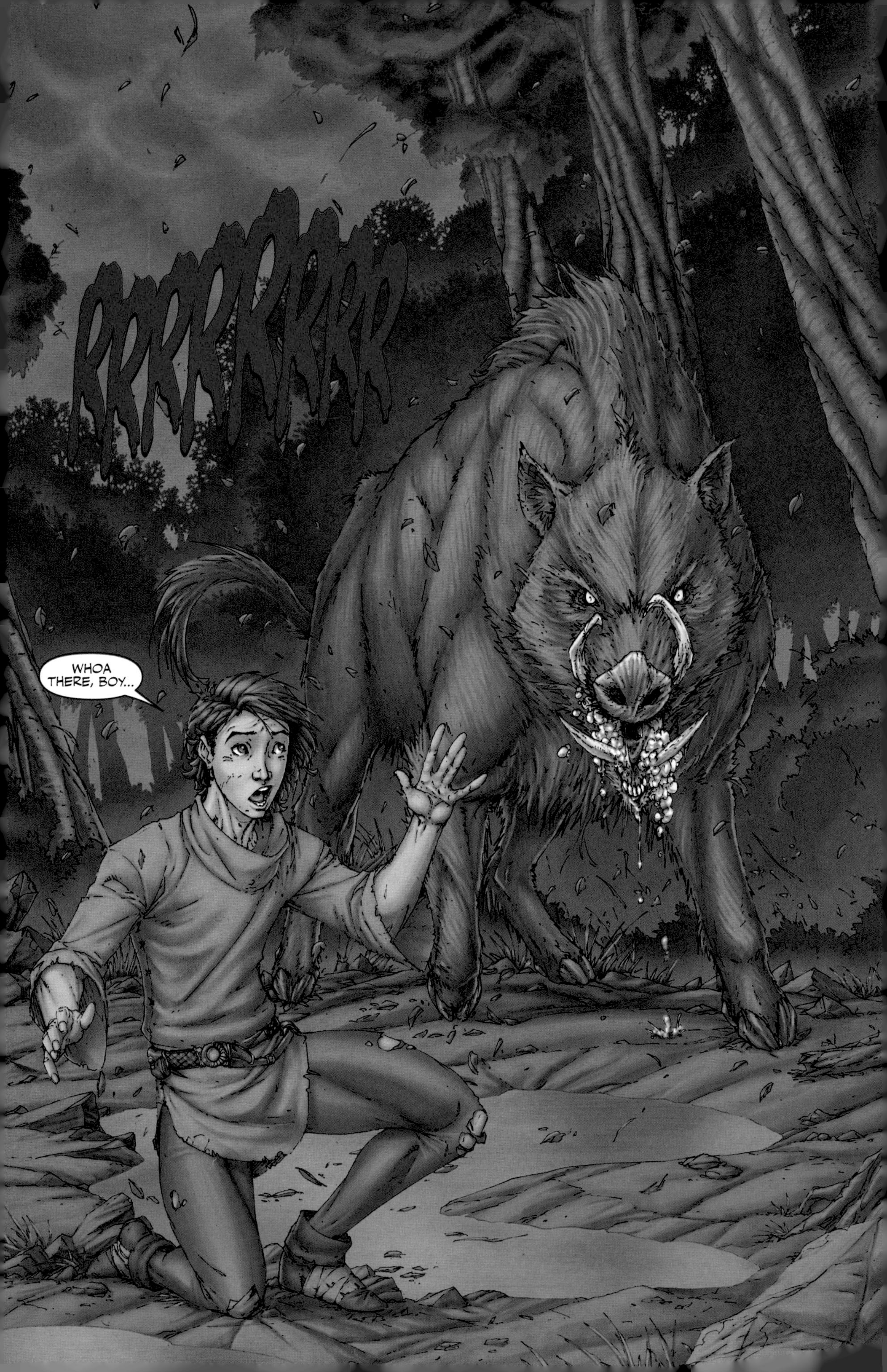
RRRRRRRRR
WHOA THERE, BOY...

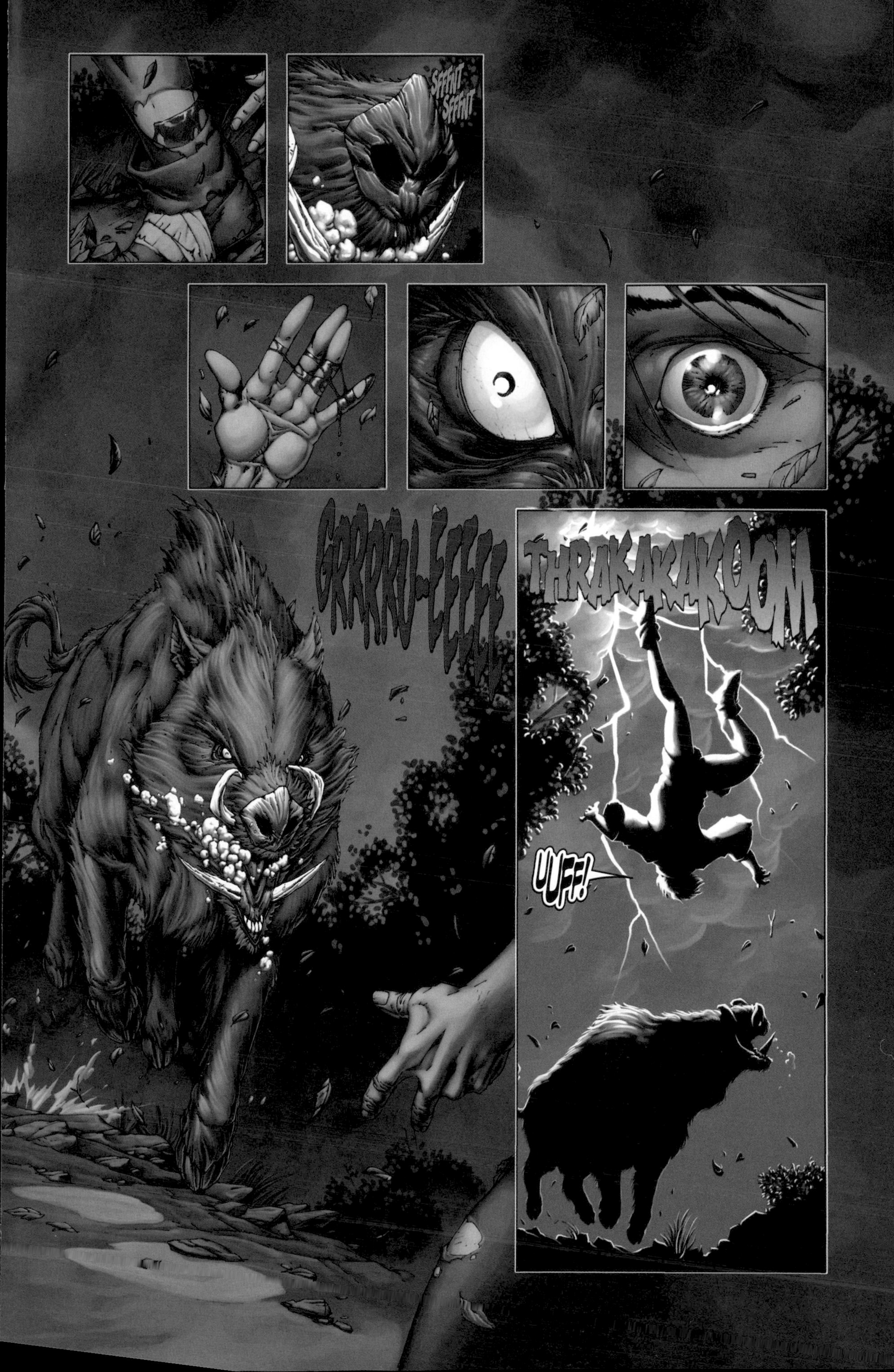
SFFFNT SFFFNT
GRRRU-EEEE
THRAKAKAKOOM
UUFF!

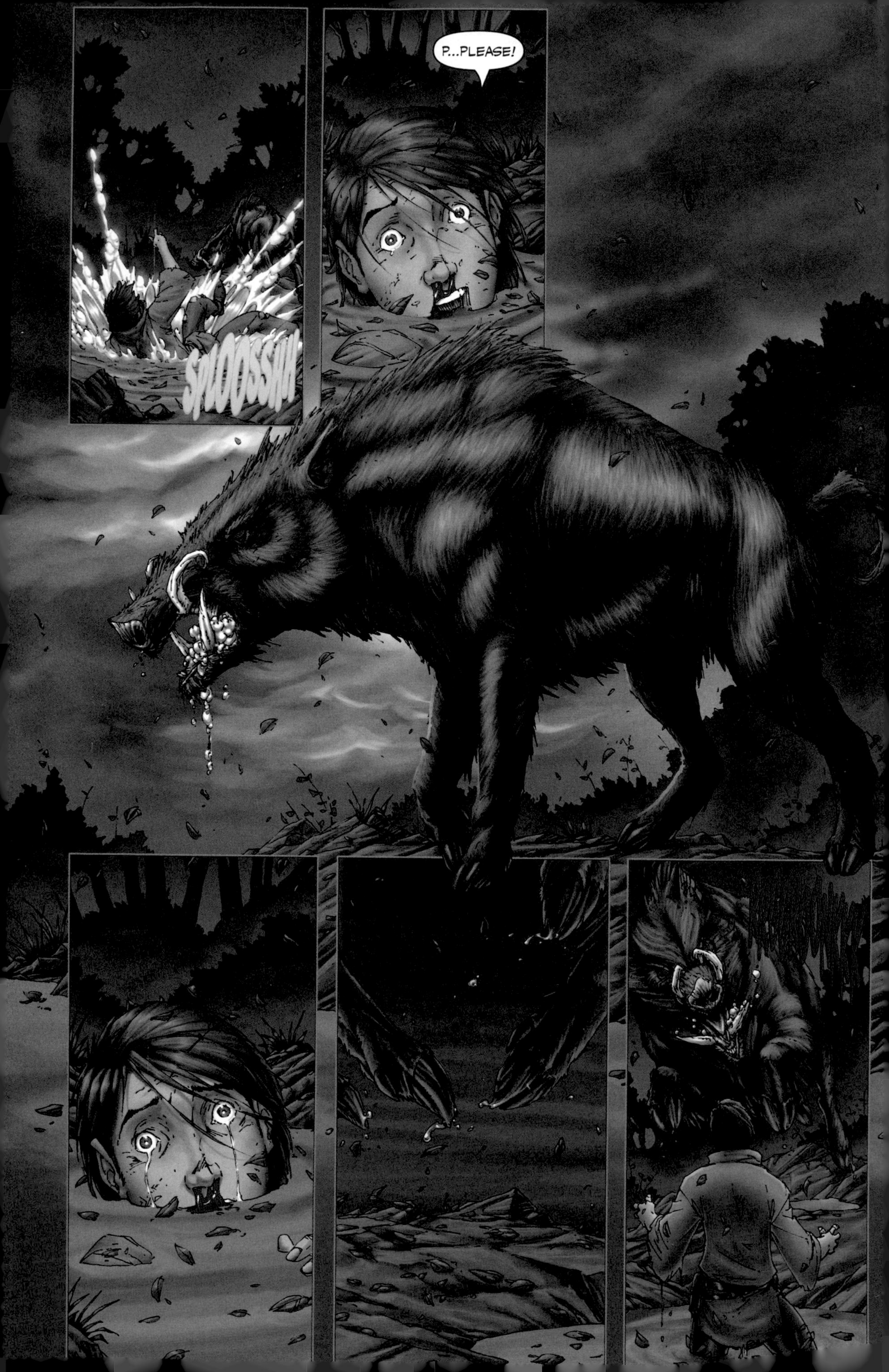
SPLOOSSHH
P...PLEASE!

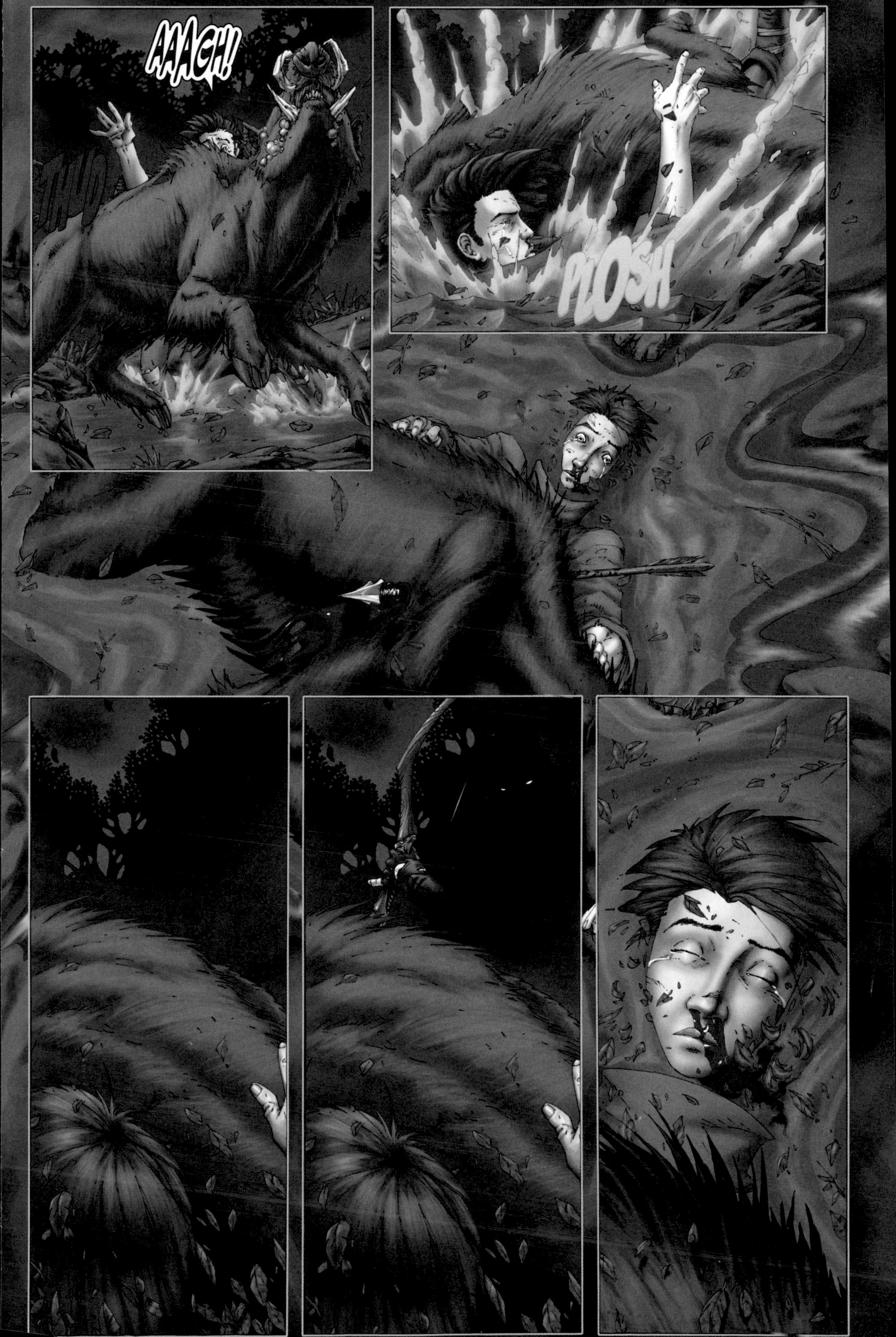
AAAGH!
PLOSH

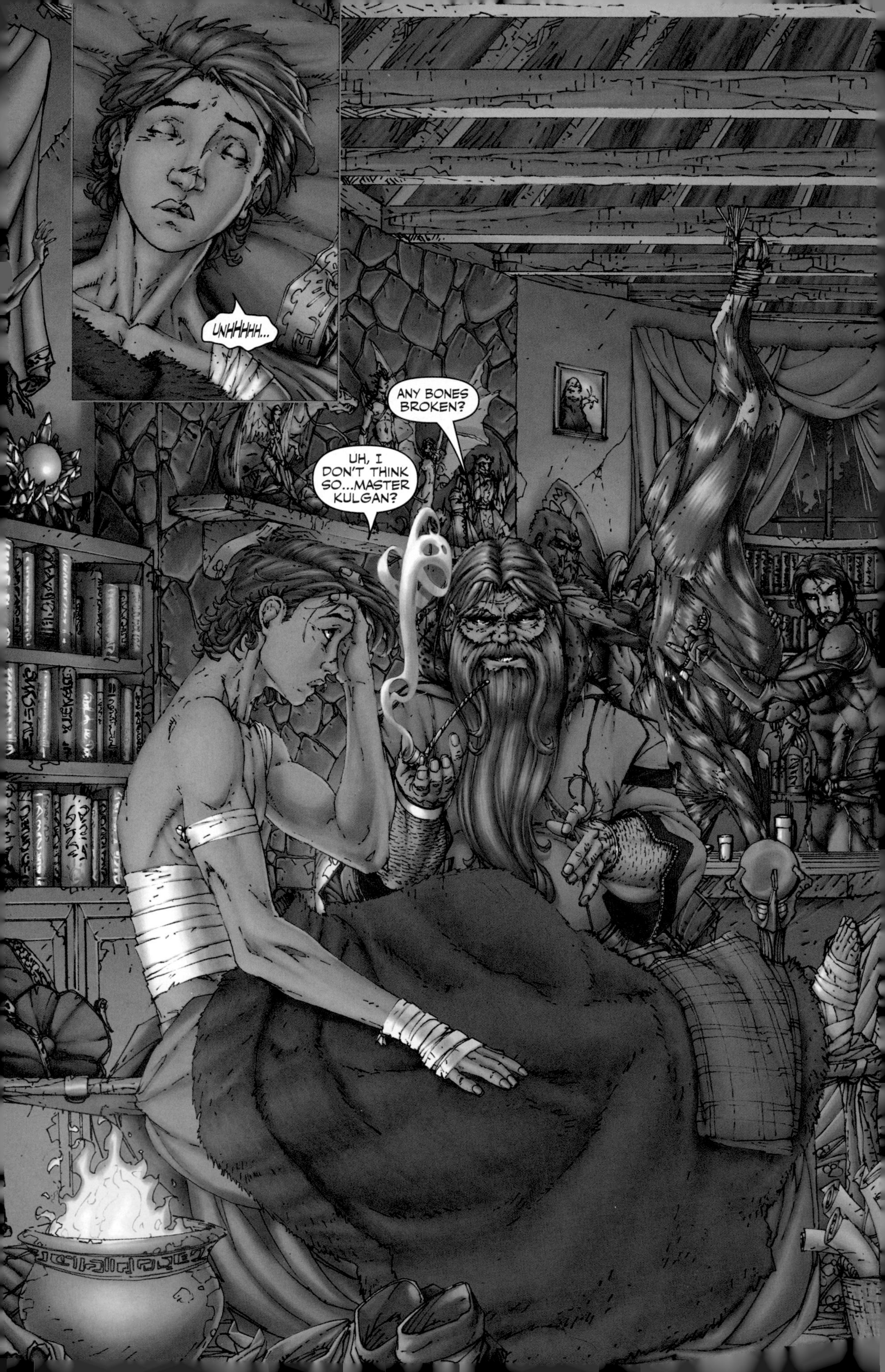
UNHHHHH...
ANY BONES BROKEN?
UH, I DON'T THINK SO...MASTER KULGAN?

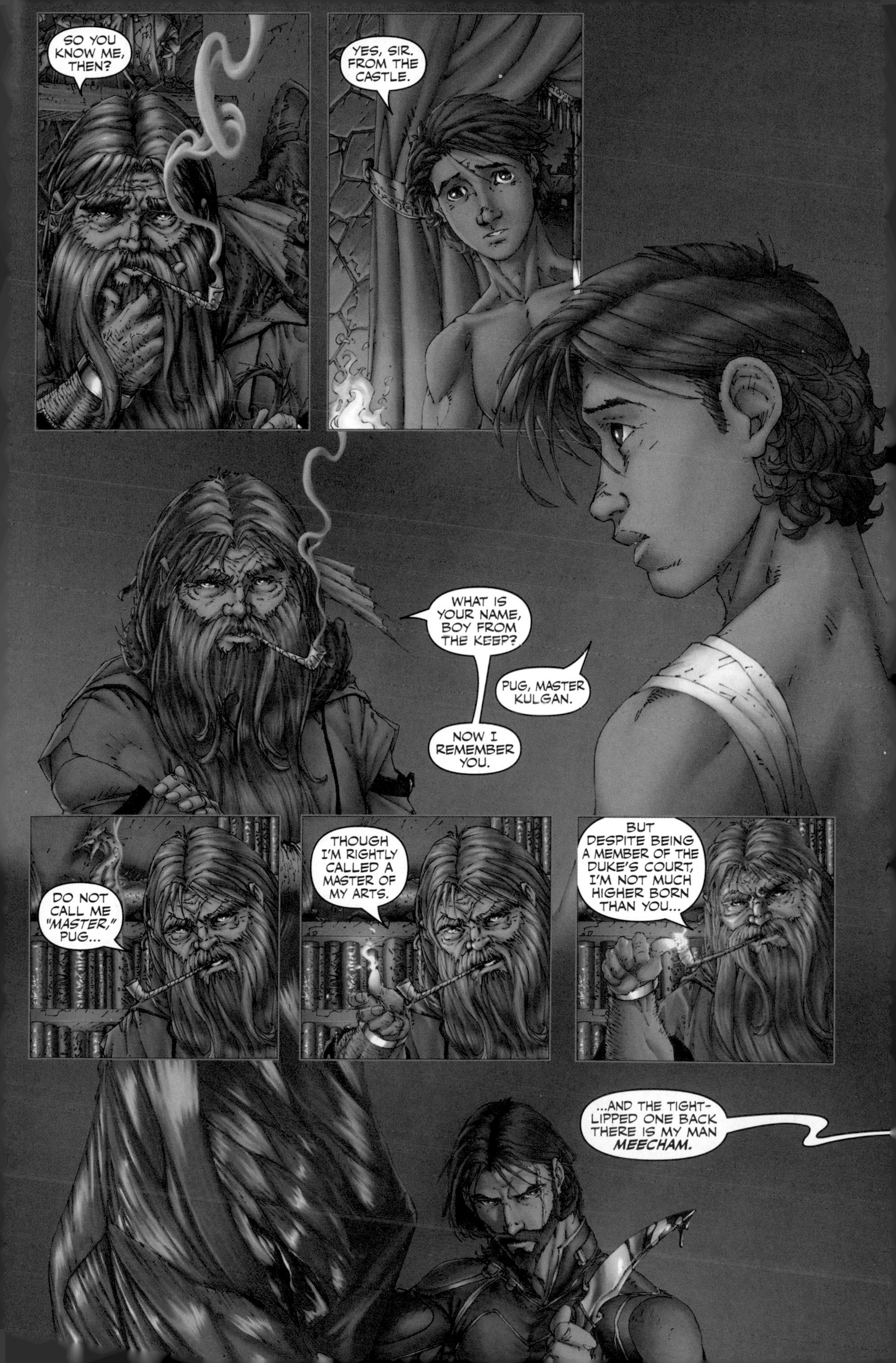
SO YOU KNOW ME, THEN?
YES, SIR. FROM THE CASTLE.
WHAT IS YOUR NAME, BOY FROM THE KEEP?
PUG, MASTER KULGAN.
NOW I REMEMBER YOU.
DO NOT CALL ME "MASTER," PUG...
THOUGH I'M RIGHTLY CALLED A MASTER OF MY ARTS.
BUT DESPITE BEING A MEMBER OF THE DUKE'S COURT, I'M NOT MUCH HIGHER BORN THAN YOU...
...AND THE TIGHT-LIPPED ONE BACK THERE IS MY MAN *MEECHAM.*

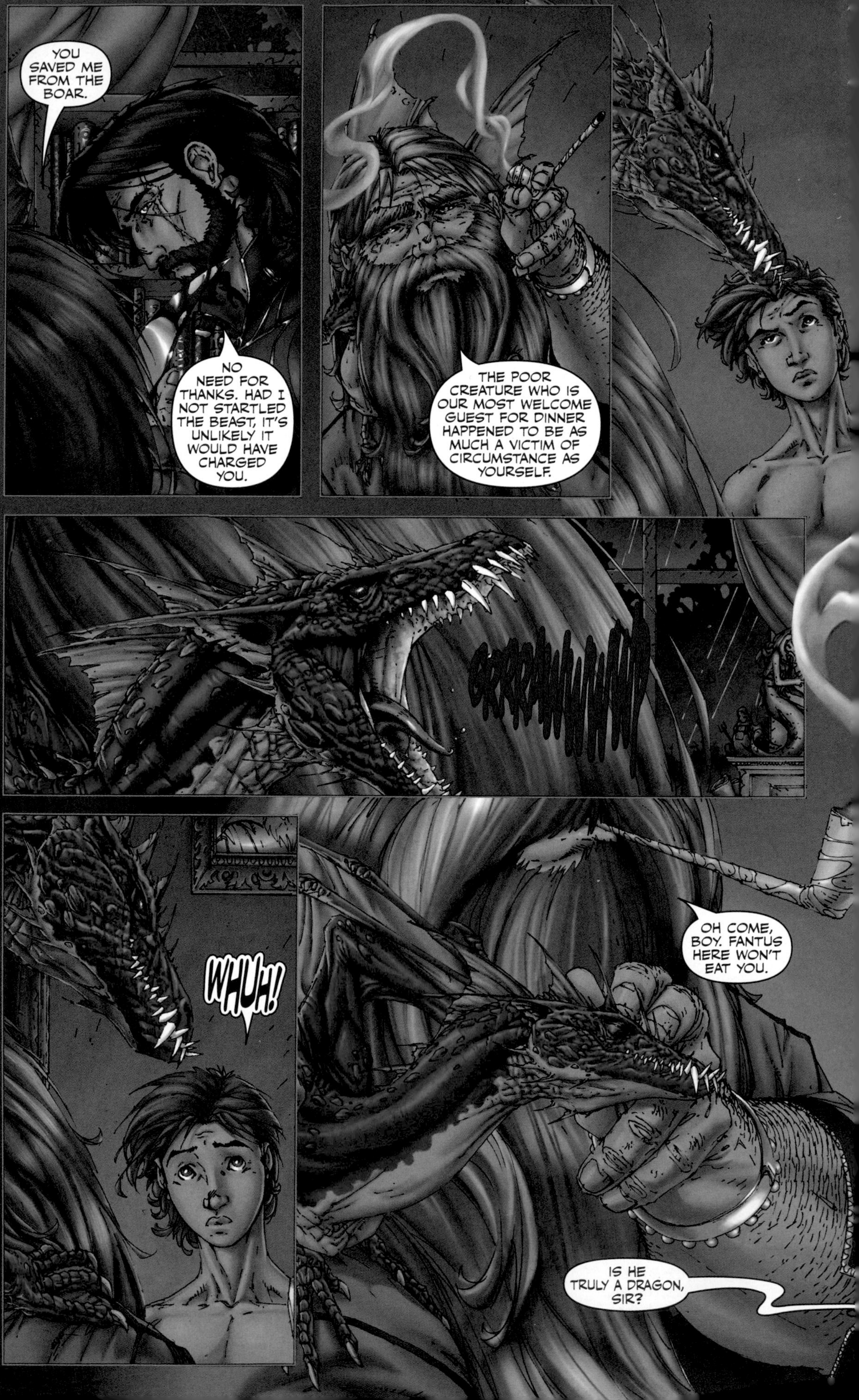

YOU SAVED ME FROM THE BOAR.
NO NEED FOR THANKS. HAD I NOT STARTLED THE BEAST, IT'S UNLIKELY IT WOULD HAVE CHARGED YOU.
THE POOR CREATURE WHO IS OUR MOST WELCOME GUEST FOR DINNER HAPPENED TO BE AS MUCH A VICTIM OF CIRCUMSTANCE AS YOURSELF.
GRRRAWWWW!
WHUH!
OH COME, BOY. FANTUS HERE WON'T EAT YOU.
IS HE TRULY A DRAGON, SIR?

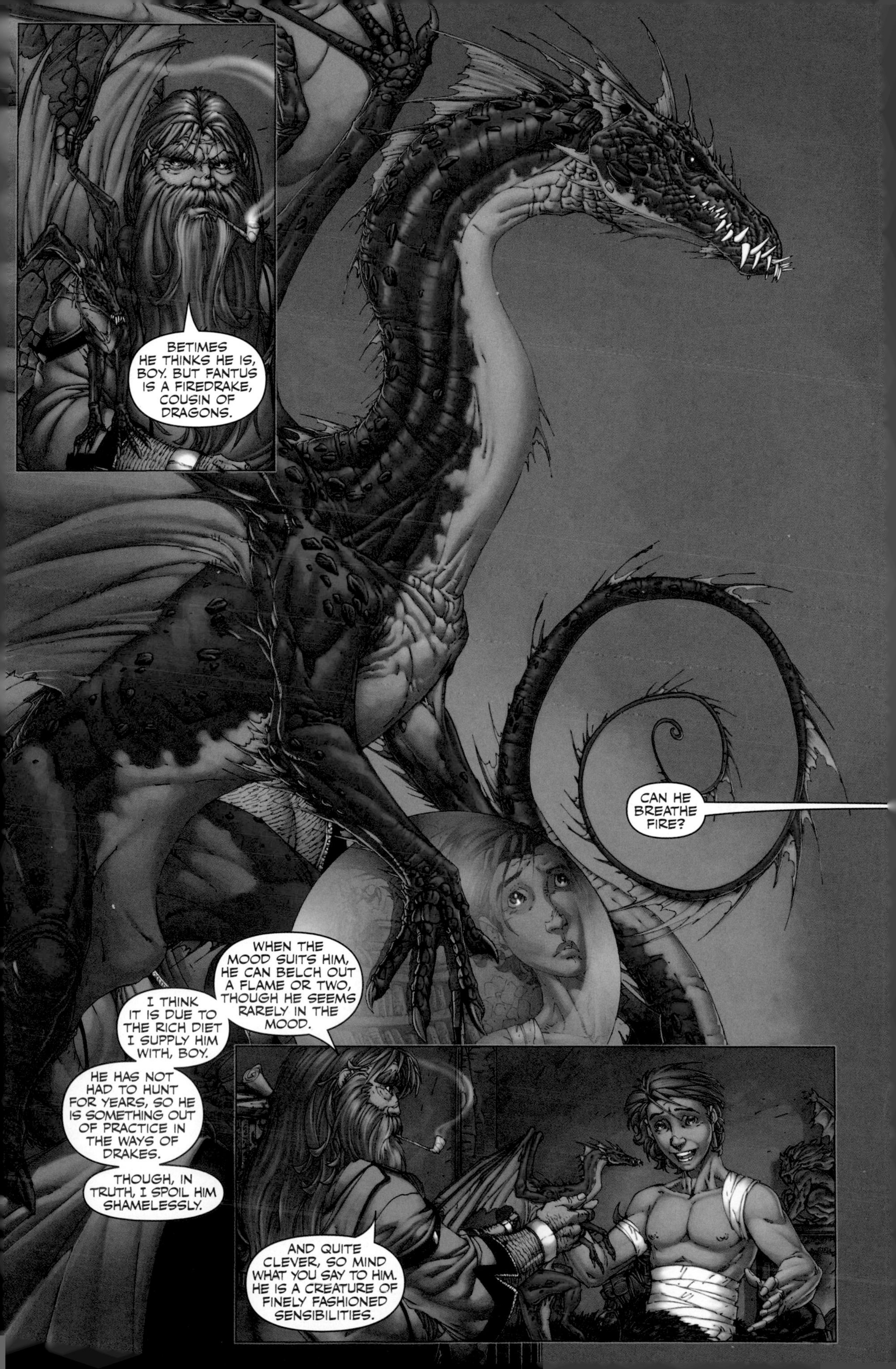
BETIMES HE THINKS HE IS, BOY. BUT FANTUS IS A FIREDRAKE, COUSIN OF DRAGONS.
CAN HE BREATHE FIRE?
WHEN THE MOOD SUITS HIM, HE CAN BELCH OUT A FLAME OR TWO, THOUGH HE SEEMS RARELY IN THE MOOD.
I THINK IT IS DUE TO THE RICH DIET I SUPPLY HIM WITH, BOY.
HE HAS NOT HAD TO HUNT FOR YEARS, SO HE IS SOMETHING OUT OF PRACTICE IN THE WAYS OF DRAKES.
THOUGH, IN TRUTH, I SPOIL HIM SHAMELESSLY.
AND QUITE CLEVER, SO MIND WHAT YOU SAY TO HIM. HE IS A CREATURE OF FINELY FASHIONED SENSIBILITIES.

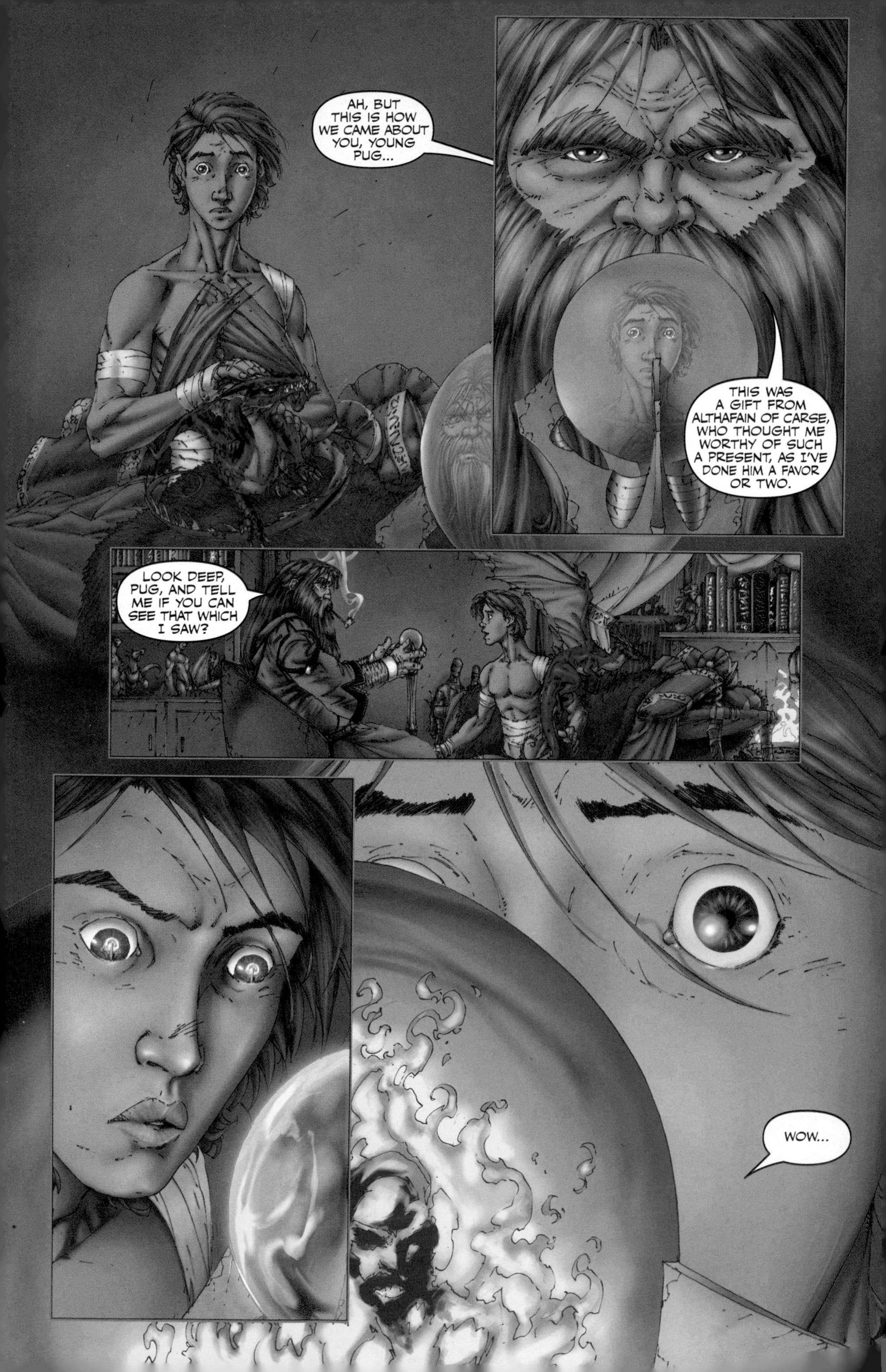
AH, BUT THIS IS HOW WE CAME ABOUT YOU, YOUNG PUG...
THIS WAS A GIFT FROM ALTHAFAIN OF CARSE, WHO THOUGHT ME WORTHY OF SUCH A PRESENT, AS I'VE DONE HIM A FAVOR OR TWO.
LOOK DEEP, PUG, AND TELL ME IF YOU CAN SEE THAT WHICH I SAW?
WOW...

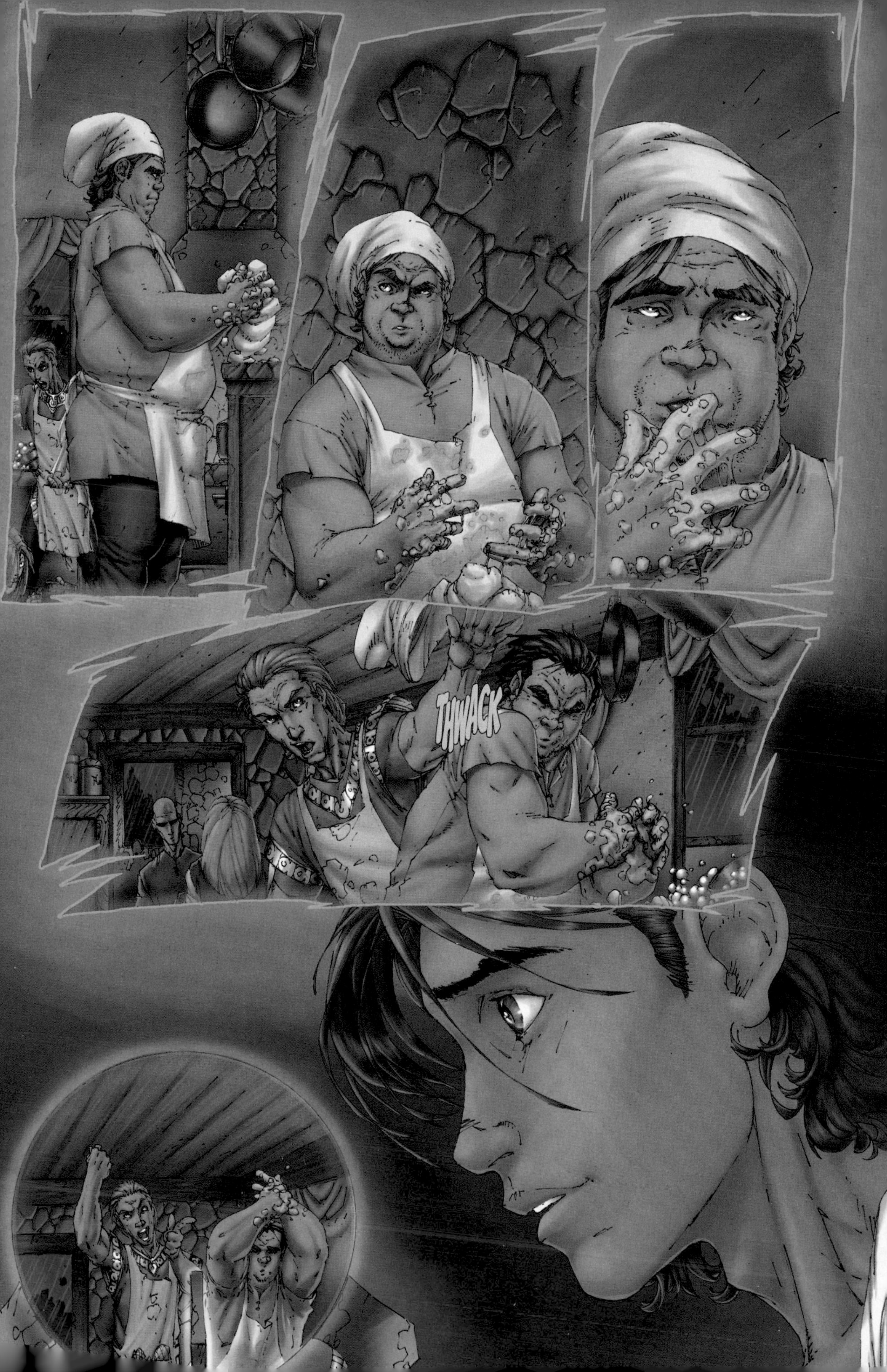
THWACK

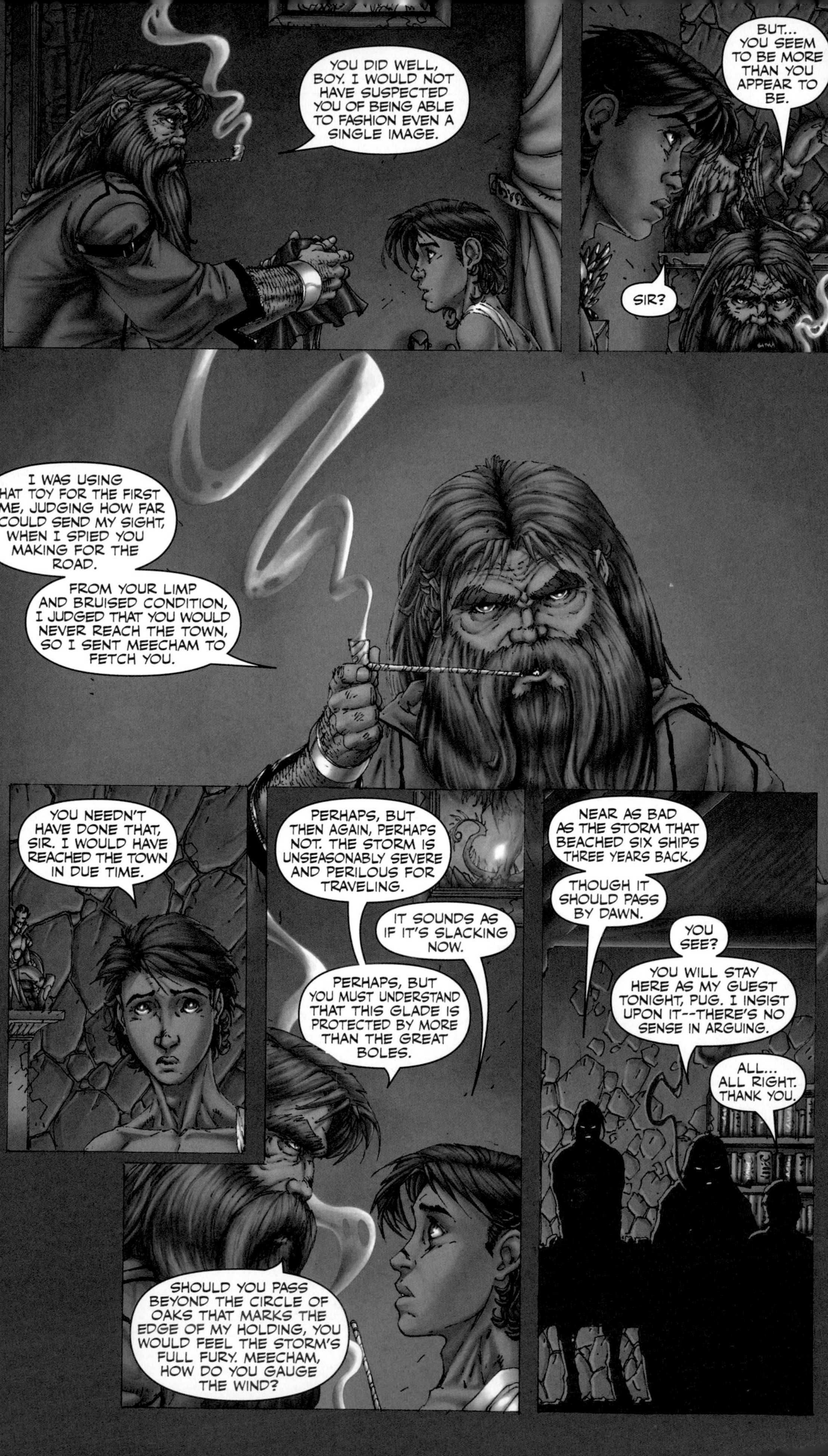
YOU DID WELL, BOY. I WOULD NOT HAVE SUSPECTED YOU OF BEING ABLE TO FASHION EVEN A SINGLE IMAGE.
BUT... YOU SEEM TO BE MORE THAN YOU APPEAR TO BE.
SIR?
I WAS USING THAT TOY FOR THE FIRST TIME, JUDGING HOW FAR I COULD SEND MY SIGHT, WHEN I SPIED YOU MAKING FOR THE ROAD.
FROM YOUR LIMP AND BRUISED CONDITION, I JUDGED THAT YOU WOULD NEVER REACH THE TOWN, SO I SENT MEECHAM TO FETCH YOU.
YOU NEEDN'T HAVE DONE THAT, SIR. I WOULD HAVE REACHED THE TOWN IN DUE TIME.
PERHAPS, BUT THEN AGAIN, PERHAPS NOT. THE STORM IS UNSEASONABLY SEVERE AND PERILOUS FOR TRAVELING.
IT SOUNDS AS IF IT'S SLACKING NOW.
PERHAPS, BUT YOU MUST UNDERSTAND THAT THIS GLADE IS PROTECTED BY MORE THAN THE GREAT BOLES.
SHOULD YOU PASS BEYOND THE CIRCLE OF OAKS THAT MARKS THE EDGE OF MY HOLDING, YOU WOULD FEEL THE STORM'S FULL FURY. MEECHAM, HOW DO YOU GAUGE THE WIND?
NEAR AS BAD AS THE STORM THAT BEACHED SIX SHIPS THREE YEARS BACK.
THOUGH IT SHOULD PASS BY DAWN.
YOU SEE?
YOU WILL STAY HERE AS MY GUEST TONIGHT, PUG. I INSIST UPON IT--THERE'S NO SENSE IN ARGUING.
ALL... ALL RIGHT. THANK YOU.

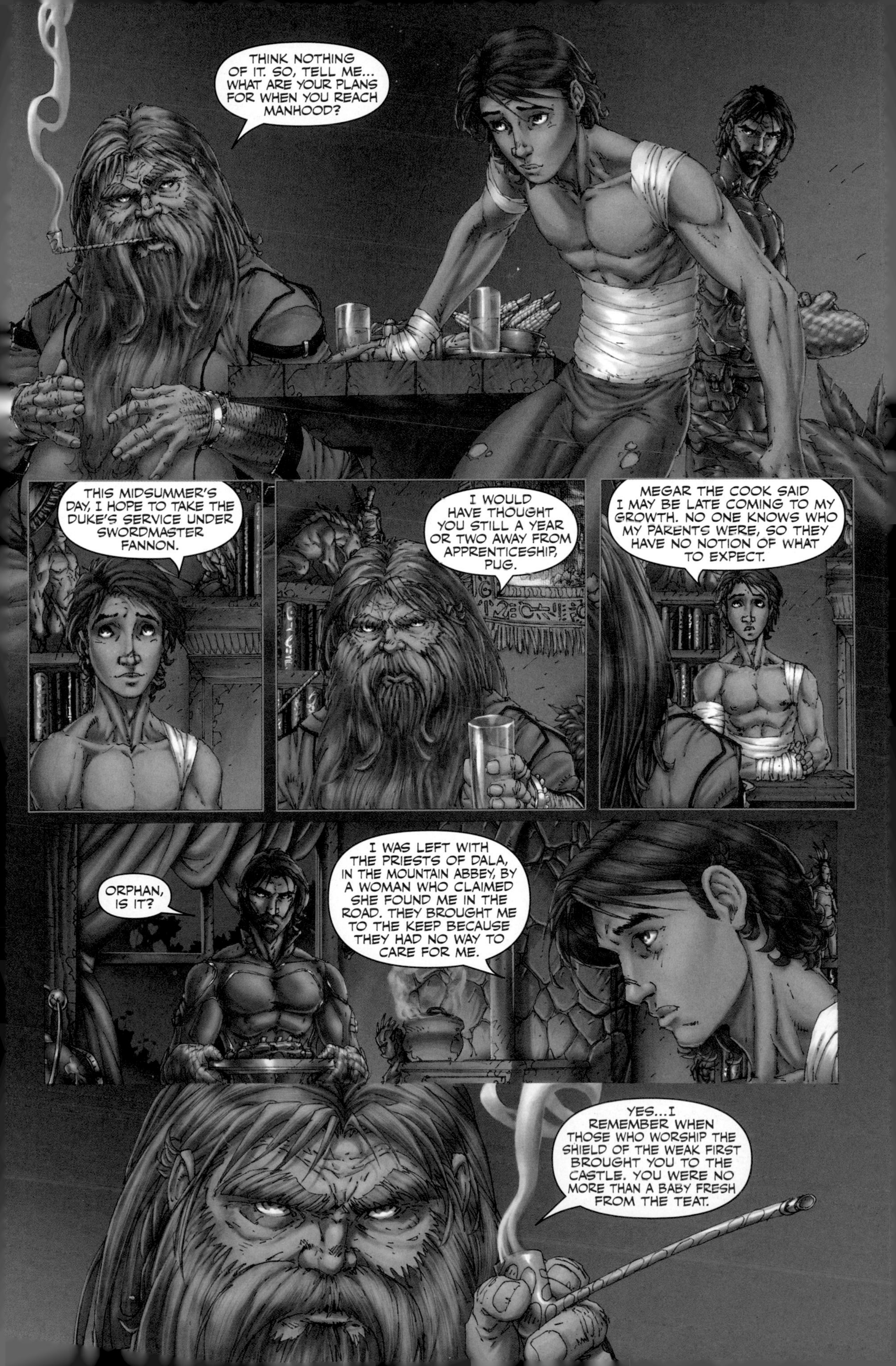
THINK NOTHING OF IT. SO, TELL ME... WHAT ARE YOUR PLANS FOR WHEN YOU REACH MANHOOD?
THIS MIDSUMMER'S DAY, I HOPE TO TAKE THE DUKE'S SERVICE UNDER SWORDMASTER FANNON.
I WOULD HAVE THOUGHT YOU STILL A YEAR OR TWO AWAY FROM APPRENTICESHIP, PUG.
MEGAR THE COOK SAID I MAY BE LATE COMING TO MY GROWTH. NO ONE KNOWS WHO MY PARENTS WERE, SO THEY HAVE NO NOTION OF WHAT TO EXPECT.
ORPHAN, IS IT?
I WAS LEFT WITH THE PRIESTS OF DALA, IN THE MOUNTAIN ABBEY, BY A WOMAN WHO CLAIMED SHE FOUND ME IN THE ROAD. THEY BROUGHT ME TO THE KEEP BECAUSE THEY HAD NO WAY TO CARE FOR ME.
YES...I REMEMBER WHEN THOSE WHO WORSHIP THE SHIELD OF THE WEAK FIRST BROUGHT YOU TO THE CASTLE. YOU WERE NO MORE THAN A BABY FRESH FROM THE TEAT.

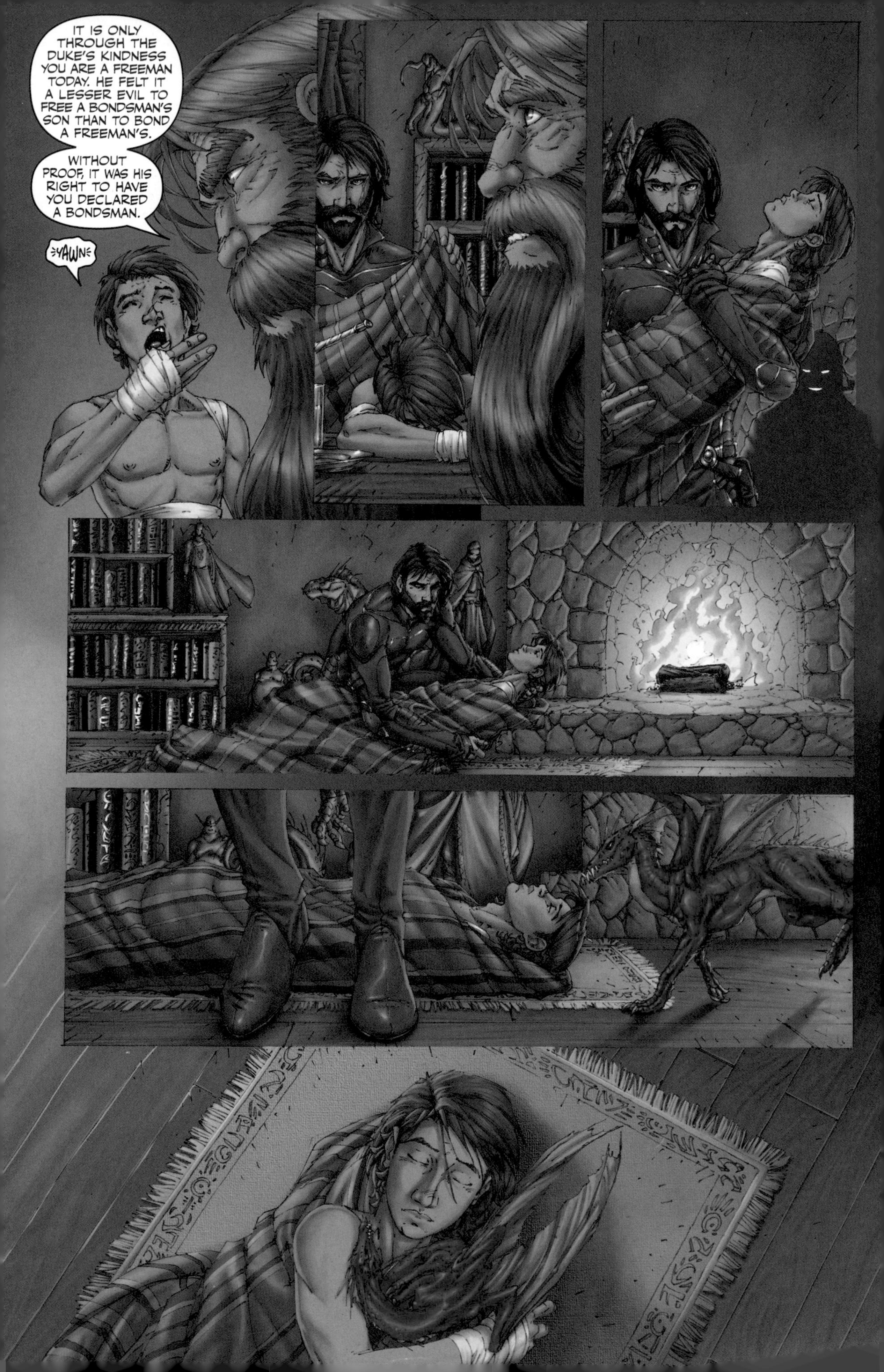
IT IS ONLY THROUGH THE DUKE'S KINDNESS YOU ARE A FREEMAN TODAY. HE FELT IT A LESSER EVIL TO FREE A BONDSMAN'S SON THAN TO BOND A FREEMAN'S.
WITHOUT PROOF, IT WAS HIS RIGHT TO HAVE YOU DECLARED A BONDSMAN.
YAWN

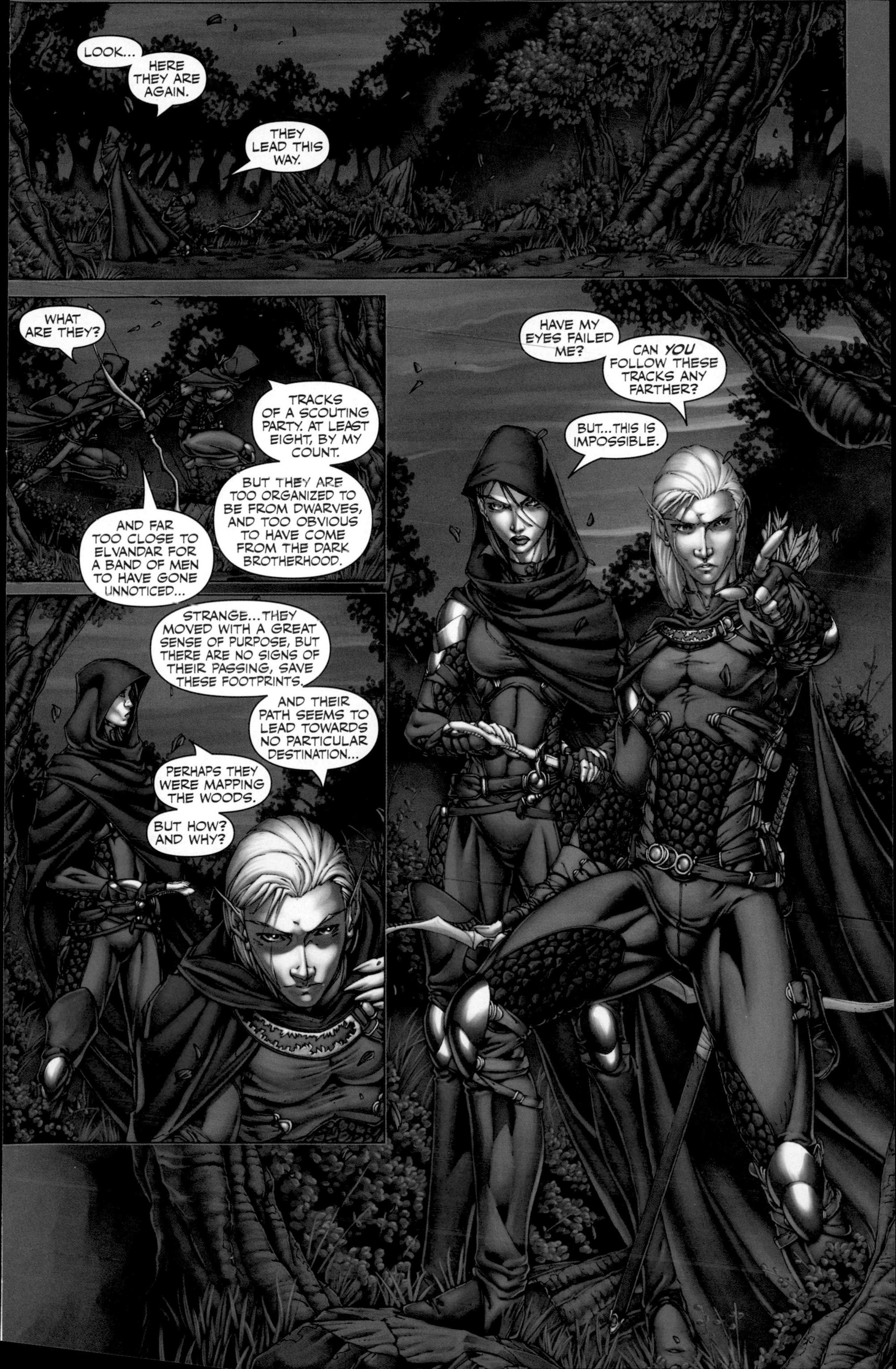

LOOK...
HERE THEY ARE AGAIN.
THEY LEAD THIS WAY.
WHAT ARE THEY?
TRACKS OF A SCOUTING PARTY. AT LEAST EIGHT, BY MY COUNT.
BUT THEY ARE TOO ORGANIZED TO BE FROM DWARVES, AND TOO OBVIOUS TO HAVE COME FROM THE DARK BROTHERHOOD.
AND FAR TOO CLOSE TO ELVANDAR FOR A BAND OF MEN TO HAVE GONE UNNOTICED...
STRANGE...THEY MOVED WITH A GREAT SENSE OF PURPOSE, BUT THERE ARE NO SIGNS OF THEIR PASSING, SAVE THESE FOOTPRINTS.
AND THEIR PATH SEEMS TO LEAD TOWARDS NO PARTICULAR DESTINATION...
PERHAPS THEY WERE MAPPING THE WOODS.
BUT HOW? AND WHY?
HAVE MY EYES FAILED ME?
CAN YOU FOLLOW THESE TRACKS ANY FARTHER?
BUT...THIS IS IMPOSSIBLE.

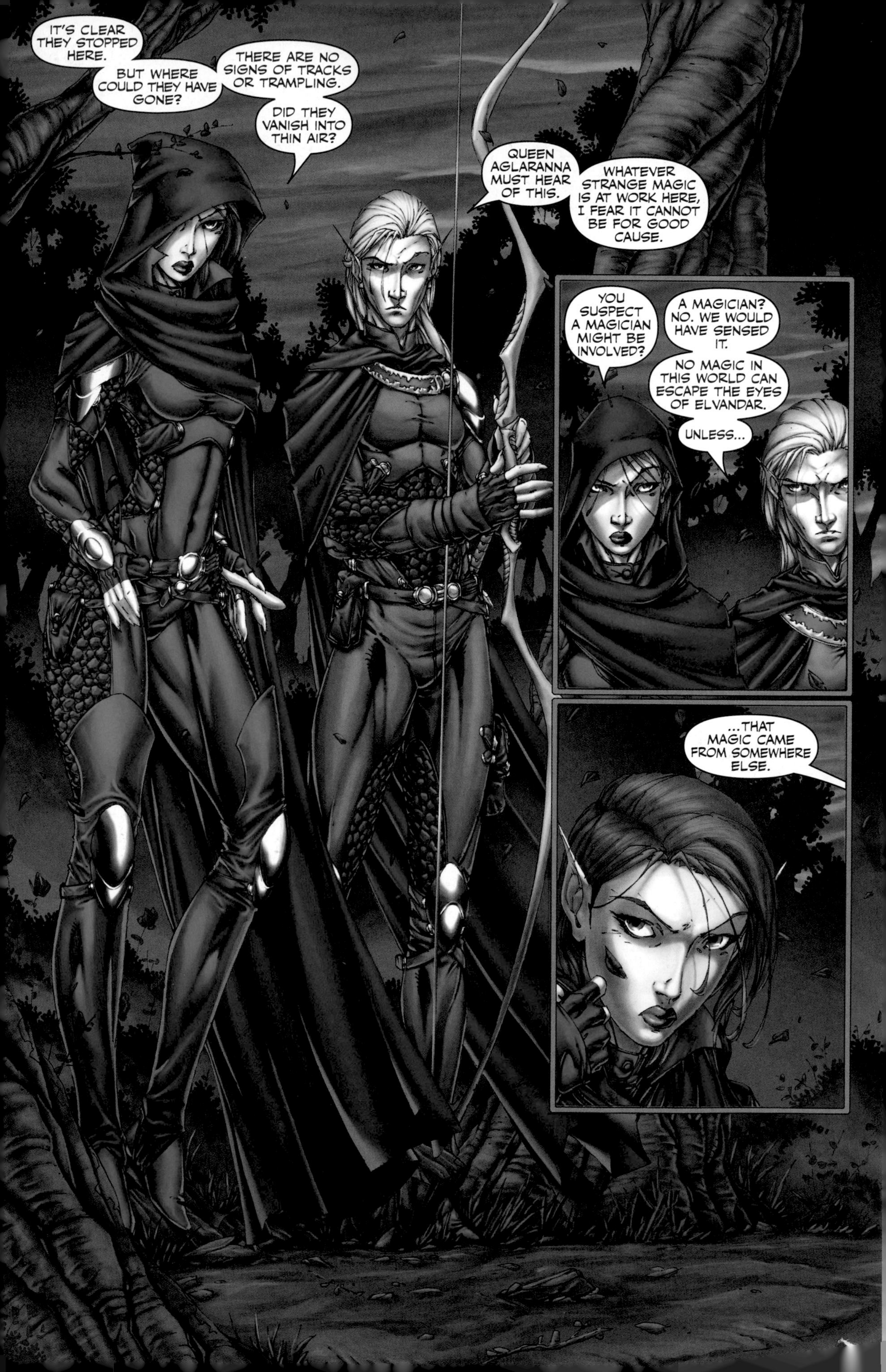
IT'S CLEAR THEY STOPPED HERE.
BUT WHERE COULD THEY HAVE GONE?
THERE ARE NO SIGNS OF TRACKS OR TRAMPLING.
DID THEY VANISH INTO THIN AIR?
QUEEN AGLARANNA MUST HEAR OF THIS.
WHATEVER STRANGE MAGIC IS AT WORK HERE, I FEAR IT CANNOT BE FOR GOOD CAUSE.
YOU SUSPECT A MAGICIAN MIGHT BE INVOLVED?
A MAGICIAN? NO. WE WOULD HAVE SENSED IT.
NO MAGIC IN THIS WORLD CAN ESCAPE THE EYES OF ELVANDAR.
UNLESS...
...THAT MAGIC CAME FROM SOMEWHERE ELSE.

MAGICIAN: APPRENTICE

CHAPTER TWO

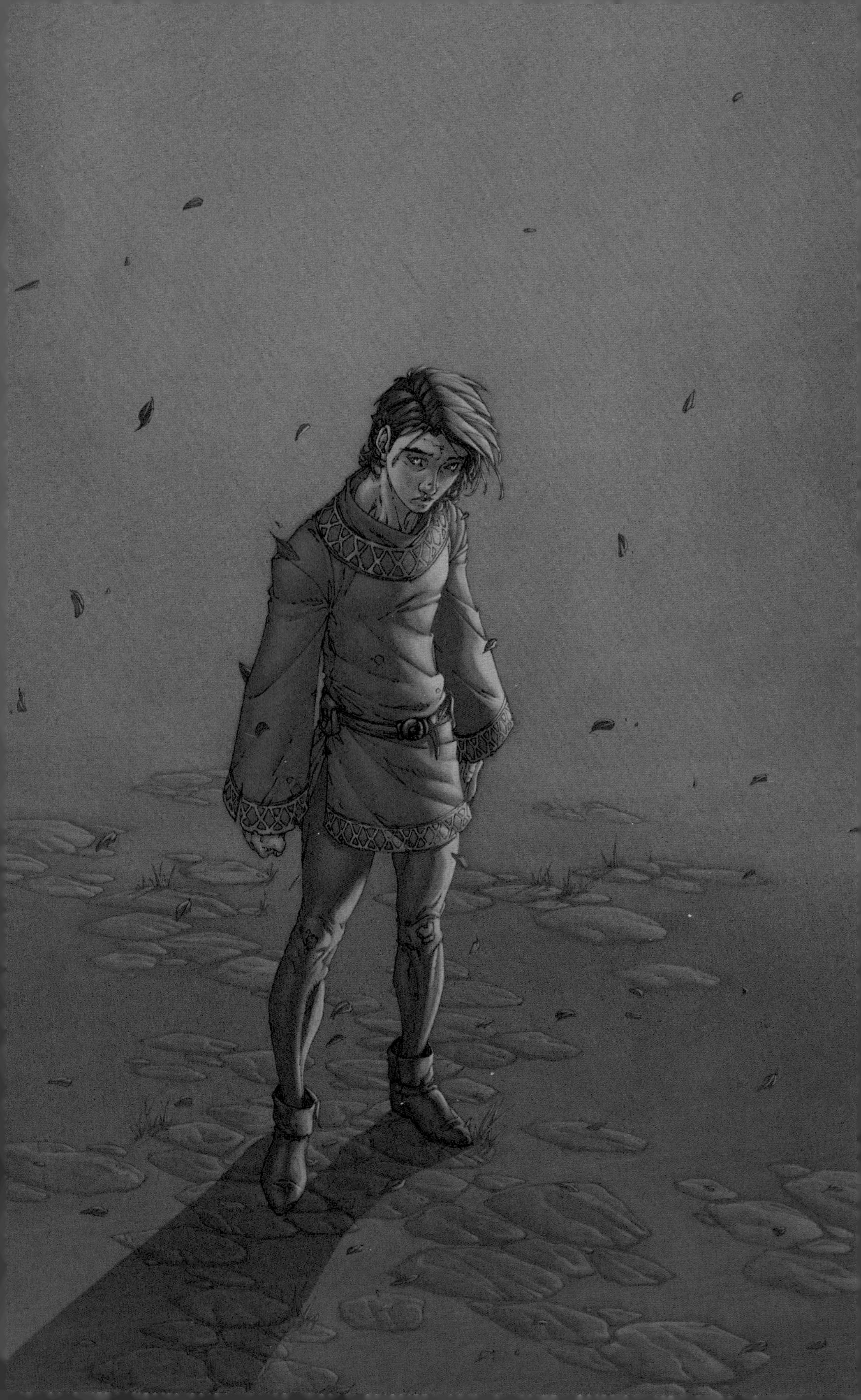

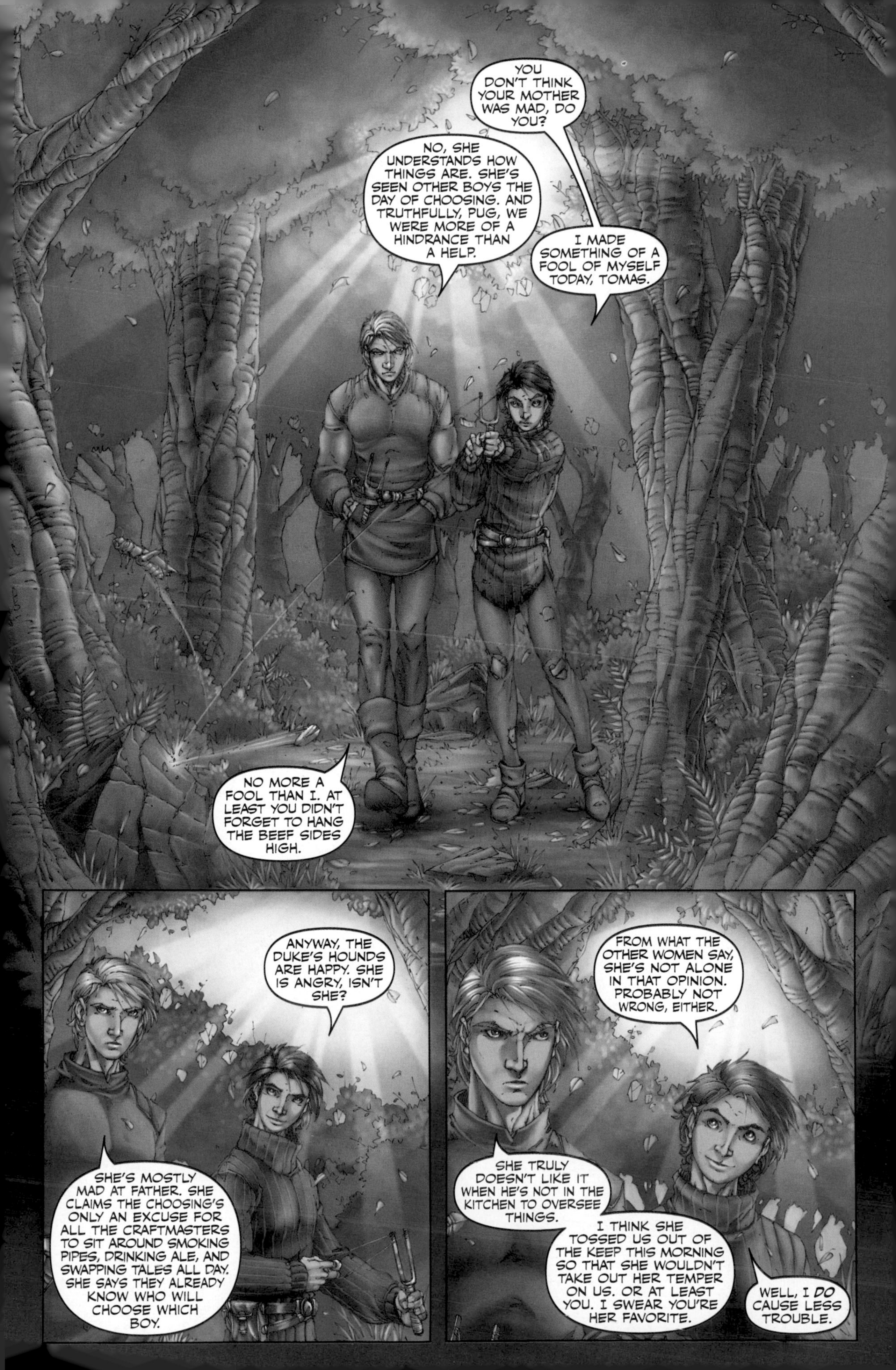
YOU DON'T THINK YOUR MOTHER WAS MAD, DO YOU?
NO, SHE UNDERSTANDS HOW THINGS ARE. SHE'S SEEN OTHER BOYS THE DAY OF CHOOSING. AND TRUTHFULLY, PUG, WE WERE MORE OF A HINDRANCE THAN A HELP.
I MADE SOMETHING OF A FOOL OF MYSELF TODAY, TOMAS.
NO MORE A FOOL THAN I. AT LEAST YOU DIDN'T FORGET TO HANG THE BEEF SIDES HIGH.
ANYWAY, THE DUKE'S HOUNDS ARE HAPPY. SHE IS ANGRY, ISN'T SHE?
SHE'S MOSTLY MAD AT FATHER. SHE CLAIMS THE CHOOSING'S ONLY AN EXCUSE FOR ALL THE CRAFTMASTERS TO SIT AROUND SMOKING PIPES, DRINKING ALE, AND SWAPPING TALES ALL DAY. SHE SAYS THEY ALREADY KNOW WHO WILL CHOOSE WHICH BOY.
FROM WHAT THE OTHER WOMEN SAY, SHE'S NOT ALONE IN THAT OPINION. PROBABLY NOT WRONG, EITHER.
SHE TRULY DOESN'T LIKE IT WHEN HE'S NOT IN THE KITCHEN TO OVERSEE THINGS.
I THINK SHE TOSSED US OUT OF THE KEEP THIS MORNING SO THAT SHE WOULDN'T TAKE OUT HER TEMPER ON US. OR AT LEAST YOU. I SWEAR YOU'RE HER FAVORITE.
WELL, I *DO* CAUSE LESS TROUBLE.

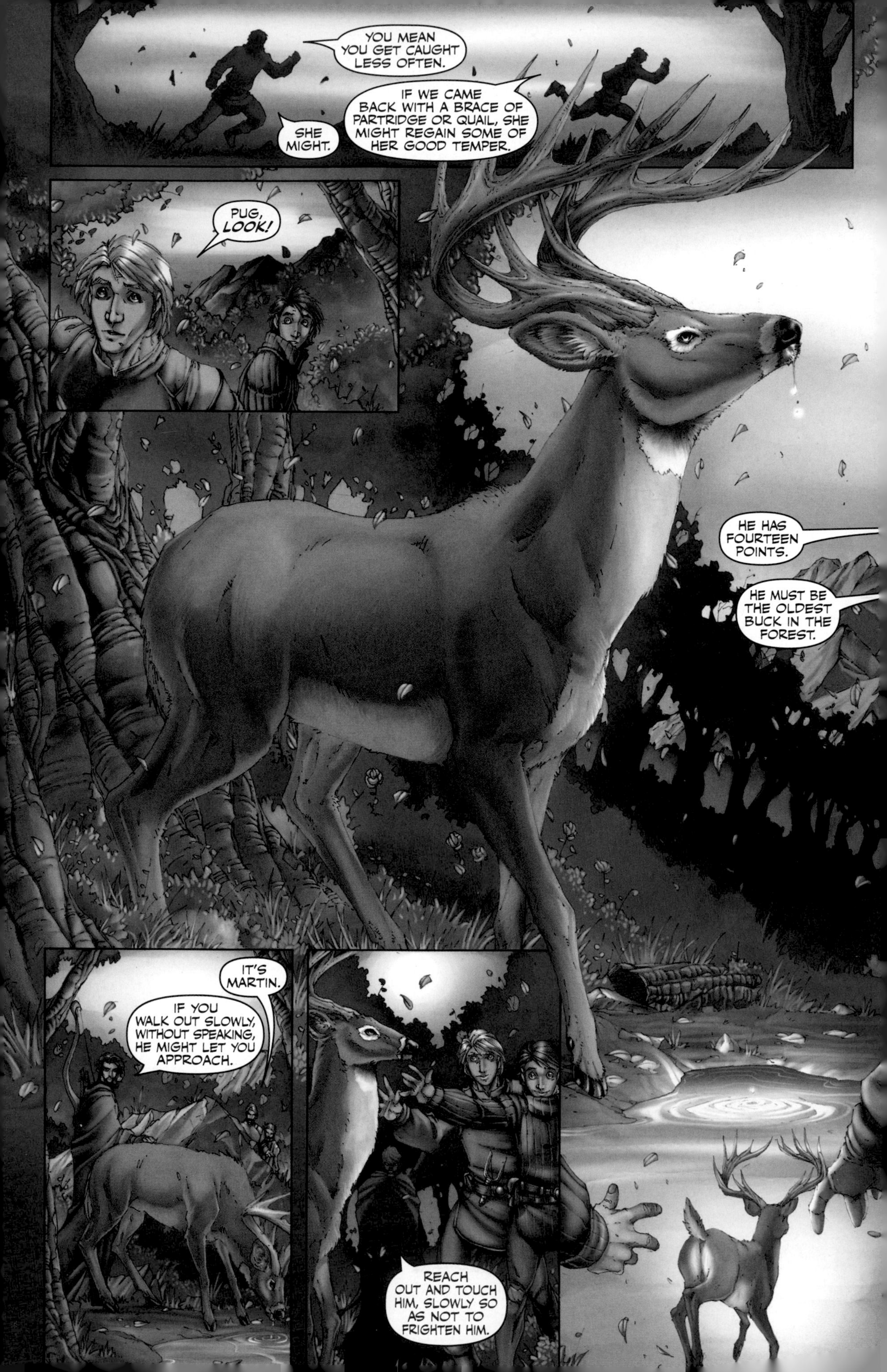
YOU MEAN YOU GET CAUGHT LESS OFTEN.
SHE MIGHT.
IF WE CAME BACK WITH A BRACE OF PARTRIDGE OR QUAIL, SHE MIGHT REGAIN SOME OF HER GOOD TEMPER.
PUG, LOOK!
HE HAS FOURTEEN POINTS.
HE MUST BE THE OLDEST BUCK IN THE FOREST.
IT'S MARTIN.
IF YOU WALK OUT SLOWLY, WITHOUT SPEAKING, HE MIGHT LET YOU APPROACH.
REACH OUT AND TOUCH HIM, SLOWLY SO AS NOT TO FRIGHTEN HIM.

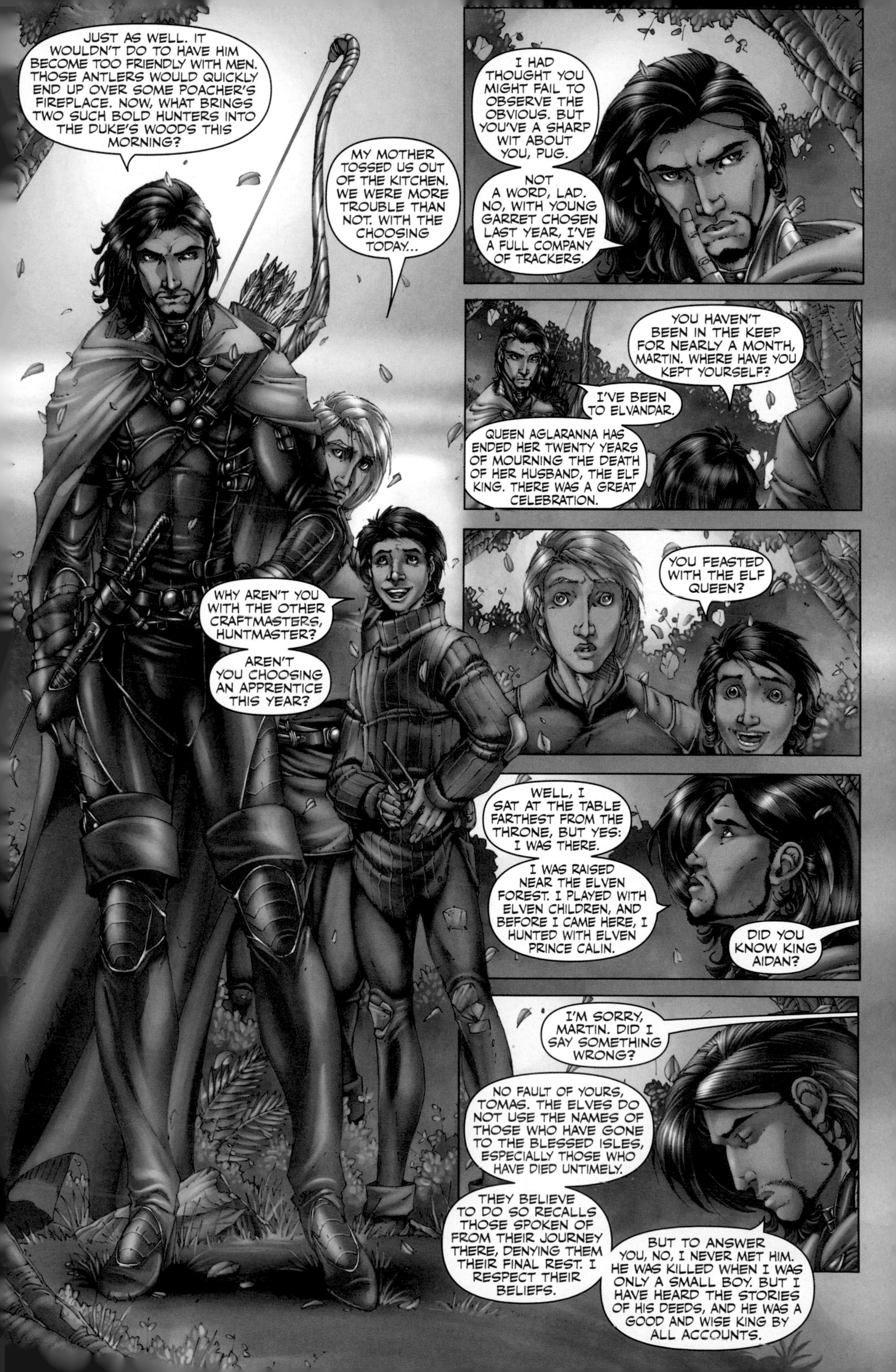
JUST AS WELL. IT WOULDN'T DO TO HAVE HIM BECOME TOO FRIENDLY WITH MEN. THOSE ANTLERS WOULD QUICKLY END UP OVER SOME POACHER'S FIREPLACE. NOW, WHAT BRINGS TWO SUCH BOLD HUNTERS INTO THE DUKE'S WOODS THIS MORNING?
MY MOTHER TOSSED US OUT OF THE KITCHEN. WE WERE MORE TROUBLE THAN NOT. WITH THE CHOOSING TODAY...
WHY AREN'T YOU WITH THE OTHER CRAFTMASTERS, HUNTMASTER?
AREN'T YOU CHOOSING AN APPRENTICE THIS YEAR?
I HAD THOUGHT YOU MIGHT FAIL TO OBSERVE THE OBVIOUS. BUT YOU'VE A SHARP WIT ABOUT YOU, PUG.
NOT A WORD, LAD. NO, WITH YOUNG GARRET CHOSEN LAST YEAR, I'VE A FULL COMPANY OF TRACKERS.
YOU HAVEN'T BEEN IN THE KEEP FOR NEARLY A MONTH, MARTIN. WHERE HAVE YOU KEPT YOURSELF?
I'VE BEEN TO ELVANDAR.
QUEEN AGLARANNA HAS ENDED HER TWENTY YEARS OF MOURNING THE DEATH OF HER HUSBAND, THE ELF KING. THERE WAS A GREAT CELEBRATION.
YOU FEASTED WITH THE ELF QUEEN?
WELL, I SAT AT THE TABLE FARTHEST FROM THE THRONE, BUT YES: I WAS THERE.
I WAS RAISED NEAR THE ELVEN FOREST. I PLAYED WITH ELVEN CHILDREN, AND BEFORE I CAME HERE, I HUNTED WITH ELVEN PRINCE CALIN.
DID YOU KNOW KING AIDAN?
I'M SORRY, MARTIN. DID I SAY SOMETHING WRONG?
NO FAULT OF YOURS, TOMAS. THE ELVES DO NOT USE THE NAMES OF THOSE WHO HAVE GONE TO THE BLESSED ISLES, ESPECIALLY THOSE WHO HAVE DIED UNTIMELY.
THEY BELIEVE TO DO SO RECALLS THOSE SPOKEN OF FROM THEIR JOURNEY THERE, DENYING THEM THEIR FINAL REST. I RESPECT THEIR BELIEFS.
BUT TO ANSWER YOU, NO, I NEVER MET HIM. HE WAS KILLED WHEN I WAS ONLY A SMALL BOY. BUT I HAVE HEARD THE STORIES OF HIS DEEDS, AND HE WAS A GOOD AND WISE KING BY ALL ACCOUNTS.

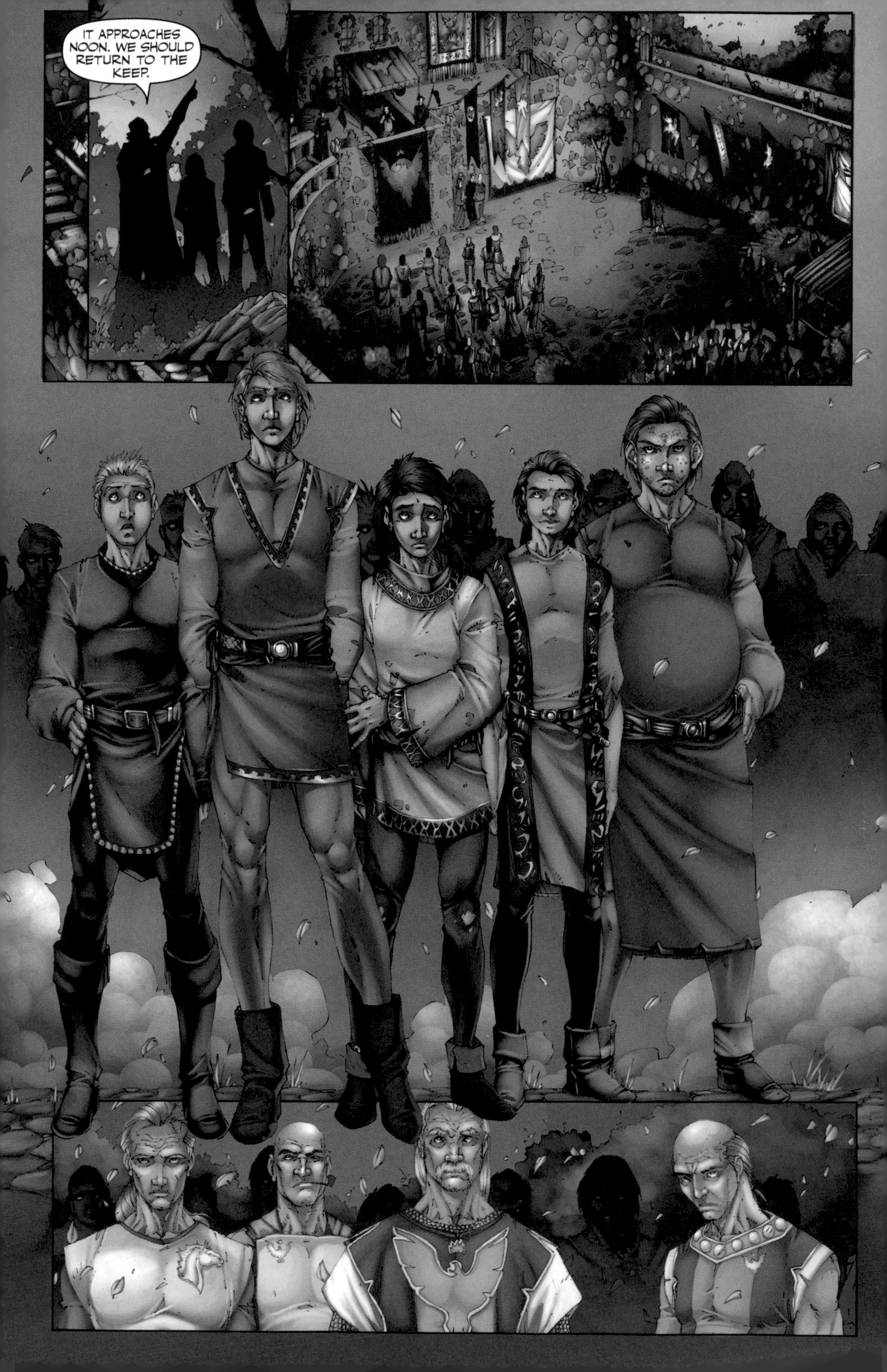
IT APPROACHES NOON. WE SHOULD RETURN TO THE KEEP.

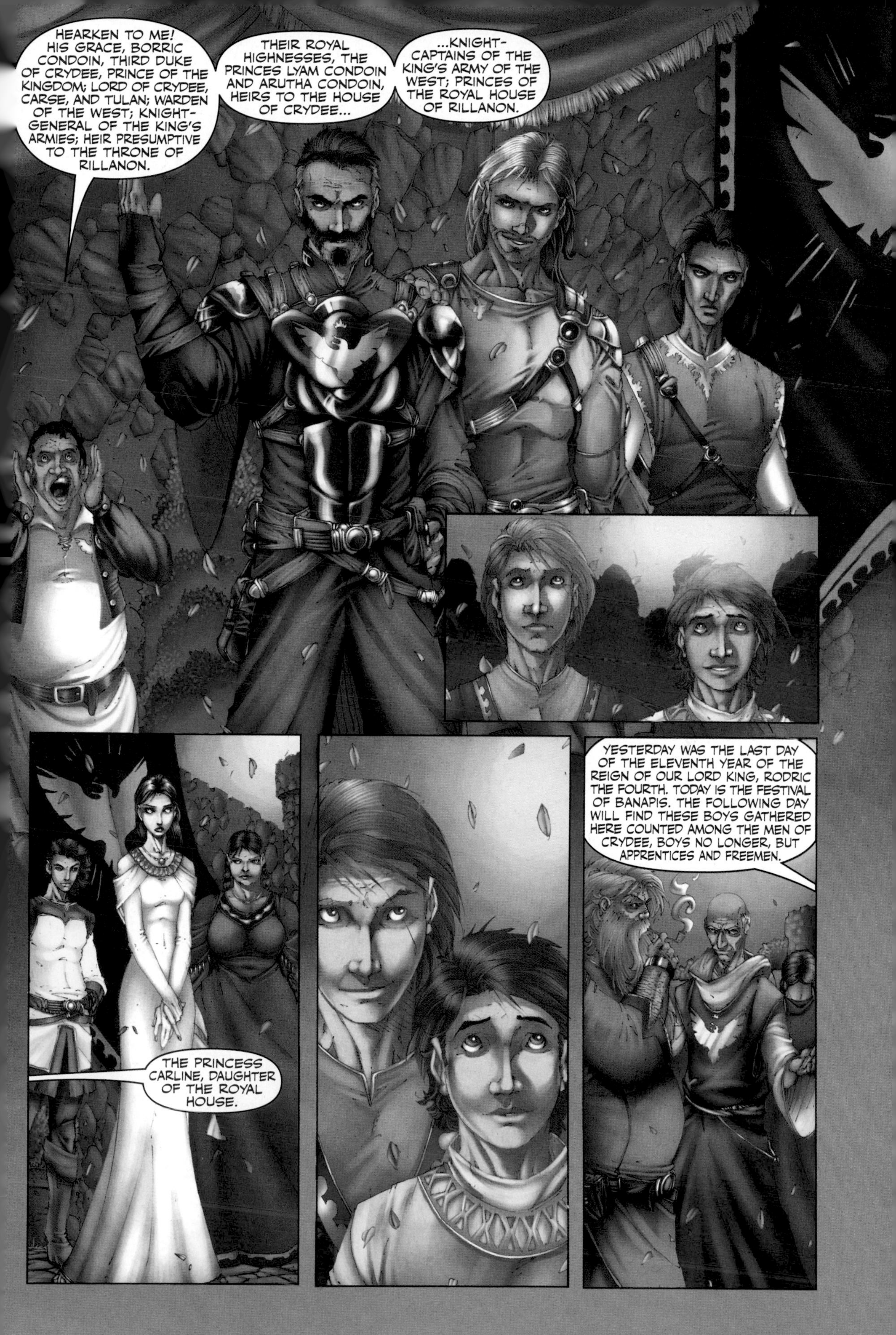
HEARKEN TO ME! HIS GRACE, BORRIC CONDOIN, THIRD DUKE OF CRYDEE, PRINCE OF THE KINGDOM; LORD OF CRYDEE, CARSE, AND TULAN; WARDEN OF THE WEST; KNIGHT-GENERAL OF THE KING'S ARMIES; HEIR PRESUMPTIVE TO THE THRONE OF RILLANON.
THEIR ROYAL HIGHNESSES, THE PRINCES LYAM CONDOIN AND ARUTHA CONDOIN, HEIRS TO THE HOUSE OF CRYDEE...
...KNIGHT-CAPTAINS OF THE KING'S ARMY OF THE WEST; PRINCES OF THE ROYAL HOUSE OF RILLANON.
THE PRINCESS CARLINE, DAUGHTER OF THE ROYAL HOUSE.
YESTERDAY WAS THE LAST DAY OF THE ELEVENTH YEAR OF THE REIGN OF OUR LORD KING, RODRIC THE FOURTH. TODAY IS THE FESTIVAL OF BANAPIS. THE FOLLOWING DAY WILL FIND THESE BOYS GATHERED HERE COUNTED AMONG THE MEN OF CRYDEE, BOYS NO LONGER, BUT APPRENTICES AND FREEMEN.

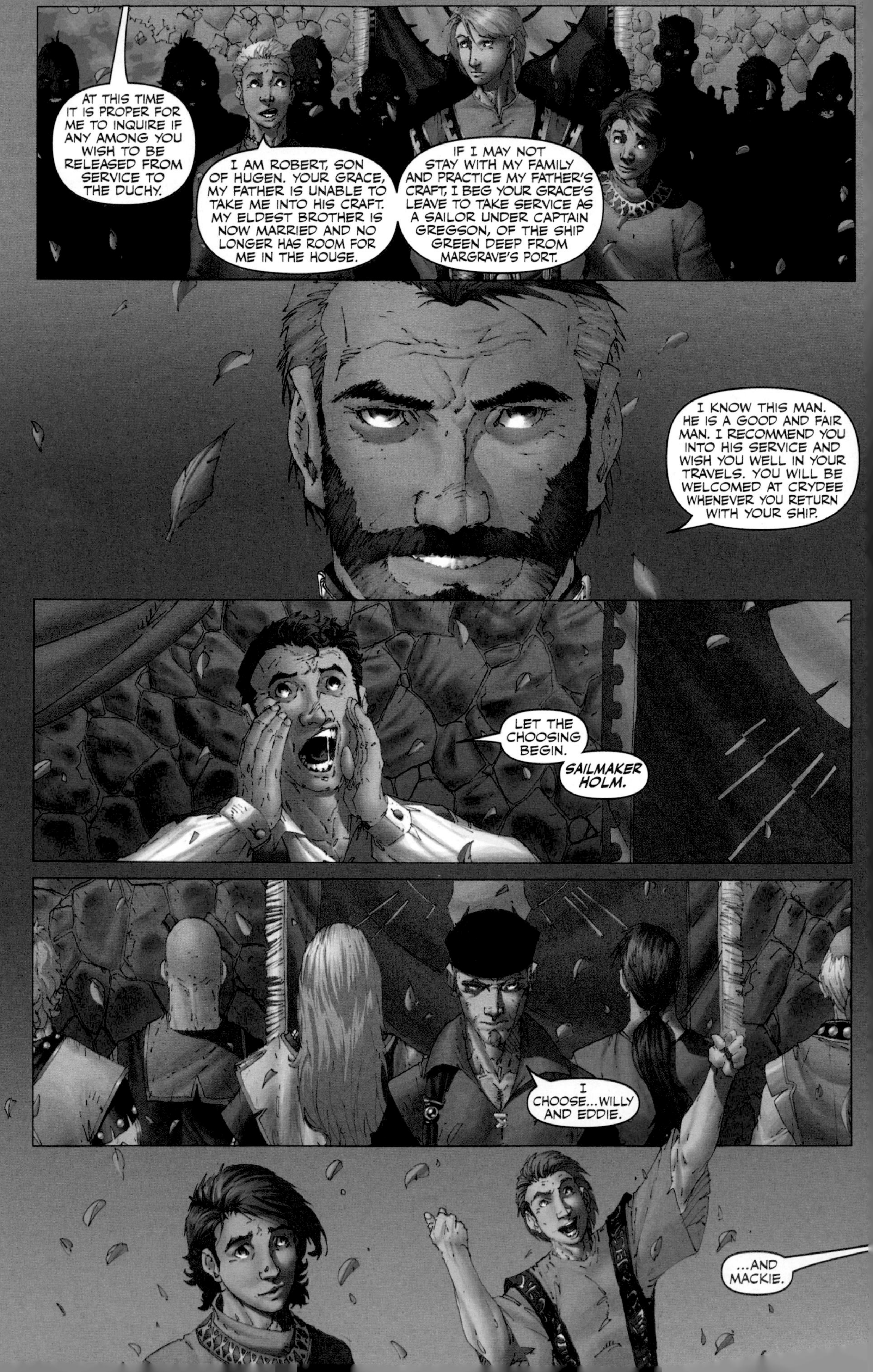

AT THIS TIME IT IS PROPER FOR ME TO INQUIRE IF ANY AMONG YOU WISH TO BE RELEASED FROM SERVICE TO THE DUCHY.
I AM ROBERT, SON OF HUGEN. YOUR GRACE, MY FATHER IS UNABLE TO TAKE ME INTO HIS CRAFT. MY ELDEST BROTHER IS NOW MARRIED AND NO LONGER HAS ROOM FOR ME IN THE HOUSE.
IF I MAY NOT STAY WITH MY FAMILY AND PRACTICE MY FATHER'S CRAFT, I BEG YOUR GRACE'S LEAVE TO TAKE SERVICE AS A SAILOR UNDER CAPTAIN GREGSON, OF THE SHIP GREEN DEEP FROM MARGRAVE'S PORT.
I KNOW THIS MAN. HE IS A GOOD AND FAIR MAN. I RECOMMEND YOU INTO HIS SERVICE AND WISH YOU WELL IN YOUR TRAVELS. YOU WILL BE WELCOMED AT CRYDEE WHENEVER YOU RETURN WITH YOUR SHIP.
LET THE CHOOSING BEGIN.
SAILMAKER HOLM.
I CHOOSE...WILLY AND EDDIE.
...AND MACKIE.

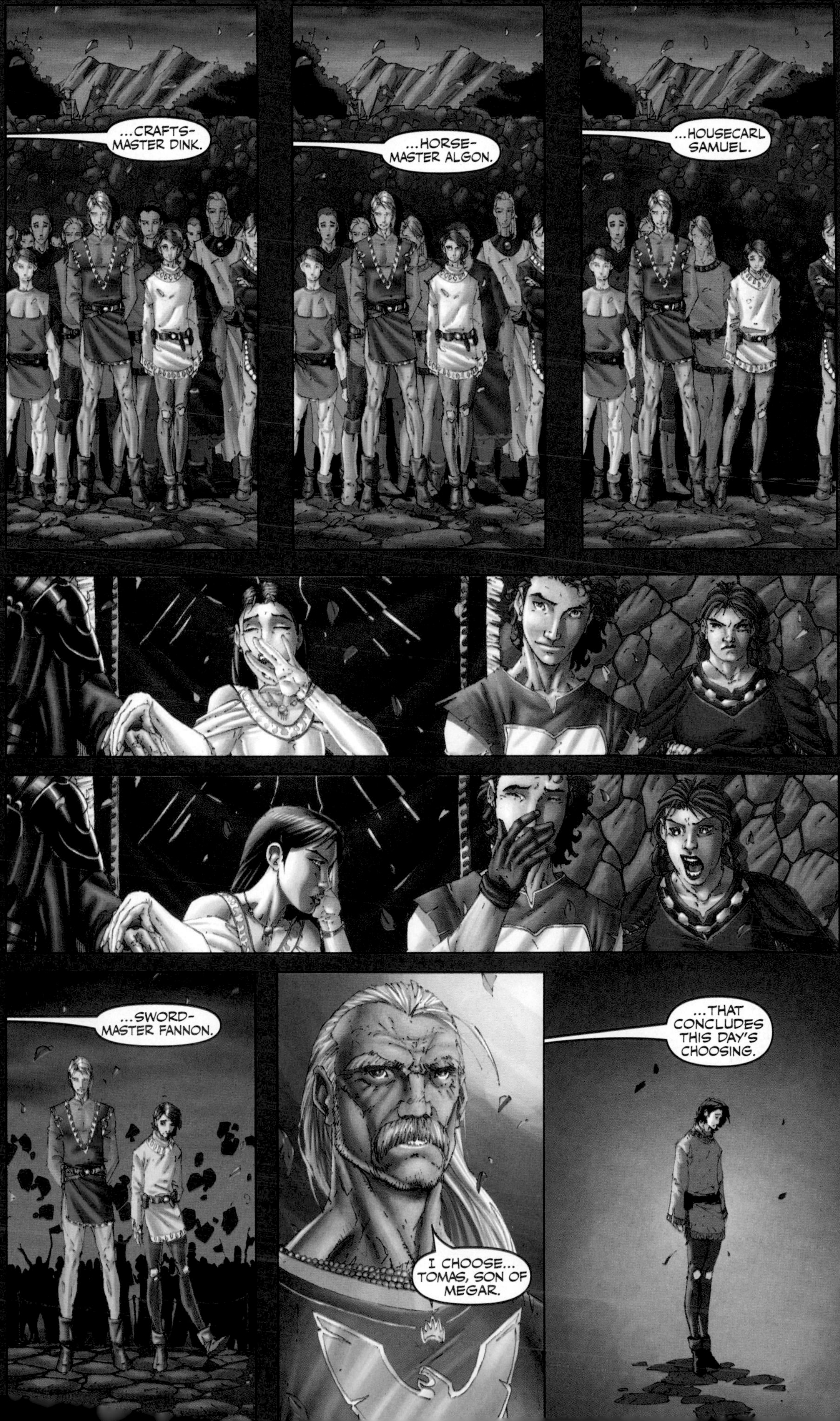
...CRAFTS-
MASTER DINK.
...HORSE-
MASTER ALGON.
...HOUSECARL
SAMUEL.
...SWORD-
MASTER FANNON.
I CHOOSE...
TOMAS, SON OF
MEGAR.
...THAT
CONCLUDES
THIS DAY'S
CHOOSING.

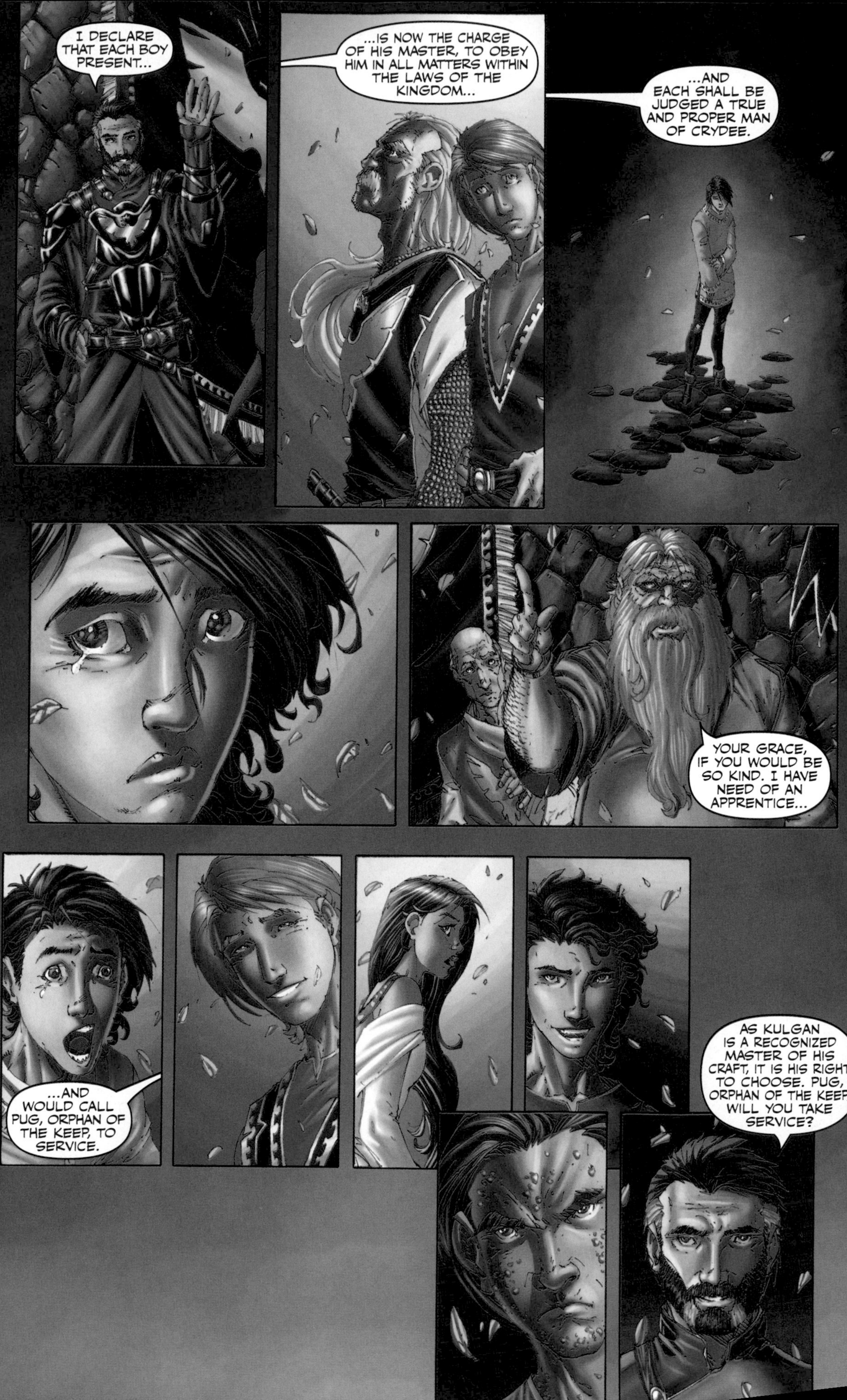
I DECLARE THAT EACH BOY PRESENT...
...IS NOW THE CHARGE OF HIS MASTER, TO OBEY HIM IN ALL MATTERS WITHIN THE LAWS OF THE KINGDOM...
...AND EACH SHALL BE JUDGED A TRUE AND PROPER MAN OF CRYDEE.
YOUR GRACE, IF YOU WOULD BE SO KIND. I HAVE NEED OF AN APPRENTICE...
...AND WOULD CALL PUG, ORPHAN OF THE KEEP, TO SERVICE.
AS KULGAN IS A RECOGNIZED MASTER OF HIS CRAFT, IT IS HIS RIGHT TO CHOOSE. PUG, ORPHAN OF THE KEEP, WILL YOU TAKE SERVICE?

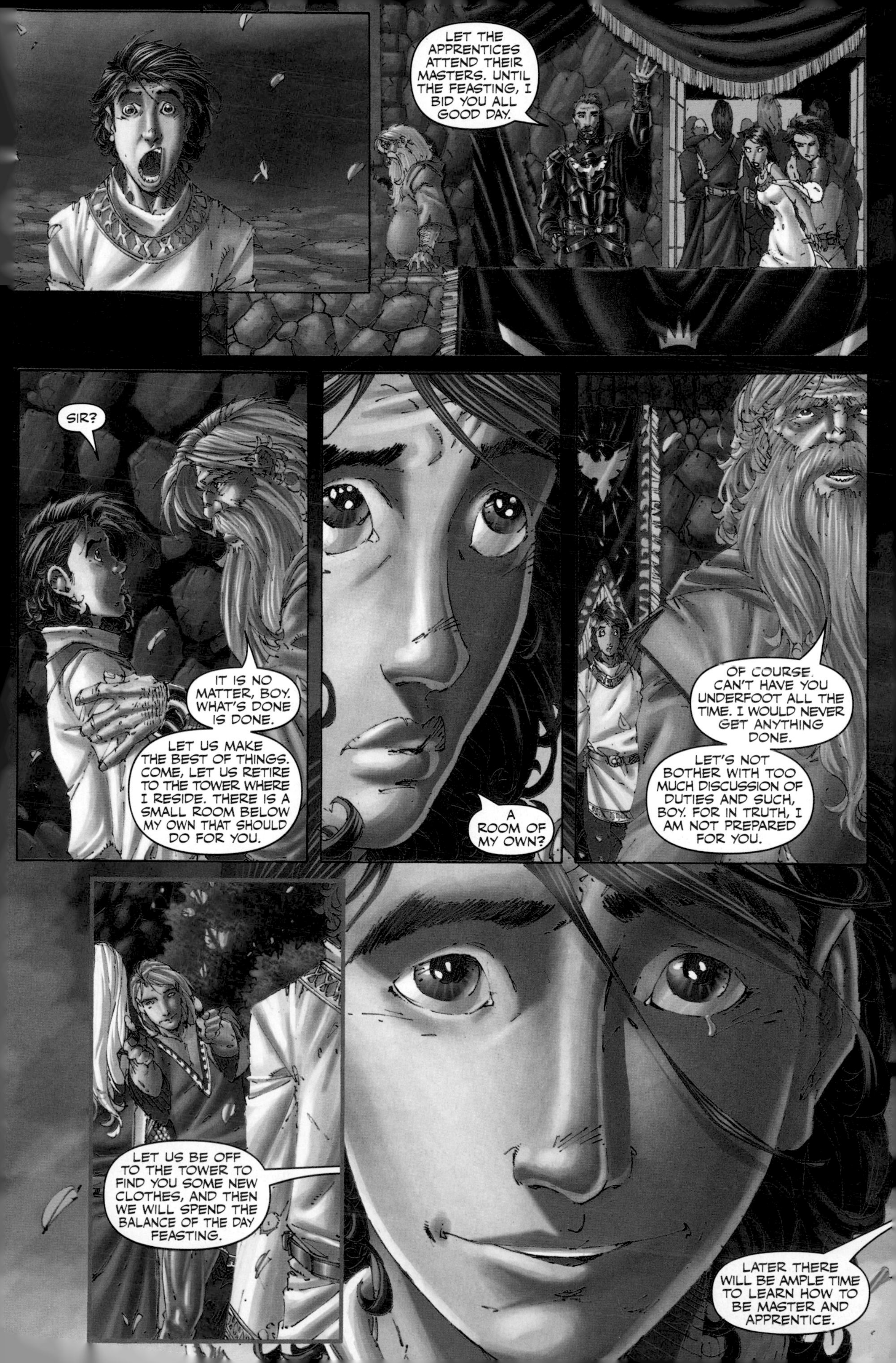
LET THE APPRENTICES ATTEND THEIR MASTERS. UNTIL THE FEASTING, I BID YOU ALL GOOD DAY.
SIR?
IT IS NO MATTER, BOY. WHAT'S DONE IS DONE.
LET US MAKE THE BEST OF THINGS. COME, LET US RETIRE TO THE TOWER WHERE I RESIDE. THERE IS A SMALL ROOM BELOW MY OWN THAT SHOULD DO FOR YOU.
A ROOM OF MY OWN?
OF COURSE. CAN'T HAVE YOU UNDERFOOT ALL THE TIME. I WOULD NEVER GET ANYTHING DONE.
LET'S NOT BOTHER WITH TOO MUCH DISCUSSION OF DUTIES AND SUCH, BOY. FOR IN TRUTH, I AM NOT PREPARED FOR YOU.
LET US BE OFF TO THE TOWER TO FIND YOU SOME NEW CLOTHES, AND THEN WE WILL SPEND THE BALANCE OF THE DAY FEASTING.
LATER THERE WILL BE AMPLE TIME TO LEARN HOW TO BE MASTER AND APPRENTICE.

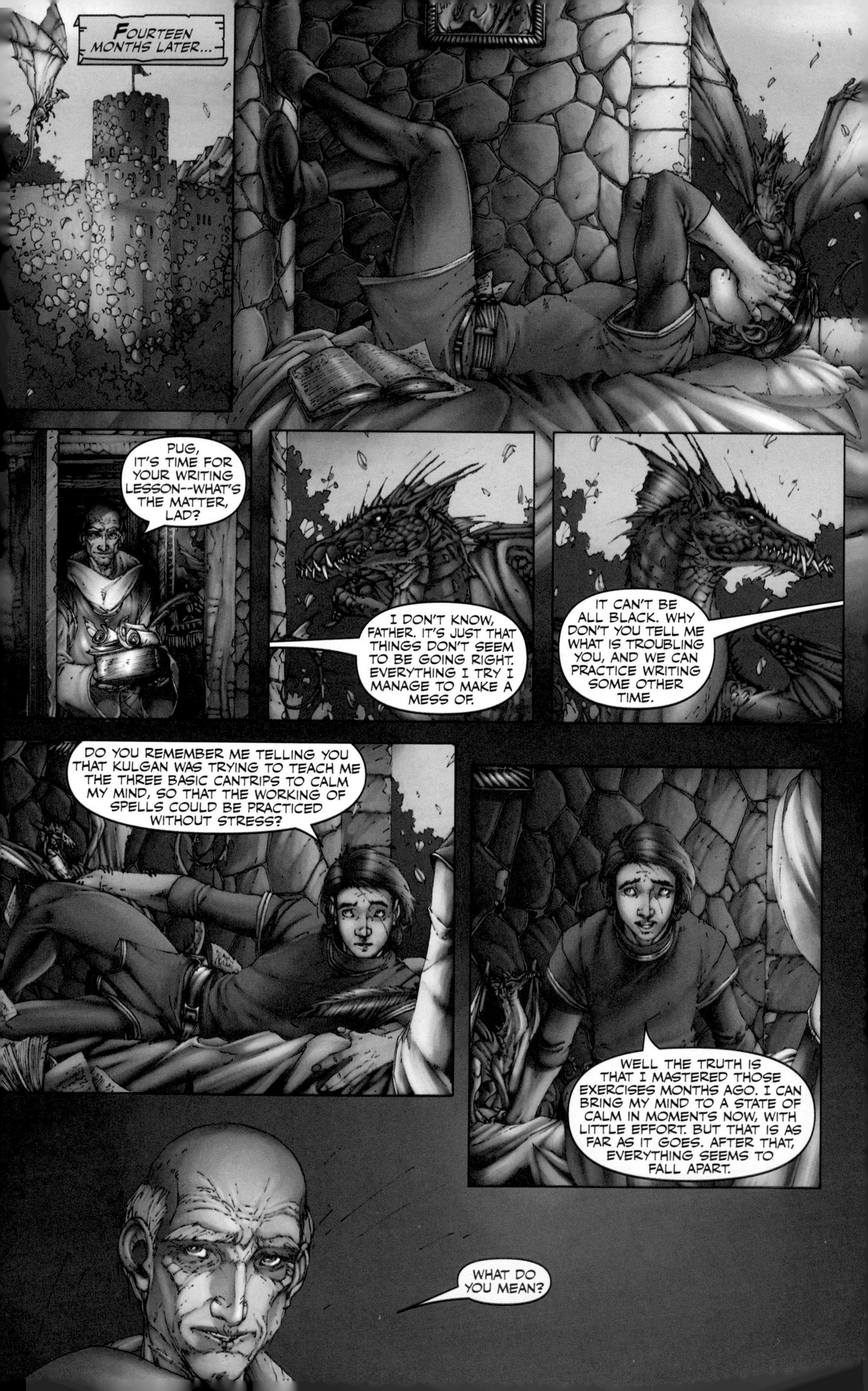
FOURTEEN MONTHS LATER...
PUG, IT'S TIME FOR YOUR WRITING LESSON--WHAT'S THE MATTER, LAD?
I DON'T KNOW, FATHER. IT'S JUST THAT THINGS DON'T SEEM TO BE GOING RIGHT. EVERYTHING I TRY I MANAGE TO MAKE A MESS OF.
IT CAN'T BE ALL BLACK. WHY DON'T YOU TELL ME WHAT IS TROUBLING YOU, AND WE CAN PRACTICE WRITING SOME OTHER TIME.
DO YOU REMEMBER ME TELLING YOU THAT KULGAN WAS TRYING TO TEACH ME THE THREE BASIC CANTRIPS TO CALM MY MIND, SO THAT THE WORKING OF SPELLS COULD BE PRACTICED WITHOUT STRESS?
WELL THE TRUTH IS THAT I MASTERED THOSE EXERCISES MONTHS AGO. I CAN BRING MY MIND TO A STATE OF CALM IN MOMENTS NOW, WITH LITTLE EFFORT. BUT THAT IS AS FAR AS IT GOES. AFTER THAT, EVERYTHING SEEMS TO FALL APART.
WHAT DO YOU MEAN?

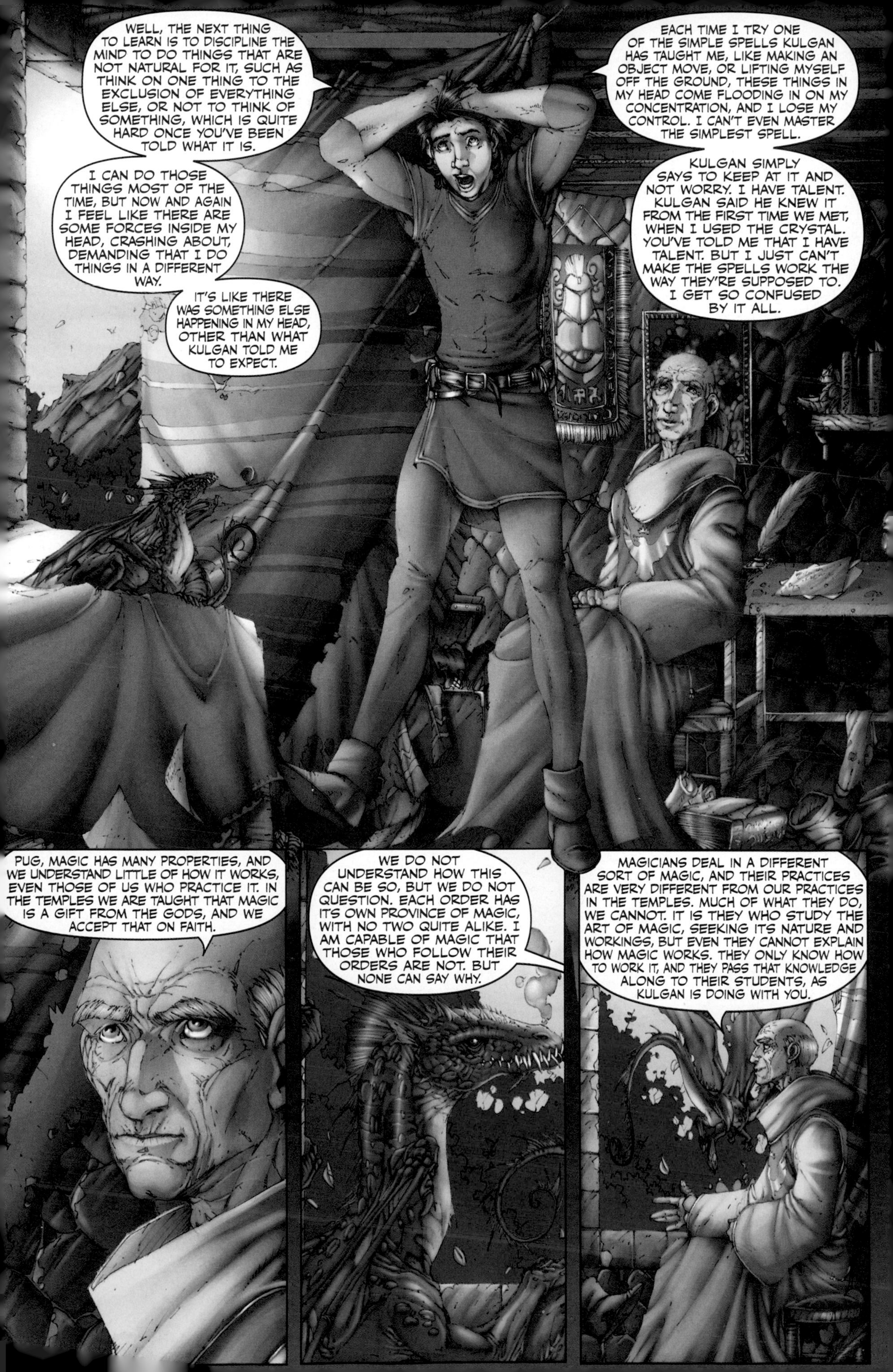
WELL, THE NEXT THING TO LEARN IS TO DISCIPLINE THE MIND TO DO THINGS THAT ARE NOT NATURAL FOR IT, SUCH AS THINK ON ONE THING TO THE EXCLUSION OF EVERYTHING ELSE, OR NOT TO THINK OF SOMETHING, WHICH IS QUITE HARD ONCE YOU'VE BEEN TOLD WHAT IT IS.
I CAN DO THOSE THINGS MOST OF THE TIME, BUT NOW AND AGAIN I FEEL LIKE THERE ARE SOME FORCES INSIDE MY HEAD, CRASHING ABOUT, DEMANDING THAT I DO THINGS IN A DIFFERENT WAY.
IT'S LIKE THERE WAS SOMETHING ELSE HAPPENING IN MY HEAD, OTHER THAN WHAT KULGAN TOLD ME TO EXPECT.
EACH TIME I TRY ONE OF THE SIMPLE SPELLS KULGAN HAS TAUGHT ME, LIKE MAKING AN OBJECT MOVE, OR LIFTING MYSELF OFF THE GROUND, THESE THINGS IN MY HEAD COME FLOODING IN ON MY CONCENTRATION, AND I LOSE MY CONTROL. I CAN'T EVEN MASTER THE SIMPLEST SPELL.
KULGAN SIMPLY SAYS TO KEEP AT IT AND NOT WORRY. I HAVE TALENT. KULGAN SAID HE KNEW IT FROM THE FIRST TIME WE MET, WHEN I USED THE CRYSTAL. YOU'VE TOLD ME THAT I HAVE TALENT. BUT I JUST CAN'T MAKE THE SPELLS WORK THE WAY THEY'RE SUPPOSED TO. I GET SO CONFUSED BY IT ALL.
PUG, MAGIC HAS MANY PROPERTIES, AND WE UNDERSTAND LITTLE OF HOW IT WORKS, EVEN THOSE OF US WHO PRACTICE IT. IN THE TEMPLES WE ARE TAUGHT THAT MAGIC IS A GIFT FROM THE GODS, AND WE ACCEPT THAT ON FAITH.
WE DO NOT UNDERSTAND HOW THIS CAN BE SO, BUT WE DO NOT QUESTION. EACH ORDER HAS ITS OWN PROVINCE OF MAGIC, WITH NO TWO QUITE ALIKE. I AM CAPABLE OF MAGIC THAT THOSE WHO FOLLOW THEIR ORDERS ARE NOT. BUT NONE CAN SAY WHY.
MAGICIANS DEAL IN A DIFFERENT SORT OF MAGIC, AND THEIR PRACTICES ARE VERY DIFFERENT FROM OUR PRACTICES IN THE TEMPLES. MUCH OF WHAT THEY DO, WE CANNOT. IT IS THEY WHO STUDY THE ART OF MAGIC, SEEKING ITS NATURE AND WORKINGS, BUT EVEN THEY CANNOT EXPLAIN HOW MAGIC WORKS. THEY ONLY KNOW HOW TO WORK IT, AND THEY PASS THAT KNOWLEDGE ALONG TO THEIR STUDENTS, AS KULGAN IS DOING WITH YOU.

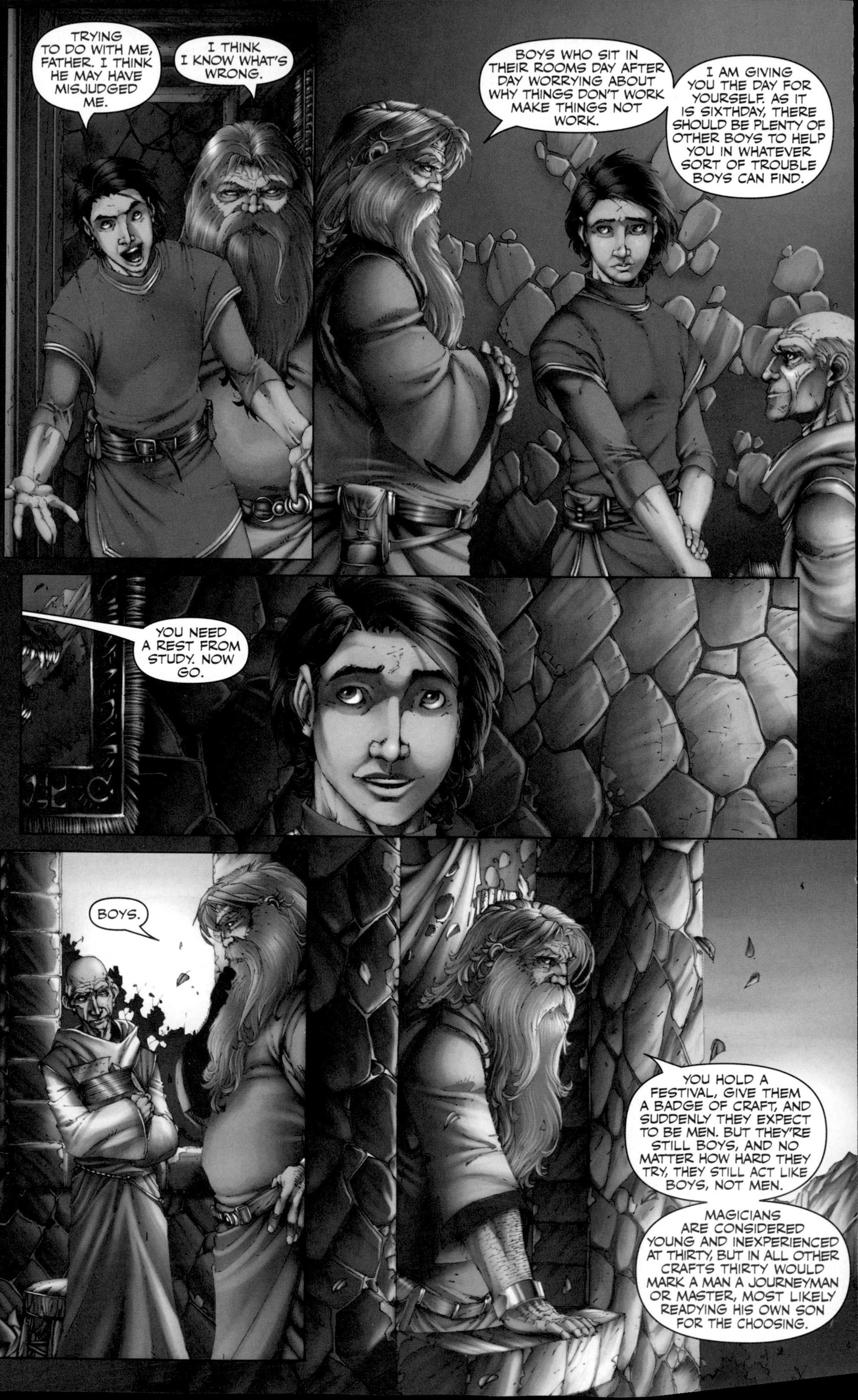
TRYING TO DO WITH ME, FATHER. I THINK HE MAY HAVE MISJUDGED ME.
I THINK I KNOW WHAT'S WRONG.
BOYS WHO SIT IN THEIR ROOMS DAY AFTER DAY WORRYING ABOUT WHY THINGS DON'T WORK MAKE THINGS NOT WORK.
I AM GIVING YOU THE DAY FOR YOURSELF. AS IT IS SIXTHDAY, THERE SHOULD BE PLENTY OF OTHER BOYS TO HELP YOU IN WHATEVER SORT OF TROUBLE BOYS CAN FIND.
YOU NEED A REST FROM STUDY. NOW GO.
BOYS.
YOU HOLD A FESTIVAL, GIVE THEM A BADGE OF CRAFT, AND SUDDENLY THEY EXPECT TO BE MEN. BUT THEY'RE STILL BOYS, AND NO MATTER HOW HARD THEY TRY, THEY STILL ACT LIKE BOYS, NOT MEN.
MAGICIANS ARE CONSIDERED YOUNG AND INEXPERIENCED AT THIRTY, BUT IN ALL OTHER CRAFTS THIRTY WOULD MARK A MAN A JOURNEYMAN OR MASTER, MOST LIKELY READYING HIS OWN SON FOR THE CHOOSING.

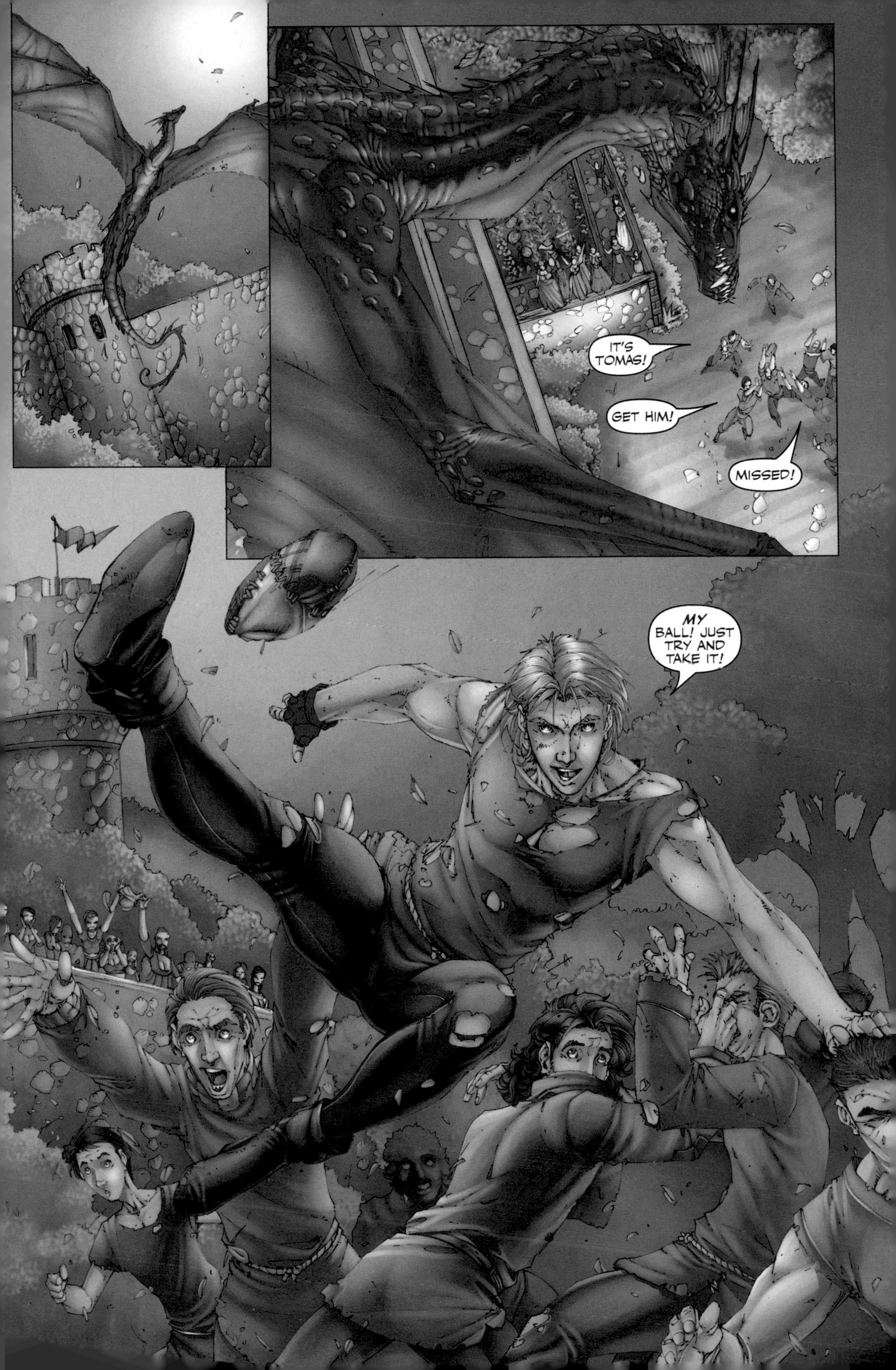
IT'S TOMAS!
GET HIM!
MISSED!
MY BALL! JUST TRY AND TAKE IT!

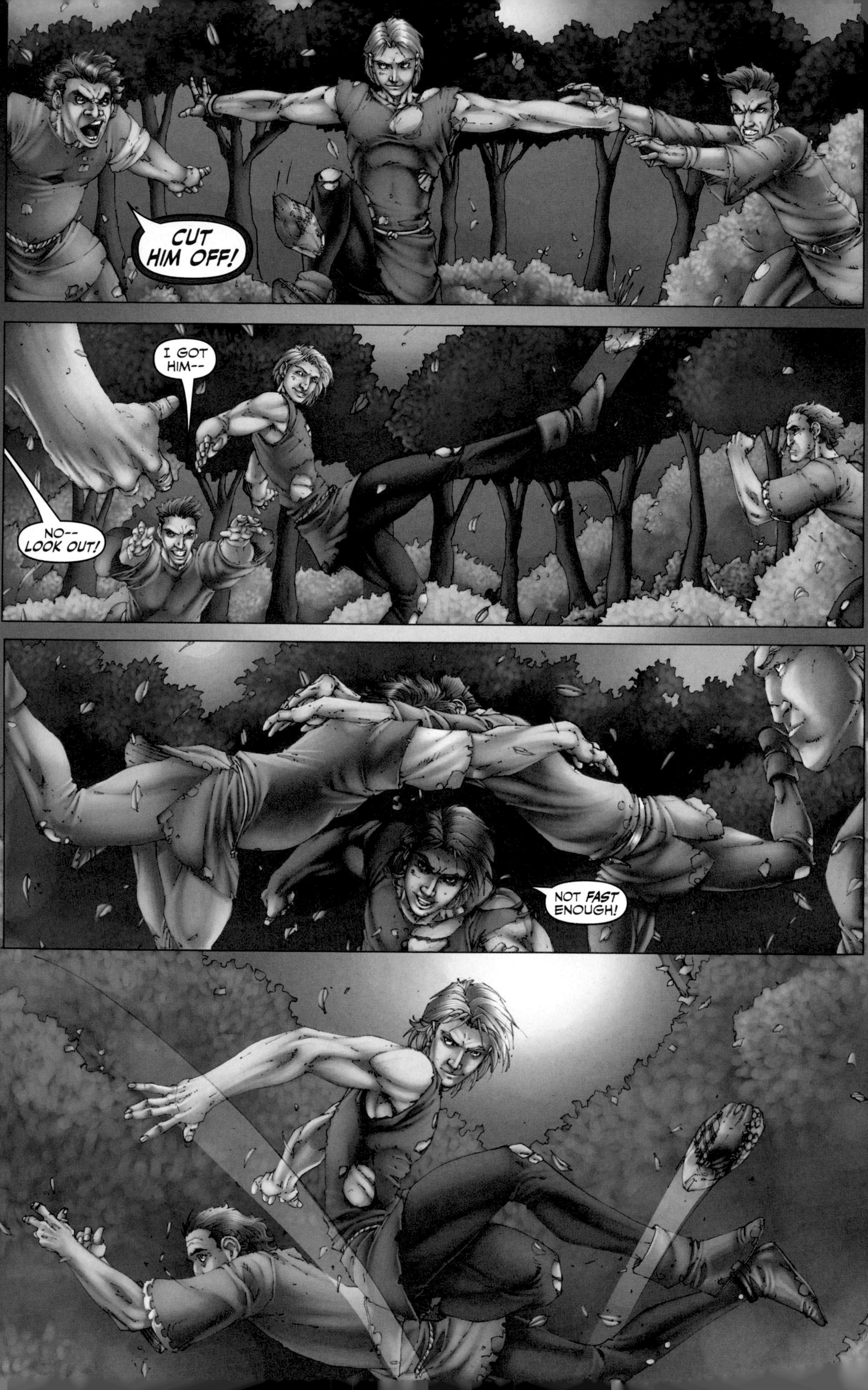
CUT HIM OFF!
I GOT HIM--
NO-- LOOK OUT!
NOT FAST ENOUGH!

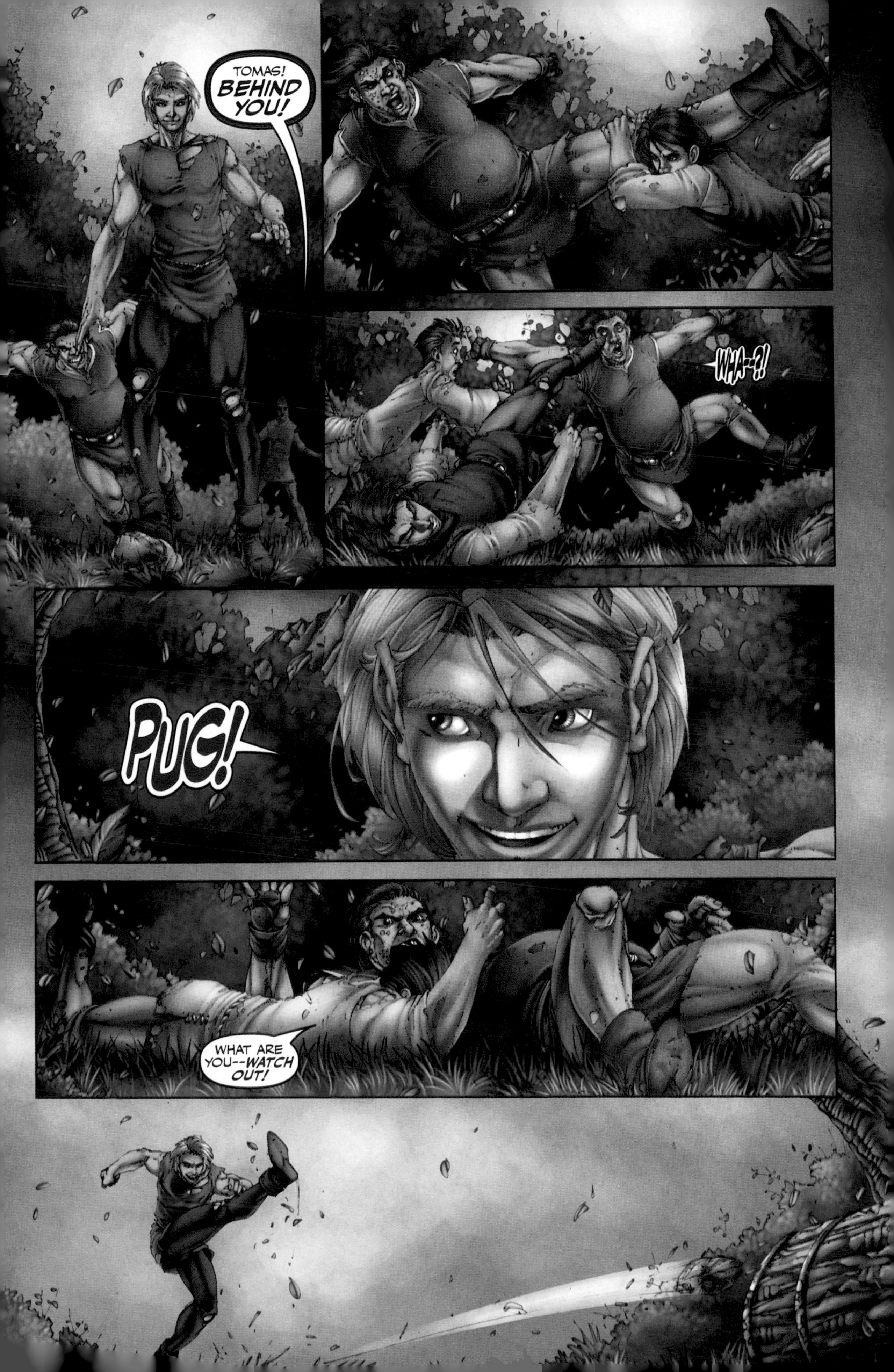

TOMAS! BEHIND YOU!
WHA--?!
PUG!
WHAT ARE YOU--WATCH OUT!

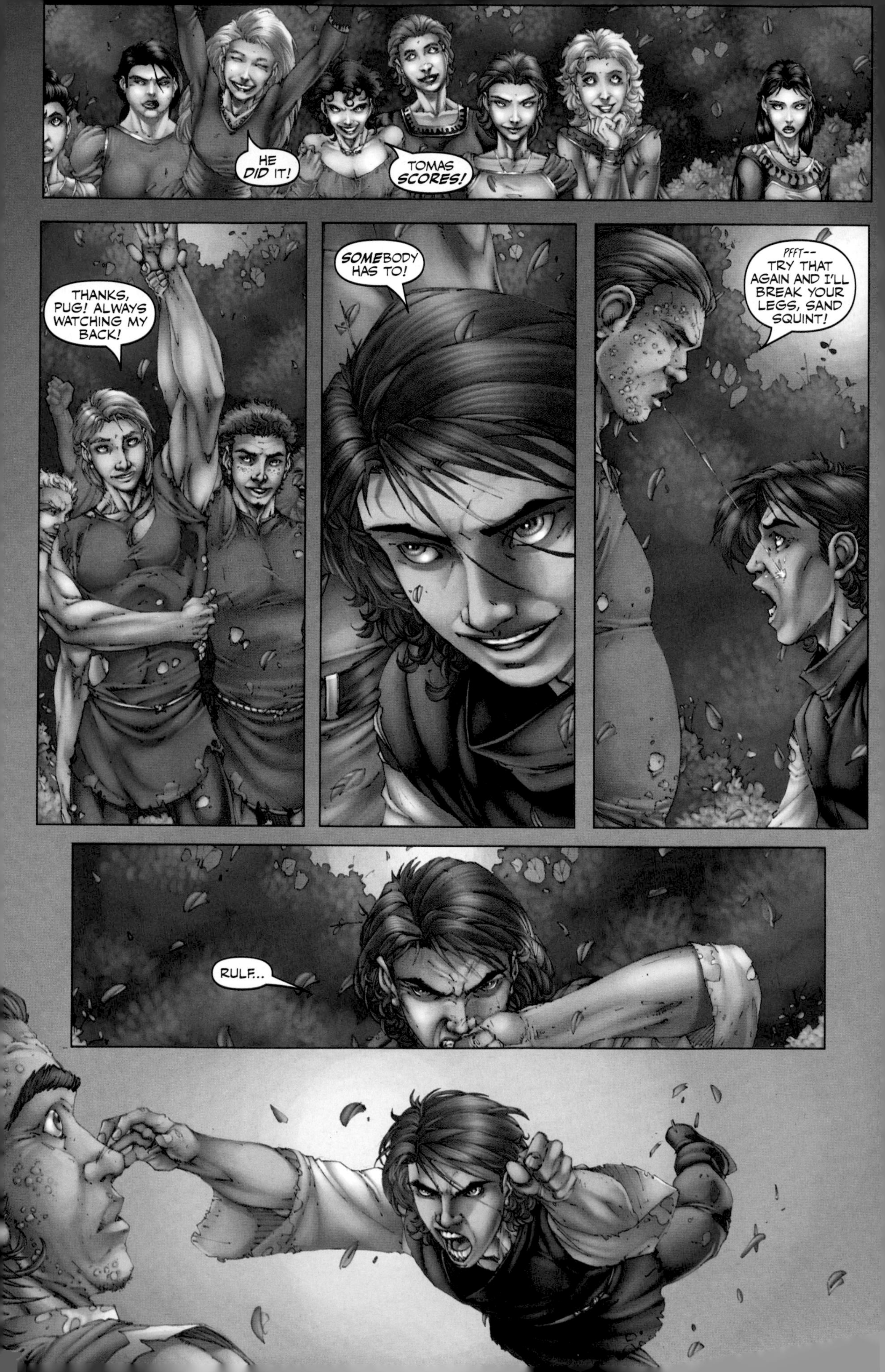
HE DID IT!
TOMAS SCORES!
THANKS, PUG! ALWAYS WATCHING MY BACK!
SOMEBODY HAS TO!
PFFT-- TRY THAT AGAIN AND I'LL BREAK YOUR LEGS, SAND SQUINT!
RULF...

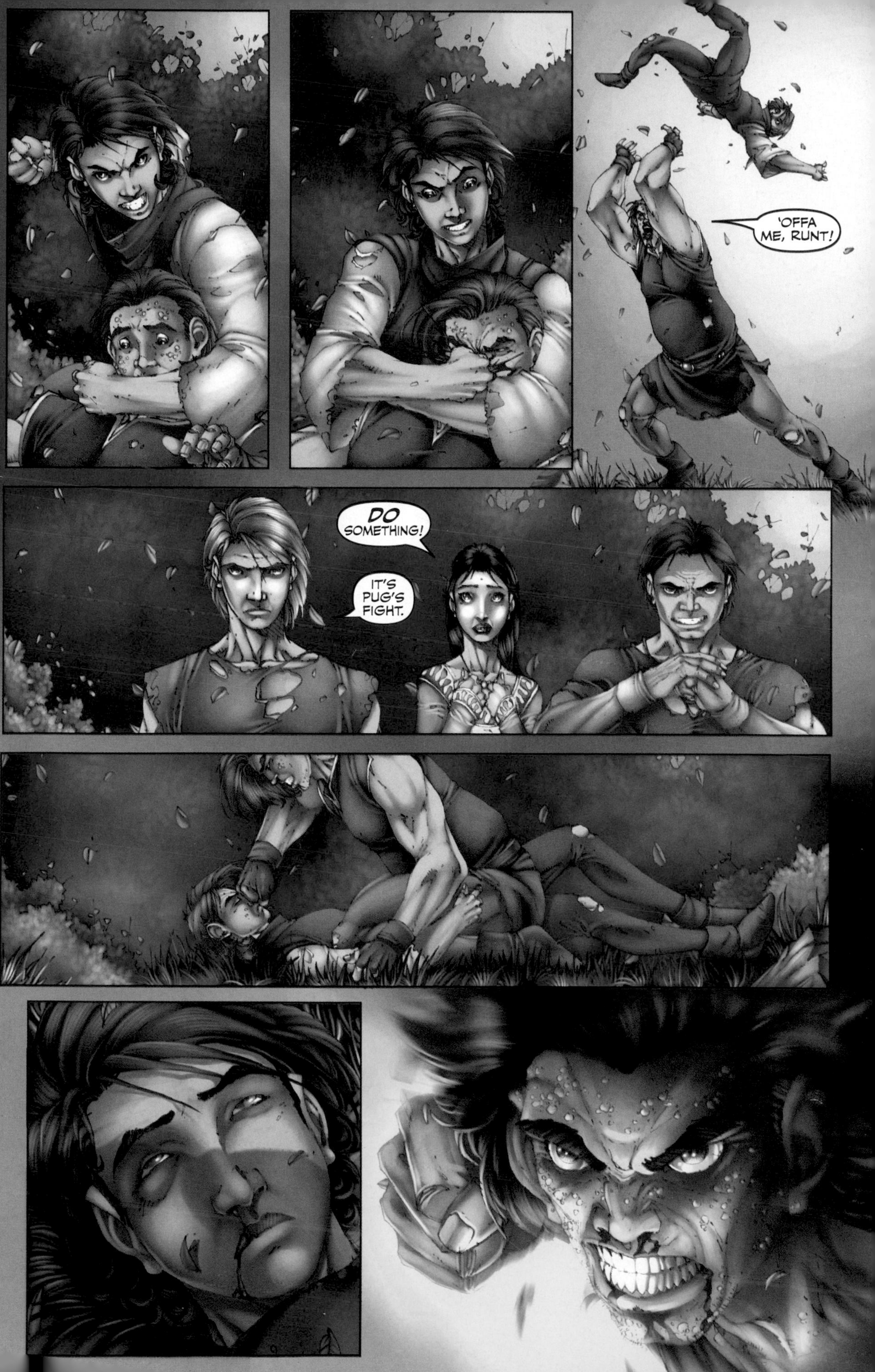
'OFFA ME, RUNT!
DO SOMETHING!
IT'S PUG'S FIGHT.

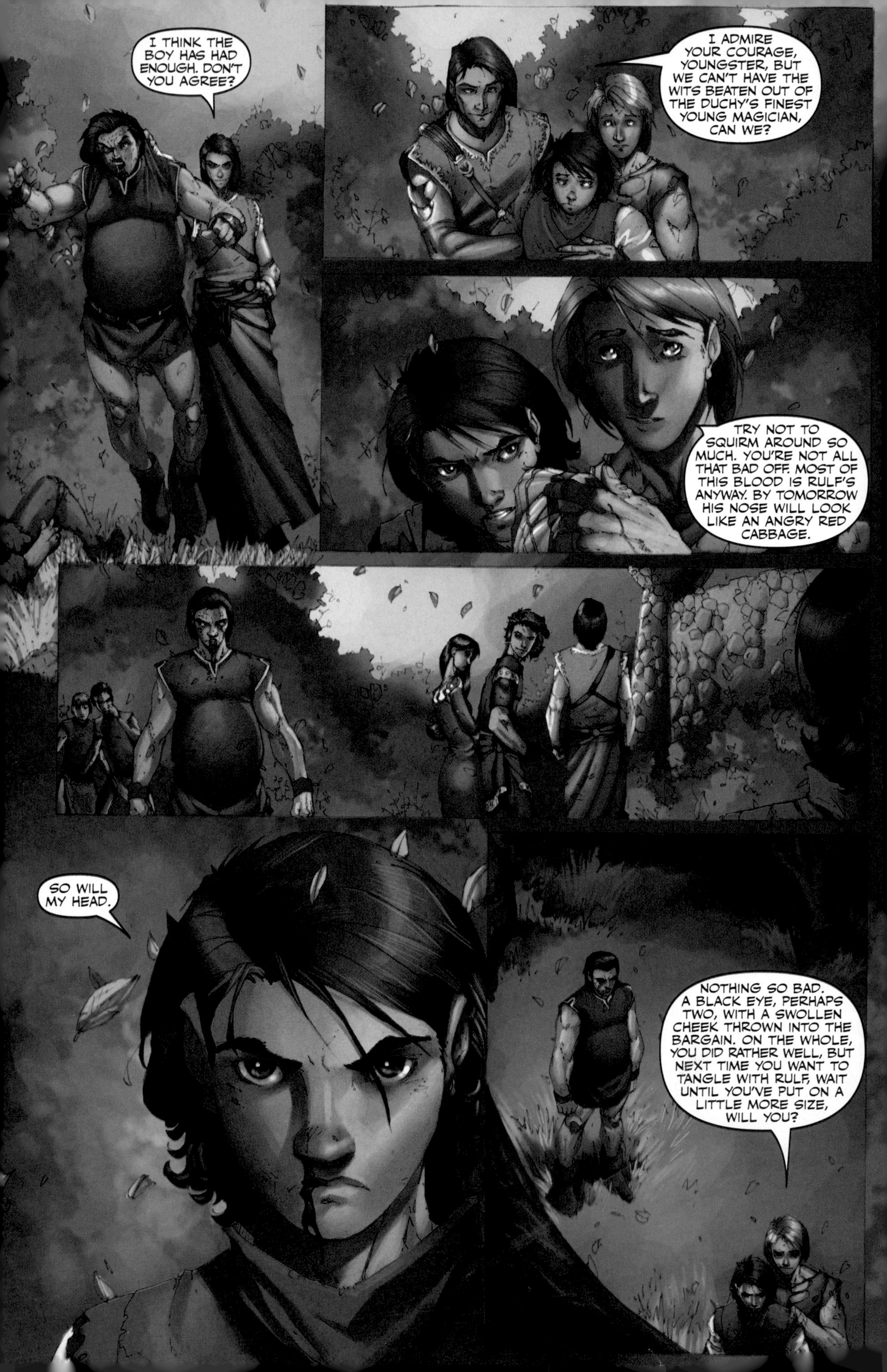
I THINK THE BOY HAS HAD ENOUGH. DON'T YOU AGREE?
I ADMIRE YOUR COURAGE, YOUNGSTER, BUT WE CAN'T HAVE THE WITS BEATEN OUT OF THE DUCHY'S FINEST YOUNG MAGICIAN, CAN WE?
TRY NOT TO SQUIRM AROUND SO MUCH. YOU'RE NOT ALL THAT BAD OFF. MOST OF THIS BLOOD IS RULF'S ANYWAY. BY TOMORROW HIS NOSE WILL LOOK LIKE AN ANGRY RED CABBAGE.
SO WILL MY HEAD.
NOTHING SO BAD. A BLACK EYE, PERHAPS TWO, WITH A SWOLLEN CHEEK THROWN INTO THE BARGAIN. ON THE WHOLE, YOU DID RATHER WELL, BUT NEXT TIME YOU WANT TO TANGLE WITH RULF, WAIT UNTIL YOU'VE PUT ON A LITTLE MORE SIZE, WILL YOU?

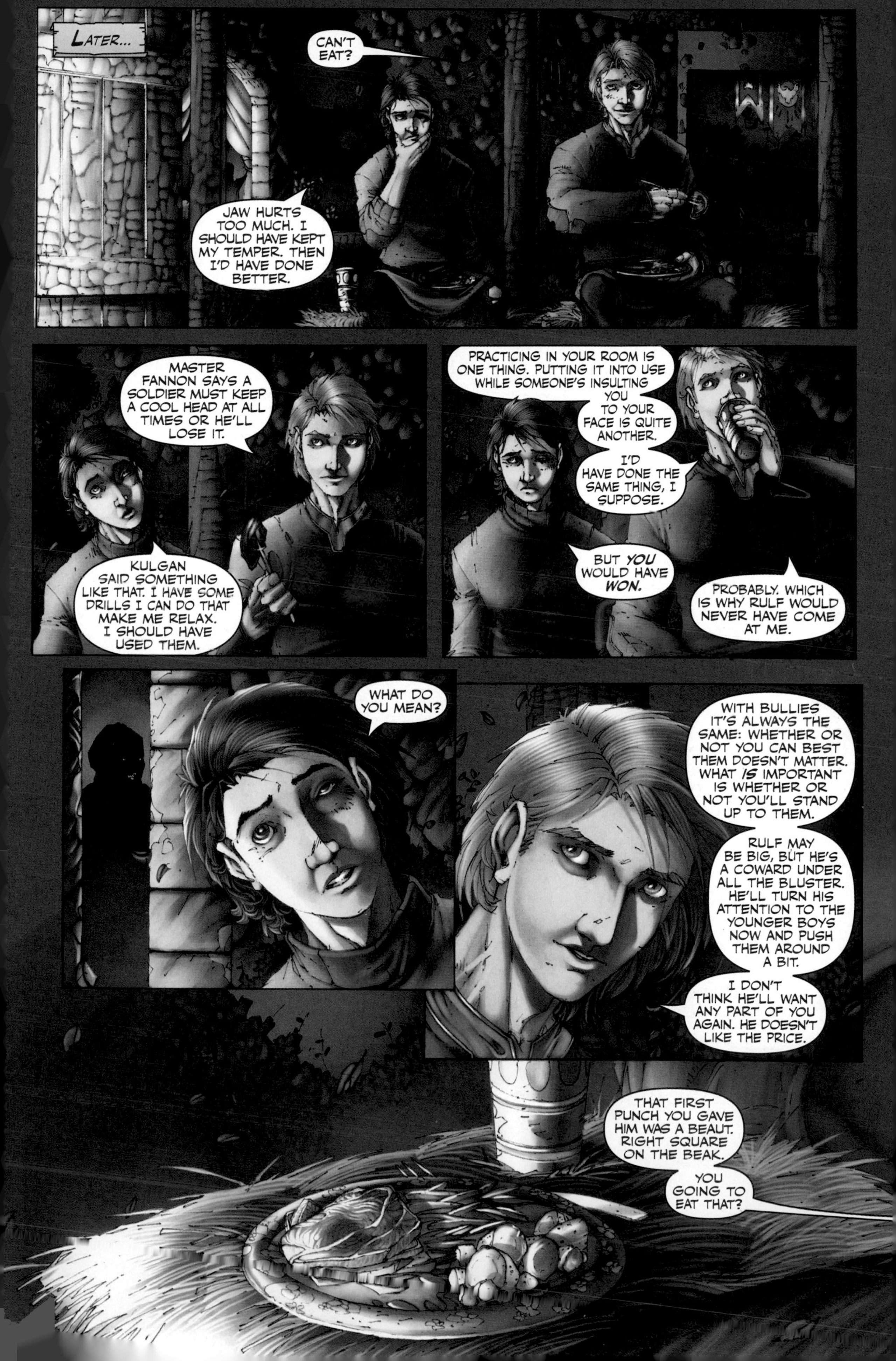
LATER...
CAN'T EAT?
JAW HURTS TOO MUCH. I SHOULD HAVE KEPT MY TEMPER. THEN I'D HAVE DONE BETTER.
MASTER FANNON SAYS A SOLDIER MUST KEEP A COOL HEAD AT ALL TIMES OR HE'LL LOSE IT.
KULGAN SAID SOMETHING LIKE THAT. I HAVE SOME DRILLS I CAN DO THAT MAKE ME RELAX. I SHOULD HAVE USED THEM.
PRACTICING IN YOUR ROOM IS ONE THING. PUTTING IT INTO USE WHILE SOMEONE'S INSULTING YOU TO YOUR FACE IS QUITE ANOTHER.
I'D HAVE DONE THE SAME THING, I SUPPOSE.
BUT *YOU* WOULD HAVE *WON.*
PROBABLY. WHICH IS WHY RULF WOULD NEVER HAVE COME AT ME.
WHAT DO YOU MEAN?
WITH BULLIES IT'S ALWAYS THE SAME: WHETHER OR NOT YOU CAN BEST THEM DOESN'T MATTER. WHAT *IS* IMPORTANT IS WHETHER OR NOT YOU'LL STAND UP TO THEM.
RULF MAY BE BIG, BUT HE'S A COWARD UNDER ALL THE BLUSTER. HE'LL TURN HIS ATTENTION TO THE YOUNGER BOYS NOW AND PUSH THEM AROUND A BIT.
I DON'T THINK HE'LL WANT ANY PART OF YOU AGAIN. HE DOESN'T LIKE THE PRICE.
THAT FIRST PUNCH YOU GAVE HIM WAS A BEAUT. RIGHT SQUARE ON THE BEAK.
YOU GOING TO EAT THAT?

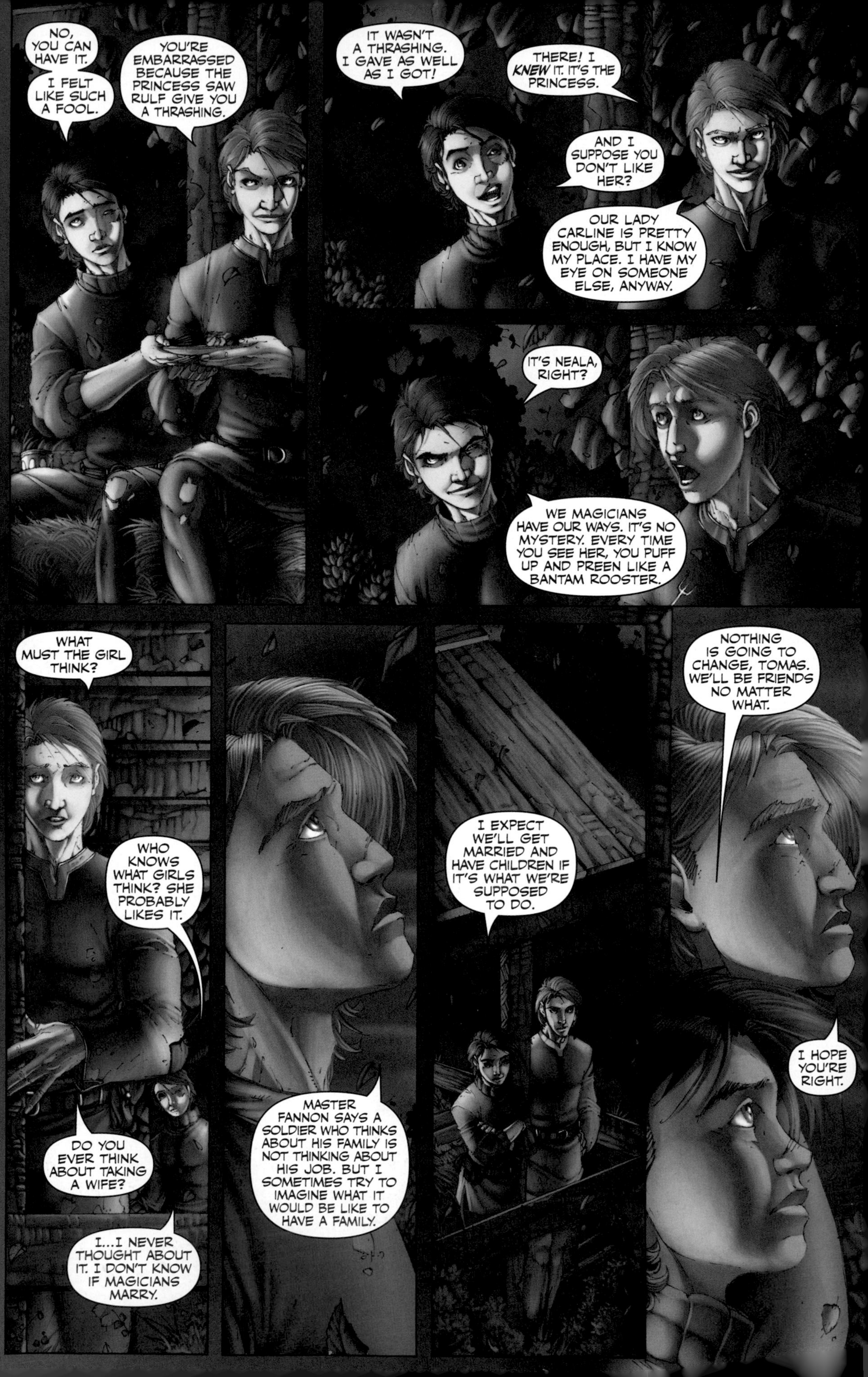

NO, YOU CAN HAVE IT.
I FELT LIKE SUCH A FOOL.
YOU'RE EMBARRASSED BECAUSE THE PRINCESS SAW RULF GIVE YOU A THRASHING.
IT WASN'T A THRASHING. I GAVE AS WELL AS I GOT!
THERE! I *KNEW* IT. IT'S THE PRINCESS.
AND I SUPPOSE YOU DON'T LIKE HER?
OUR LADY CARLINE IS PRETTY ENOUGH, BUT I KNOW MY PLACE. I HAVE MY EYE ON SOMEONE ELSE, ANYWAY.
IT'S NEALA, RIGHT?
WE MAGICIANS HAVE OUR WAYS. IT'S NO MYSTERY. EVERY TIME YOU SEE HER, YOU PUFF UP AND PREEN LIKE A BANTAM ROOSTER.
WHAT MUST THE GIRL THINK?
WHO KNOWS WHAT GIRLS THINK? SHE PROBABLY LIKES IT.
DO YOU EVER THINK ABOUT TAKING A WIFE?
I...I NEVER THOUGHT ABOUT IT. I DON'T KNOW IF MAGICIANS MARRY.
MASTER FANNON SAYS A SOLDIER WHO THINKS ABOUT HIS FAMILY IS NOT THINKING ABOUT HIS JOB. BUT I SOMETIMES TRY TO IMAGINE WHAT IT WOULD BE LIKE TO HAVE A FAMILY.
I EXPECT WE'LL GET MARRIED AND HAVE CHILDREN IF IT'S WHAT WE'RE SUPPOSED TO DO.
NOTHING IS GOING TO CHANGE, TOMAS. WE'LL BE FRIENDS NO MATTER WHAT.
I HOPE YOU'RE RIGHT.

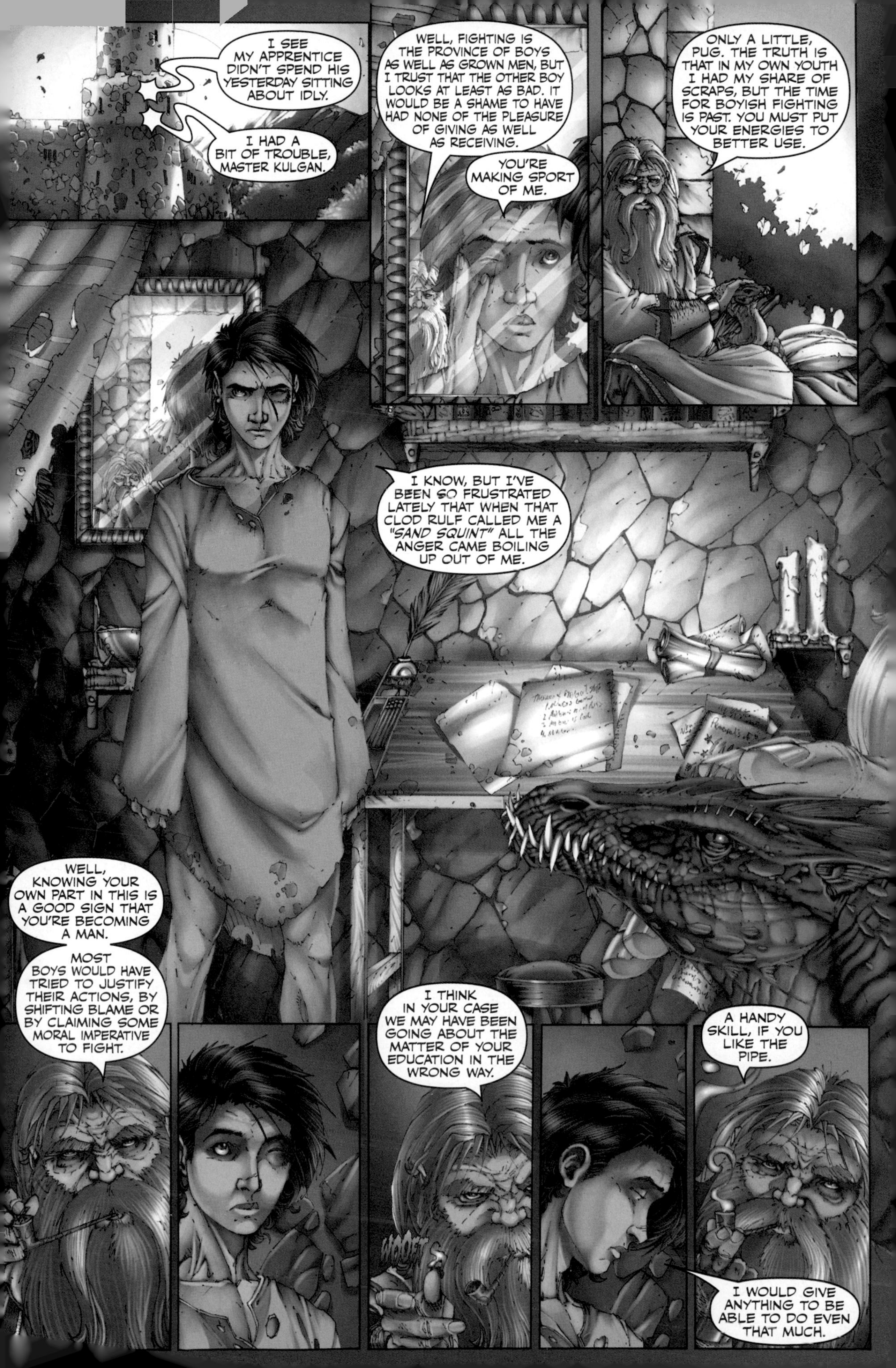
I SEE MY APPRENTICE DIDN'T SPEND HIS YESTERDAY SITTING ABOUT IDLY.
I HAD A BIT OF TROUBLE, MASTER KULGAN.
WELL, FIGHTING IS THE PROVINCE OF BOYS AS WELL AS GROWN MEN, BUT I TRUST THAT THE OTHER BOY LOOKS AT LEAST AS BAD. IT WOULD BE A SHAME TO HAVE HAD NONE OF THE PLEASURE OF GIVING AS WELL AS RECEIVING.
YOU'RE MAKING SPORT OF ME.
ONLY A LITTLE, PUG. THE TRUTH IS THAT IN MY OWN YOUTH I HAD MY SHARE OF SCRAPS, BUT THE TIME FOR BOYISH FIGHTING IS PAST. YOU MUST PUT YOUR ENERGIES TO BETTER USE.
I KNOW, BUT I'VE BEEN SO FRUSTRATED LATELY THAT WHEN THAT CLOD RULF CALLED ME A "SAND SQUINT" ALL THE ANGER CAME BOILING UP OUT OF ME.
WELL, KNOWING YOUR OWN PART IN THIS IS A GOOD SIGN THAT YOU'RE BECOMING A MAN.
MOST BOYS WOULD HAVE TRIED TO JUSTIFY THEIR ACTIONS, BY SHIFTING BLAME OR BY CLAIMING SOME MORAL IMPERATIVE TO FIGHT.
I THINK IN YOUR CASE WE MAY HAVE BEEN GOING ABOUT THE MATTER OF YOUR EDUCATION IN THE WRONG WAY.
WOOF
A HANDY SKILL, IF YOU LIKE THE PIPE.
I WOULD GIVE ANYTHING TO BE ABLE TO DO EVEN THAT MUCH.

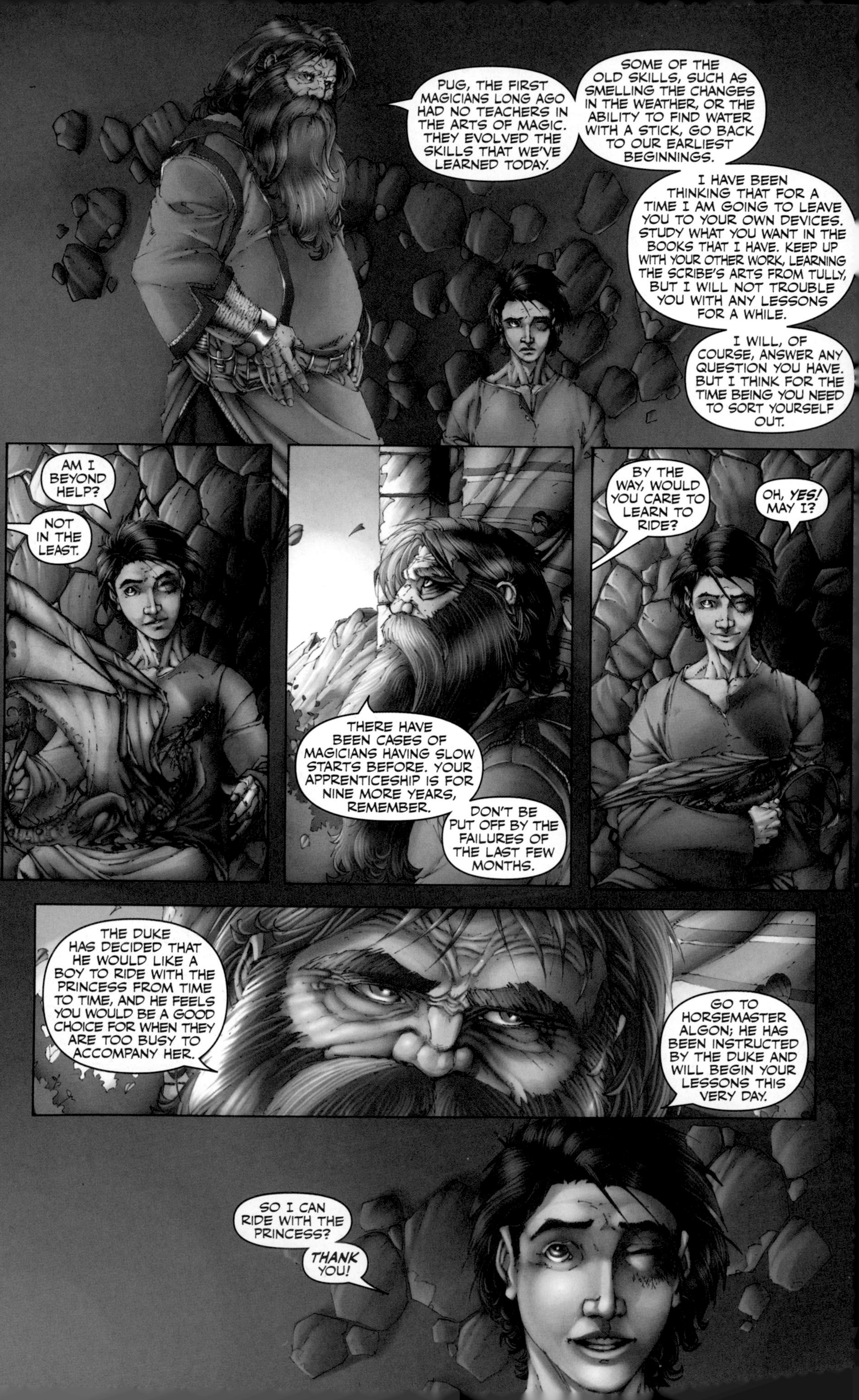
PUG, THE FIRST MAGICIANS LONG AGO HAD NO TEACHERS IN THE ARTS OF MAGIC. THEY EVOLVED THE SKILLS THAT WE'VE LEARNED TODAY.
SOME OF THE OLD SKILLS, SUCH AS SMELLING THE CHANGES IN THE WEATHER, OR THE ABILITY TO FIND WATER WITH A STICK, GO BACK TO OUR EARLIEST BEGINNINGS.
I HAVE BEEN THINKING THAT FOR A TIME I AM GOING TO LEAVE YOU TO YOUR OWN DEVICES. STUDY WHAT YOU WANT IN THE BOOKS THAT I HAVE. KEEP UP WITH YOUR OTHER WORK, LEARNING THE SCRIBE'S ARTS FROM TULLY, BUT I WILL NOT TROUBLE YOU WITH ANY LESSONS FOR A WHILE.
I WILL, OF COURSE, ANSWER ANY QUESTION YOU HAVE. BUT I THINK FOR THE TIME BEING YOU NEED TO SORT YOURSELF OUT.
AM I BEYOND HELP?
NOT IN THE LEAST.
THERE HAVE BEEN CASES OF MAGICIANS HAVING SLOW STARTS BEFORE. YOUR APPRENTICESHIP IS FOR NINE MORE YEARS, REMEMBER.
DON'T BE PUT OFF BY THE FAILURES OF THE LAST FEW MONTHS.
BY THE WAY, WOULD YOU CARE TO LEARN TO RIDE?
OH, *YES!* MAY I?
THE DUKE HAS DECIDED THAT HE WOULD LIKE A BOY TO RIDE WITH THE PRINCESS FROM TIME TO TIME, AND HE FEELS YOU WOULD BE A GOOD CHOICE FOR WHEN THEY ARE TOO BUSY TO ACCOMPANY HER.
GO TO HORSEMASTER ALGON; HE HAS BEEN INSTRUCTED BY THE DUKE AND WILL BEGIN YOUR LESSONS THIS VERY DAY.
SO I CAN RIDE WITH THE PRINCESS?
THANK YOU!

MAGICIAN: APPRENTICE
CHAPTER THREE

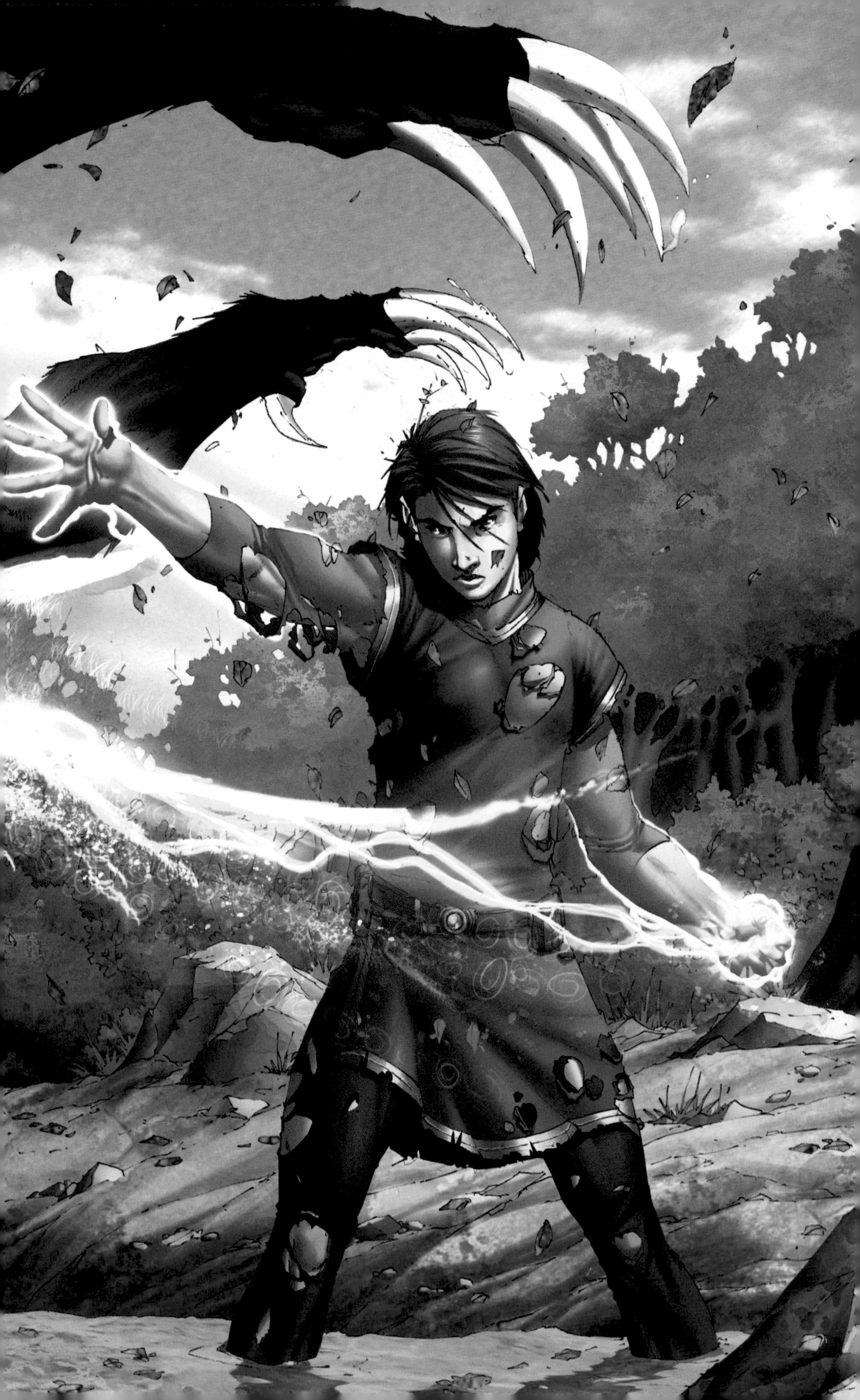

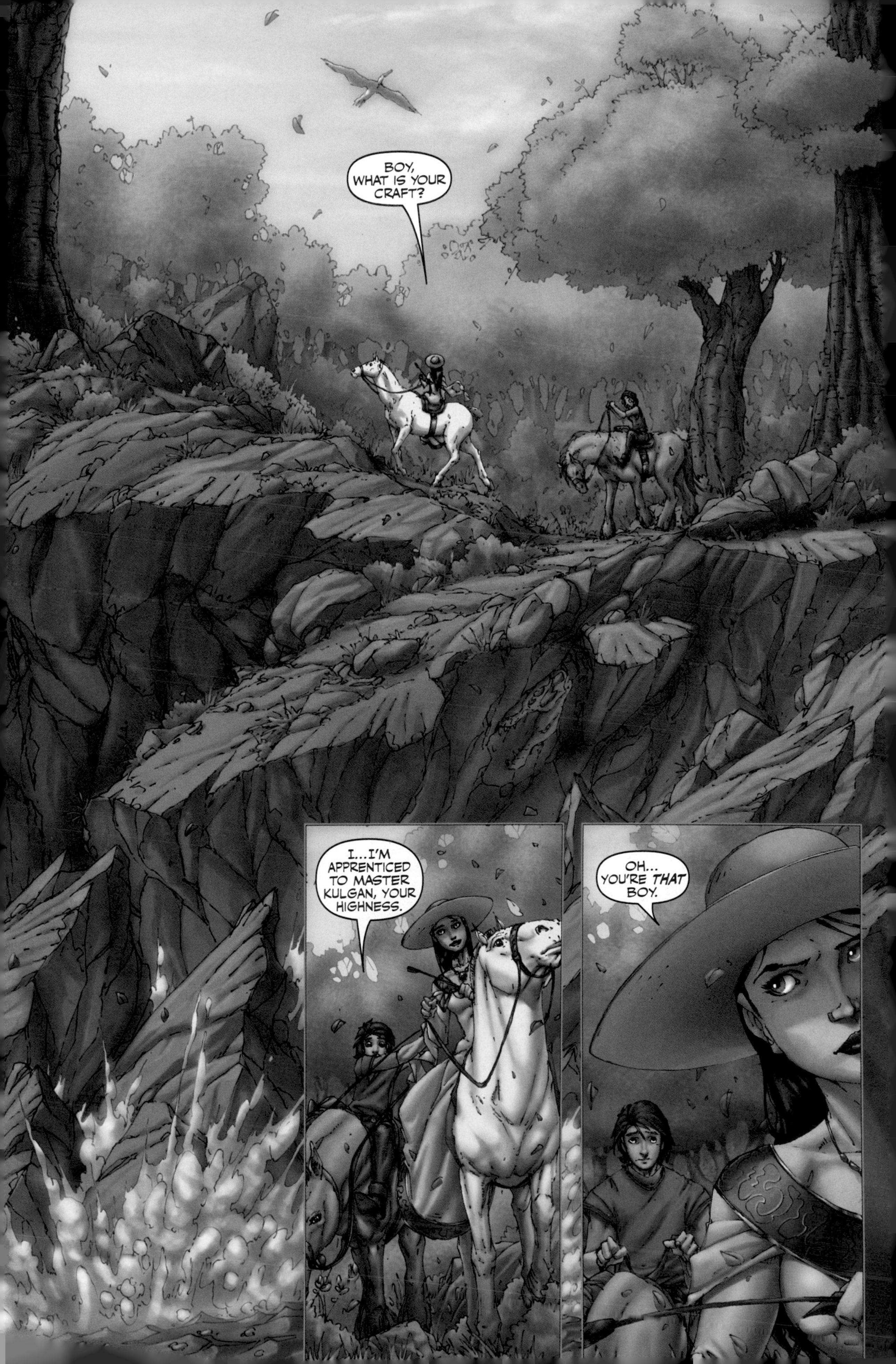
BOY, WHAT IS YOUR CRAFT?
I...I'M APPRENTICED TO MASTER KULGAN, YOUR HIGHNESS.
OH... YOU'RE *THAT* BOY.

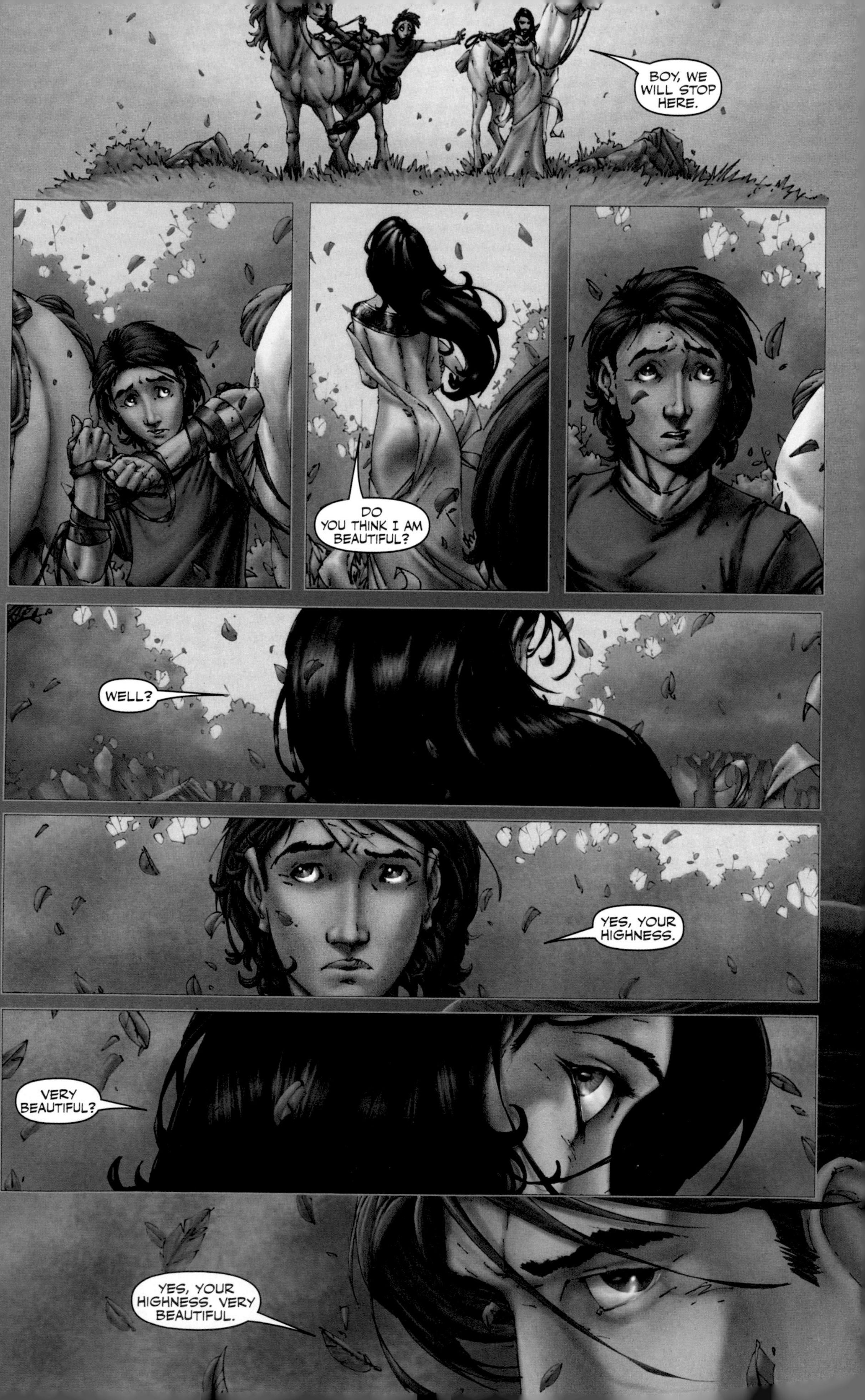
BOY, WE WILL STOP HERE.
DO YOU THINK I AM BEAUTIFUL?
WELL?
YES, YOUR HIGHNESS.
VERY BEAUTIFUL?
YES, YOUR HIGHNESS. VERY BEAUTIFUL.

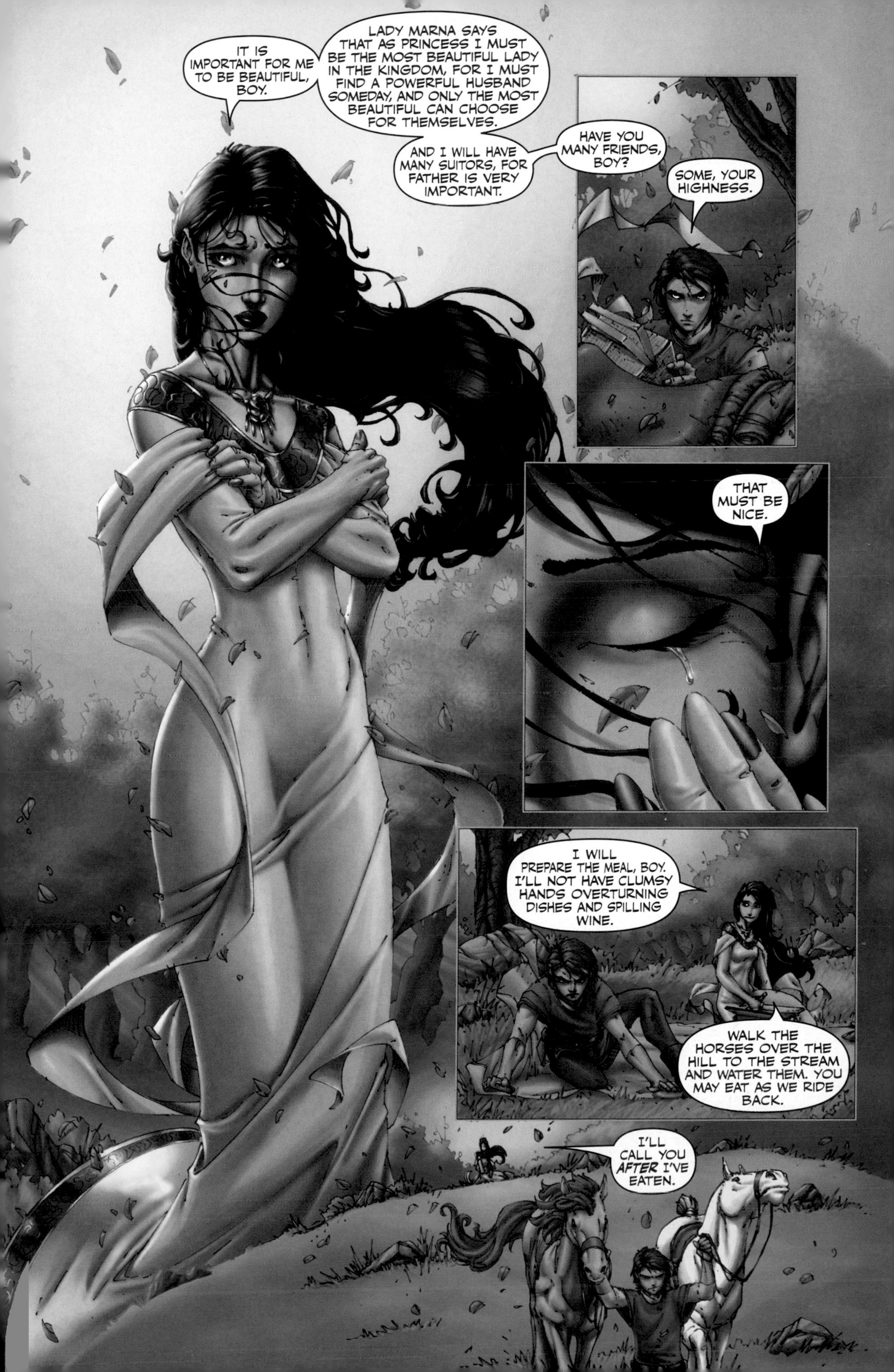
IT IS IMPORTANT FOR ME TO BE BEAUTIFUL, BOY.
LADY MARNA SAYS THAT AS PRINCESS I MUST BE THE MOST BEAUTIFUL LADY IN THE KINGDOM, FOR I MUST FIND A POWERFUL HUSBAND SOMEDAY, AND ONLY THE MOST BEAUTIFUL CAN CHOOSE FOR THEMSELVES.
AND I WILL HAVE MANY SUITORS, FOR FATHER IS VERY IMPORTANT.
HAVE YOU MANY FRIENDS, BOY?
SOME, YOUR HIGHNESS.
THAT MUST BE NICE.
I WILL PREPARE THE MEAL, BOY. I'LL NOT HAVE CLUMSY HANDS OVERTURNING DISHES AND SPILLING WINE.
WALK THE HORSES OVER THE HILL TO THE STREAM AND WATER THEM. YOU MAY EAT AS WE RIDE BACK.
I'LL CALL YOU *AFTER* I'VE EATEN.

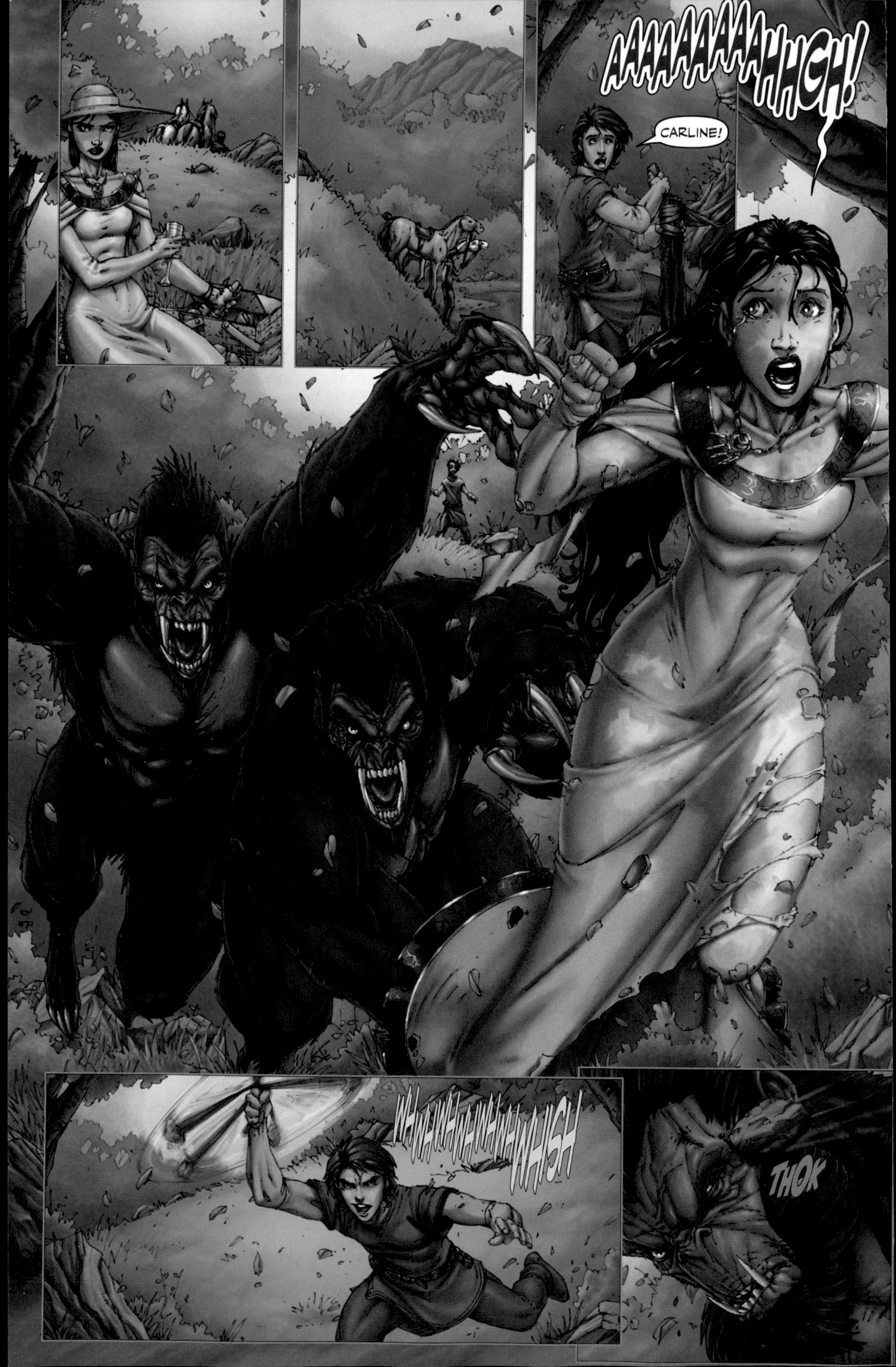
AAAAAAAAHHGH!
CARLINE!
WHWHWHWHWHWHWHISH
THOK

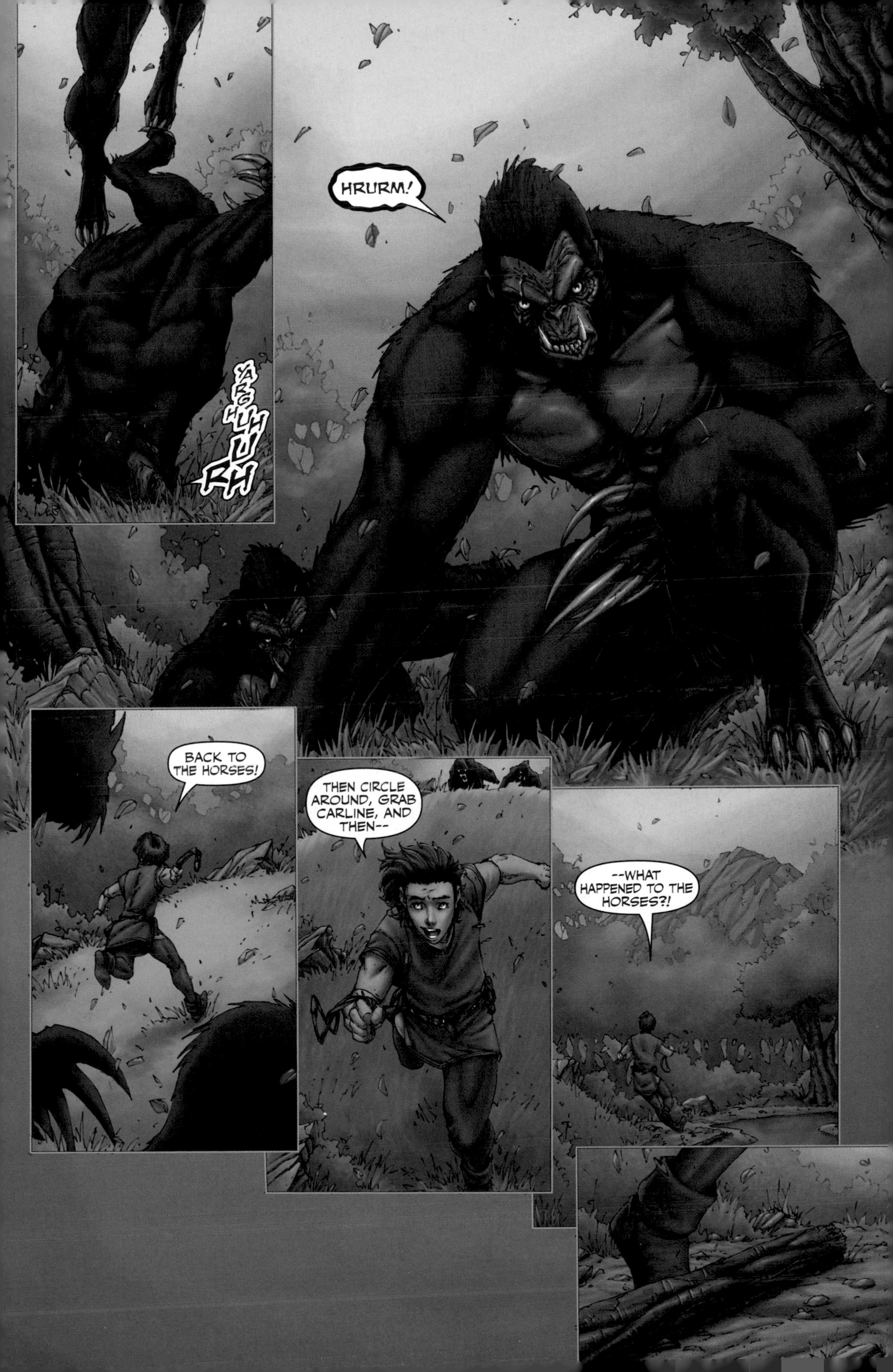
YARGHUHURH
HRURM!
BACK TO THE HORSES!
THEN CIRCLE AROUND, GRAB CARLINE, AND THEN--
--WHAT HAPPENED TO THE HORSES?!

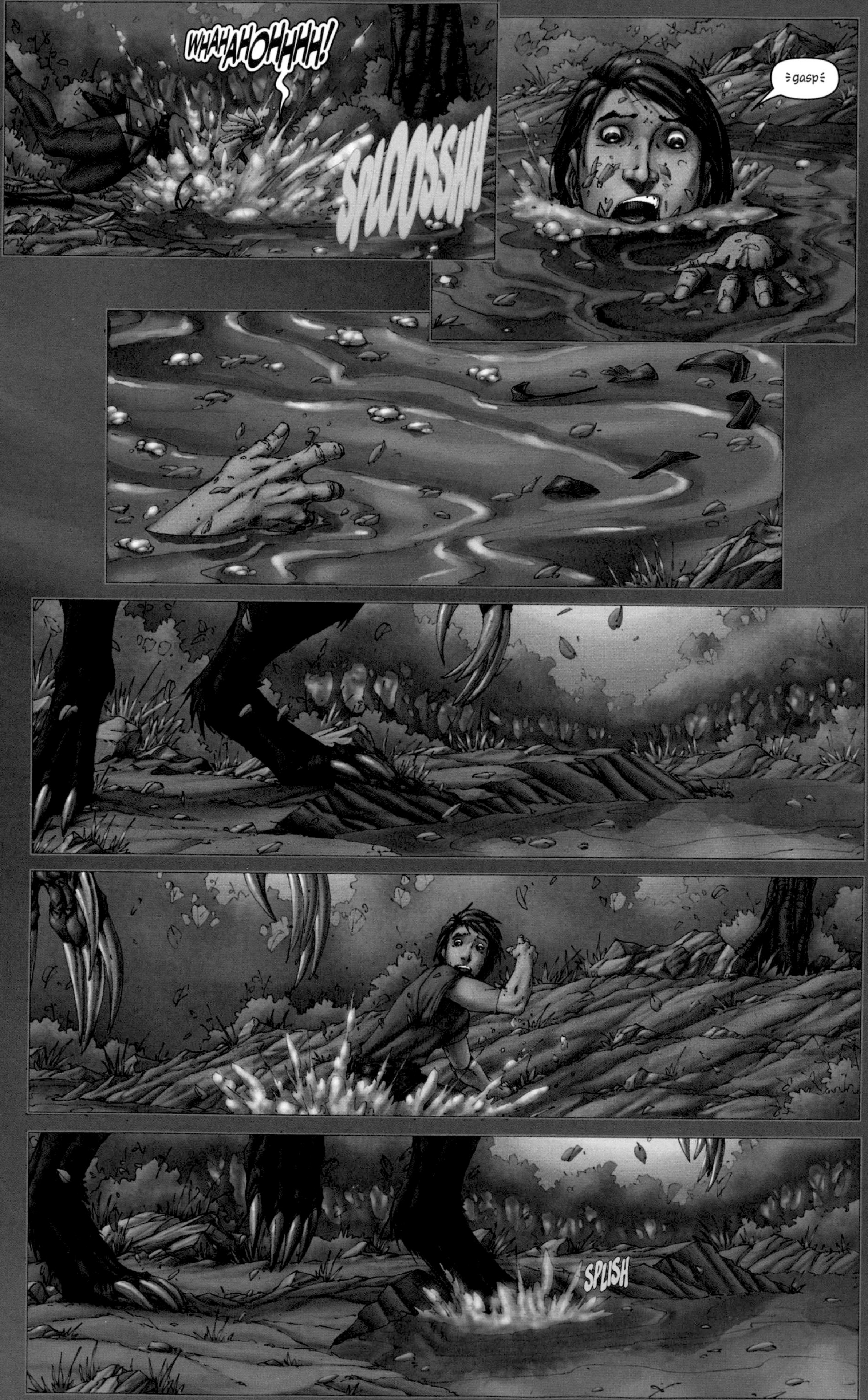
WHAHAHOHHH!
SPLOOSSHH
gasp
SPLISH

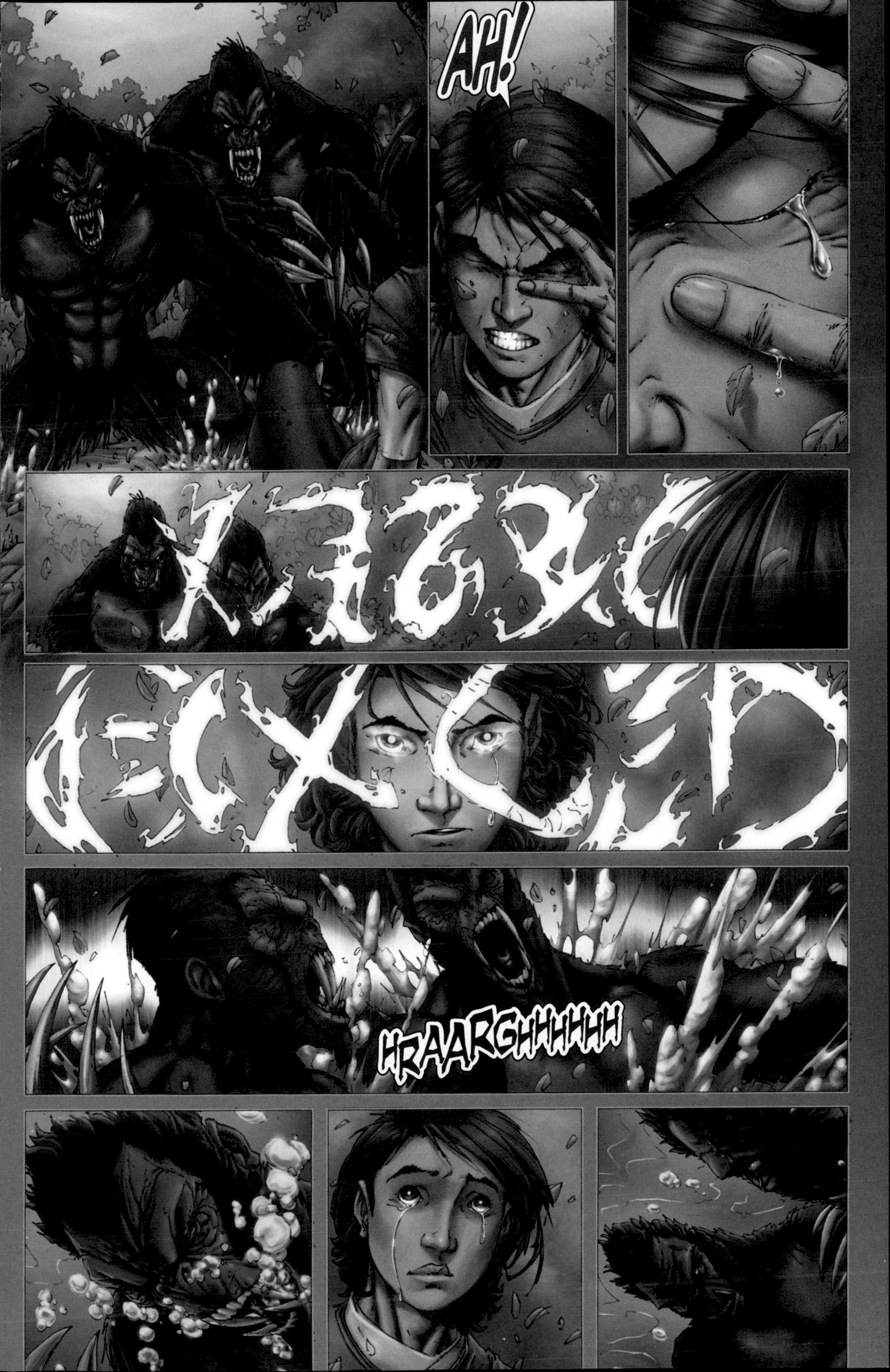
AH!
HRAARGHHHHH

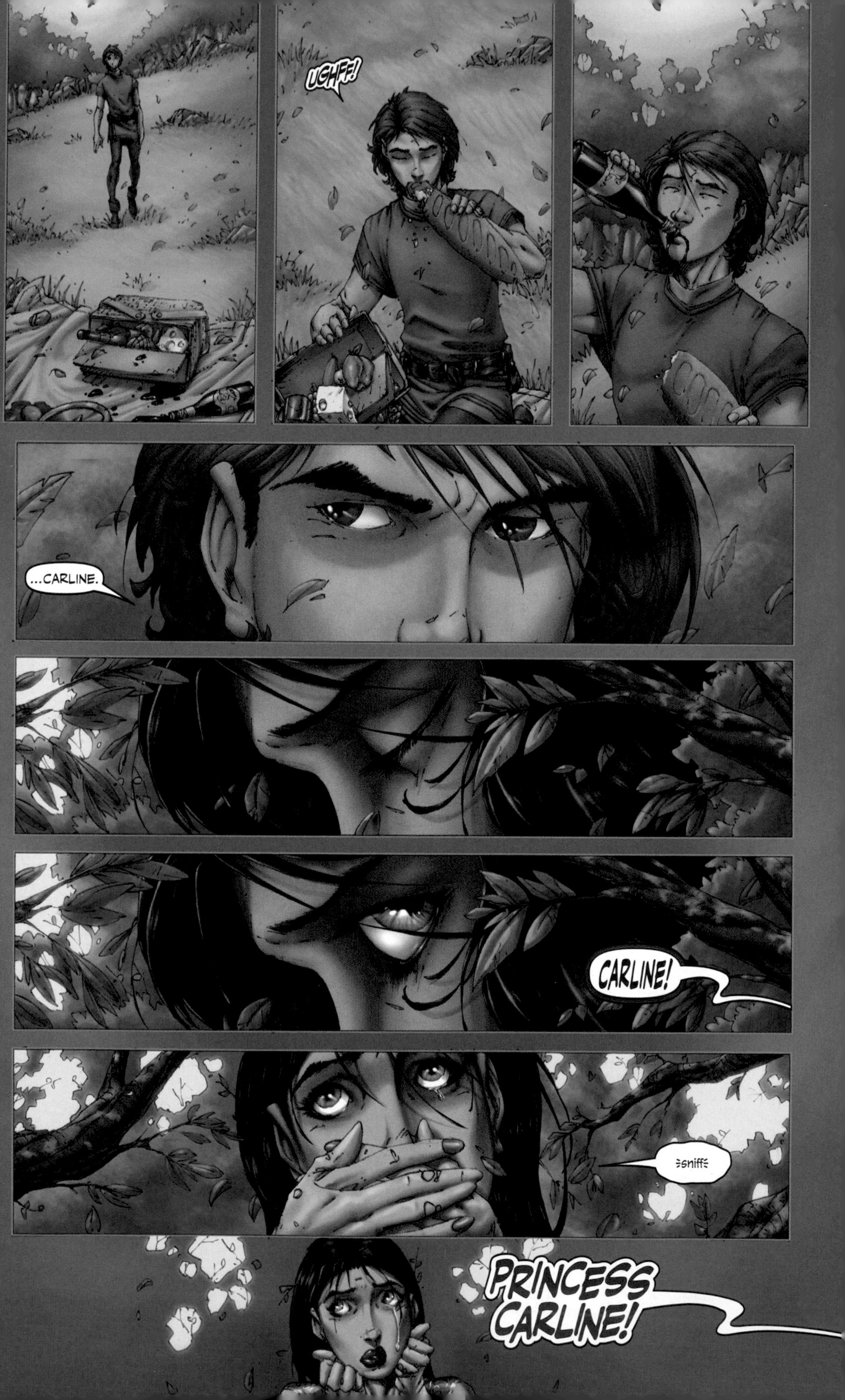
UGHFF!
...CARLINE.
CARLINE!
sniff
PRINCESS CARLINE!

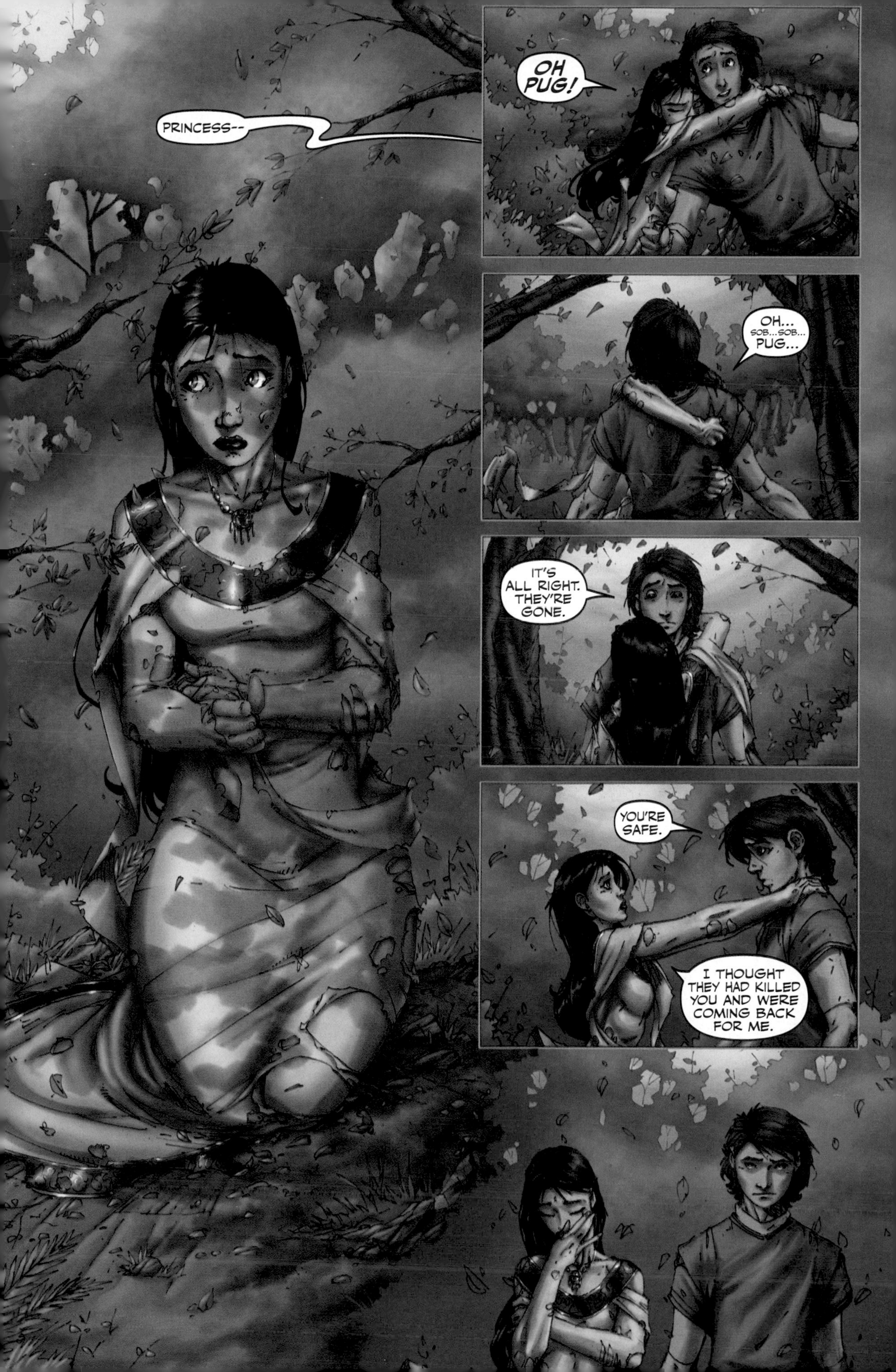
OH PUG!
PRINCESS--
OH... SOB...SOB... PUG...
IT'S ALL RIGHT. THEY'RE GONE.
YOU'RE SAFE.
I THOUGHT THEY HAD KILLED YOU AND WERE COMING BACK FOR ME.

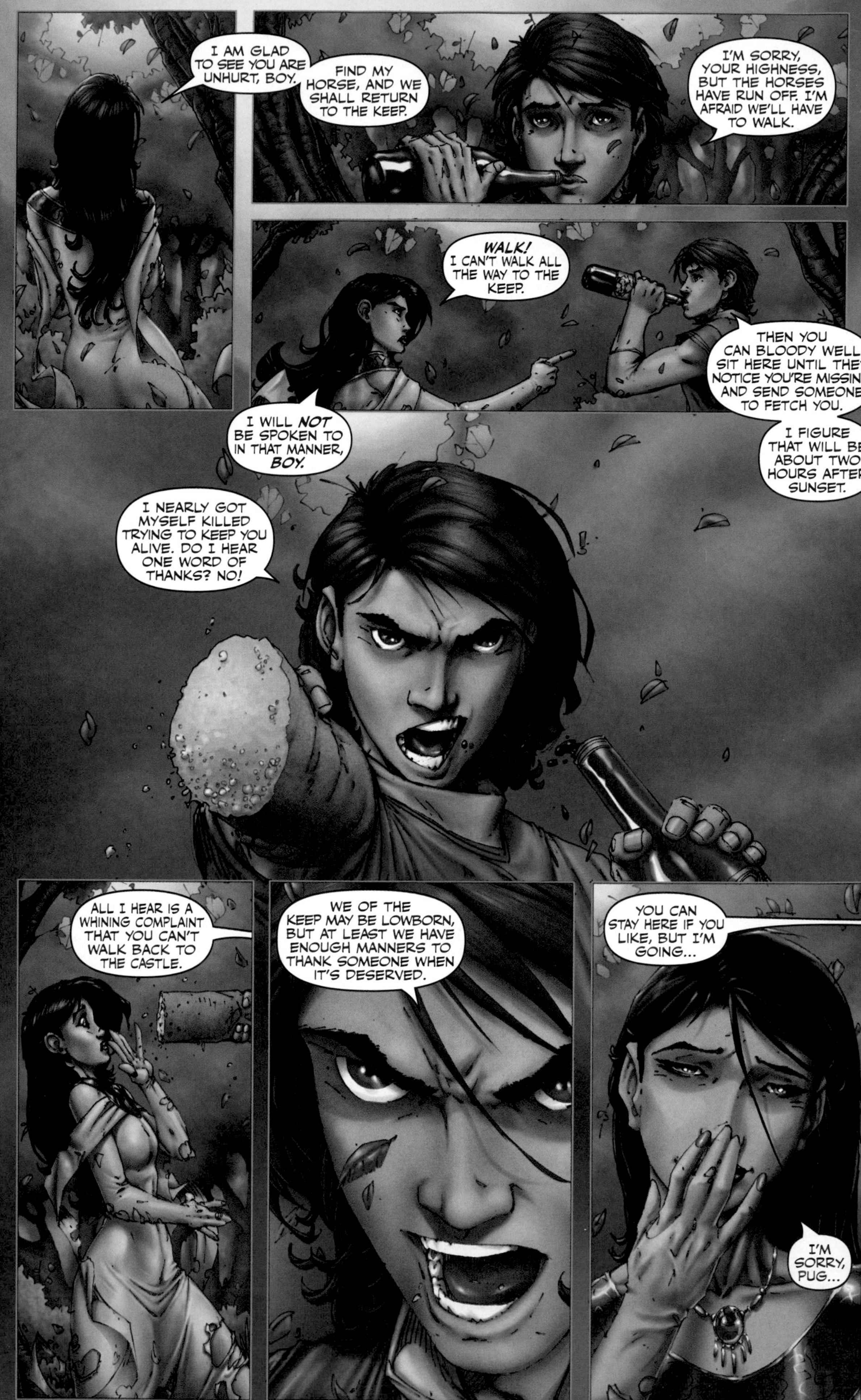
I AM GLAD TO SEE YOU ARE UNHURT, BOY.
FIND MY HORSE, AND WE SHALL RETURN TO THE KEEP.
I'M SORRY, YOUR HIGHNESS, BUT THE HORSES HAVE RUN OFF. I'M AFRAID WE'LL HAVE TO WALK.
WALK! I CAN'T WALK ALL THE WAY TO THE KEEP.
THEN YOU CAN BLOODY WELL SIT HERE UNTIL THEY NOTICE YOU'RE MISSING AND SEND SOMEONE TO FETCH YOU.
I FIGURE THAT WILL BE ABOUT TWO HOURS AFTER SUNSET.
I WILL NOT BE SPOKEN TO IN THAT MANNER, BOY.
I NEARLY GOT MYSELF KILLED TRYING TO KEEP YOU ALIVE. DO I HEAR ONE WORD OF THANKS? NO!
ALL I HEAR IS A WHINING COMPLAINT THAT YOU CAN'T WALK BACK TO THE CASTLE.
WE OF THE KEEP MAY BE LOWBORN, BUT AT LEAST WE HAVE ENOUGH MANNERS TO THANK SOMEONE WHEN IT'S DESERVED.
YOU CAN STAY HERE IF YOU LIKE, BUT I'M GOING...
I'M SORRY, PUG...

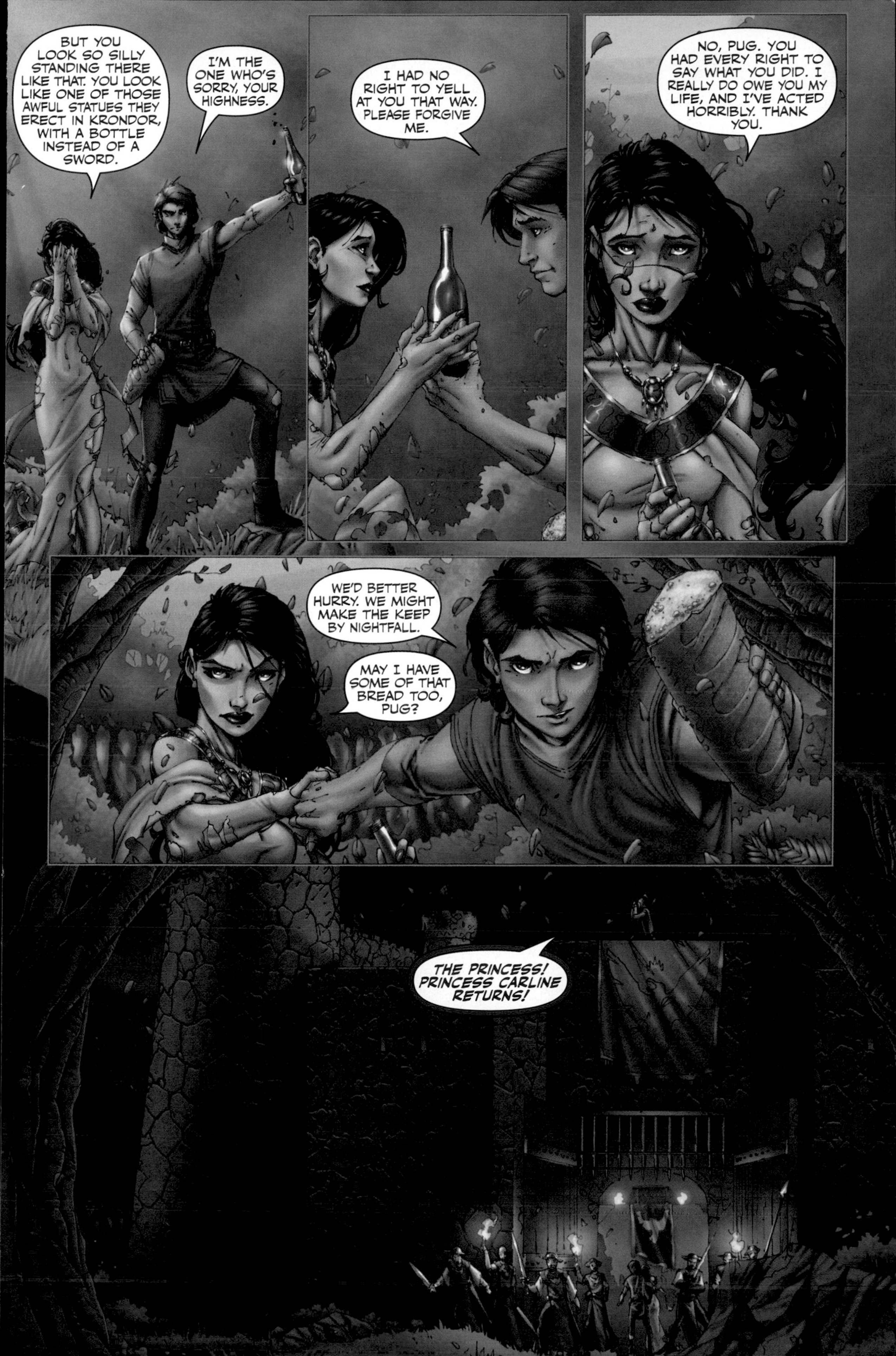

BUT YOU LOOK SO SILLY STANDING THERE LIKE THAT. YOU LOOK LIKE ONE OF THOSE AWFUL STATUES THEY ERECT IN KRONDOR, WITH A BOTTLE INSTEAD OF A SWORD.
I'M THE ONE WHO'S SORRY, YOUR HIGHNESS.
I HAD NO RIGHT TO YELL AT YOU THAT WAY. PLEASE FORGIVE ME.
NO, PUG. YOU HAD EVERY RIGHT TO SAY WHAT YOU DID. I REALLY DO OWE YOU MY LIFE, AND I'VE ACTED HORRIBLY. THANK YOU.
WE'D BETTER HURRY. WE MIGHT MAKE THE KEEP BY NIGHTFALL.
MAY I HAVE SOME OF THAT BREAD TOO, PUG?
THE PRINCESS! PRINCESS CARLINE RETURNS!

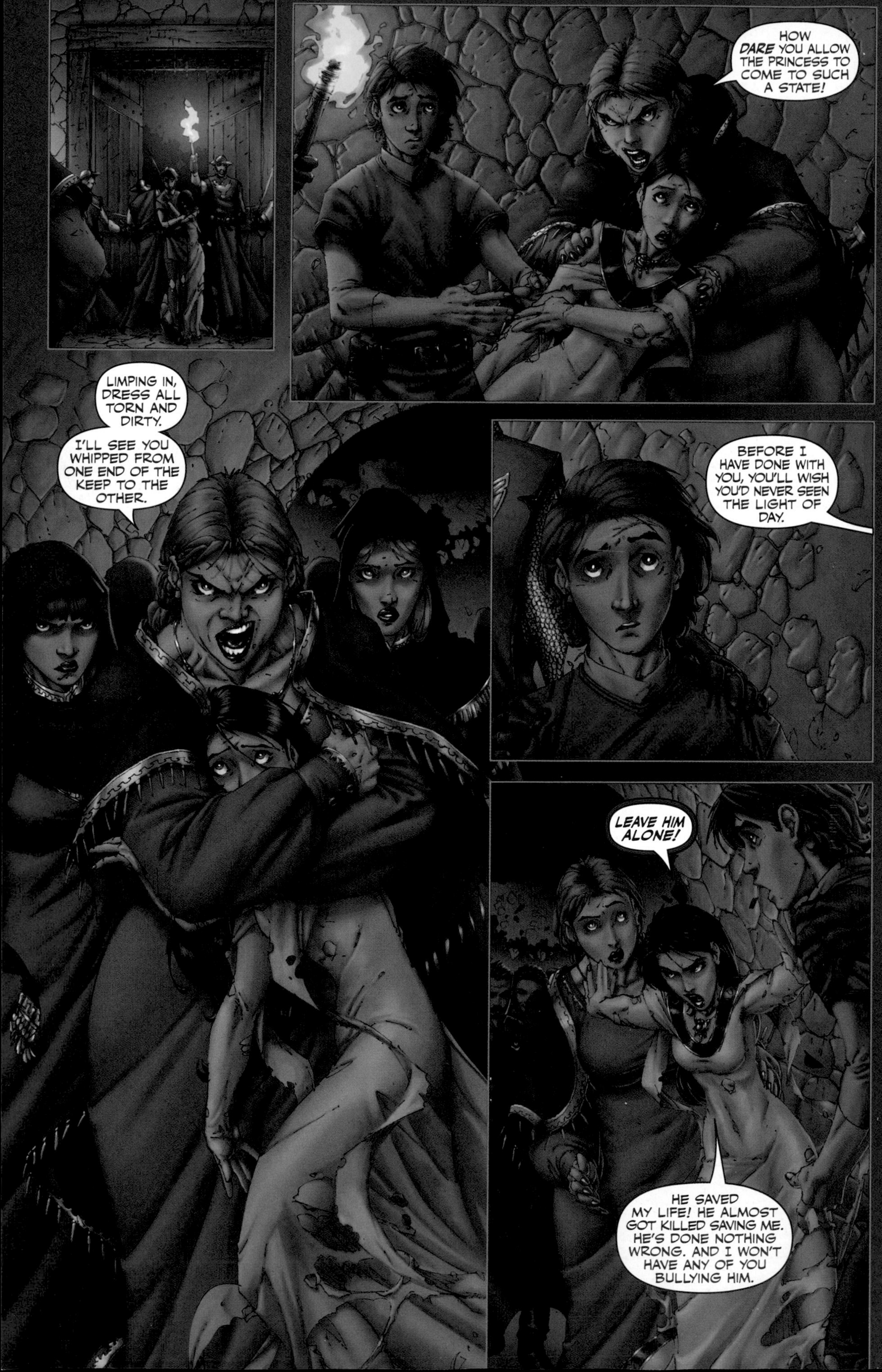
HOW *DARE* YOU ALLOW THE PRINCESS TO COME TO SUCH A STATE!
LIMPING IN, DRESS ALL TORN AND DIRTY.
I'LL SEE YOU WHIPPED FROM ONE END OF THE KEEP TO THE OTHER.
BEFORE I HAVE DONE WITH YOU, YOU'LL WISH YOU'D NEVER SEEN THE LIGHT OF DAY.
LEAVE HIM ALONE!
HE SAVED MY LIFE! HE ALMOST GOT KILLED SAVING ME. HE'S DONE NOTHING WRONG. AND I WON'T HAVE ANY OF YOU BULLYING HIM.

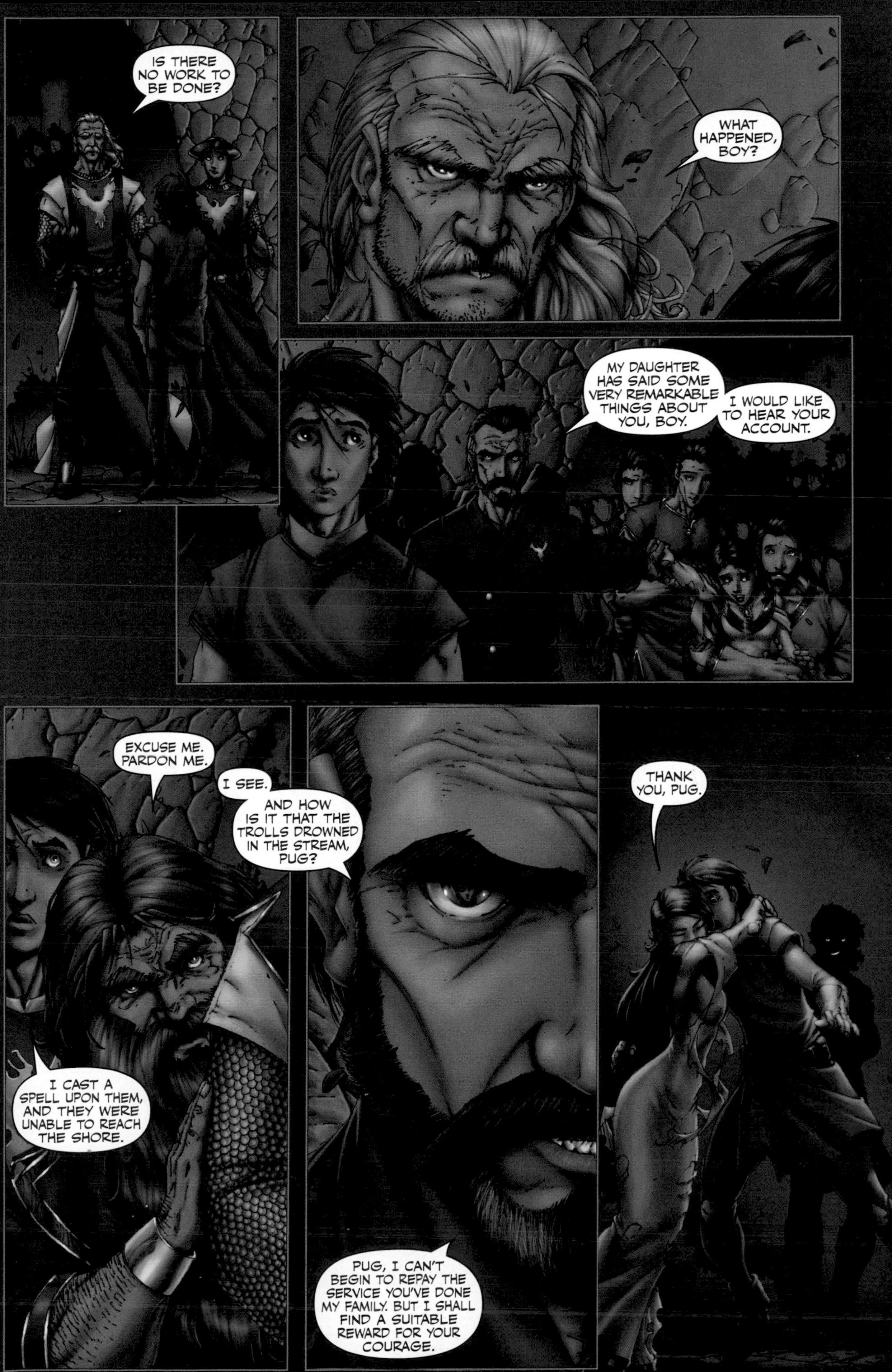
IS THERE NO WORK TO BE DONE?
WHAT HAPPENED, BOY?
MY DAUGHTER HAS SAID SOME VERY REMARKABLE THINGS ABOUT YOU, BOY.
I WOULD LIKE TO HEAR YOUR ACCOUNT.
EXCUSE ME. PARDON ME.
I SEE.
AND HOW IS IT THAT THE TROLLS DROWNED IN THE STREAM, PUG?
I CAST A SPELL UPON THEM, AND THEY WERE UNABLE TO REACH THE SHORE.
PUG, I CAN'T BEGIN TO REPAY THE SERVICE YOU'VE DONE MY FAMILY. BUT I SHALL FIND A SUITABLE REWARD FOR YOUR COURAGE.
THANK YOU, PUG.

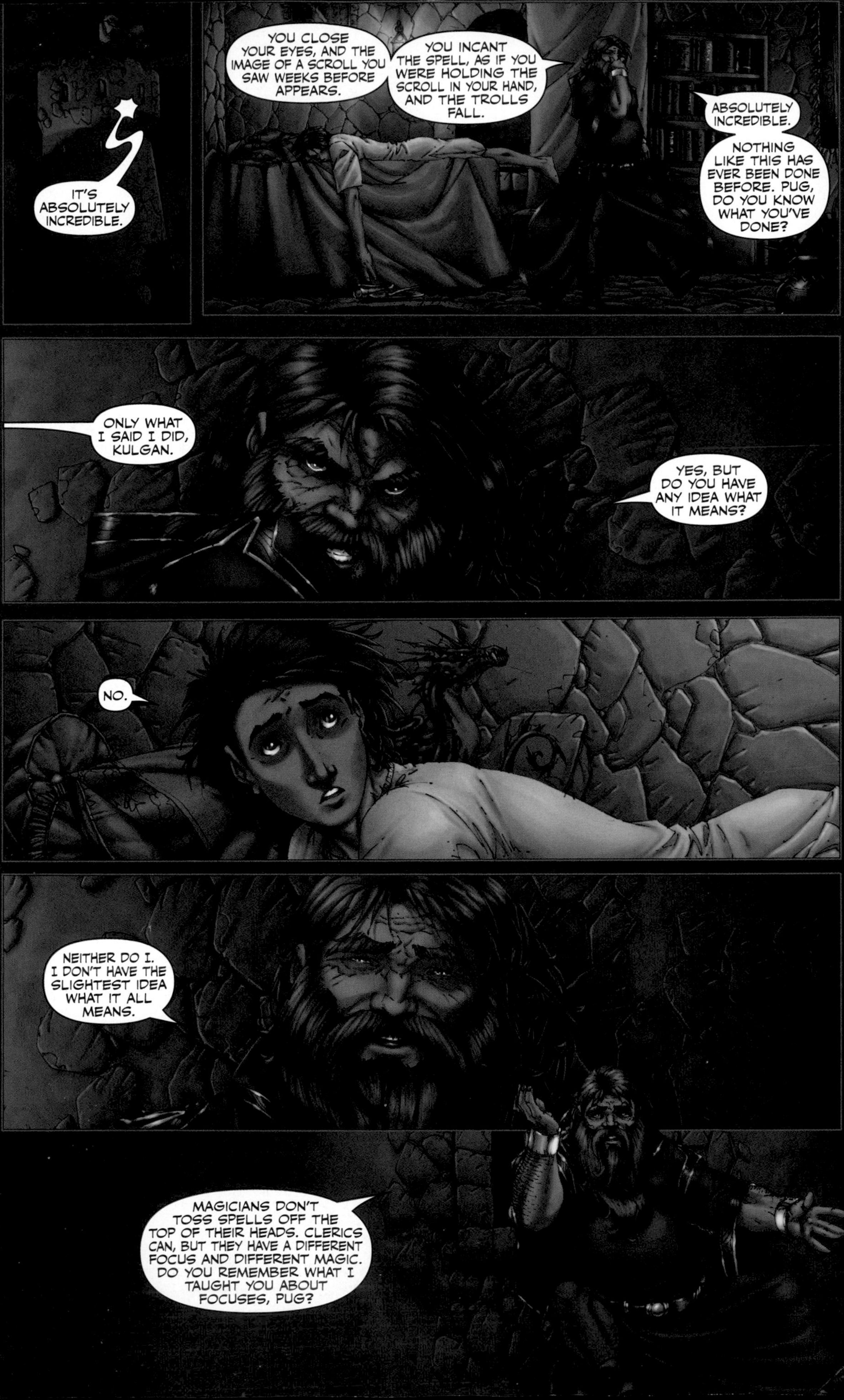
IT'S ABSOLUTELY INCREDIBLE.
YOU CLOSE YOUR EYES, AND THE IMAGE OF A SCROLL YOU SAW WEEKS BEFORE APPEARS.
YOU INCANT THE SPELL, AS IF YOU WERE HOLDING THE SCROLL IN YOUR HAND, AND THE TROLLS FALL.
ABSOLUTELY INCREDIBLE.
NOTHING LIKE THIS HAS EVER BEEN DONE BEFORE. PUG, DO YOU KNOW WHAT YOU'VE DONE?
ONLY WHAT I SAID I DID, KULGAN.
YES, BUT DO YOU HAVE ANY IDEA WHAT IT MEANS?
NO.
NEITHER DO I. I DON'T HAVE THE SLIGHTEST IDEA WHAT IT ALL MEANS.
MAGICIANS DON'T TOSS SPELLS OFF THE TOP OF THEIR HEADS. CLERICS CAN, BUT THEY HAVE A DIFFERENT FOCUS AND DIFFERENT MAGIC. DO YOU REMEMBER WHAT I TAUGHT YOU ABOUT FOCUSES, PUG?

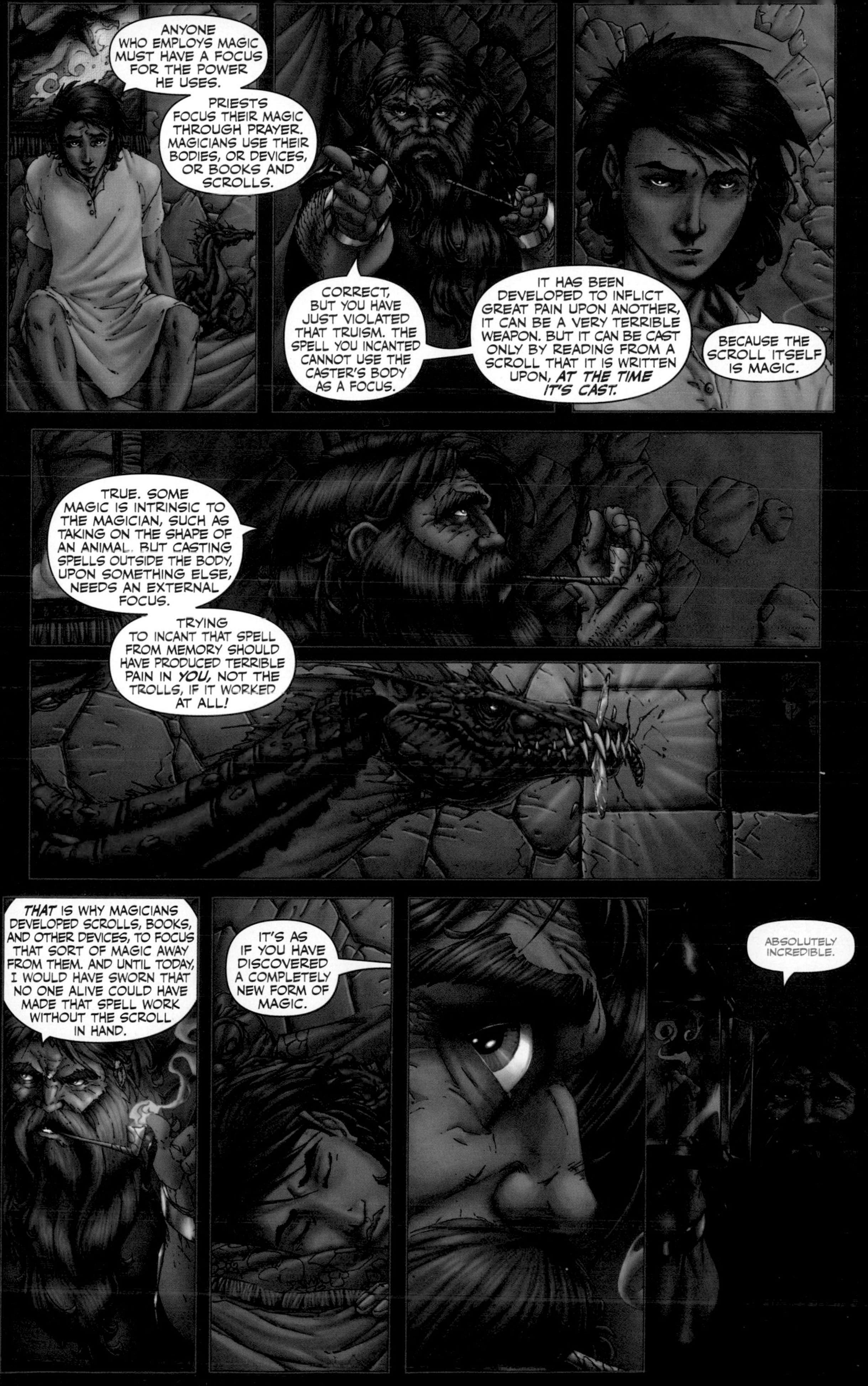
ANYONE WHO EMPLOYS MAGIC MUST HAVE A FOCUS FOR THE POWER HE USES.
PRIESTS FOCUS THEIR MAGIC THROUGH PRAYER. MAGICIANS USE THEIR BODIES, OR DEVICES, OR BOOKS AND SCROLLS.
CORRECT, BUT YOU HAVE JUST VIOLATED THAT TRUISM. THE SPELL YOU INCANTED CANNOT USE THE CASTER'S BODY AS A FOCUS.
IT HAS BEEN DEVELOPED TO INFLICT GREAT PAIN UPON ANOTHER, IT CAN BE A VERY TERRIBLE WEAPON. BUT IT CAN BE CAST ONLY BY READING FROM A SCROLL THAT IT IS WRITTEN UPON, *AT THE TIME IT'S CAST.*
BECAUSE THE SCROLL ITSELF IS MAGIC.
TRUE. SOME MAGIC IS INTRINSIC TO THE MAGICIAN, SUCH AS TAKING ON THE SHAPE OF AN ANIMAL. BUT CASTING SPELLS OUTSIDE THE BODY, UPON SOMETHING ELSE, NEEDS AN EXTERNAL FOCUS.
TRYING TO INCANT THAT SPELL FROM MEMORY SHOULD HAVE PRODUCED TERRIBLE PAIN IN *YOU,* NOT THE TROLLS, IF IT WORKED AT ALL!
THAT IS WHY MAGICIANS DEVELOPED SCROLLS, BOOKS, AND OTHER DEVICES, TO FOCUS THAT SORT OF MAGIC AWAY FROM THEM. AND UNTIL TODAY, I WOULD HAVE SWORN THAT NO ONE ALIVE COULD HAVE MADE THAT SPELL WORK WITHOUT THE SCROLL IN HAND.
IT'S AS IF YOU HAVE DISCOVERED A COMPLETELY NEW FORM OF MAGIC.
ABSOLUTELY INCREDIBLE.

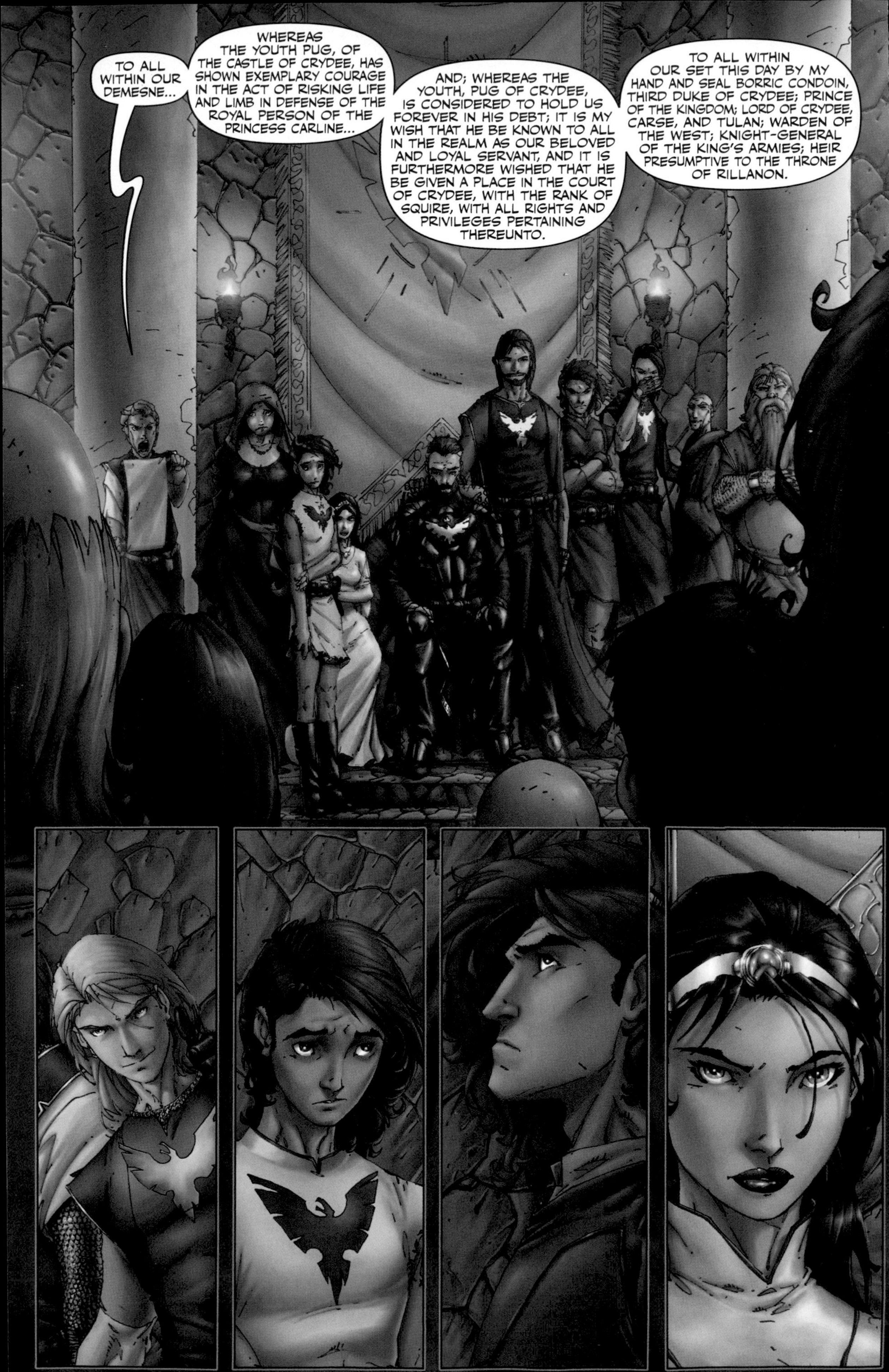
TO ALL WITHIN OUR DEMESNE...
WHEREAS THE YOUTH PUG, OF THE CASTLE OF CRYDEE, HAS SHOWN EXEMPLARY COURAGE IN THE ACT OF RISKING LIFE AND LIMB IN DEFENSE OF THE ROYAL PERSON OF THE PRINCESS CARLINE...
AND; WHEREAS THE YOUTH, PUG OF CRYDEE, IS CONSIDERED TO HOLD US FOREVER IN HIS DEBT; IT IS MY WISH THAT HE BE KNOWN TO ALL IN THE REALM AS OUR BELOVED AND LOYAL SERVANT, AND IT IS FURTHERMORE WISHED THAT HE BE GIVEN A PLACE IN THE COURT OF CRYDEE, WITH THE RANK OF SQUIRE, WITH ALL RIGHTS AND PRIVILEGES PERTAINING THEREUNTO.
TO ALL WITHIN OUR SET THIS DAY BY MY HAND AND SEAL BORRIC CONDOIN, THIRD DUKE OF CRYDEE; PRINCE OF THE KINGDOM; LORD OF CRYDEE, CARSE, AND TULAN; WARDEN OF THE WEST; KNIGHT-GENERAL OF THE KING'S ARMIES; HEIR PRESUMPTIVE TO THE THRONE OF RILLANON.

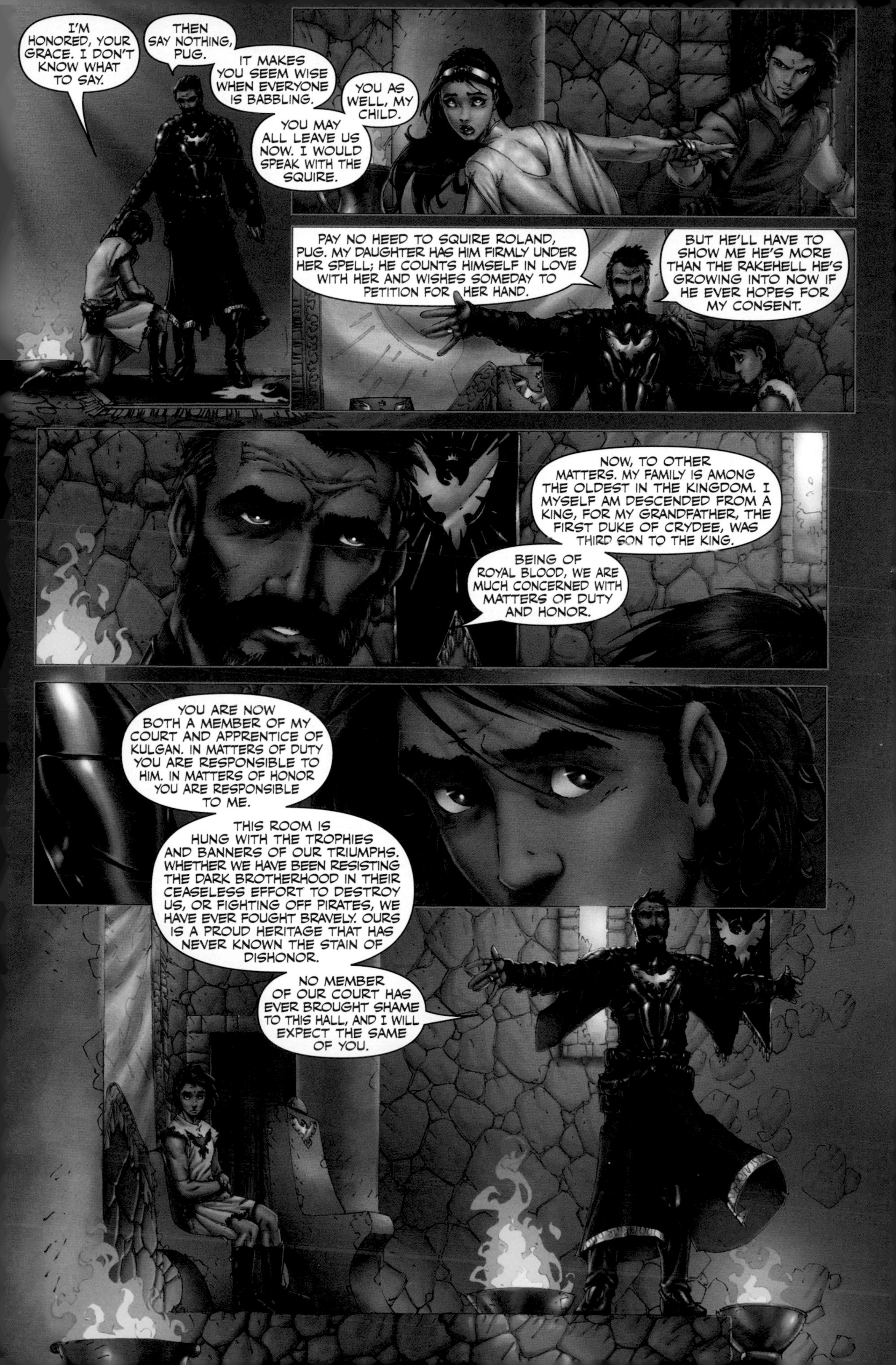
I'M HONORED, YOUR GRACE. I DON'T KNOW WHAT TO SAY.
THEN SAY NOTHING, PUG.
IT MAKES YOU SEEM WISE WHEN EVERYONE IS BABBLING.
YOU AS WELL, MY CHILD.
YOU MAY ALL LEAVE US NOW. I WOULD SPEAK WITH THE SQUIRE.
PAY NO HEED TO SQUIRE ROLAND, PUG. MY DAUGHTER HAS HIM FIRMLY UNDER HER SPELL; HE COUNTS HIMSELF IN LOVE WITH HER AND WISHES SOMEDAY TO PETITION FOR HER HAND.
BUT HE'LL HAVE TO SHOW ME HE'S MORE THAN THE RAKEHELL HE'S GROWING INTO NOW IF HE EVER HOPES FOR MY CONSENT.
NOW, TO OTHER MATTERS. MY FAMILY IS AMONG THE OLDEST IN THE KINGDOM. I MYSELF AM DESCENDED FROM A KING, FOR MY GRANDFATHER, THE FIRST DUKE OF CRYDEE, WAS THIRD SON TO THE KING.
BEING OF ROYAL BLOOD, WE ARE MUCH CONCERNED WITH MATTERS OF DUTY AND HONOR.
YOU ARE NOW BOTH A MEMBER OF MY COURT AND APPRENTICE OF KULGAN. IN MATTERS OF DUTY YOU ARE RESPONSIBLE TO HIM. IN MATTERS OF HONOR YOU ARE RESPONSIBLE TO ME.
THIS ROOM IS HUNG WITH THE TROPHIES AND BANNERS OF OUR TRIUMPHS. WHETHER WE HAVE BEEN RESISTING THE DARK BROTHERHOOD IN THEIR CEASELESS EFFORT TO DESTROY US, OR FIGHTING OFF PIRATES, WE HAVE EVER FOUGHT BRAVELY. OURS IS A PROUD HERITAGE THAT HAS NEVER KNOWN THE STAIN OF DISHONOR.
NO MEMBER OF OUR COURT HAS EVER BROUGHT SHAME TO THIS HALL, AND I WILL EXPECT THE SAME OF YOU.

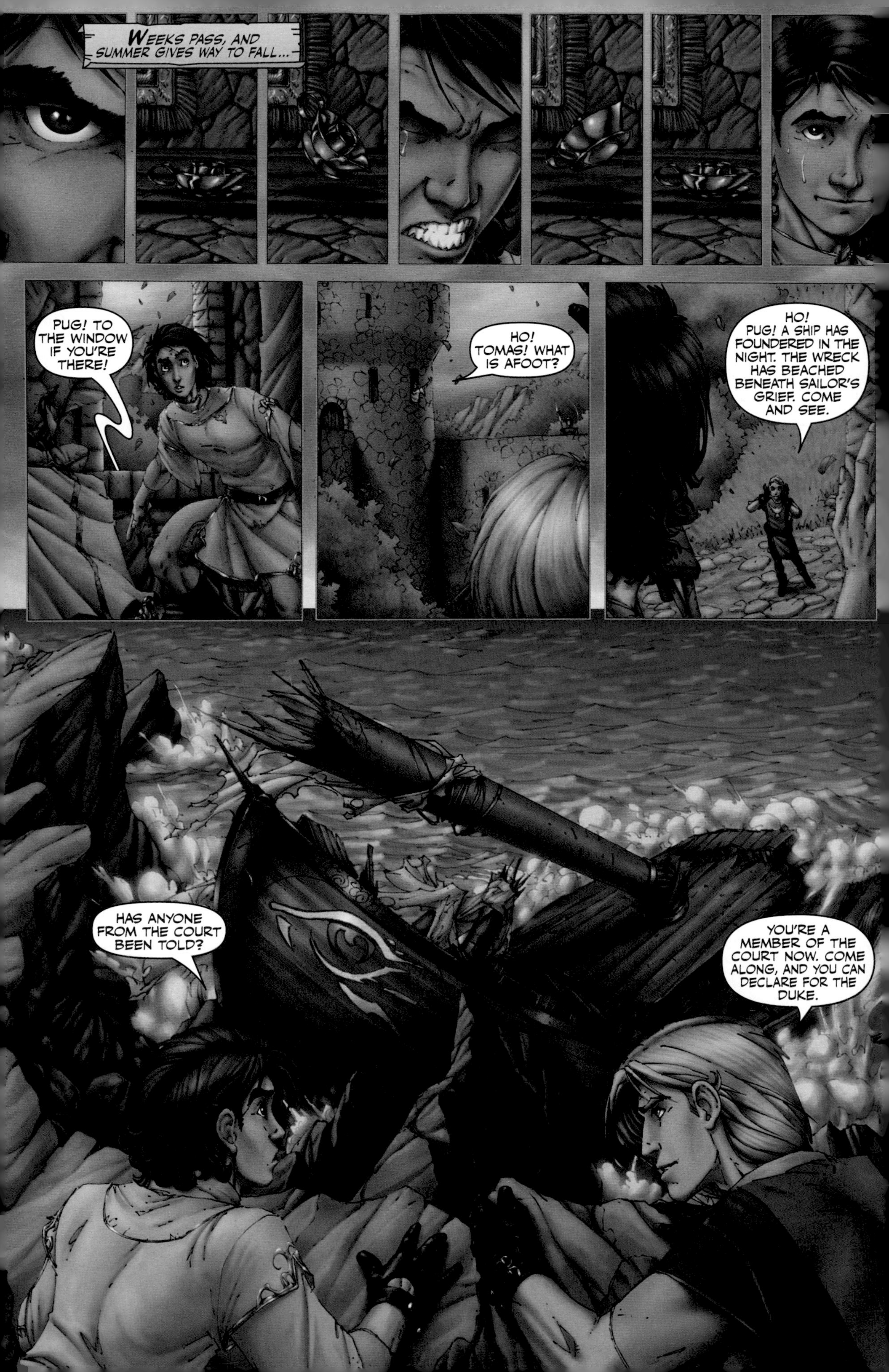
WEEKS PASS, AND SUMMER GIVES WAY TO FALL...
PUG! TO THE WINDOW IF YOU'RE THERE!
HO! TOMAS! WHAT IS AFOOT?
HO! PUG! A SHIP HAS FOUNDERED IN THE NIGHT. THE WRECK HAS BEACHED BENEATH SAILOR'S GRIEF. COME AND SEE.
HAS ANYONE FROM THE COURT BEEN TOLD?
YOU'RE A MEMBER OF THE COURT NOW. COME ALONG, AND YOU CAN DECLARE FOR THE DUKE.

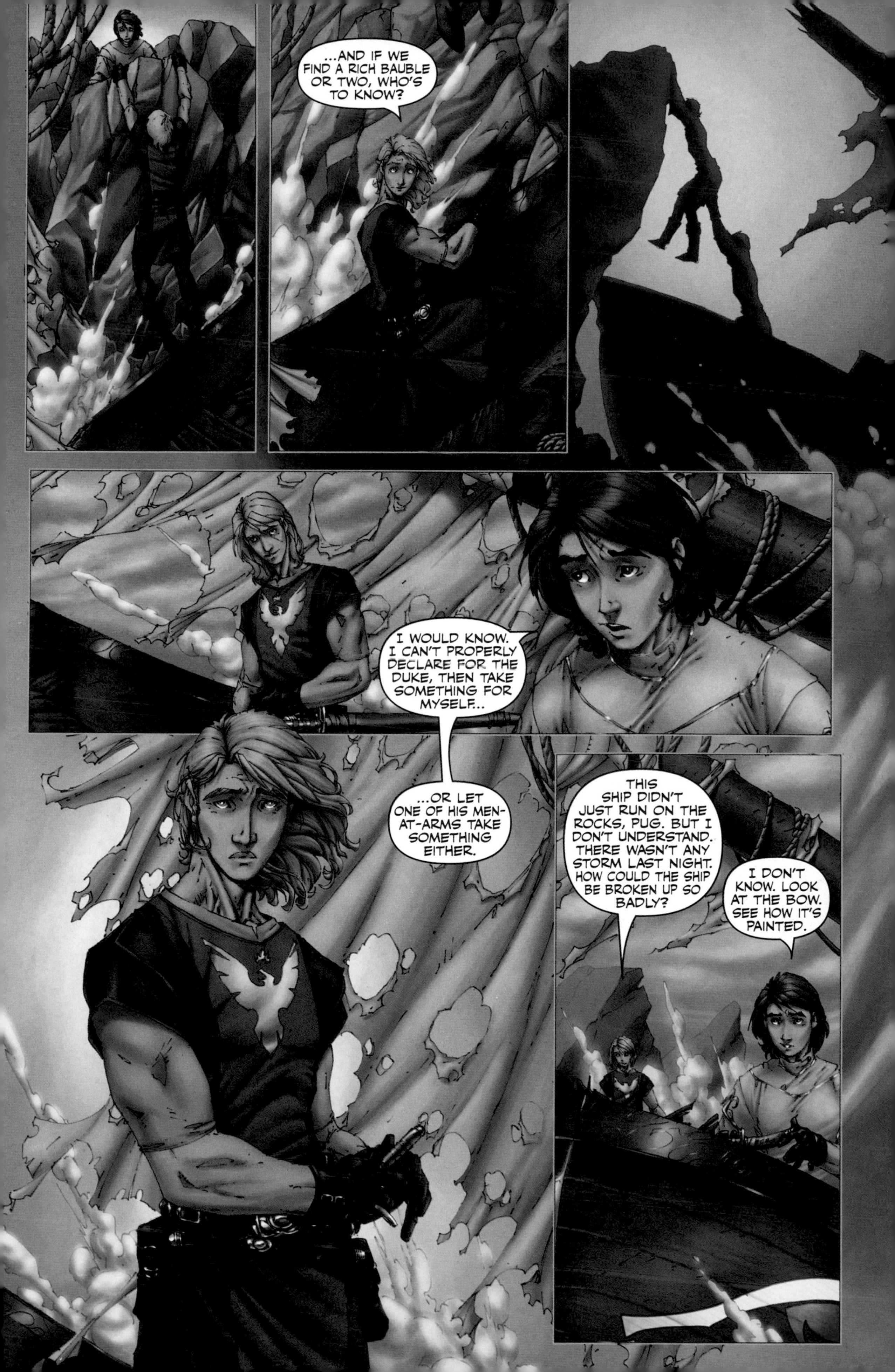
...AND IF WE FIND A RICH BAUBLE OR TWO, WHO'S TO KNOW?
I WOULD KNOW. I CAN'T PROPERLY DECLARE FOR THE DUKE, THEN TAKE SOMETHING FOR MYSELF...
...OR LET ONE OF HIS MEN-AT-ARMS TAKE SOMETHING EITHER.
THIS SHIP DIDN'T JUST RUN ON THE ROCKS, PUG. BUT I DON'T UNDERSTAND. THERE WASN'T ANY STORM LAST NIGHT. HOW COULD THE SHIP BE BROKEN UP SO BADLY?
I DON'T KNOW. LOOK AT THE BOW. SEE HOW IT'S PAINTED.

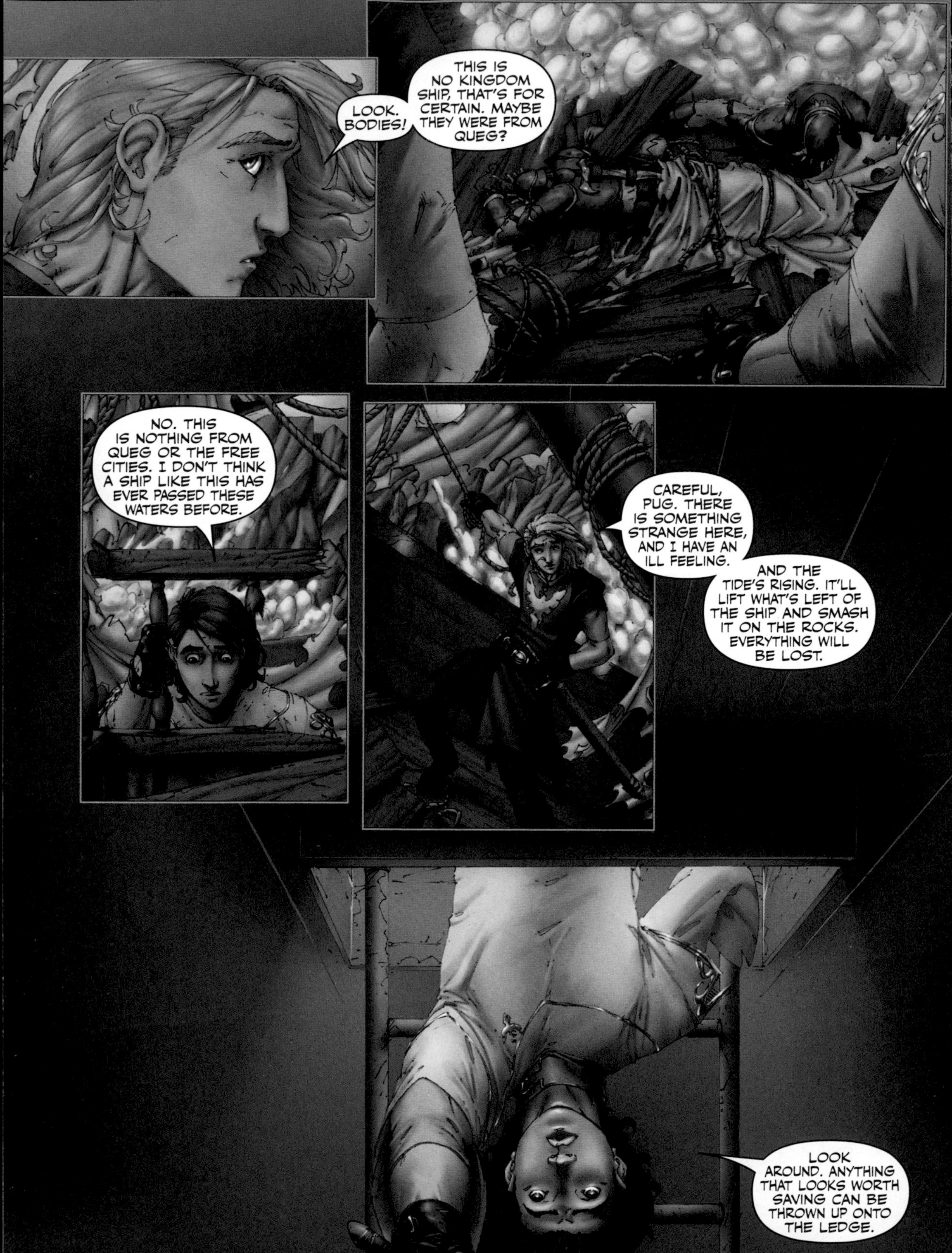
LOOK. BODIES!
THIS IS NO KINGDOM SHIP, THAT'S FOR CERTAIN. MAYBE THEY WERE FROM QUEG?
NO. THIS IS NOTHING FROM QUEG OR THE FREE CITIES. I DON'T THINK A SHIP LIKE THIS HAS EVER PASSED THESE WATERS BEFORE.
CAREFUL, PUG. THERE IS SOMETHING STRANGE HERE, AND I HAVE AN ILL FEELING.
AND THE TIDE'S RISING. IT'LL LIFT WHAT'S LEFT OF THE SHIP AND SMASH IT ON THE ROCKS. EVERYTHING WILL BE LOST.
LOOK AROUND. ANYTHING THAT LOOKS WORTH SAVING CAN BE THROWN UP ONTO THE LEDGE.

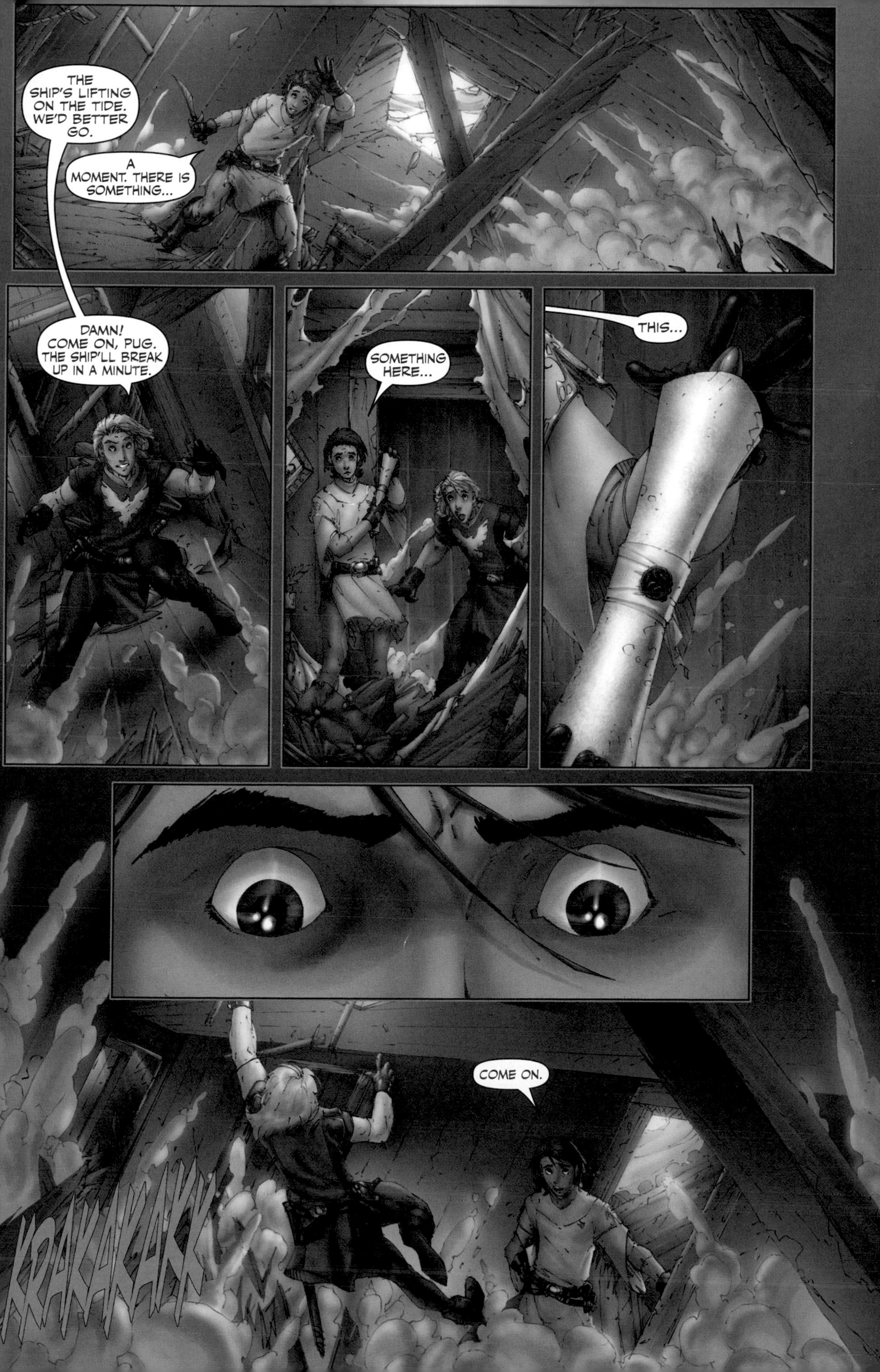
THE SHIP'S LIFTING ON THE TIDE. WE'D BETTER GO.
A MOMENT. THERE IS SOMETHING...
DAMN! COME ON, PUG. THE SHIP'LL BREAK UP IN A MINUTE.
SOMETHING HERE...
THIS...
COME ON.
KRAKAKAKK

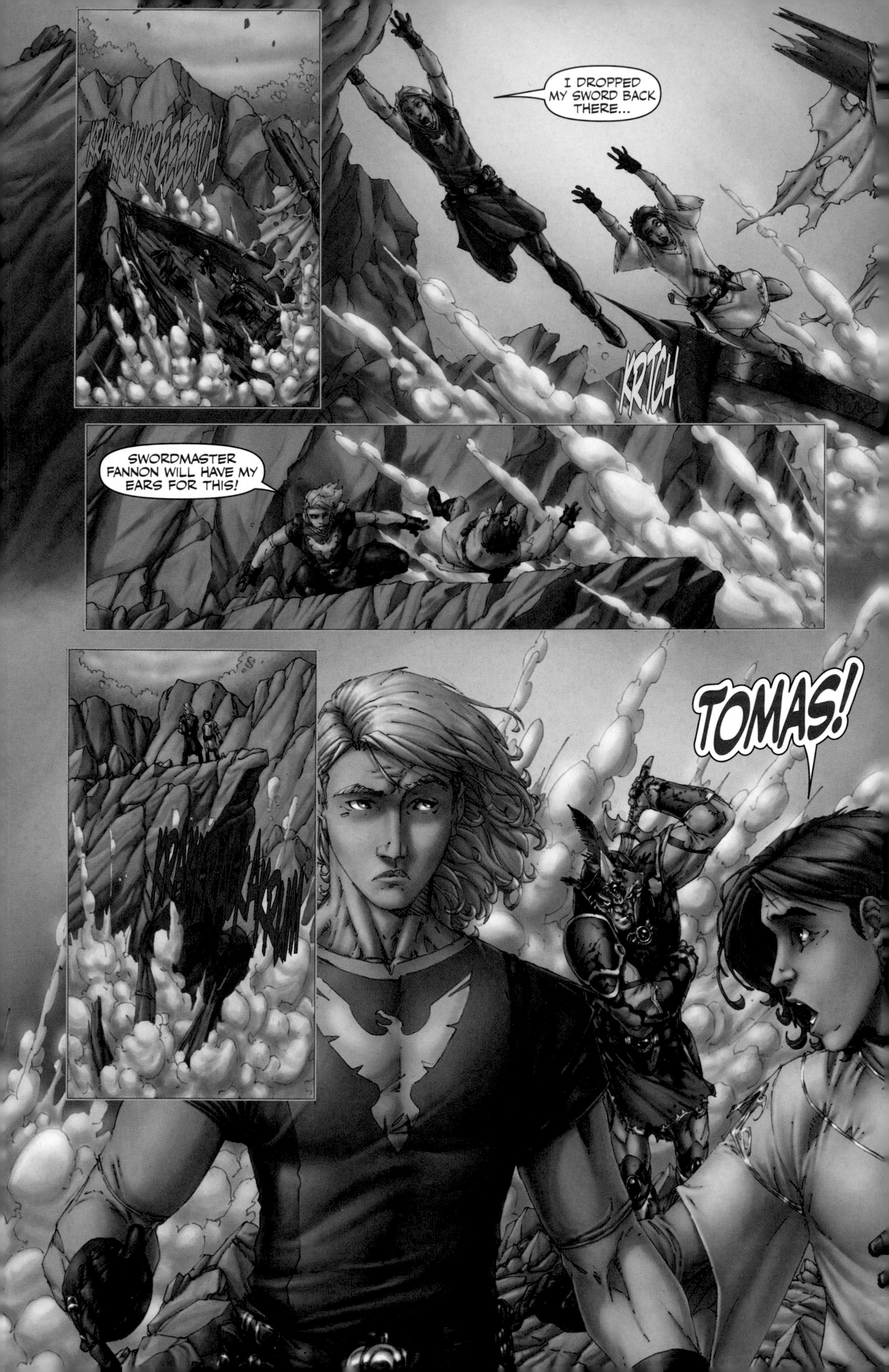
I DROPPED MY SWORD BACK THERE...
KRTCH
SWORDMASTER FANNON WILL HAVE MY EARS FOR THIS!
TOMAS!

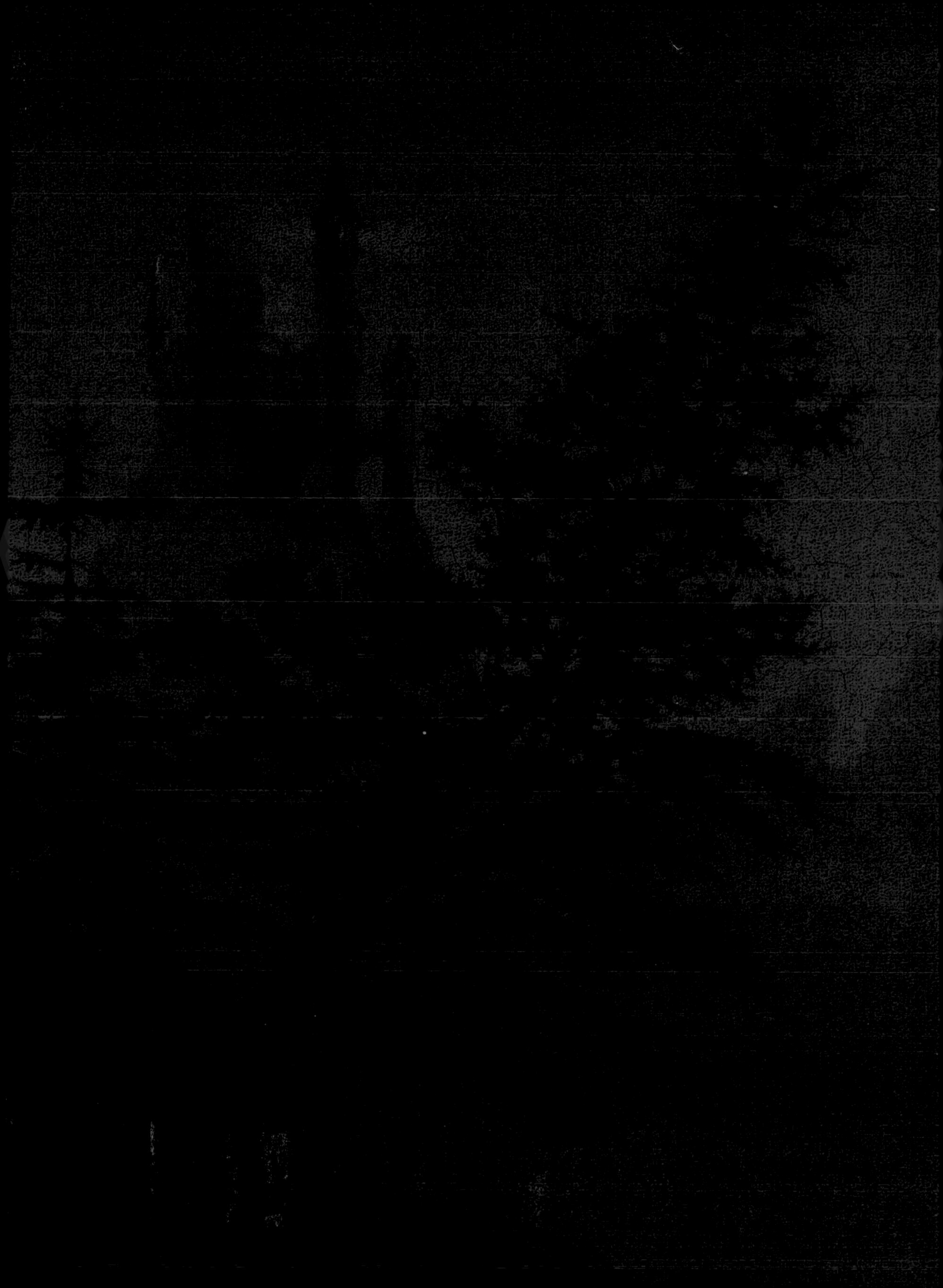

MAGICIAN: APPRENTICE

CHAPTER FOUR

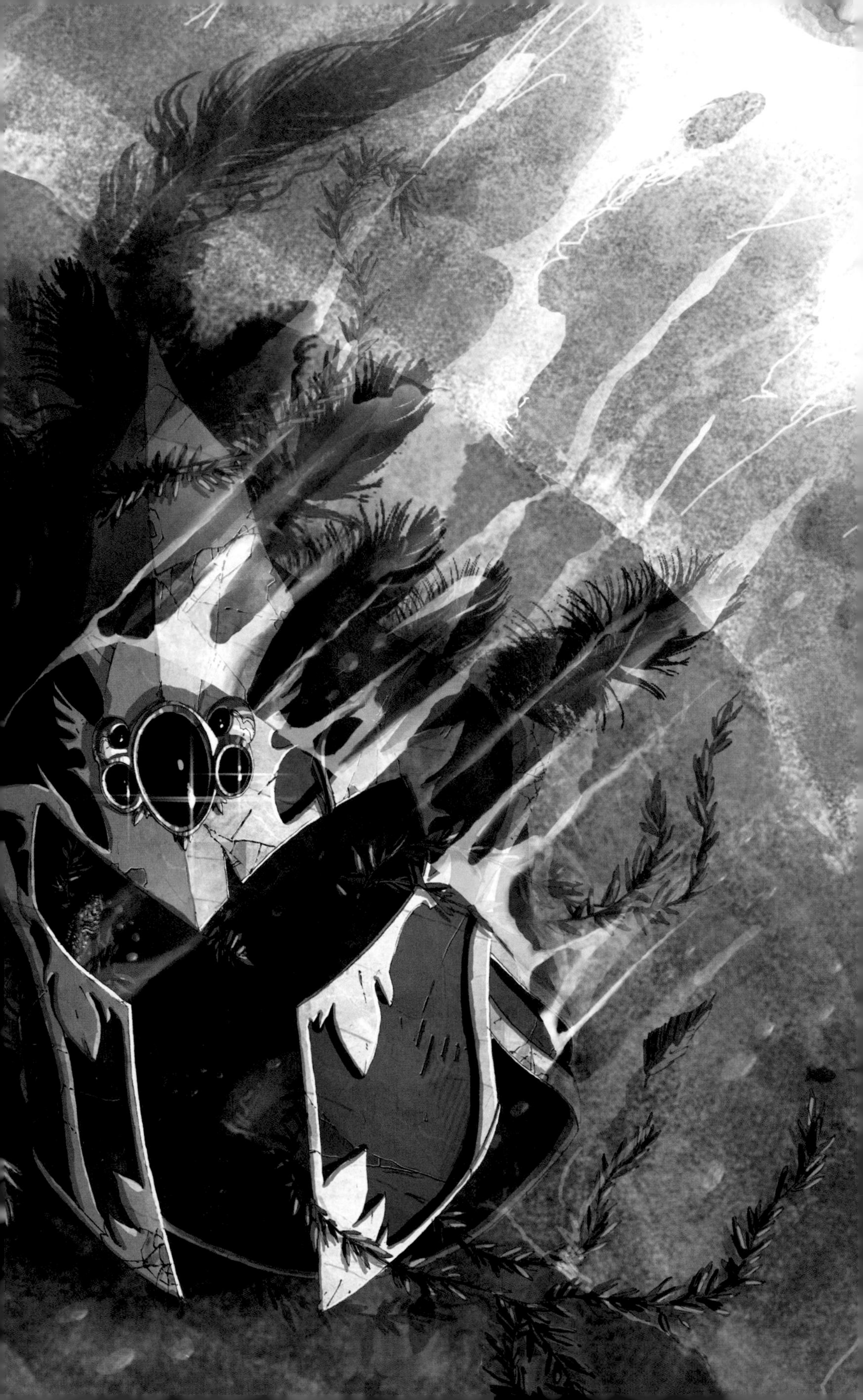

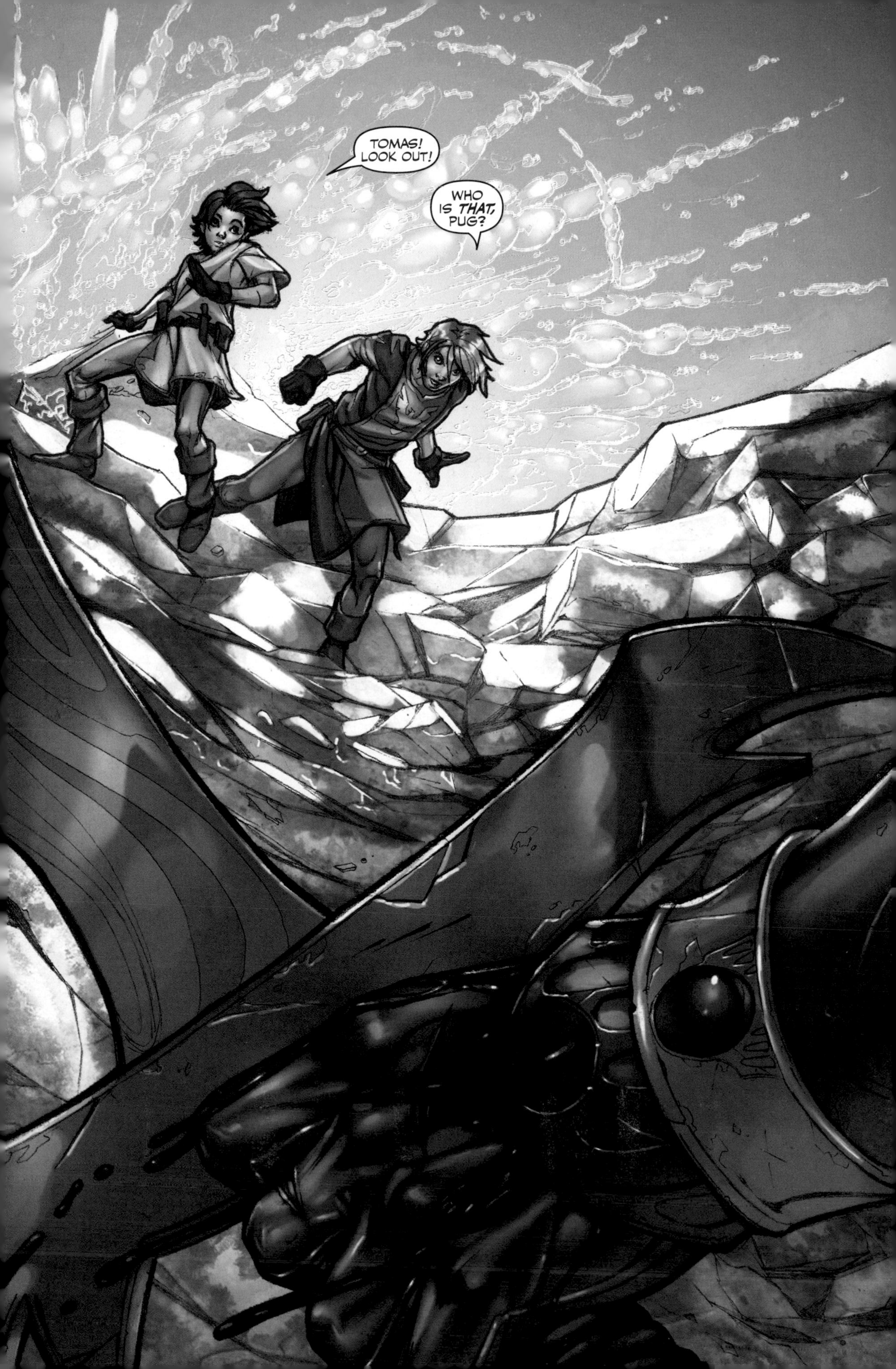
TOMAS! LOOK OUT!
WHO IS *THAT,* PUG?

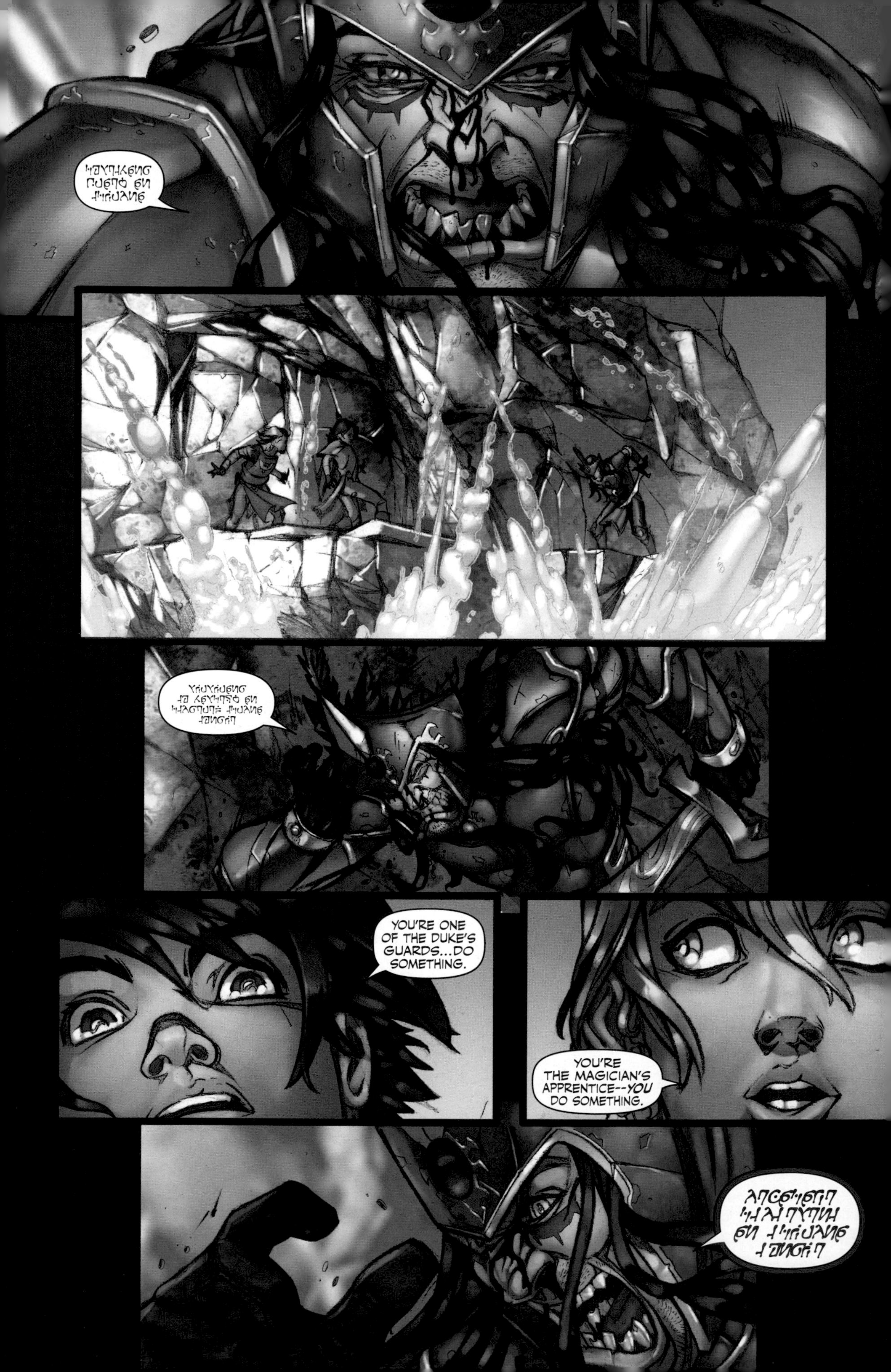
YOU'RE ONE OF THE DUKE'S GUARDS...DO SOMETHING.
YOU'RE THE MAGICIAN'S APPRENTICE--*YOU* DO SOMETHING.

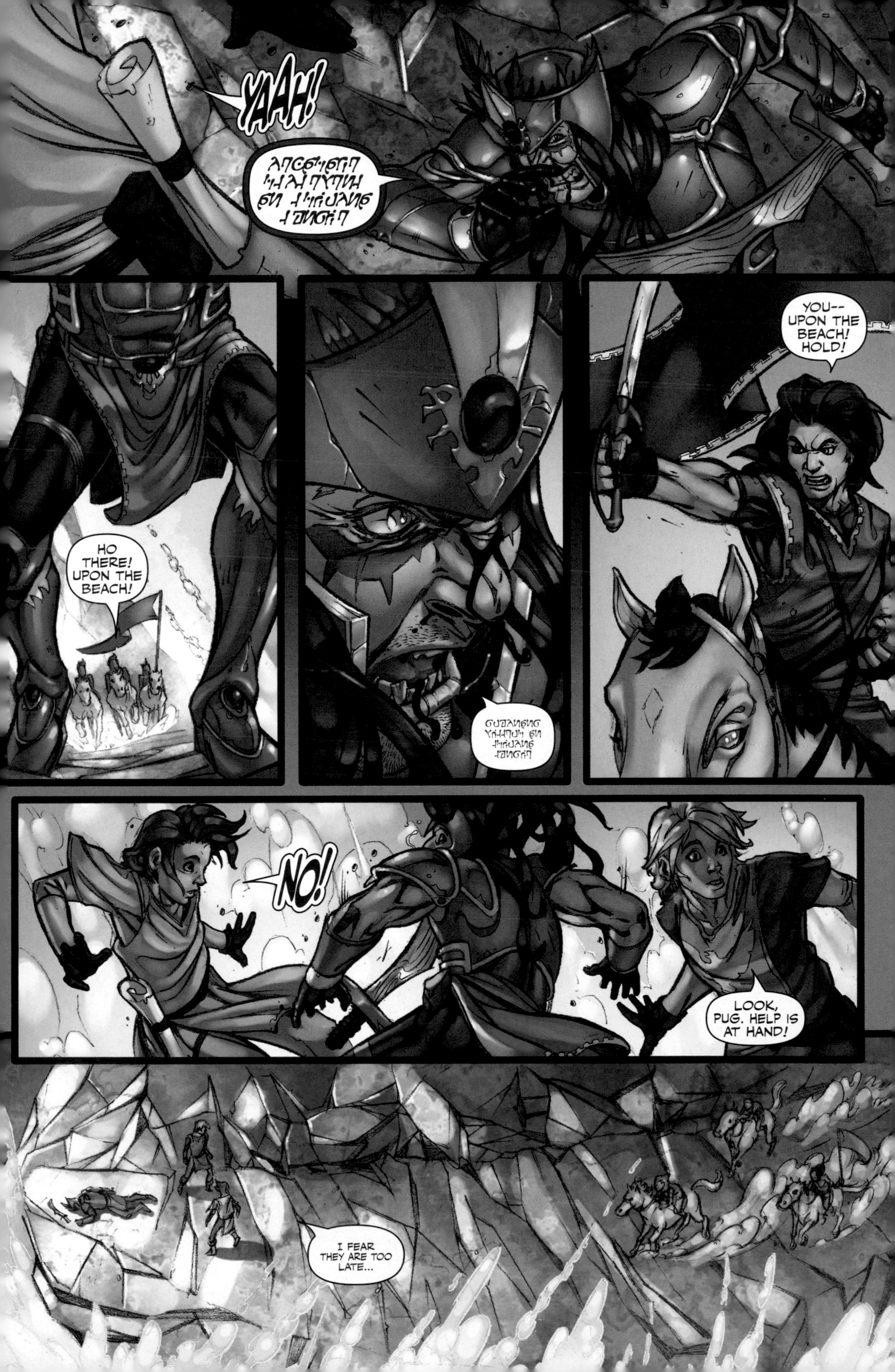
YAAH!
HO THERE! UPON THE BEACH!
YOU-- UPON THE BEACH! HOLD!
NO!
LOOK, PUG. HELP IS AT HAND!
I FEAR THEY ARE TOO LATE...

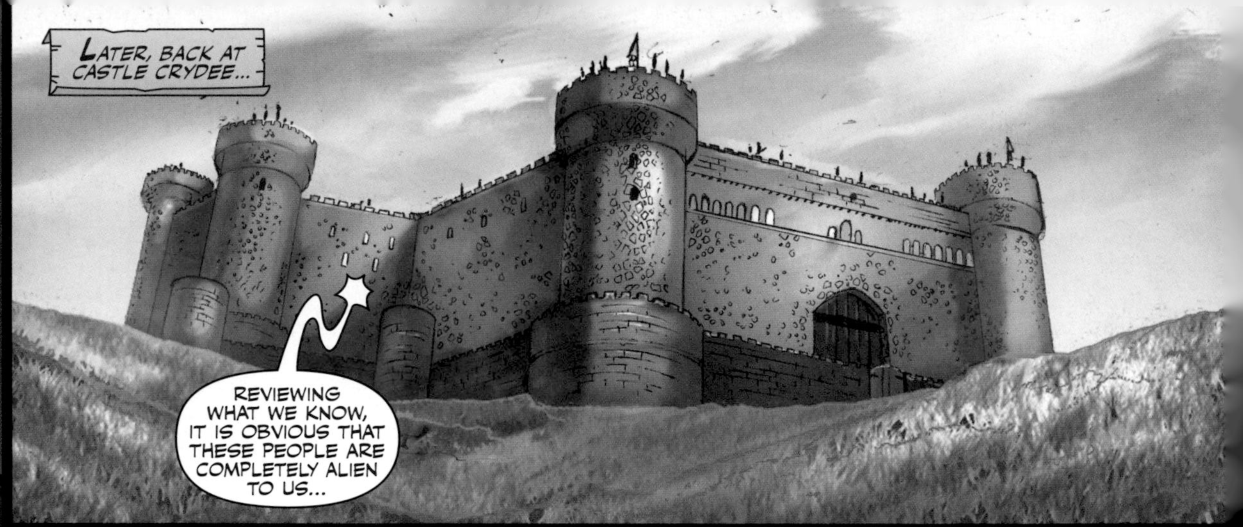
LATER, BACK AT CASTLE CRYDEE...
REVIEWING WHAT WE KNOW, IT IS OBVIOUS THAT THESE PEOPLE ARE COMPLETELY ALIEN TO US...

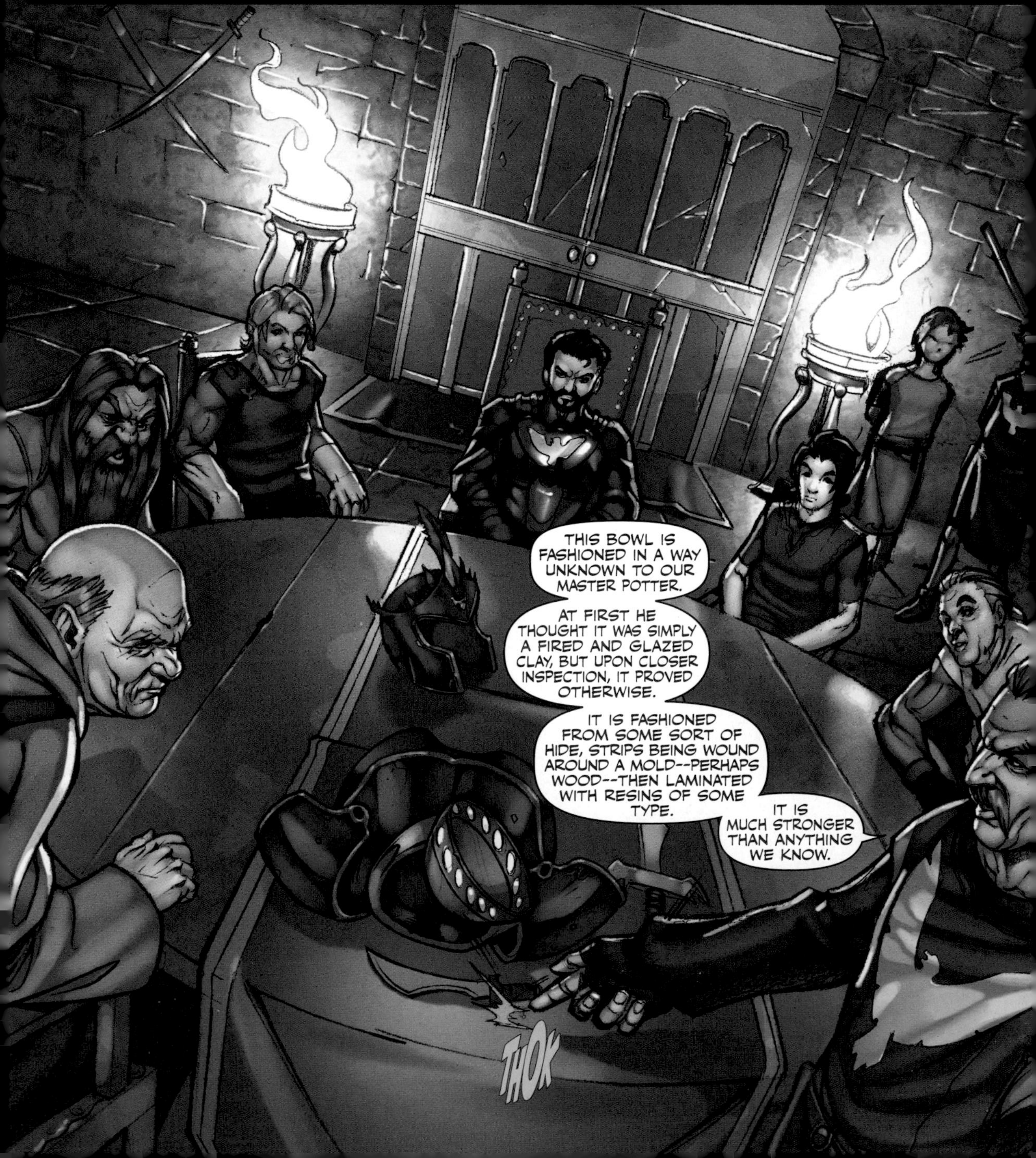
THIS BOWL IS FASHIONED IN A WAY UNKNOWN TO OUR MASTER POTTER.
AT FIRST HE THOUGHT IT WAS SIMPLY A FIRED AND GLAZED CLAY, BUT UPON CLOSER INSPECTION, IT PROVED OTHERWISE.
IT IS FASHIONED FROM SOME SORT OF HIDE, STRIPS BEING WOUND AROUND A MOLD--PERHAPS WOOD--THEN LAMINATED WITH RESINS OF SOME TYPE.
IT IS MUCH STRONGER THAN ANYTHING WE KNOW.
THOK

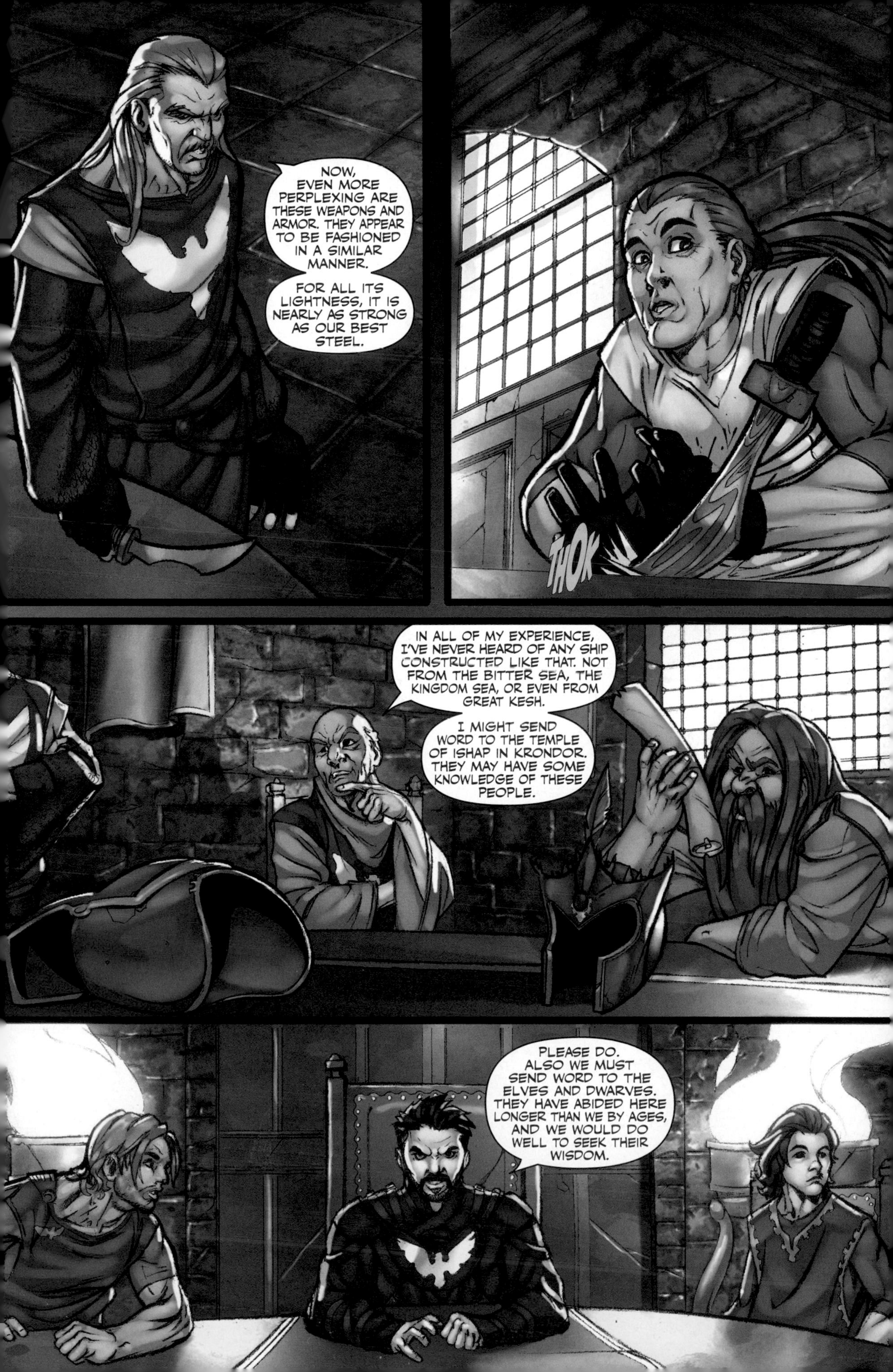
NOW, EVEN MORE PERPLEXING ARE THESE WEAPONS AND ARMOR. THEY APPEAR TO BE FASHIONED IN A SIMILAR MANNER.
FOR ALL ITS LIGHTNESS, IT IS NEARLY AS STRONG AS OUR BEST STEEL.
THOK
IN ALL OF MY EXPERIENCE, I'VE NEVER HEARD OF ANY SHIP CONSTRUCTED LIKE THAT. NOT FROM THE BITTER SEA, THE KINGDOM SEA, OR EVEN FROM GREAT KESH.
I MIGHT SEND WORD TO THE TEMPLE OF ISHAP IN KRONDOR. THEY MAY HAVE SOME KNOWLEDGE OF THESE PEOPLE.
PLEASE DO. ALSO WE MUST SEND WORD TO THE ELVES AND DWARVES. THEY HAVE ABIDED HERE LONGER THAN WE BY AGES, AND WE WOULD DO WELL TO SEEK THEIR WISDOM.

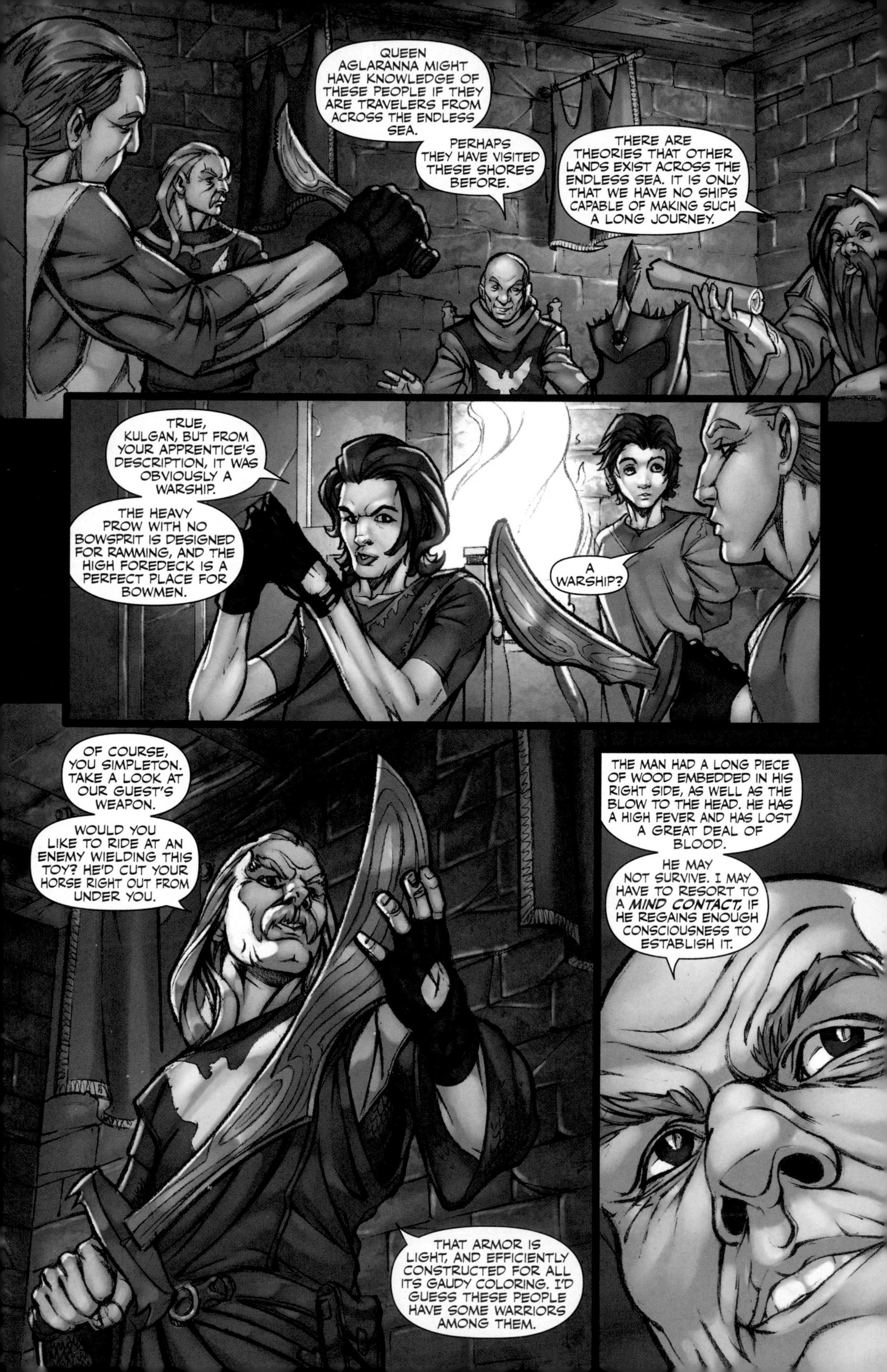
QUEEN AGLARANNA MIGHT HAVE KNOWLEDGE OF THESE PEOPLE IF THEY ARE TRAVELERS FROM ACROSS THE ENDLESS SEA.
PERHAPS THEY HAVE VISITED THESE SHORES BEFORE.
THERE ARE THEORIES THAT OTHER LANDS EXIST ACROSS THE ENDLESS SEA. IT IS ONLY THAT WE HAVE NO SHIPS CAPABLE OF MAKING SUCH A LONG JOURNEY.
TRUE, KULGAN, BUT FROM YOUR APPRENTICE'S DESCRIPTION, IT WAS OBVIOUSLY A WARSHIP.
THE HEAVY PROW WITH NO BOWSPRIT IS DESIGNED FOR RAMMING, AND THE HIGH FOREDECK IS A PERFECT PLACE FOR BOWMEN.
A WARSHIP?
OF COURSE, YOU SIMPLETON. TAKE A LOOK AT OUR GUEST'S WEAPON.
WOULD YOU LIKE TO RIDE AT AN ENEMY WIELDING THIS TOY? HE'D CUT YOUR HORSE RIGHT OUT FROM UNDER YOU.
THAT ARMOR IS LIGHT, AND EFFICIENTLY CONSTRUCTED FOR ALL ITS GAUDY COLORING. I'D GUESS THESE PEOPLE HAVE SOME WARRIORS AMONG THEM.
THE MAN HAD A LONG PIECE OF WOOD EMBEDDED IN HIS RIGHT SIDE, AS WELL AS THE BLOW TO THE HEAD. HE HAS A HIGH FEVER AND HAS LOST A GREAT DEAL OF BLOOD.
HE MAY NOT SURVIVE. I MAY HAVE TO RESORT TO A *MIND CONTACT,* IF HE REGAINS ENOUGH CONSCIOUSNESS TO ESTABLISH IT.

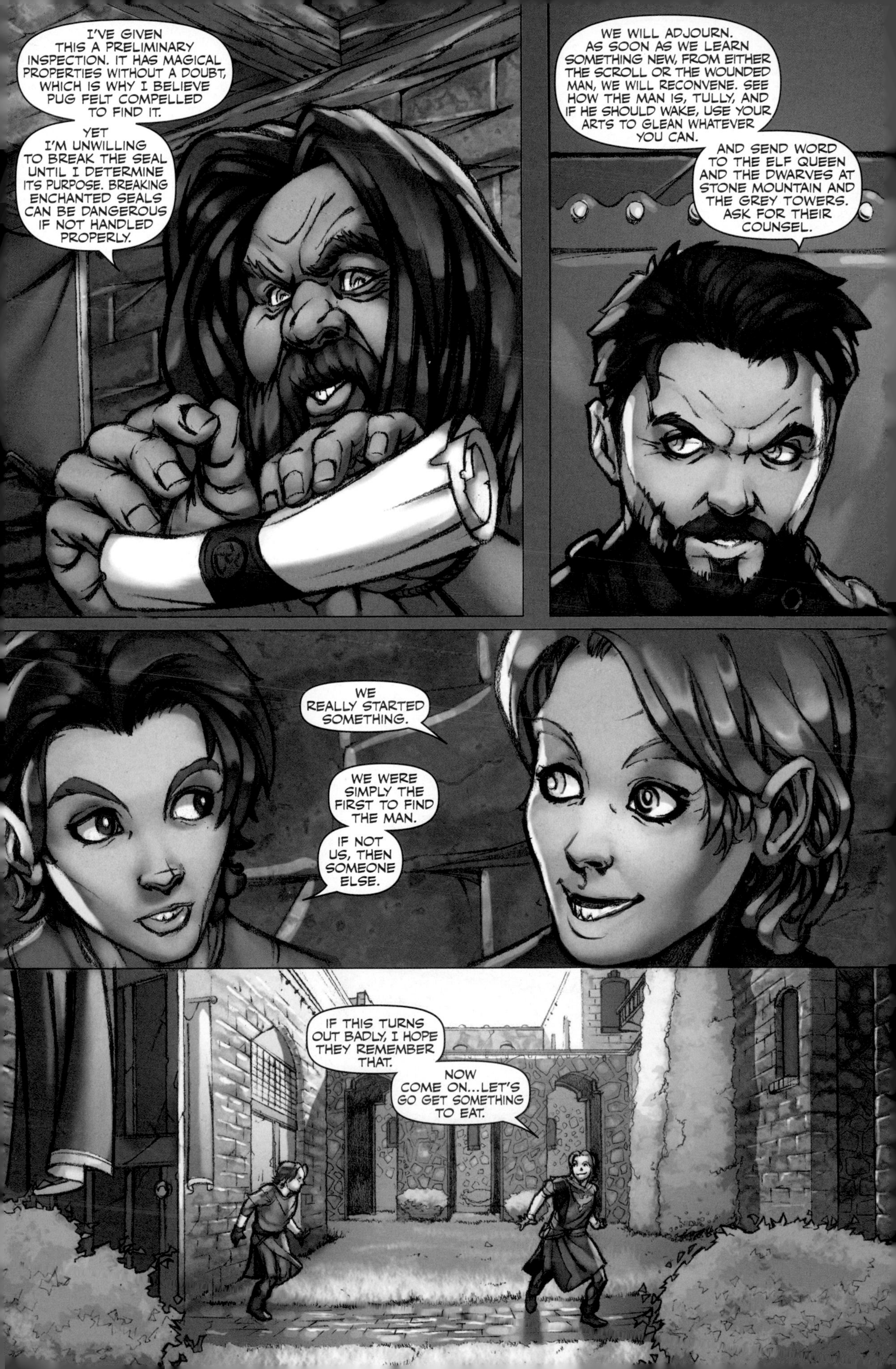
I'VE GIVEN THIS A PRELIMINARY INSPECTION. IT HAS MAGICAL PROPERTIES WITHOUT A DOUBT, WHICH IS WHY I BELIEVE PUG FELT COMPELLED TO FIND IT.
YET I'M UNWILLING TO BREAK THE SEAL UNTIL I DETERMINE ITS PURPOSE. BREAKING ENCHANTED SEALS CAN BE DANGEROUS IF NOT HANDLED PROPERLY.
WE WILL ADJOURN. AS SOON AS WE LEARN SOMETHING NEW, FROM EITHER THE SCROLL OR THE WOUNDED MAN, WE WILL RECONVENE. SEE HOW THE MAN IS, TULLY, AND IF HE SHOULD WAKE, USE YOUR ARTS TO GLEAN WHATEVER YOU CAN.
AND SEND WORD TO THE ELF QUEEN AND THE DWARVES AT STONE MOUNTAIN AND THE GREY TOWERS. ASK FOR THEIR COUNSEL.
WE REALLY STARTED SOMETHING.
WE WERE SIMPLY THE FIRST TO FIND THE MAN.
IF NOT US, THEN SOMEONE ELSE.
IF THIS TURNS OUT BADLY, I HOPE THEY REMEMBER THAT.
NOW COME ON...LET'S GO GET SOMETHING TO EAT.

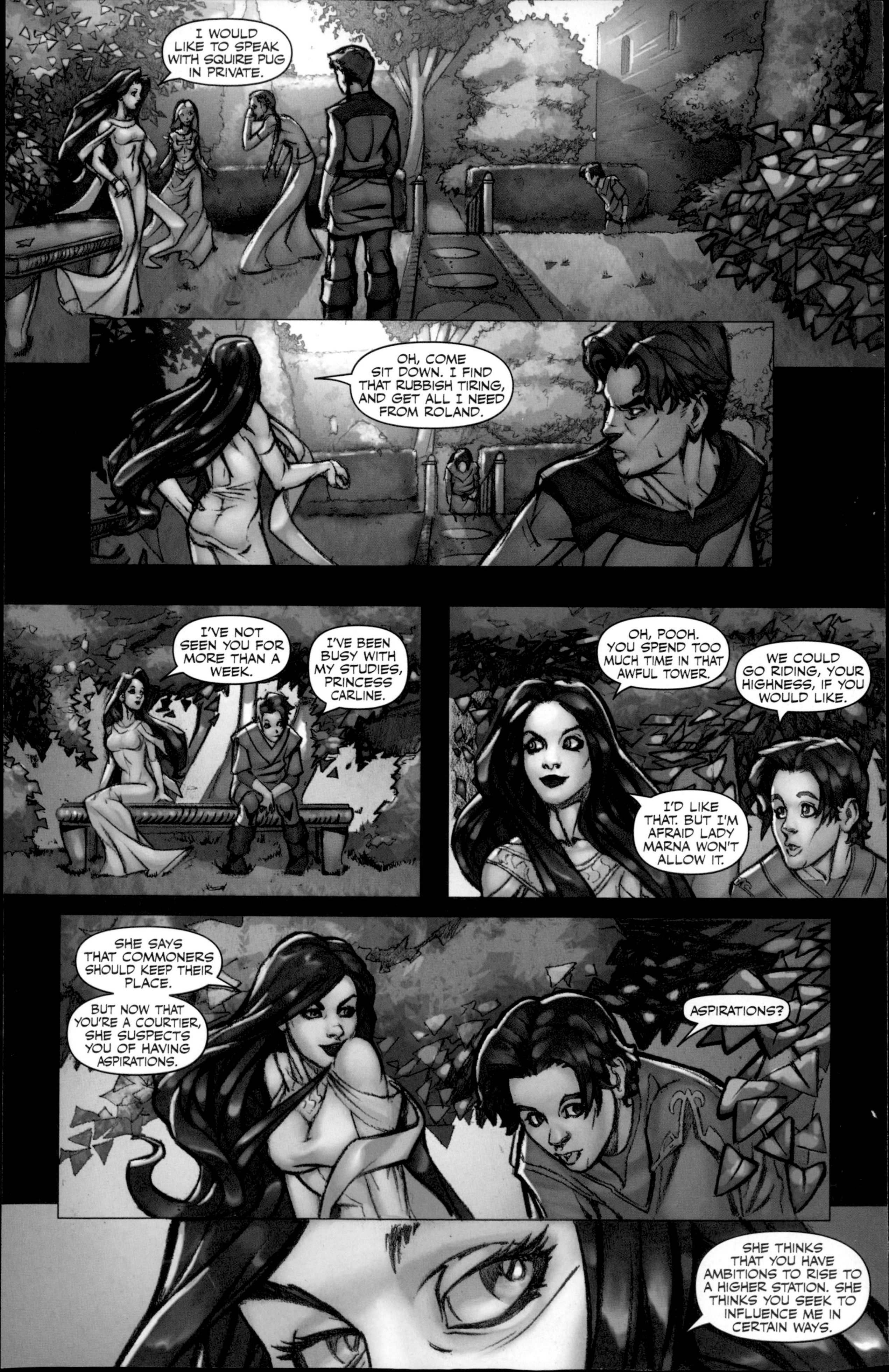
I WOULD LIKE TO SPEAK WITH SQUIRE PUG IN PRIVATE.
OH, COME SIT DOWN. I FIND THAT RUBBISH TIRING, AND GET ALL I NEED FROM ROLAND.
I'VE NOT SEEN YOU FOR MORE THAN A WEEK.
I'VE BEEN BUSY WITH MY STUDIES, PRINCESS CARLINE.
OH, POOH. YOU SPEND TOO MUCH TIME IN THAT AWFUL TOWER.
WE COULD GO RIDING, YOUR HIGHNESS, IF YOU WOULD LIKE.
I'D LIKE THAT. BUT I'M AFRAID LADY MARNA WON'T ALLOW IT.
SHE SAYS THAT COMMONERS SHOULD KEEP THEIR PLACE.
BUT NOW THAT YOU'RE A COURTIER, SHE SUSPECTS YOU OF HAVING ASPIRATIONS.
ASPIRATIONS?
SHE THINKS THAT YOU HAVE AMBITIONS TO RISE TO A HIGHER STATION. SHE THINKS YOU SEEK TO INFLUENCE ME IN CERTAIN WAYS.

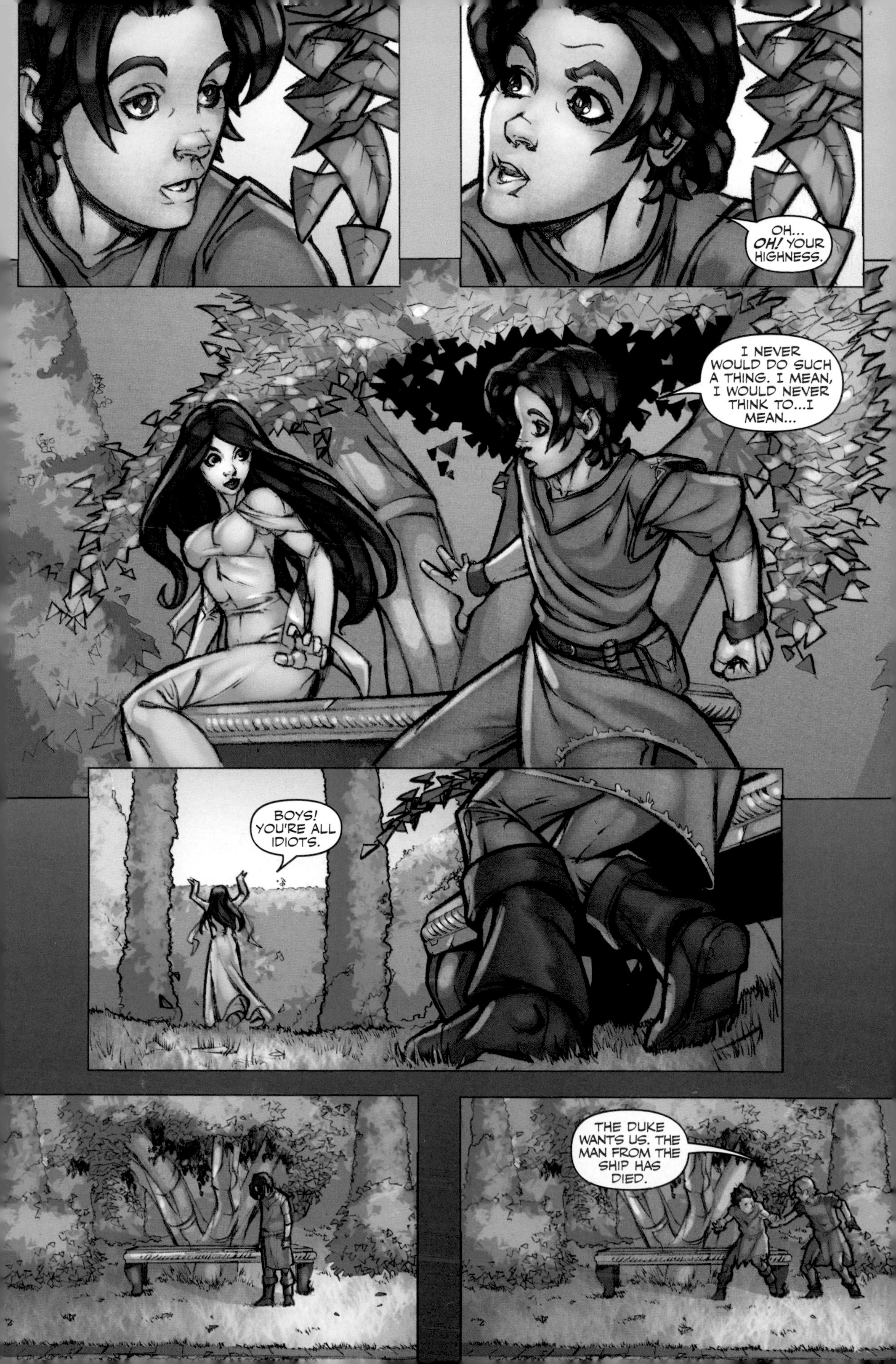
OH... *OH!* YOUR HIGHNESS.
I NEVER WOULD DO SUCH A THING. I MEAN, I WOULD NEVER THINK TO...I MEAN...
BOYS! YOU'RE ALL IDIOTS.
THE DUKE WANTS US. THE MAN FROM THE SHIP HAS DIED.

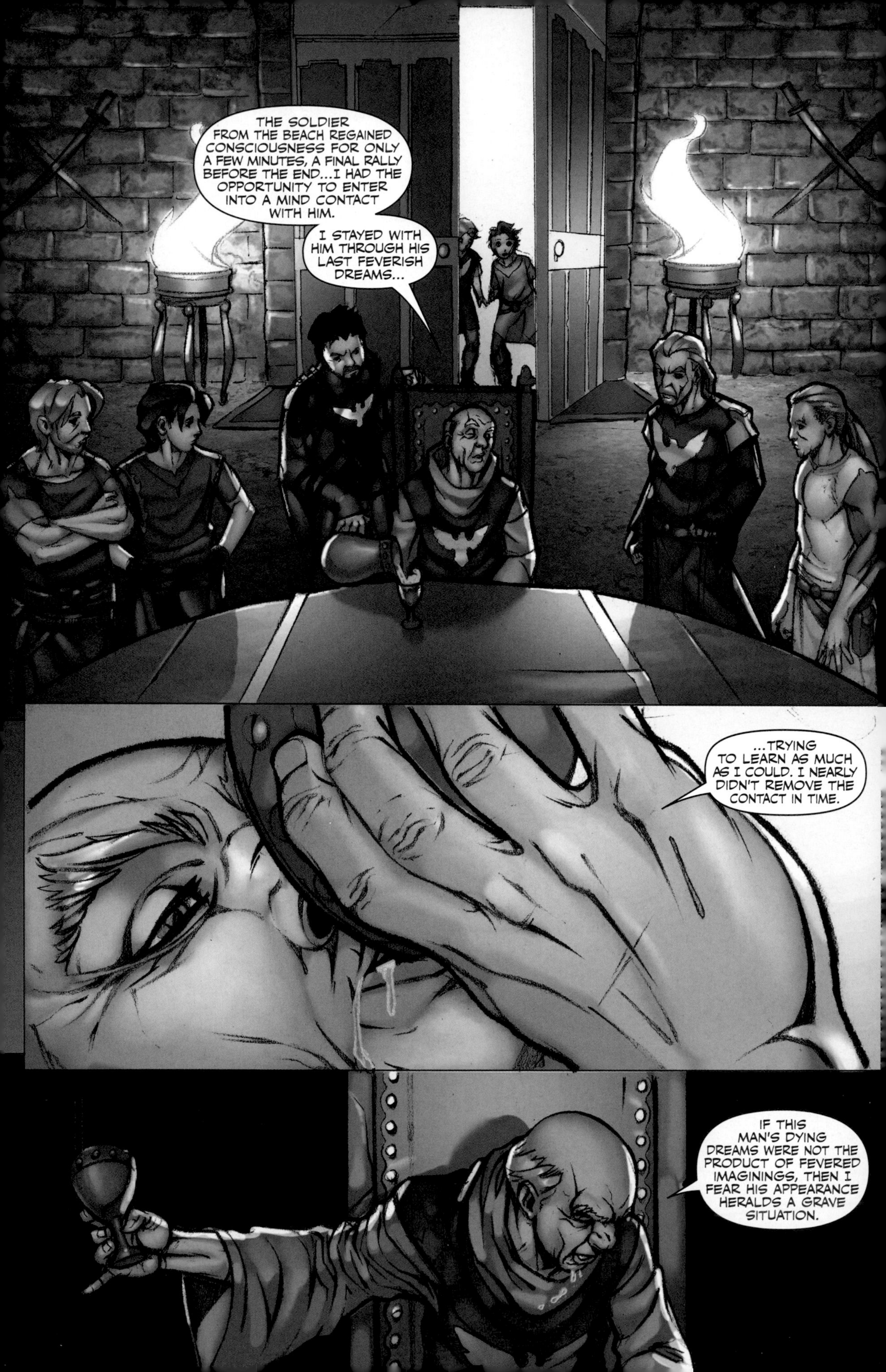
THE SOLDIER FROM THE BEACH REGAINED CONSCIOUSNESS FOR ONLY A FEW MINUTES, A FINAL RALLY BEFORE THE END...I HAD THE OPPORTUNITY TO ENTER INTO A MIND CONTACT WITH HIM.
I STAYED WITH HIM THROUGH HIS LAST FEVERISH DREAMS...
...TRYING TO LEARN AS MUCH AS I COULD. I NEARLY DIDN'T REMOVE THE CONTACT IN TIME.
IF THIS MAN'S DYING DREAMS WERE NOT THE PRODUCT OF FEVERED IMAGININGS, THEN I FEAR HIS APPEARANCE HERALDS A GRAVE SITUATION.

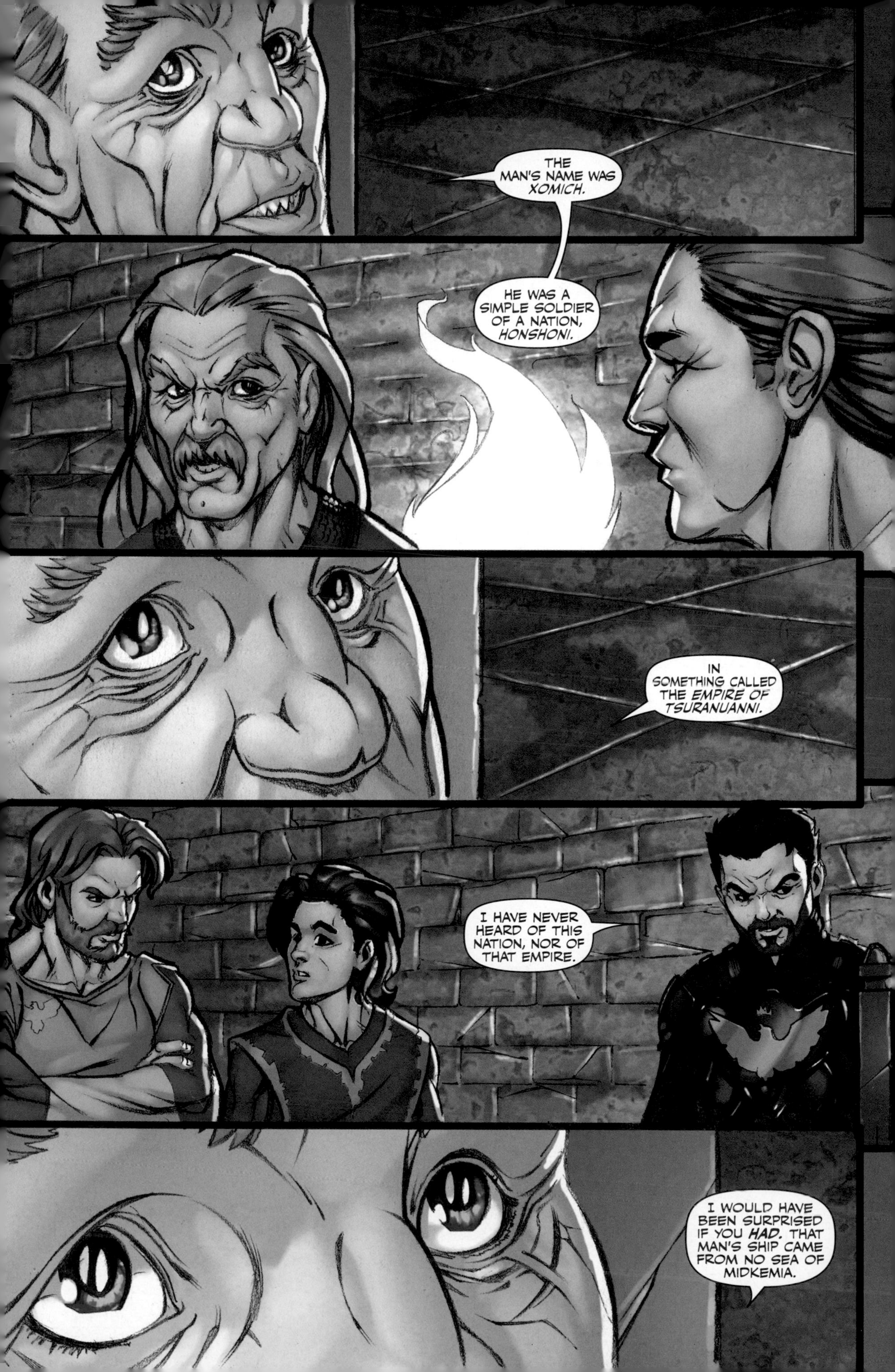
THE MAN'S NAME WAS XOMICH.
HE WAS A SIMPLE SOLDIER OF A NATION, HONSHONI.
IN SOMETHING CALLED THE EMPIRE OF TSURANUANNI.
I HAVE NEVER HEARD OF THIS NATION, NOR OF THAT EMPIRE.
I WOULD HAVE BEEN SURPRISED IF YOU HAD. THAT MAN'S SHIP CAME FROM NO SEA OF MIDKEMIA.

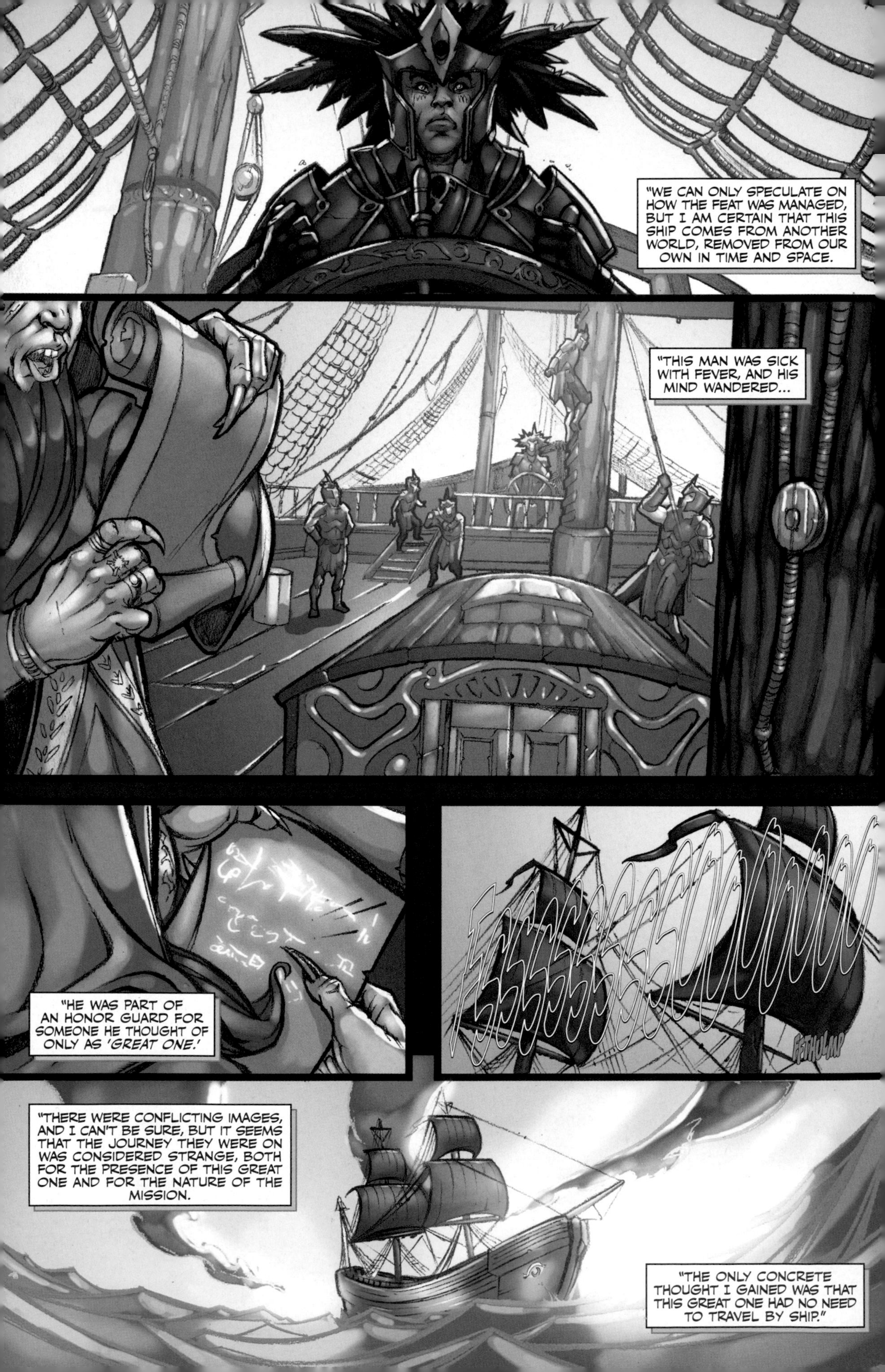
"WE CAN ONLY SPECULATE ON HOW THE FEAT WAS MANAGED, BUT I AM CERTAIN THAT THIS SHIP COMES FROM ANOTHER WORLD, REMOVED FROM OUR OWN IN TIME AND SPACE.
"THIS MAN WAS SICK WITH FEVER, AND HIS MIND WANDERED...
"HE WAS PART OF AN HONOR GUARD FOR SOMEONE HE THOUGHT OF ONLY AS 'GREAT ONE.'
FSSSSSSSSOOOOOOO
FFTHUMP
"THERE WERE CONFLICTING IMAGES, AND I CAN'T BE SURE, BUT IT SEEMS THAT THE JOURNEY THEY WERE ON WAS CONSIDERED STRANGE, BOTH FOR THE PRESENCE OF THIS GREAT ONE AND FOR THE NATURE OF THE MISSION.
"THE ONLY CONCRETE THOUGHT I GAINED WAS THAT THIS GREAT ONE HAD NO NEED TO TRAVEL BY SHIP."

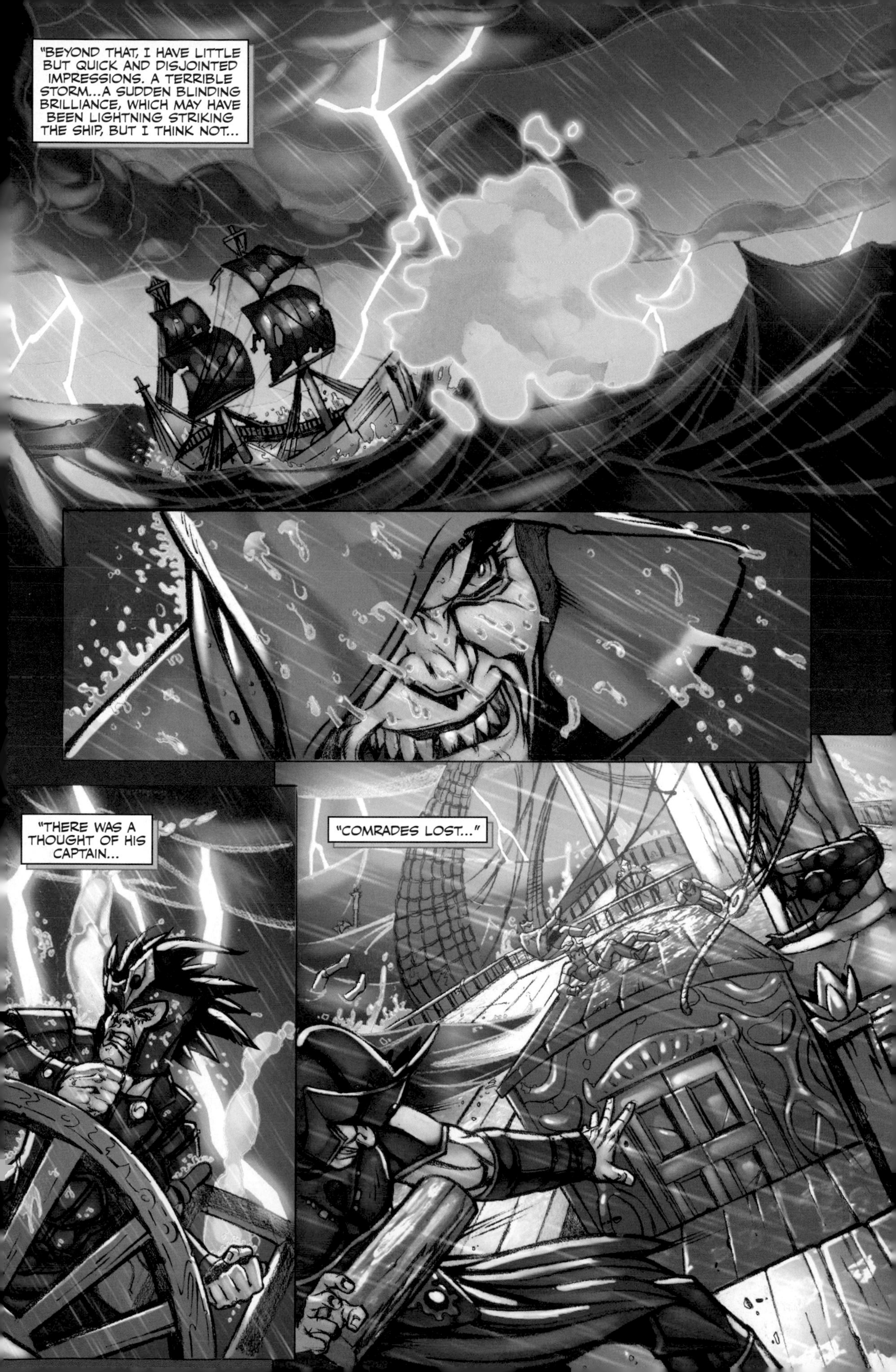
"BEYOND THAT, I HAVE LITTLE BUT QUICK AND DISJOINTED IMPRESSIONS. A TERRIBLE STORM...A SUDDEN BLINDING BRILLIANCE, WHICH MAY HAVE BEEN LIGHTNING STRIKING THE SHIP, BUT I THINK NOT...
"THERE WAS A THOUGHT OF HIS CAPTAIN...
"COMRADES LOST..."

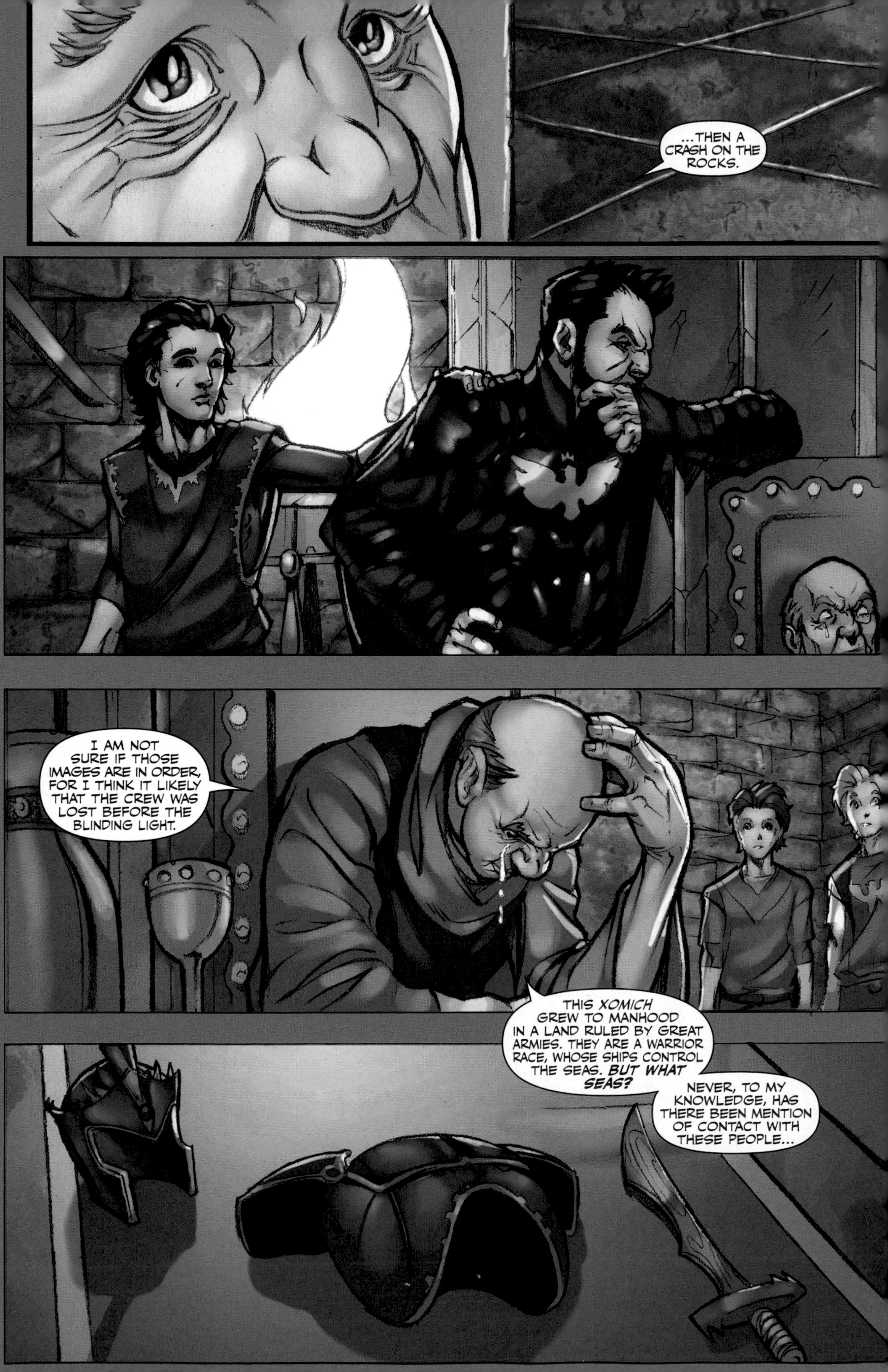
...THEN A CRASH ON THE ROCKS.
I AM NOT SURE IF THOSE IMAGES ARE IN ORDER, FOR I THINK IT LIKELY THAT THE CREW WAS LOST BEFORE THE BLINDING LIGHT.
THIS *XOMICH* GREW TO MANHOOD IN A LAND RULED BY GREAT ARMIES. THEY ARE A WARRIOR RACE, WHOSE SHIPS CONTROL THE SEAS. ***BUT WHAT SEAS?***
NEVER, TO MY KNOWLEDGE, HAS THERE BEEN MENTION OF CONTACT WITH THESE PEOPLE...

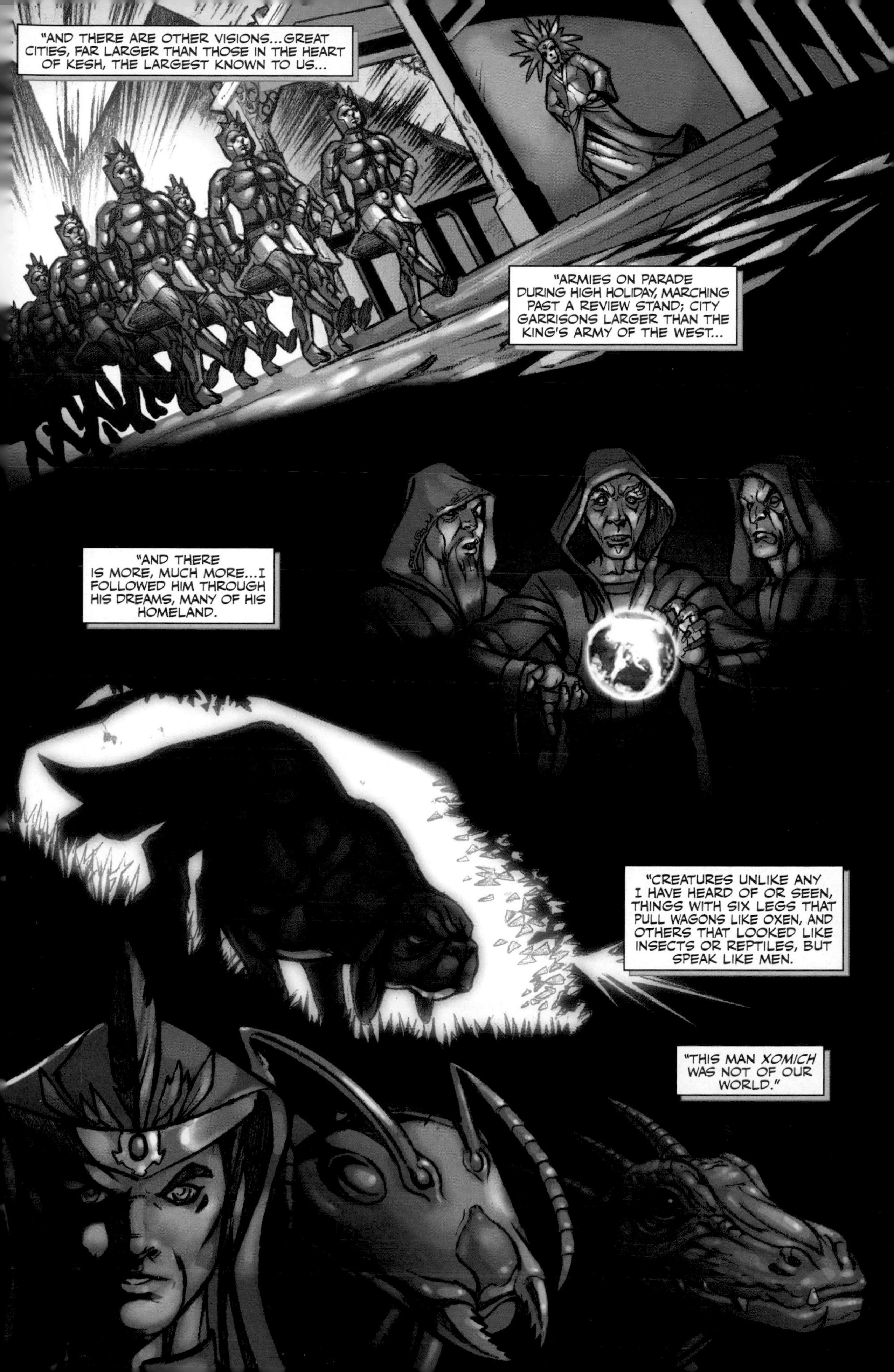
"AND THERE ARE OTHER VISIONS...GREAT CITIES, FAR LARGER THAN THOSE IN THE HEART OF KESH, THE LARGEST KNOWN TO US...
"ARMIES ON PARADE DURING HIGH HOLIDAY, MARCHING PAST A REVIEW STAND; CITY GARRISONS LARGER THAN THE KING'S ARMY OF THE WEST...
"AND THERE IS MORE, MUCH MORE...I FOLLOWED HIM THROUGH HIS DREAMS, MANY OF HIS HOMELAND.
"CREATURES UNLIKE ANY I HAVE HEARD OF OR SEEN, THINGS WITH SIX LEGS THAT PULL WAGONS LIKE OXEN, AND OTHERS THAT LOOKED LIKE INSECTS OR REPTILES, BUT SPEAK LIKE MEN.
"THIS MAN *XOMICH* WAS NOT OF OUR WORLD."

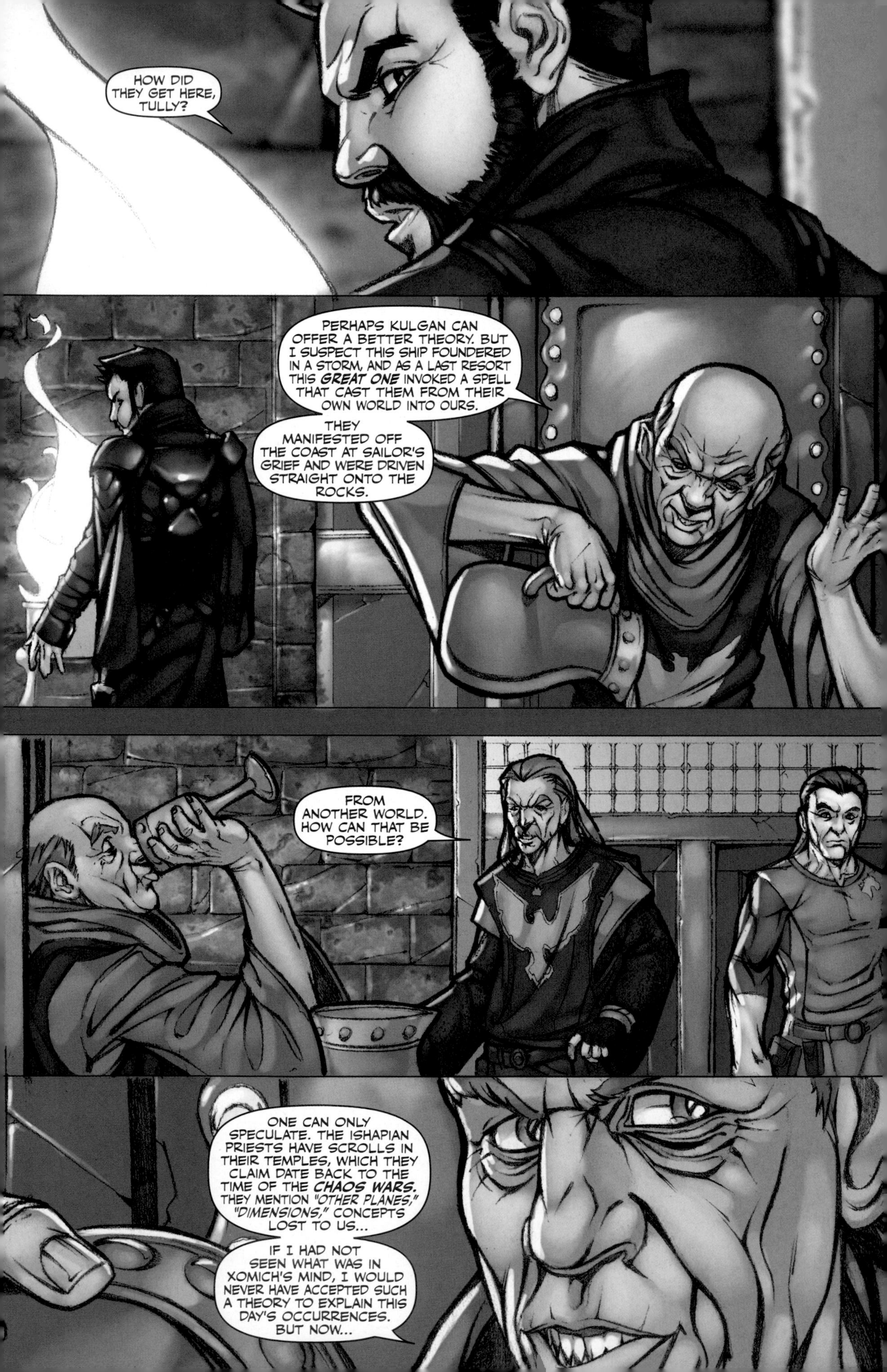
HOW DID THEY GET HERE, TULLY?
PERHAPS KULGAN CAN OFFER A BETTER THEORY. BUT I SUSPECT THIS SHIP FOUNDERED IN A STORM, AND AS A LAST RESORT THIS *GREAT ONE* INVOKED A SPELL THAT CAST THEM FROM THEIR OWN WORLD INTO OURS.
THEY MANIFESTED OFF THE COAST AT SAILOR'S GRIEF AND WERE DRIVEN STRAIGHT ONTO THE ROCKS.
FROM ANOTHER WORLD. HOW CAN THAT BE POSSIBLE?
ONE CAN ONLY SPECULATE. THE ISHAPIAN PRIESTS HAVE SCROLLS IN THEIR TEMPLES, WHICH THEY CLAIM DATE BACK TO THE TIME OF THE *CHAOS WARS.* THEY MENTION *"OTHER PLANES," "DIMENSIONS,"* CONCEPTS LOST TO US...
IF I HAD NOT SEEN WHAT WAS IN XOMICH'S MIND, I WOULD NEVER HAVE ACCEPTED SUCH A THEORY TO EXPLAIN THIS DAY'S OCCURRENCES. BUT NOW...

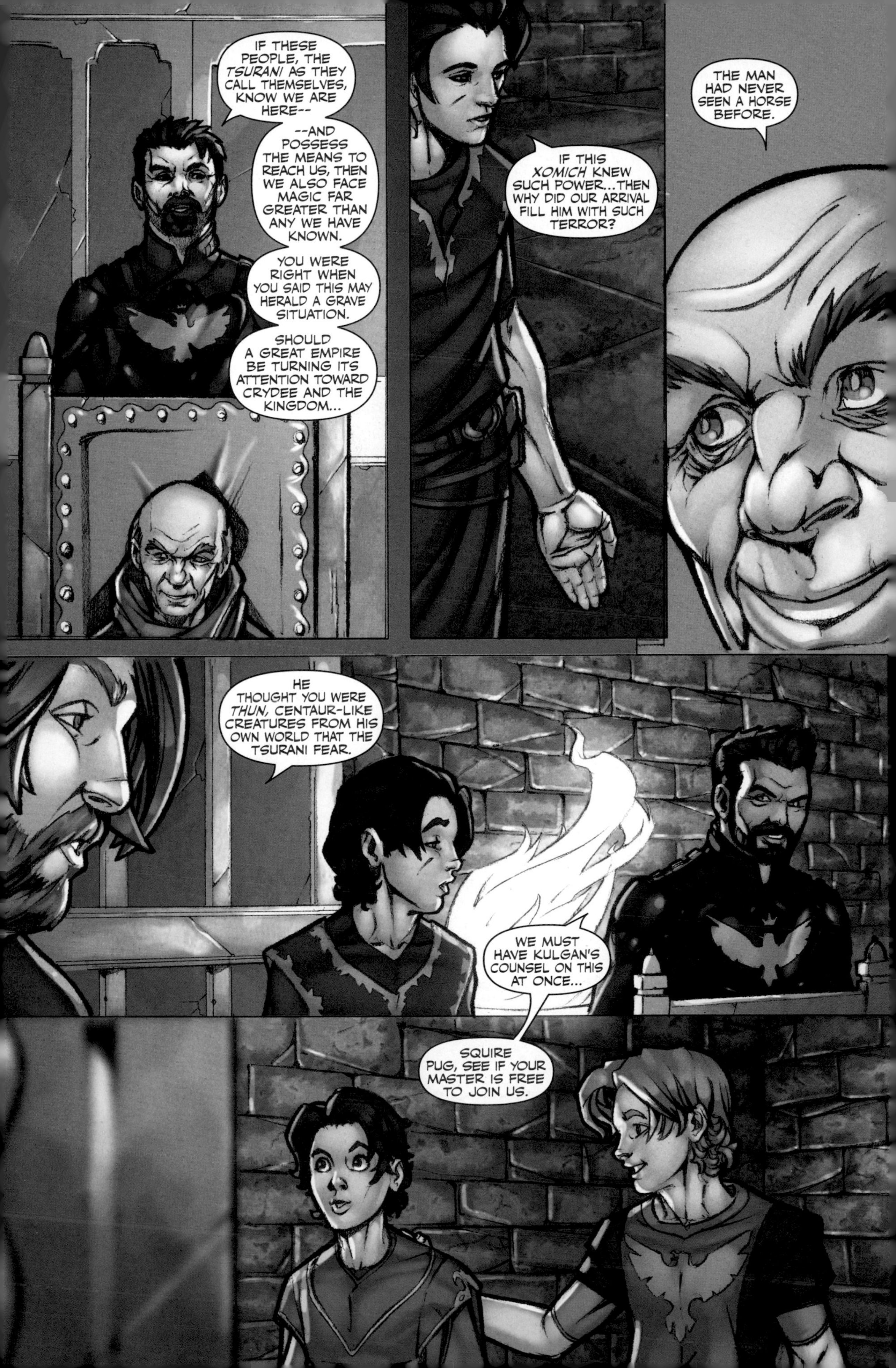
IF THESE PEOPLE, THE TSURANI AS THEY CALL THEMSELVES, KNOW WE ARE HERE--
--AND POSSESS THE MEANS TO REACH US, THEN WE ALSO FACE MAGIC FAR GREATER THAN ANY WE HAVE KNOWN.
YOU WERE RIGHT WHEN YOU SAID THIS MAY HERALD A GRAVE SITUATION.
SHOULD A GREAT EMPIRE BE TURNING ITS ATTENTION TOWARD CRYDEE AND THE KINGDOM...
IF THIS XOMICH KNEW SUCH POWER...THEN WHY DID OUR ARRIVAL FILL HIM WITH SUCH TERROR?
THE MAN HAD NEVER SEEN A HORSE BEFORE.
HE THOUGHT YOU WERE THUN, CENTAUR-LIKE CREATURES FROM HIS OWN WORLD THAT THE TSURANI FEAR.
WE MUST HAVE KULGAN'S COUNSEL ON THIS AT ONCE...
SQUIRE PUG, SEE IF YOUR MASTER IS FREE TO JOIN US.

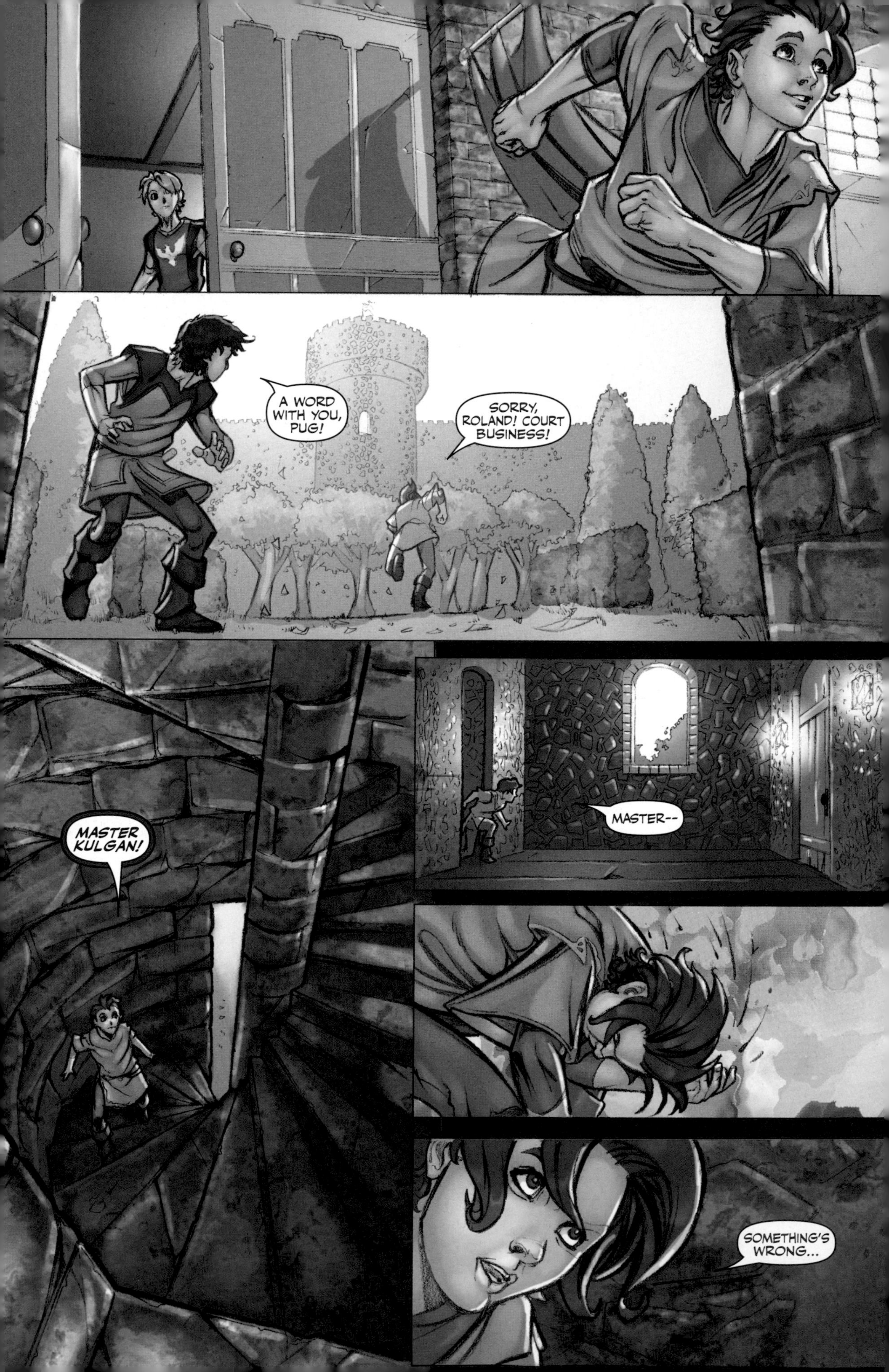
A WORD WITH YOU, PUG!
SORRY, ROLAND! COURT BUSINESS!
MASTER KULGAN!
MASTER--
SOMETHING'S WRONG...

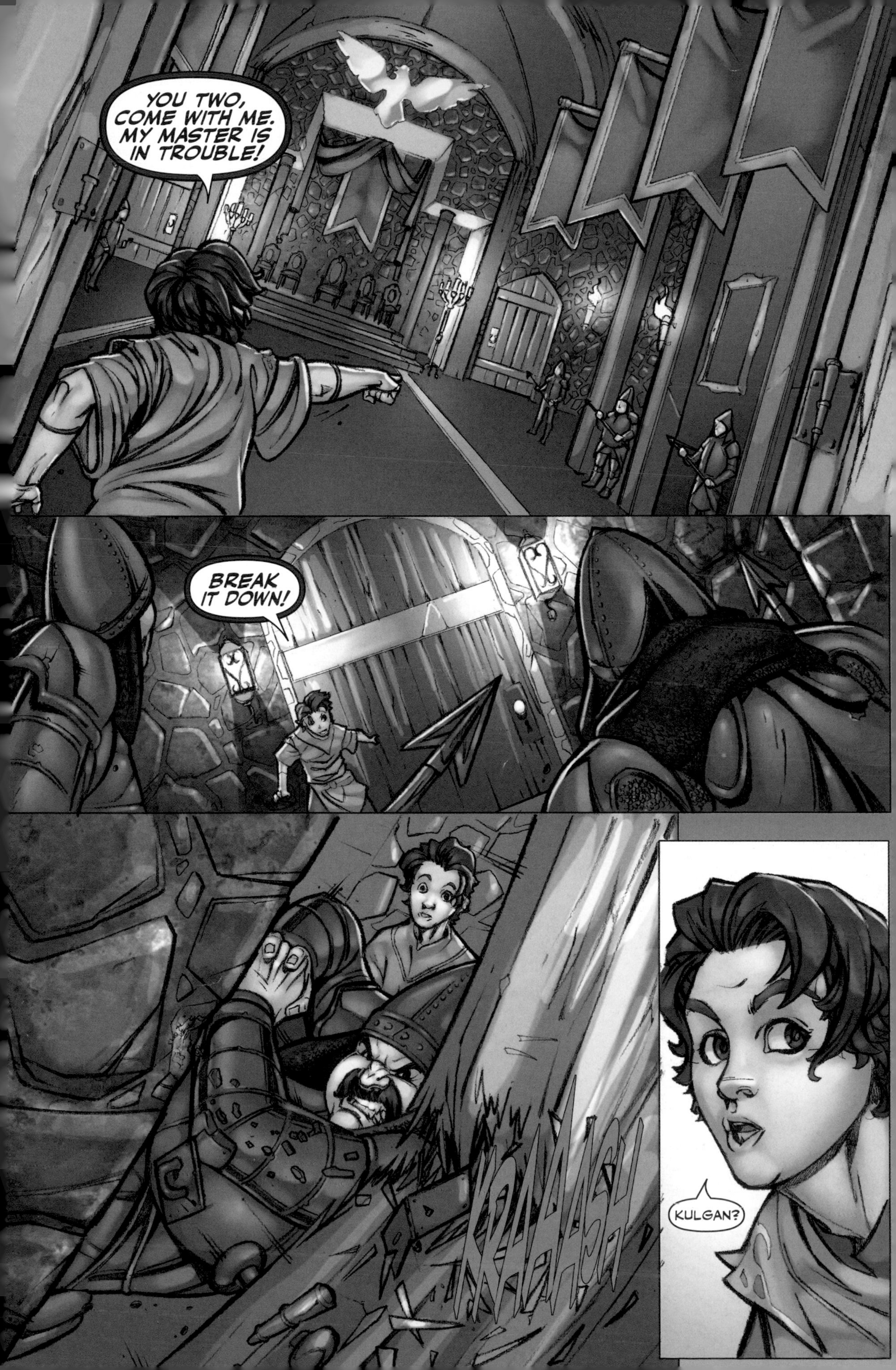
YOU TWO, COME WITH ME. MY MASTER IS IN TROUBLE!
BREAK IT DOWN!
KRAAASH
KULGAN?

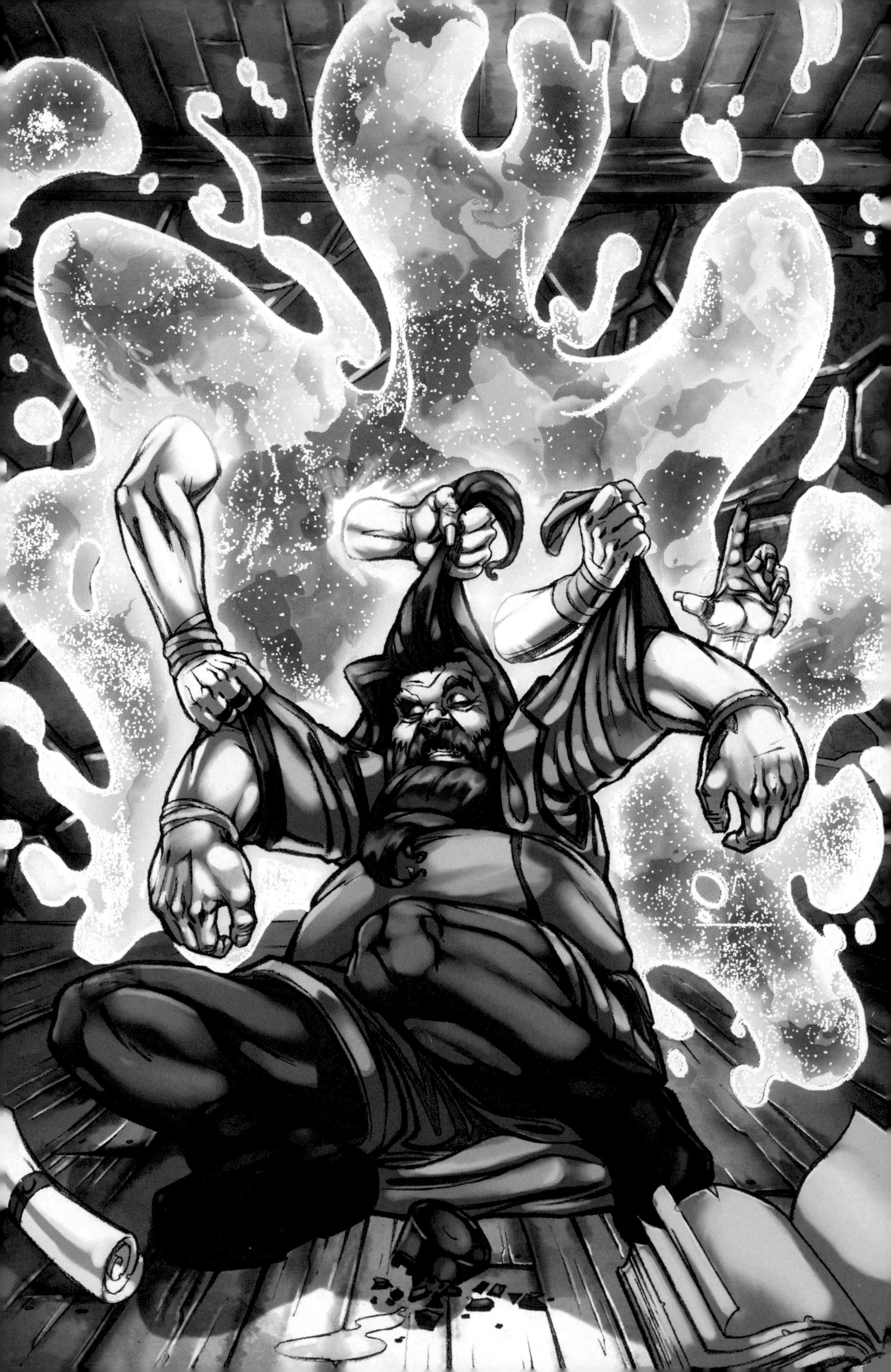

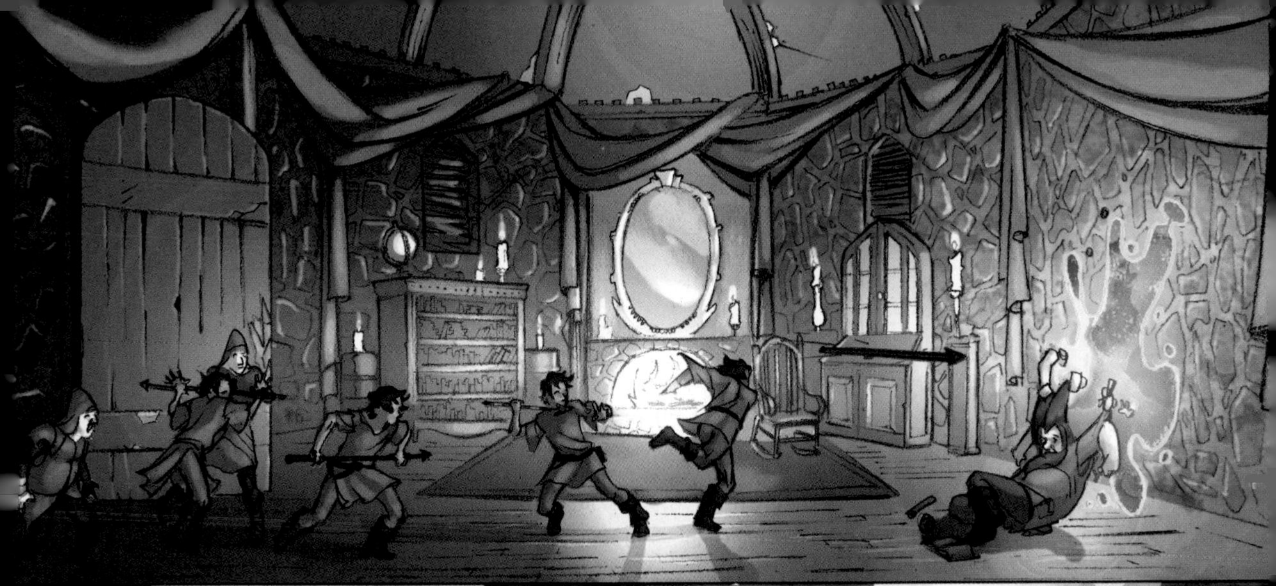

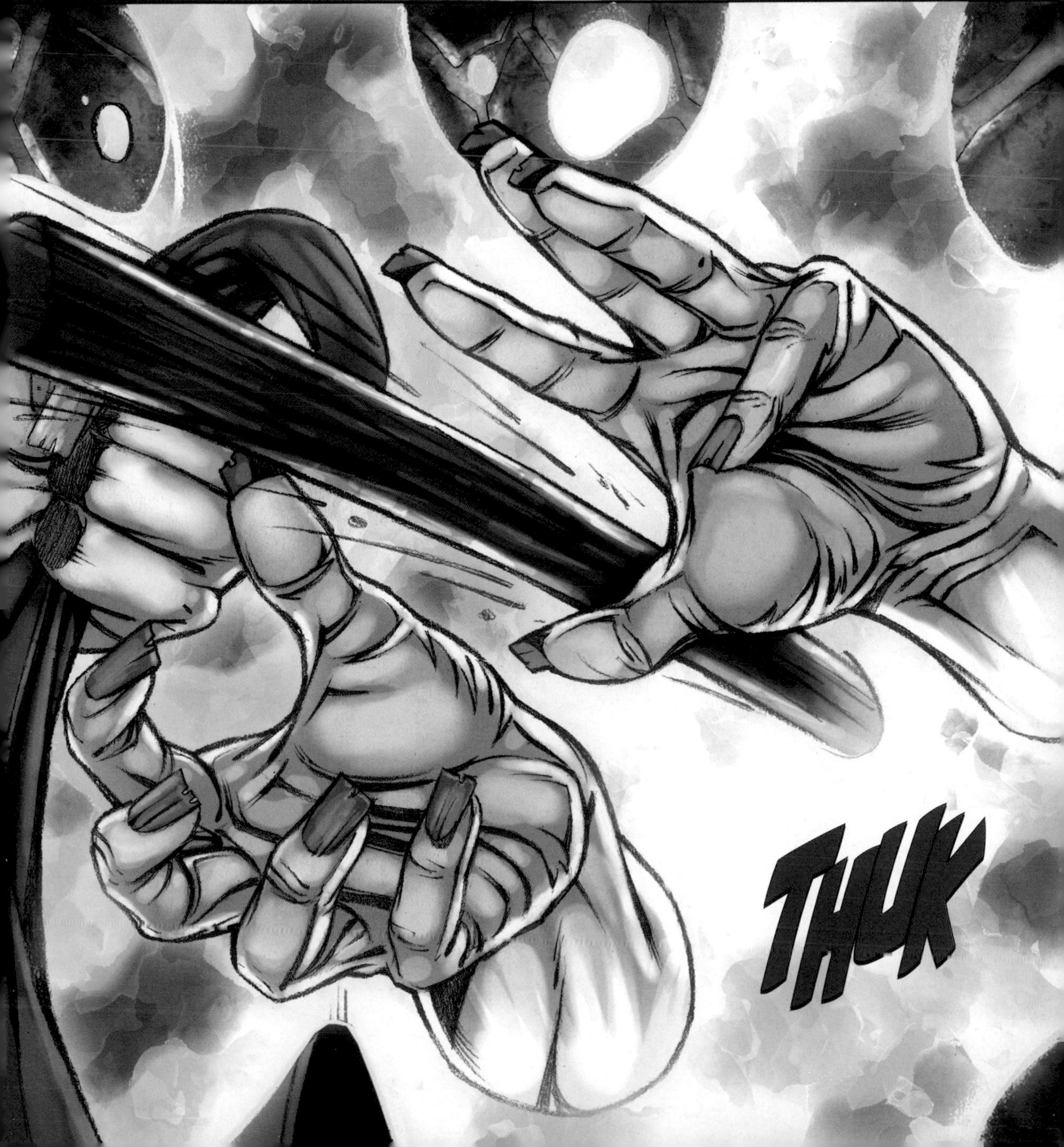
THUK

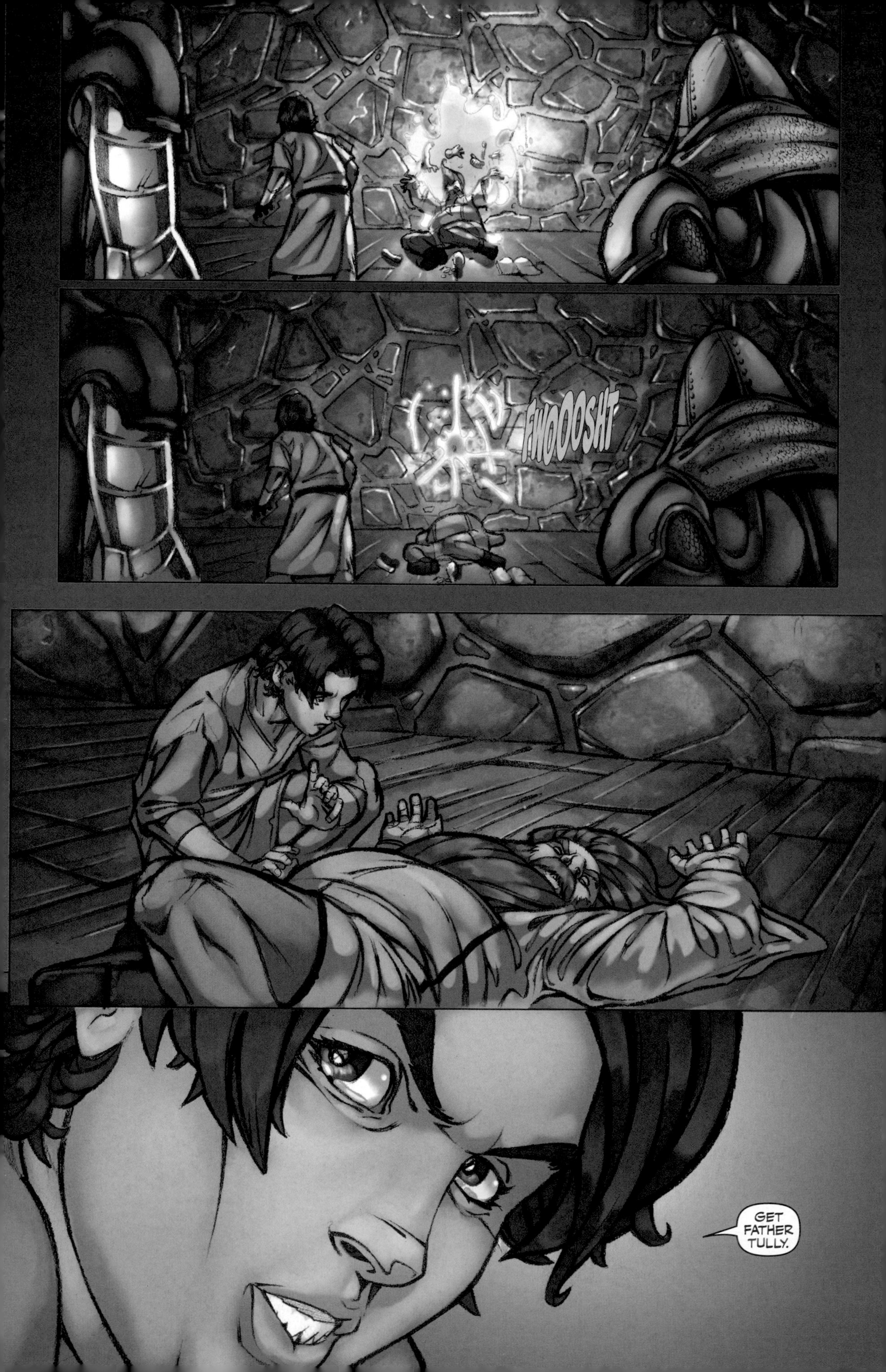
FWOOOSHT
GET FATHER TULLY.

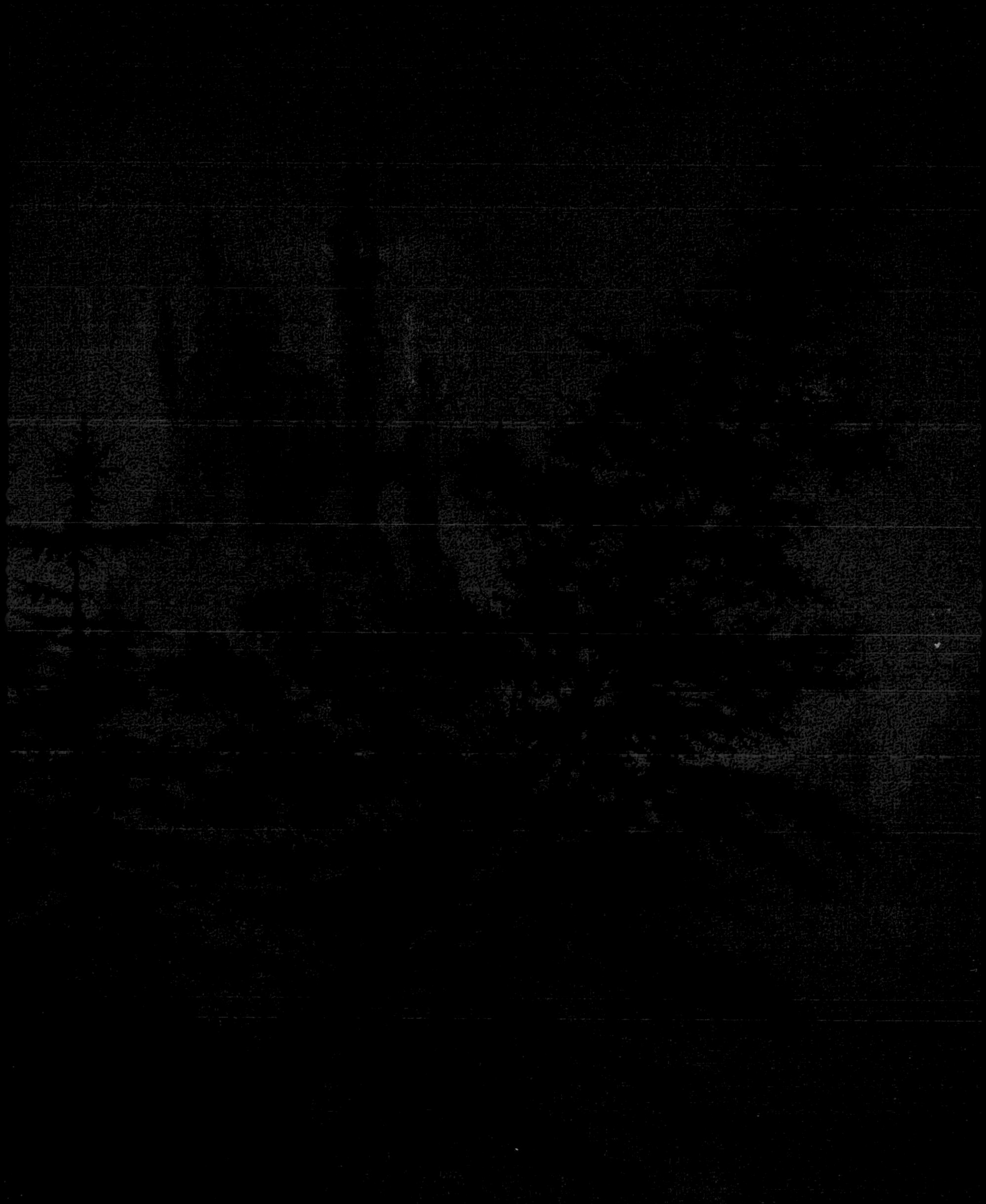

MAGICIAN: APPRENTICE

CHAPTER FIVE

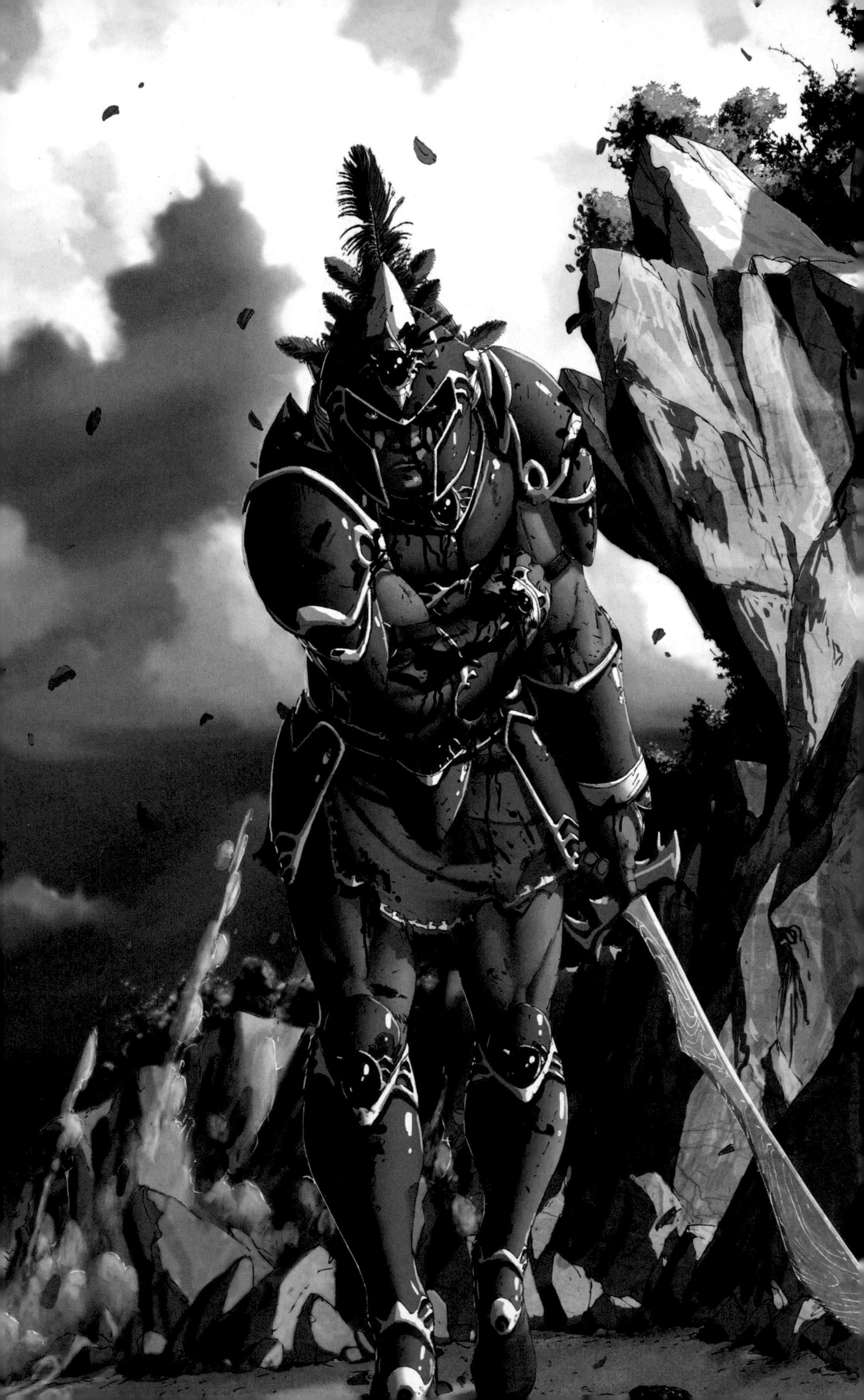

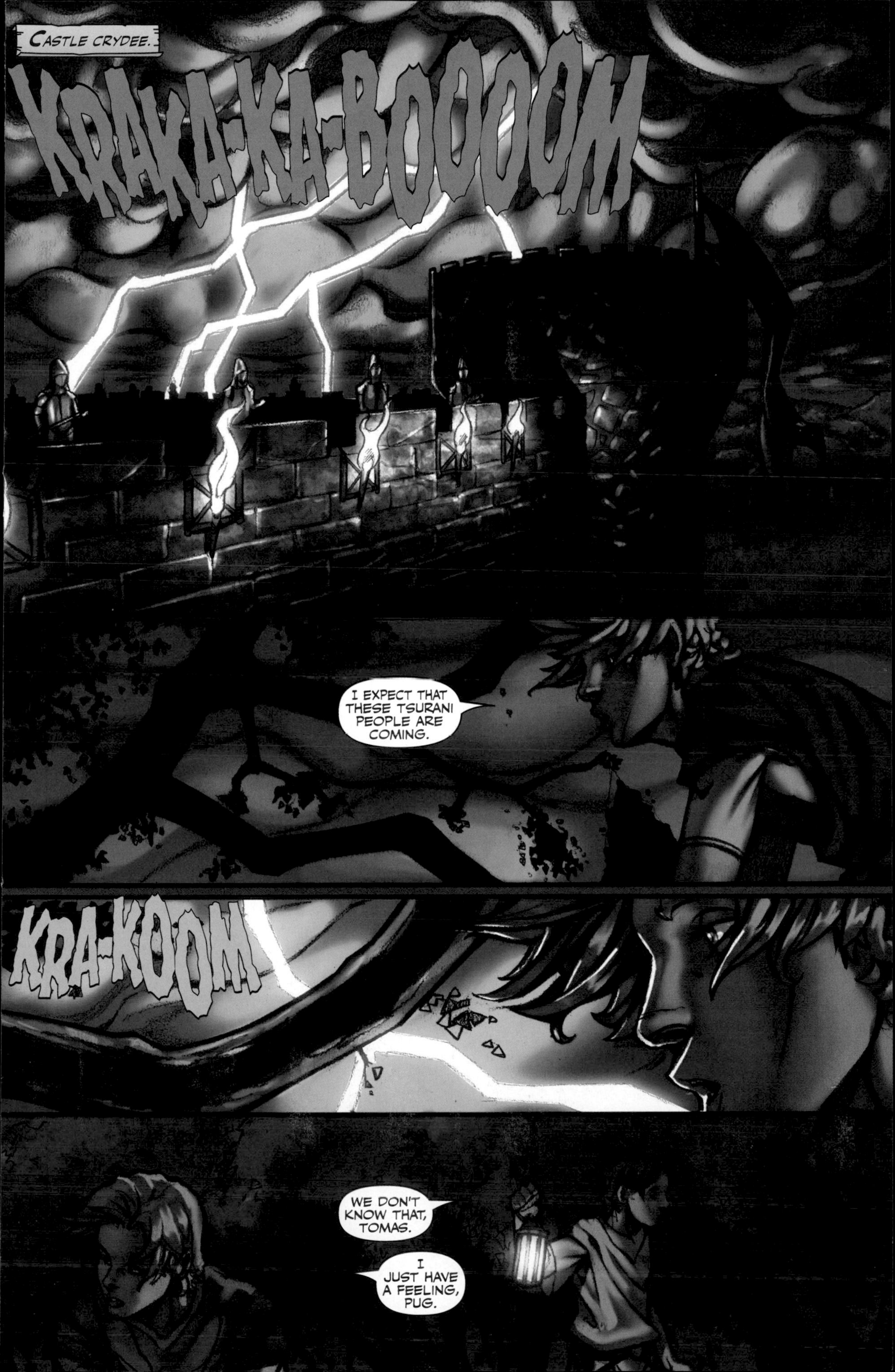
CASTLE CRYDEE.
KRAKA-KA-BOOOOM
I EXPECT THAT THESE TSURANI PEOPLE ARE COMING.
KRA-KOOM
WE DON'T KNOW THAT, TOMAS.
I JUST HAVE A FEELING, PUG.

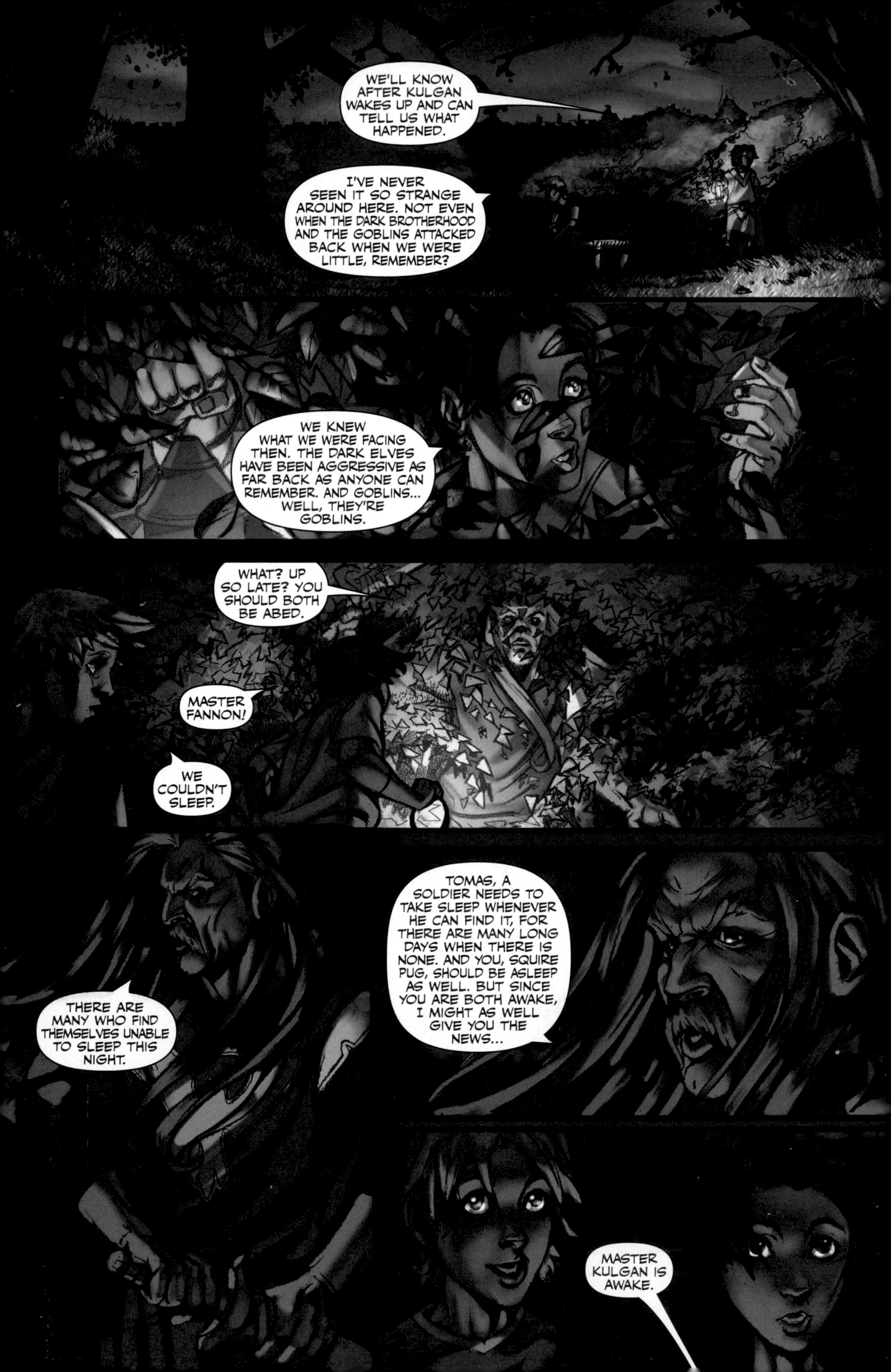

WE'LL KNOW AFTER KULGAN WAKES UP AND CAN TELL US WHAT HAPPENED.
I'VE NEVER SEEN IT SO STRANGE AROUND HERE. NOT EVEN WHEN THE DARK BROTHERHOOD AND THE GOBLINS ATTACKED BACK WHEN WE WERE LITTLE, REMEMBER?
WE KNEW WHAT WE WERE FACING THEN. THE DARK ELVES HAVE BEEN AGGRESSIVE AS FAR BACK AS ANYONE CAN REMEMBER. AND GOBLINS... WELL, THEY'RE GOBLINS.
WHAT? UP SO LATE? YOU SHOULD BOTH BE ABED.
MASTER FANNON!
WE COULDN'T SLEEP.
THERE ARE MANY WHO FIND THEMSELVES UNABLE TO SLEEP THIS NIGHT.
TOMAS, A SOLDIER NEEDS TO TAKE SLEEP WHENEVER HE CAN FIND IT, FOR THERE ARE MANY LONG DAYS WHEN THERE IS NONE. AND YOU, SQUIRE PUG, SHOULD BE ASLEEP AS WELL. BUT SINCE YOU ARE BOTH AWAKE, I MIGHT AS WELL GIVE YOU THE NEWS...
MASTER KULGAN IS AWAKE.

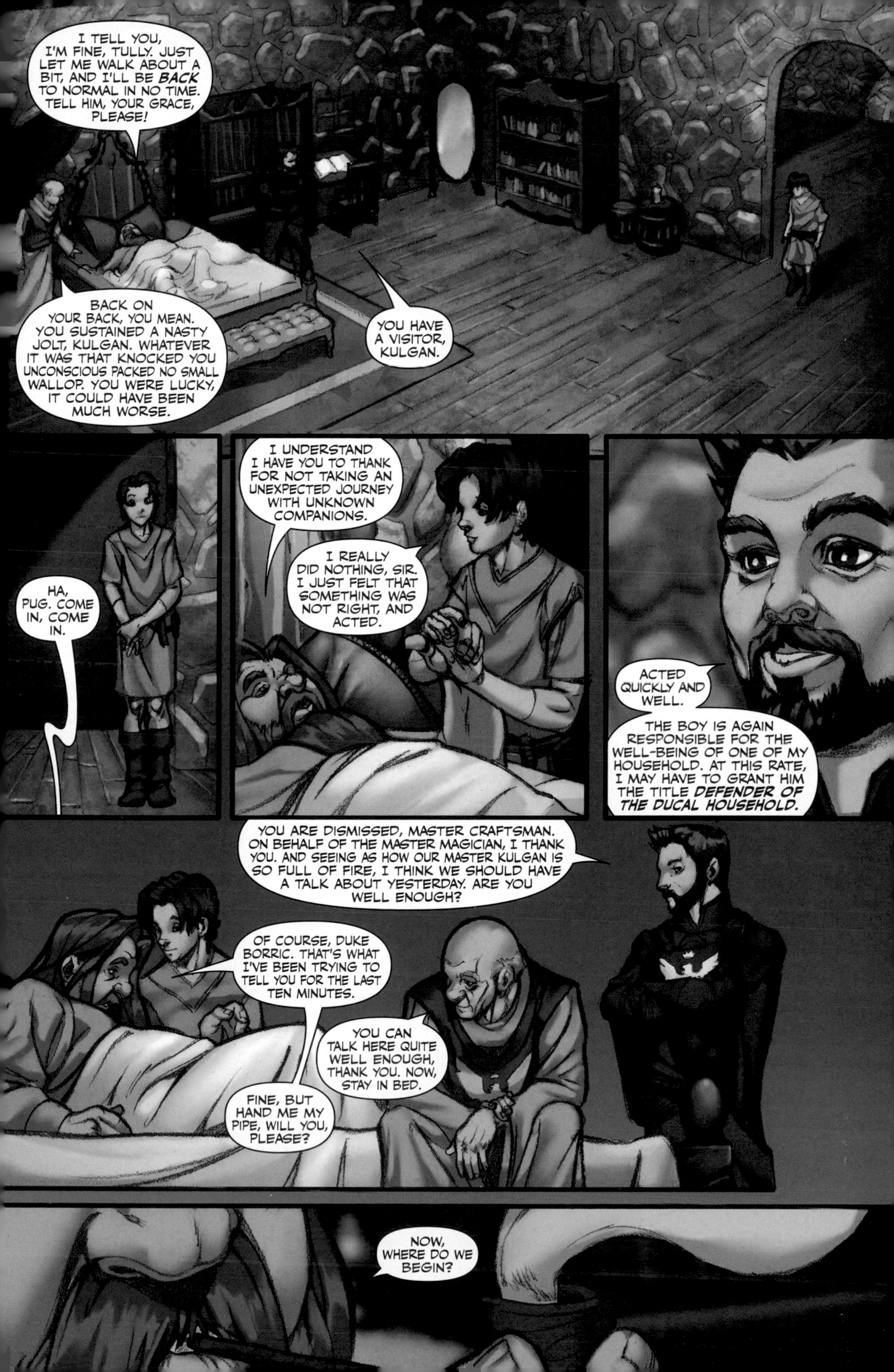
I TELL YOU, I'M FINE, TULLY. JUST LET ME WALK ABOUT A BIT, AND I'LL BE *BACK* TO NORMAL IN NO TIME. TELL HIM, YOUR GRACE, PLEASE!
BACK ON YOUR BACK, YOU MEAN. YOU SUSTAINED A NASTY JOLT, KULGAN. WHATEVER IT WAS THAT KNOCKED YOU UNCONSCIOUS PACKED NO SMALL WALLOP. YOU WERE LUCKY, IT COULD HAVE BEEN MUCH WORSE.
YOU HAVE A VISITOR, KULGAN.
HA, PUG. COME IN, COME IN.
I UNDERSTAND I HAVE YOU TO THANK FOR NOT TAKING AN UNEXPECTED JOURNEY WITH UNKNOWN COMPANIONS.
I REALLY DID NOTHING, SIR. I JUST FELT THAT SOMETHING WAS NOT RIGHT, AND ACTED.
ACTED QUICKLY AND WELL.
THE BOY IS AGAIN RESPONSIBLE FOR THE WELL-BEING OF ONE OF MY HOUSEHOLD. AT THIS RATE, I MAY HAVE TO GRANT HIM THE TITLE *DEFENDER OF THE DUCAL HOUSEHOLD.*
YOU ARE DISMISSED, MASTER CRAFTSMAN. ON BEHALF OF THE MASTER MAGICIAN, I THANK YOU. AND SEEING AS HOW OUR MASTER KULGAN IS SO FULL OF FIRE, I THINK WE SHOULD HAVE A TALK ABOUT YESTERDAY. ARE YOU WELL ENOUGH?
OF COURSE, DUKE BORRIC. THAT'S WHAT I'VE BEEN TRYING TO TELL YOU FOR THE LAST TEN MINUTES.
YOU CAN TALK HERE QUITE WELL ENOUGH, THANK YOU. NOW, STAY IN BED.
FINE, BUT HAND ME MY PIPE, WILL YOU, PLEASE?
NOW, WHERE DO WE BEGIN?

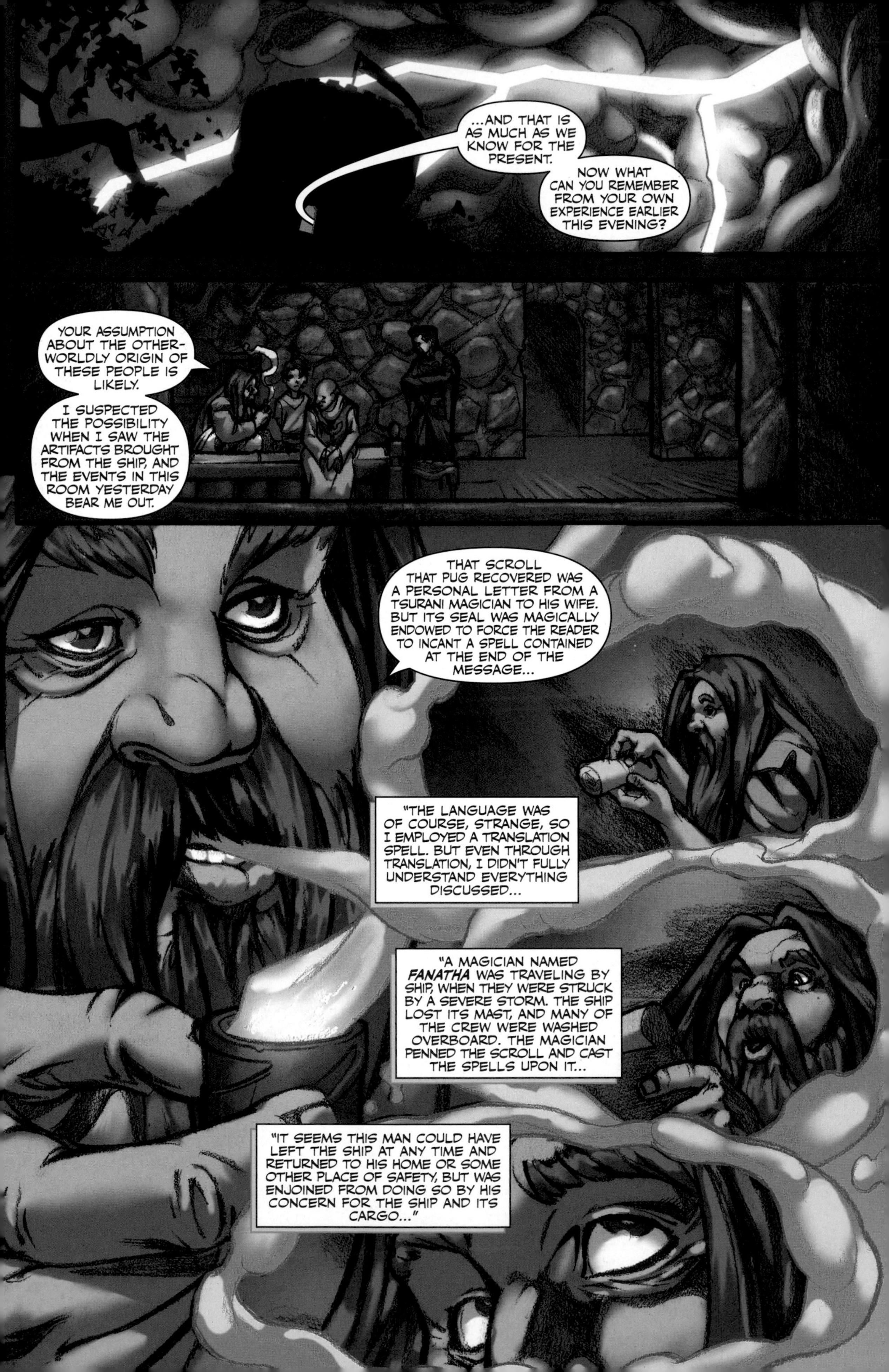
...AND THAT IS AS MUCH AS WE KNOW FOR THE PRESENT.
NOW WHAT CAN YOU REMEMBER FROM YOUR OWN EXPERIENCE EARLIER THIS EVENING?
YOUR ASSUMPTION ABOUT THE OTHER-WORLDLY ORIGIN OF THESE PEOPLE IS LIKELY.
I SUSPECTED THE POSSIBILITY WHEN I SAW THE ARTIFACTS BROUGHT FROM THE SHIP, AND THE EVENTS IN THIS ROOM YESTERDAY BEAR ME OUT.
THAT SCROLL THAT PUG RECOVERED WAS A PERSONAL LETTER FROM A TSURANI MAGICIAN TO HIS WIFE. BUT ITS SEAL WAS MAGICALLY ENDOWED TO FORCE THE READER TO INCANT A SPELL CONTAINED AT THE END OF THE MESSAGE...
"THE LANGUAGE WAS OF COURSE, STRANGE, SO I EMPLOYED A TRANSLATION SPELL. BUT EVEN THROUGH TRANSLATION, I DIDN'T FULLY UNDERSTAND EVERYTHING DISCUSSED...
"A MAGICIAN NAMED ***FANATHA*** WAS TRAVELING BY SHIP, WHEN THEY WERE STRUCK BY A SEVERE STORM. THE SHIP LOST ITS MAST, AND MANY OF THE CREW WERE WASHED OVERBOARD. THE MAGICIAN PENNED THE SCROLL AND CAST THE SPELLS UPON IT...
"IT SEEMS THIS MAN COULD HAVE LEFT THE SHIP AT ANY TIME AND RETURNED TO HIS HOME OR SOME OTHER PLACE OF SAFETY, BUT WAS ENJOINED FROM DOING SO BY HIS CONCERN FOR THE SHIP AND ITS CARGO..."

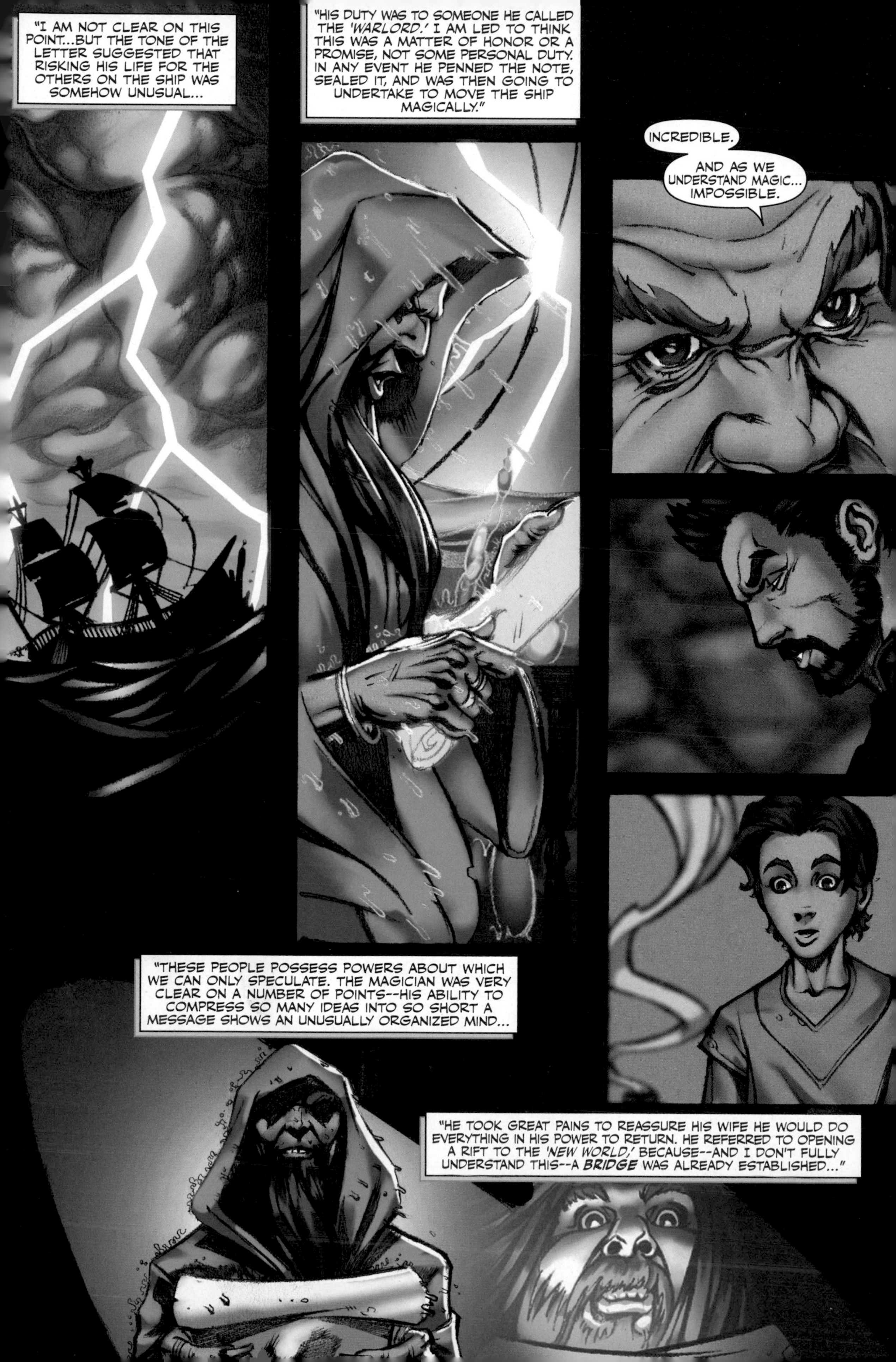
"I AM NOT CLEAR ON THIS POINT...BUT THE TONE OF THE LETTER SUGGESTED THAT RISKING HIS LIFE FOR THE OTHERS ON THE SHIP WAS SOMEHOW UNUSUAL...
"HIS DUTY WAS TO SOMEONE HE CALLED THE 'WARLORD.' I AM LED TO THINK THIS WAS A MATTER OF HONOR OR A PROMISE, NOT SOME PERSONAL DUTY. IN ANY EVENT HE PENNED THE NOTE, SEALED IT, AND WAS THEN GOING TO UNDERTAKE TO MOVE THE SHIP MAGICALLY."
INCREDIBLE.
AND AS WE UNDERSTAND MAGIC... IMPOSSIBLE.
"THESE PEOPLE POSSESS POWERS ABOUT WHICH WE CAN ONLY SPECULATE. THE MAGICIAN WAS VERY CLEAR ON A NUMBER OF POINTS--HIS ABILITY TO COMPRESS SO MANY IDEAS INTO SO SHORT A MESSAGE SHOWS AN UNUSUALLY ORGANIZED MIND...
"HE TOOK GREAT PAINS TO REASSURE HIS WIFE HE WOULD DO EVERYTHING IN HIS POWER TO RETURN. HE REFERRED TO OPENING A RIFT TO THE 'NEW WORLD,' BECAUSE--AND I DON'T FULLY UNDERSTAND THIS--A BRIDGE WAS ALREADY ESTABLISHED..."

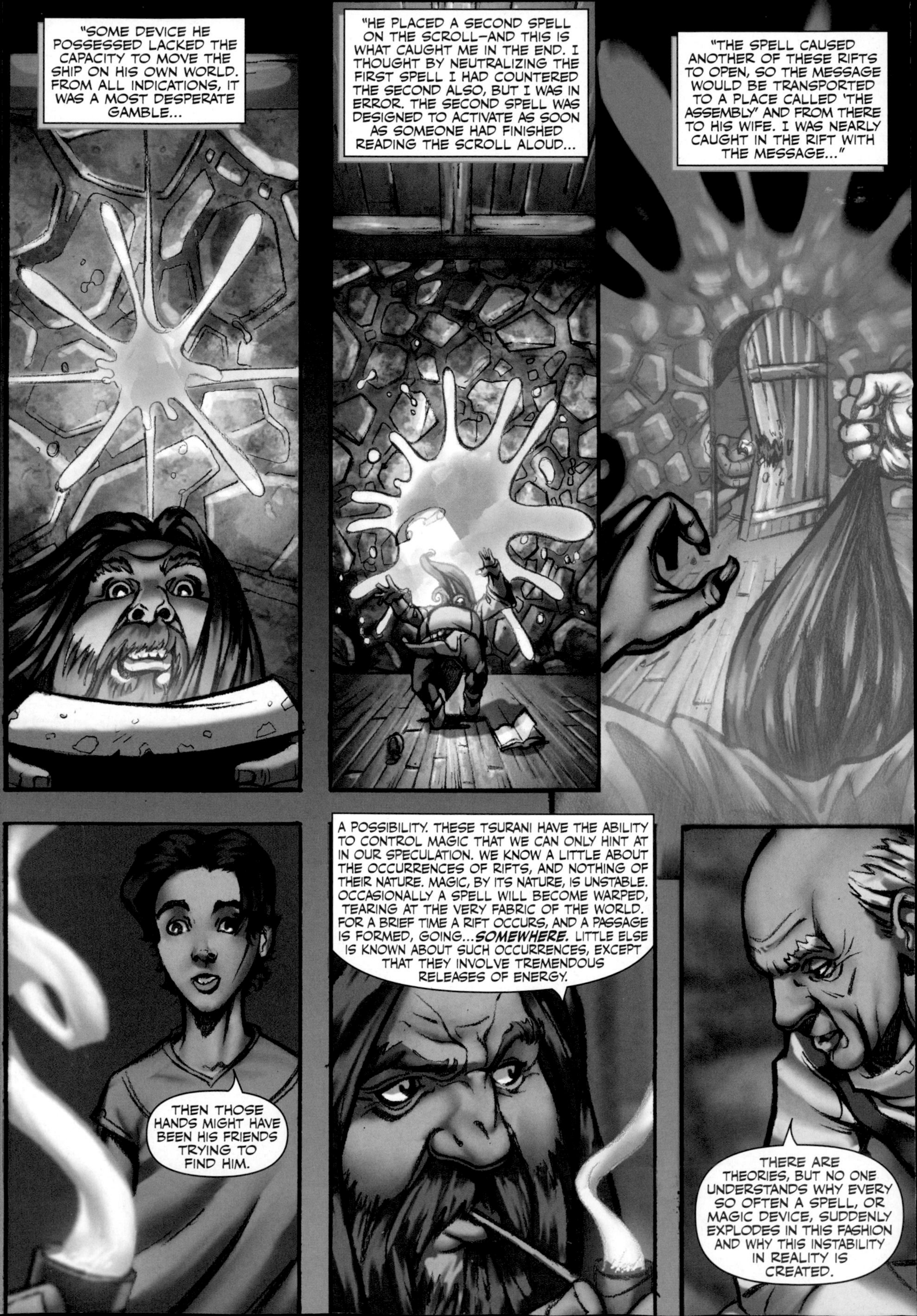
"SOME DEVICE HE POSSESSED LACKED THE CAPACITY TO MOVE THE SHIP ON HIS OWN WORLD. FROM ALL INDICATIONS, IT WAS A MOST DESPERATE GAMBLE...
"HE PLACED A SECOND SPELL ON THE SCROLL—AND THIS IS WHAT CAUGHT ME IN THE END. I THOUGHT BY NEUTRALIZING THE FIRST SPELL I HAD COUNTERED THE SECOND ALSO, BUT I WAS IN ERROR. THE SECOND SPELL WAS DESIGNED TO ACTIVATE AS SOON AS SOMEONE HAD FINISHED READING THE SCROLL ALOUD...
"THE SPELL CAUSED ANOTHER OF THESE RIFTS TO OPEN, SO THE MESSAGE WOULD BE TRANSPORTED TO A PLACE CALLED 'THE ASSEMBLY' AND FROM THERE TO HIS WIFE. I WAS NEARLY CAUGHT IN THE RIFT WITH THE MESSAGE..."
THEN THOSE HANDS MIGHT HAVE BEEN HIS FRIENDS TRYING TO FIND HIM.
A POSSIBILITY. THESE TSURANI HAVE THE ABILITY TO CONTROL MAGIC THAT WE CAN ONLY HINT AT IN OUR SPECULATION. WE KNOW A LITTLE ABOUT THE OCCURRENCES OF RIFTS, AND NOTHING OF THEIR NATURE. MAGIC, BY ITS NATURE, IS UNSTABLE. OCCASIONALLY A SPELL WILL BECOME WARPED, TEARING AT THE VERY FABRIC OF THE WORLD. FOR A BRIEF TIME A RIFT OCCURS, AND A PASSAGE IS FORMED, GOING...SOMEWHERE. LITTLE ELSE IS KNOWN ABOUT SUCH OCCURRENCES, EXCEPT THAT THEY INVOLVE TREMENDOUS RELEASES OF ENERGY.
THERE ARE THEORIES, BUT NO ONE UNDERSTANDS WHY EVERY SO OFTEN A SPELL, OR MAGIC DEVICE, SUDDENLY EXPLODES IN THIS FASHION AND WHY THIS INSTABILITY IN REALITY IS CREATED.

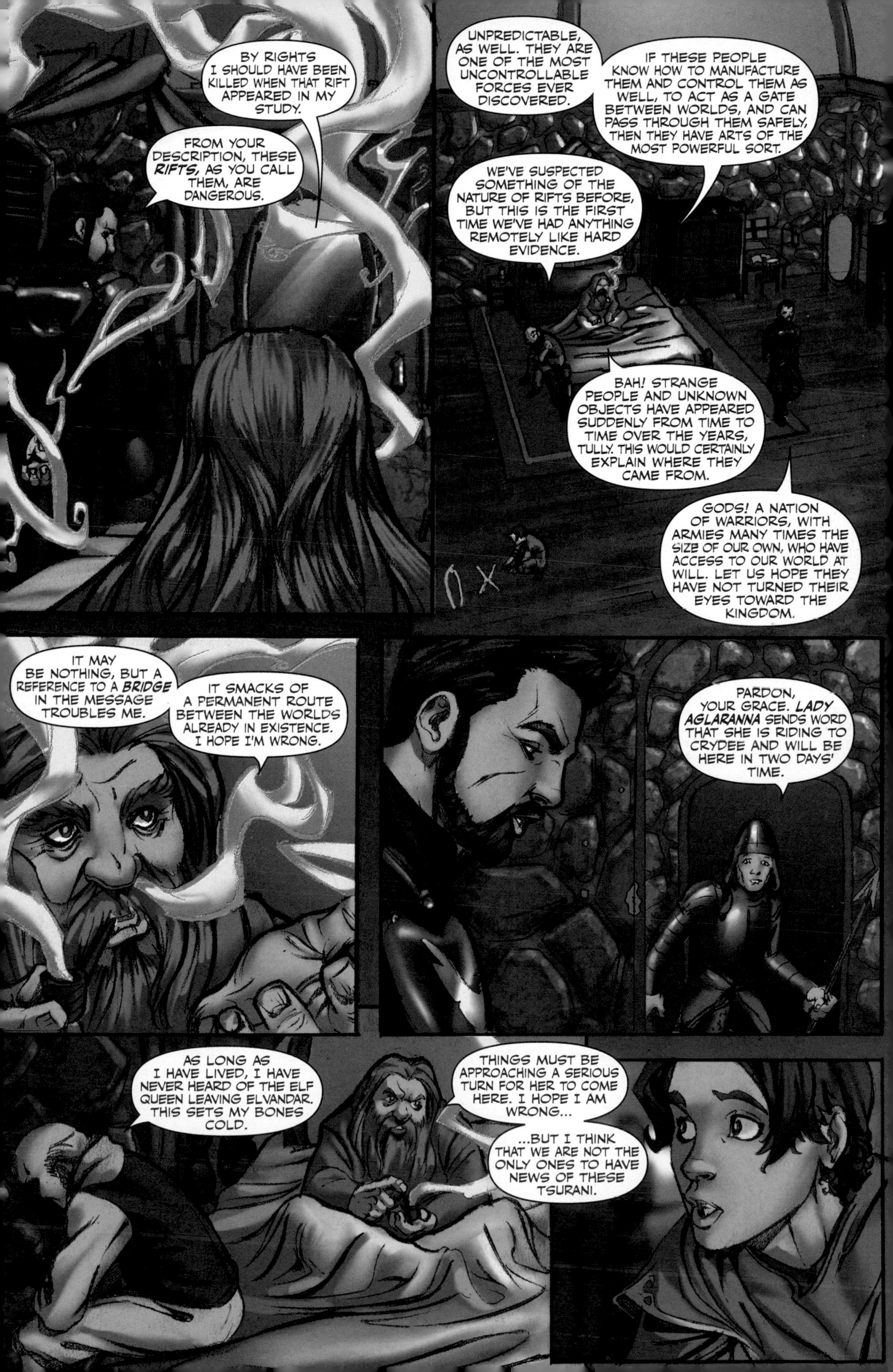
BY RIGHTS I SHOULD HAVE BEEN KILLED WHEN THAT RIFT APPEARED IN MY STUDY.
FROM YOUR DESCRIPTION, THESE RIFTS, AS YOU CALL THEM, ARE DANGEROUS.
UNPREDICTABLE, AS WELL. THEY ARE ONE OF THE MOST UNCONTROLLABLE FORCES EVER DISCOVERED.
IF THESE PEOPLE KNOW HOW TO MANUFACTURE THEM AND CONTROL THEM AS WELL, TO ACT AS A GATE BETWEEN WORLDS, AND CAN PASS THROUGH THEM SAFELY, THEN THEY HAVE ARTS OF THE MOST POWERFUL SORT.
WE'VE SUSPECTED SOMETHING OF THE NATURE OF RIFTS BEFORE, BUT THIS IS THE FIRST TIME WE'VE HAD ANYTHING REMOTELY LIKE HARD EVIDENCE.
BAH! STRANGE PEOPLE AND UNKNOWN OBJECTS HAVE APPEARED SUDDENLY FROM TIME TO TIME OVER THE YEARS, TULLY. THIS WOULD CERTAINLY EXPLAIN WHERE THEY CAME FROM.
GODS! A NATION OF WARRIORS, WITH ARMIES MANY TIMES THE SIZE OF OUR OWN, WHO HAVE ACCESS TO OUR WORLD AT WILL. LET US HOPE THEY HAVE NOT TURNED THEIR EYES TOWARD THE KINGDOM.
IT MAY BE NOTHING, BUT A REFERENCE TO A BRIDGE IN THE MESSAGE TROUBLES ME.
IT SMACKS OF A PERMANENT ROUTE BETWEEN THE WORLDS ALREADY IN EXISTENCE. I HOPE I'M WRONG.
PARDON, YOUR GRACE. LADY AGLARANNA SENDS WORD THAT SHE IS RIDING TO CRYDEE AND WILL BE HERE IN TWO DAYS' TIME.
AS LONG AS I HAVE LIVED, I HAVE NEVER HEARD OF THE ELF QUEEN LEAVING ELVANDAR. THIS SETS MY BONES COLD.
THINGS MUST BE APPROACHING A SERIOUS TURN FOR HER TO COME HERE. I HOPE I AM WRONG...
...BUT I THINK THAT WE ARE NOT THE ONLY ONES TO HAVE NEWS OF THESE TSURANI.

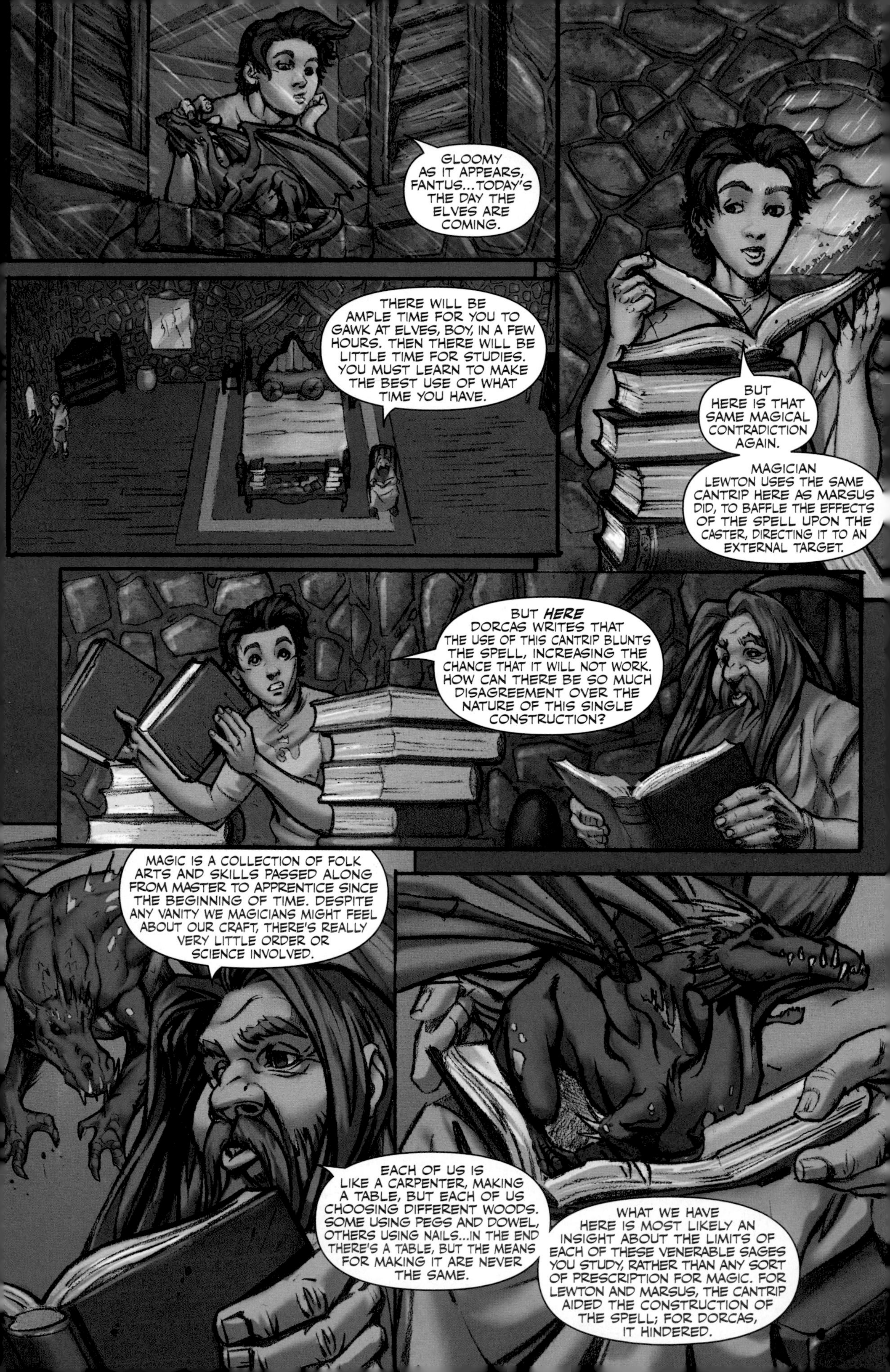
GLOOMY AS IT APPEARS, FANTUS...TODAY'S THE DAY THE ELVES ARE COMING.
THERE WILL BE AMPLE TIME FOR YOU TO GAWK AT ELVES, BOY, IN A FEW HOURS. THEN THERE WILL BE LITTLE TIME FOR STUDIES. YOU MUST LEARN TO MAKE THE BEST USE OF WHAT TIME YOU HAVE.
BUT HERE IS THAT SAME MAGICAL CONTRADICTION AGAIN.
MAGICIAN LEWTON USES THE SAME CANTRIP HERE AS MARSUS DID, TO BAFFLE THE EFFECTS OF THE SPELL UPON THE CASTER, DIRECTING IT TO AN EXTERNAL TARGET.
BUT ***HERE*** DORCAS WRITES THAT THE USE OF THIS CANTRIP BLUNTS THE SPELL, INCREASING THE CHANCE THAT IT WILL NOT WORK. HOW CAN THERE BE SO MUCH DISAGREEMENT OVER THE NATURE OF THIS SINGLE CONSTRUCTION?
MAGIC IS A COLLECTION OF FOLK ARTS AND SKILLS PASSED ALONG FROM MASTER TO APPRENTICE SINCE THE BEGINNING OF TIME. DESPITE ANY VANITY WE MAGICIANS MIGHT FEEL ABOUT OUR CRAFT, THERE'S REALLY VERY LITTLE ORDER OR SCIENCE INVOLVED.
EACH OF US IS LIKE A CARPENTER, MAKING A TABLE, BUT EACH OF US CHOOSING DIFFERENT WOODS. SOME USING PEGS AND DOWEL, OTHERS USING NAILS...IN THE END THERE'S A TABLE, BUT THE MEANS FOR MAKING IT ARE NEVER THE SAME.
WHAT WE HAVE HERE IS MOST LIKELY AN INSIGHT ABOUT THE LIMITS OF EACH OF THESE VENERABLE SAGES YOU STUDY, RATHER THAN ANY SORT OF PRESCRIPTION FOR MAGIC. FOR LEWTON AND MARSUS, THE CANTRIP AIDED THE CONSTRUCTION OF THE SPELL; FOR DORCAS, IT HINDERED.

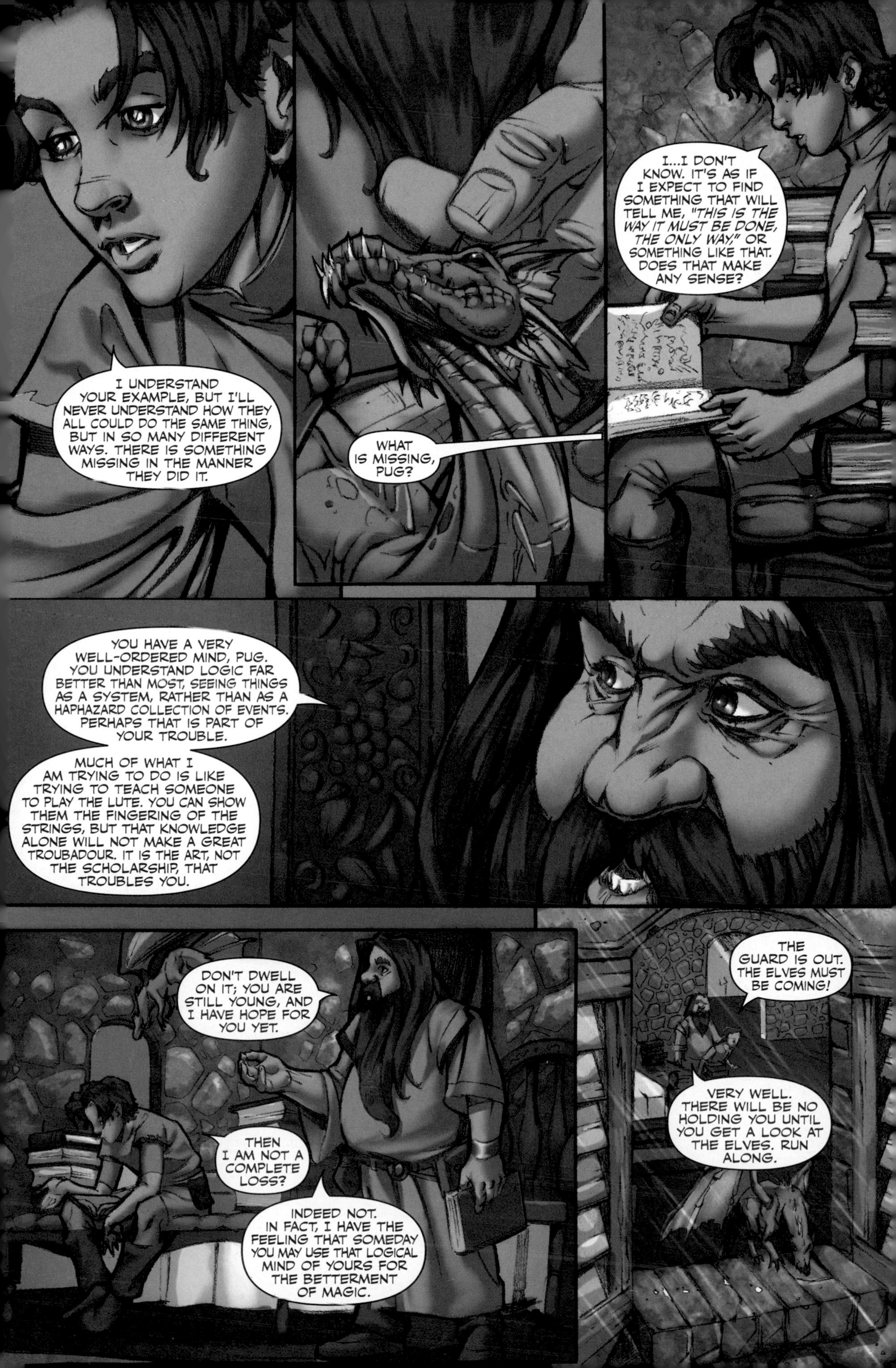
I UNDERSTAND YOUR EXAMPLE, BUT I'LL NEVER UNDERSTAND HOW THEY ALL COULD DO THE SAME THING, BUT IN SO MANY DIFFERENT WAYS. THERE IS SOMETHING MISSING IN THE MANNER THEY DID IT.
WHAT IS MISSING, PUG?
I...I DON'T KNOW. IT'S AS IF I EXPECT TO FIND SOMETHING THAT WILL TELL ME, *"THIS IS THE WAY IT MUST BE DONE, THE ONLY WAY,"* OR SOMETHING LIKE THAT. DOES THAT MAKE ANY SENSE?
YOU HAVE A VERY WELL-ORDERED MIND, PUG. YOU UNDERSTAND LOGIC FAR BETTER THAN MOST, SEEING THINGS AS A SYSTEM, RATHER THAN AS A HAPHAZARD COLLECTION OF EVENTS. PERHAPS THAT IS PART OF YOUR TROUBLE.
MUCH OF WHAT I AM TRYING TO DO IS LIKE TRYING TO TEACH SOMEONE TO PLAY THE LUTE. YOU CAN SHOW THEM THE FINGERING OF THE STRINGS, BUT THAT KNOWLEDGE ALONE WILL NOT MAKE A GREAT TROUBADOUR. IT IS THE ART, NOT THE SCHOLARSHIP, THAT TROUBLES YOU.
DON'T DWELL ON IT; YOU ARE STILL YOUNG, AND I HAVE HOPE FOR YOU YET.
THEN I AM NOT A COMPLETE LOSS?
INDEED NOT. IN FACT, I HAVE THE FEELING THAT SOMEDAY YOU MAY USE THAT LOGICAL MIND OF YOURS FOR THE BETTERMENT OF MAGIC.
THE GUARD IS OUT. THE ELVES MUST BE COMING!
VERY WELL. THERE WILL BE NO HOLDING YOU UNTIL YOU GET A LOOK AT THE ELVES. RUN ALONG.

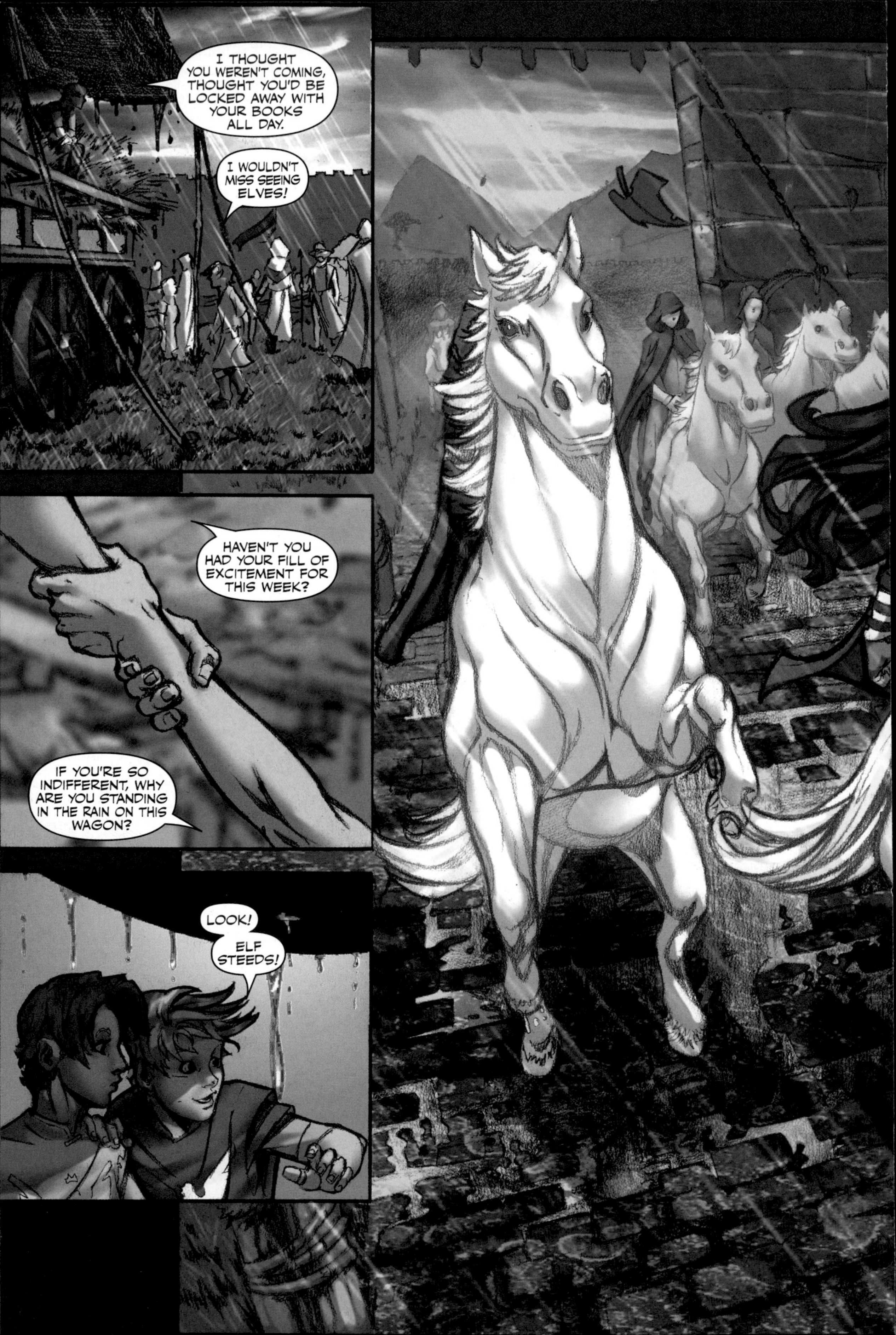
I THOUGHT YOU WEREN'T COMING, THOUGHT YOU'D BE LOCKED AWAY WITH YOUR BOOKS ALL DAY.
I WOULDN'T MISS SEEING ELVES!
HAVEN'T YOU HAD YOUR FILL OF EXCITEMENT FOR THIS WEEK?
IF YOU'RE SO INDIFFERENT, WHY ARE YOU STANDING IN THE RAIN ON THIS WAGON?
LOOK!
ELF STEEDS!

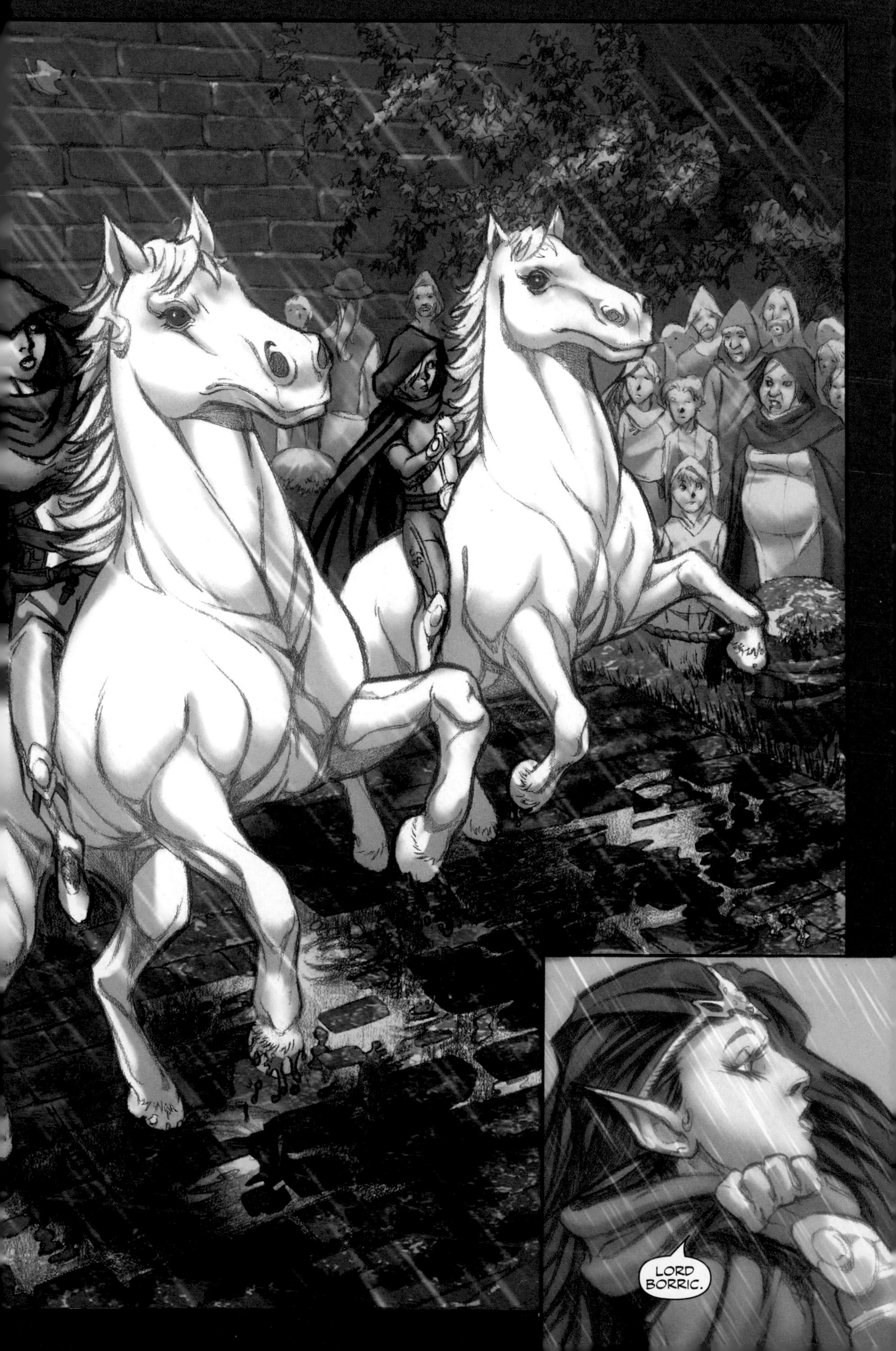
LORD BORRIC.

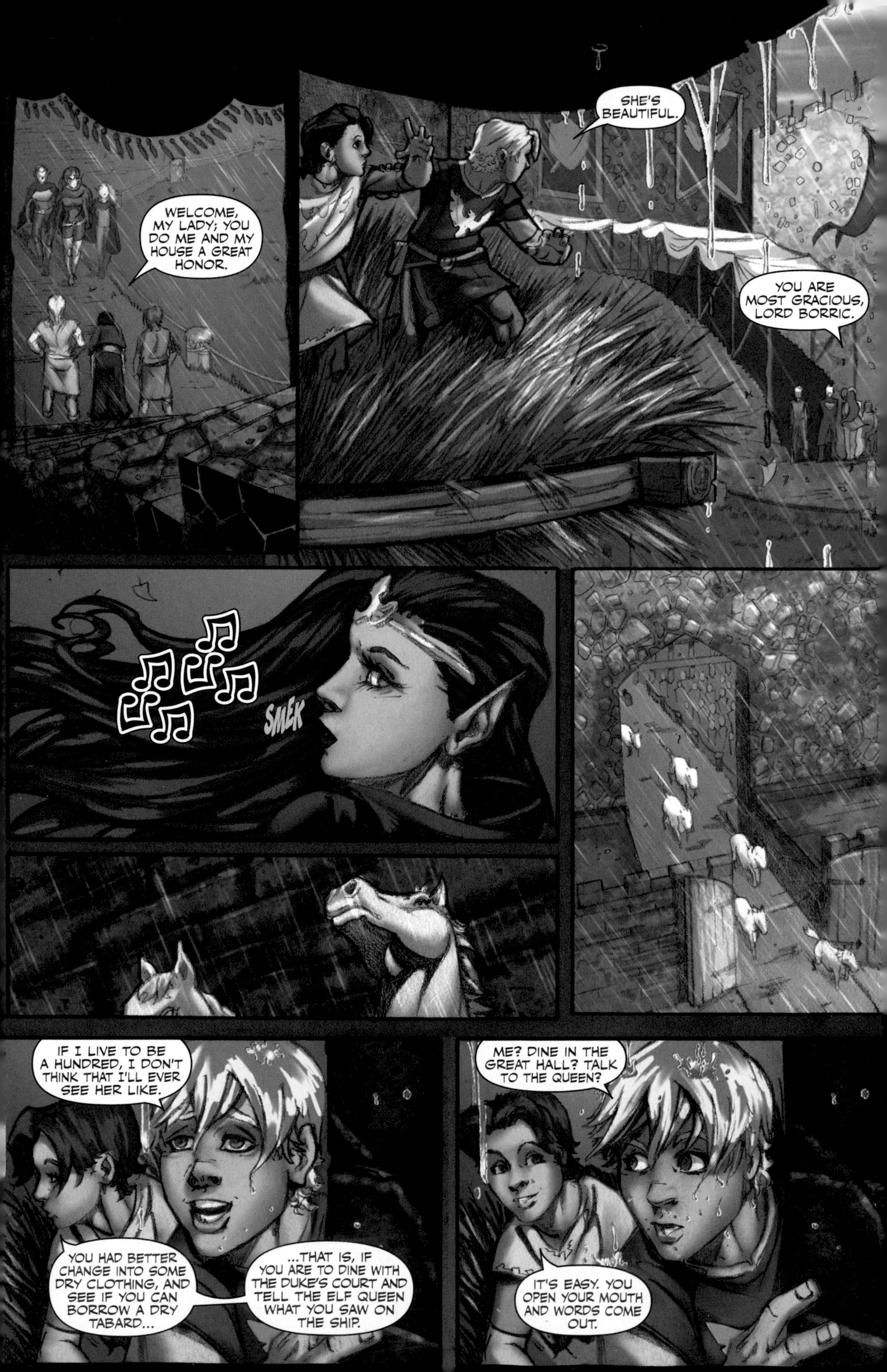
WELCOME, MY LADY; YOU DO ME AND MY HOUSE A GREAT HONOR.
SHE'S BEAUTIFUL.
YOU ARE MOST GRACIOUS, LORD BORRIC.
SMEK
IF I LIVE TO BE A HUNDRED, I DON'T THINK THAT I'LL EVER SEE HER LIKE.
YOU HAD BETTER CHANGE INTO SOME DRY CLOTHING, AND SEE IF YOU CAN BORROW A DRY TABARD...
...THAT IS, IF YOU ARE TO DINE WITH THE DUKE'S COURT AND TELL THE ELF QUEEN WHAT YOU SAW ON THE SHIP.
ME? DINE IN THE GREAT HALL? TALK TO THE QUEEN?
IT'S EASY. YOU OPEN YOUR MOUTH AND WORDS COME OUT.

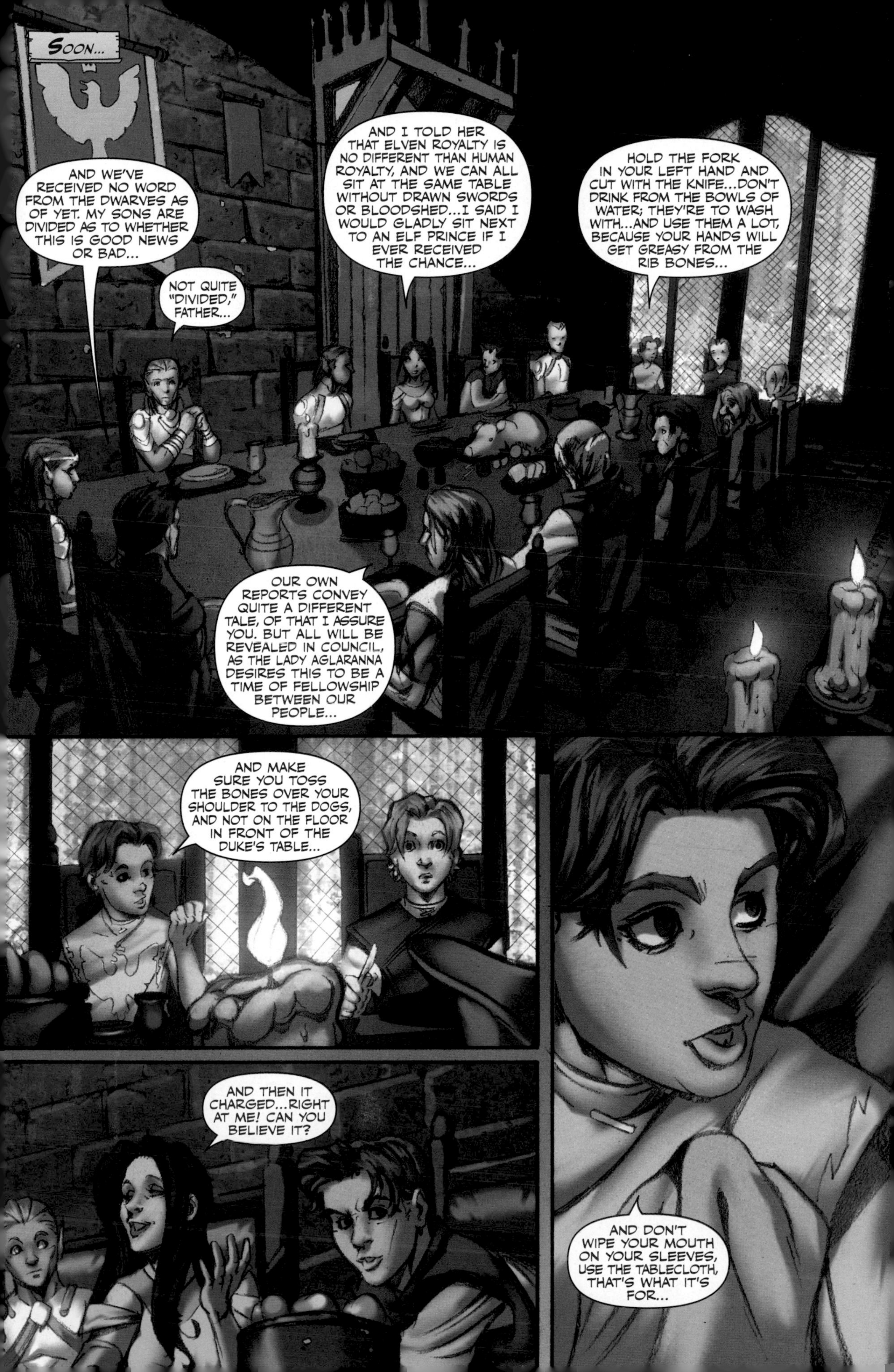
SOON...
AND WE'VE RECEIVED NO WORD FROM THE DWARVES AS OF YET. MY SONS ARE DIVIDED AS TO WHETHER THIS IS GOOD NEWS OR BAD...
NOT QUITE "DIVIDED," FATHER...
AND I TOLD HER THAT ELVEN ROYALTY IS NO DIFFERENT THAN HUMAN ROYALTY, AND WE CAN ALL SIT AT THE SAME TABLE WITHOUT DRAWN SWORDS OR BLOODSHED...I SAID I WOULD GLADLY SIT NEXT TO AN ELF PRINCE IF I EVER RECEIVED THE CHANCE...
HOLD THE FORK IN YOUR LEFT HAND AND CUT WITH THE KNIFE...DON'T DRINK FROM THE BOWLS OF WATER; THEY'RE TO WASH WITH...AND USE THEM A LOT, BECAUSE YOUR HANDS WILL GET GREASY FROM THE RIB BONES...
OUR OWN REPORTS CONVEY QUITE A DIFFERENT TALE, OF THAT I ASSURE YOU. BUT ALL WILL BE REVEALED IN COUNCIL, AS THE LADY AGLARANNA DESIRES THIS TO BE A TIME OF FELLOWSHIP BETWEEN OUR PEOPLE...
AND MAKE SURE YOU TOSS THE BONES OVER YOUR SHOULDER TO THE DOGS, AND NOT ON THE FLOOR IN FRONT OF THE DUKE'S TABLE...
AND THEN IT CHARGED...RIGHT AT ME! CAN YOU BELIEVE IT?
AND DON'T WIPE YOUR MOUTH ON YOUR SLEEVES, USE THE TABLECLOTH, THAT'S WHAT IT'S FOR...

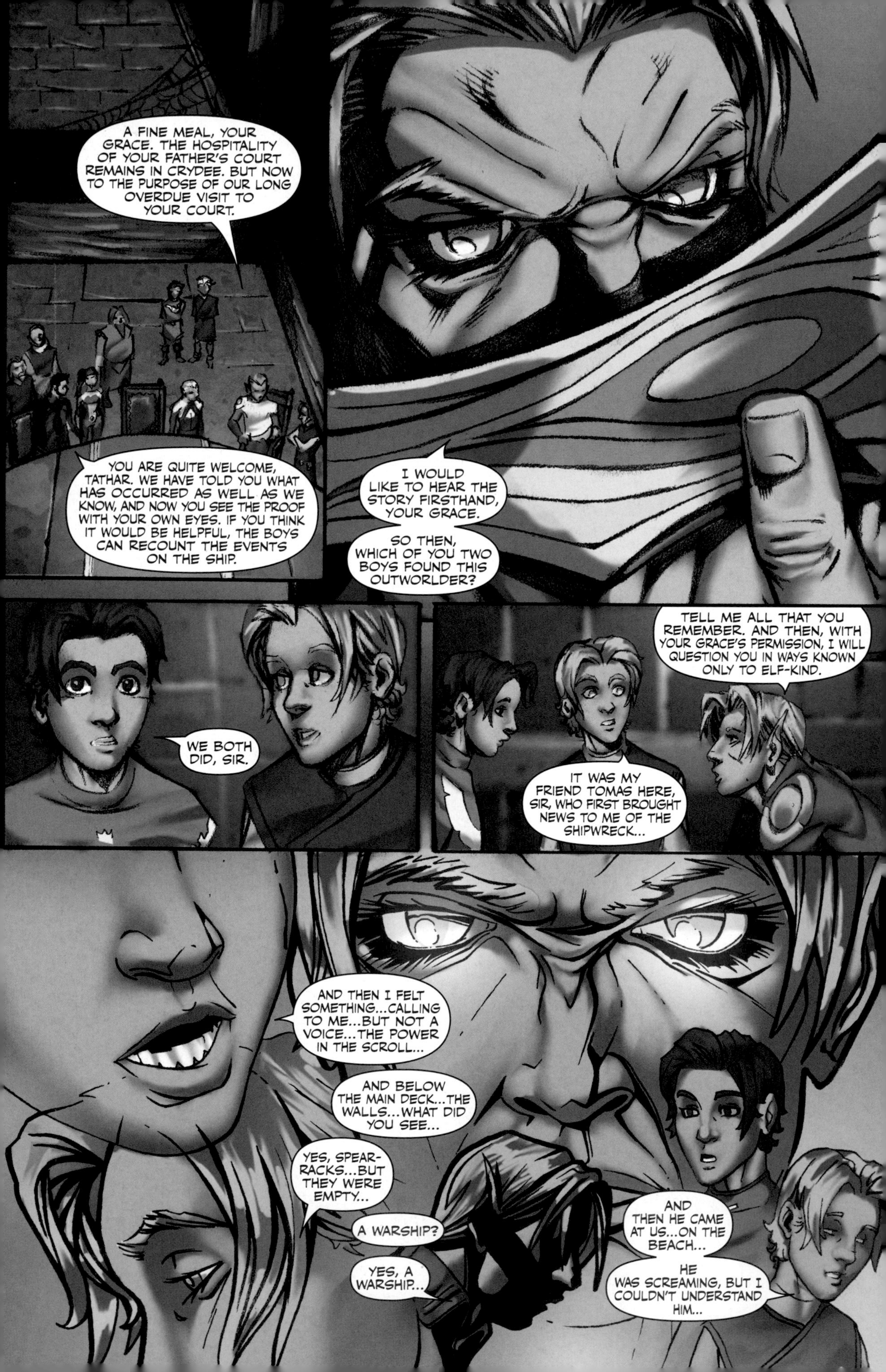
A FINE MEAL, YOUR GRACE. THE HOSPITALITY OF YOUR FATHER'S COURT REMAINS IN CRYDEE. BUT NOW TO THE PURPOSE OF OUR LONG OVERDUE VISIT TO YOUR COURT.
YOU ARE QUITE WELCOME, TATHAR. WE HAVE TOLD YOU WHAT HAS OCCURRED AS WELL AS WE KNOW, AND NOW YOU SEE THE PROOF WITH YOUR OWN EYES. IF YOU THINK IT WOULD BE HELPFUL, THE BOYS CAN RECOUNT THE EVENTS ON THE SHIP.
I WOULD LIKE TO HEAR THE STORY FIRSTHAND, YOUR GRACE.
SO THEN, WHICH OF YOU TWO BOYS FOUND THIS OUTWORLDER?
WE BOTH DID, SIR.
TELL ME ALL THAT YOU REMEMBER. AND THEN, WITH YOUR GRACE'S PERMISSION, I WILL QUESTION YOU IN WAYS KNOWN ONLY TO ELF-KIND.
IT WAS MY FRIEND TOMAS HERE, SIR, WHO FIRST BROUGHT NEWS TO ME OF THE SHIPWRECK...
AND THEN I FELT SOMETHING...CALLING TO ME...BUT NOT A VOICE...THE POWER IN THE SCROLL...
AND BELOW THE MAIN DECK...THE WALLS...WHAT DID YOU SEE...
YES, SPEAR-RACKS...BUT THEY WERE EMPTY...
A WARSHIP?
YES, A WARSHIP...
AND THEN HE CAME AT US...ON THE BEACH...
HE WAS SCREAMING, BUT I COULDN'T UNDERSTAND HIM...

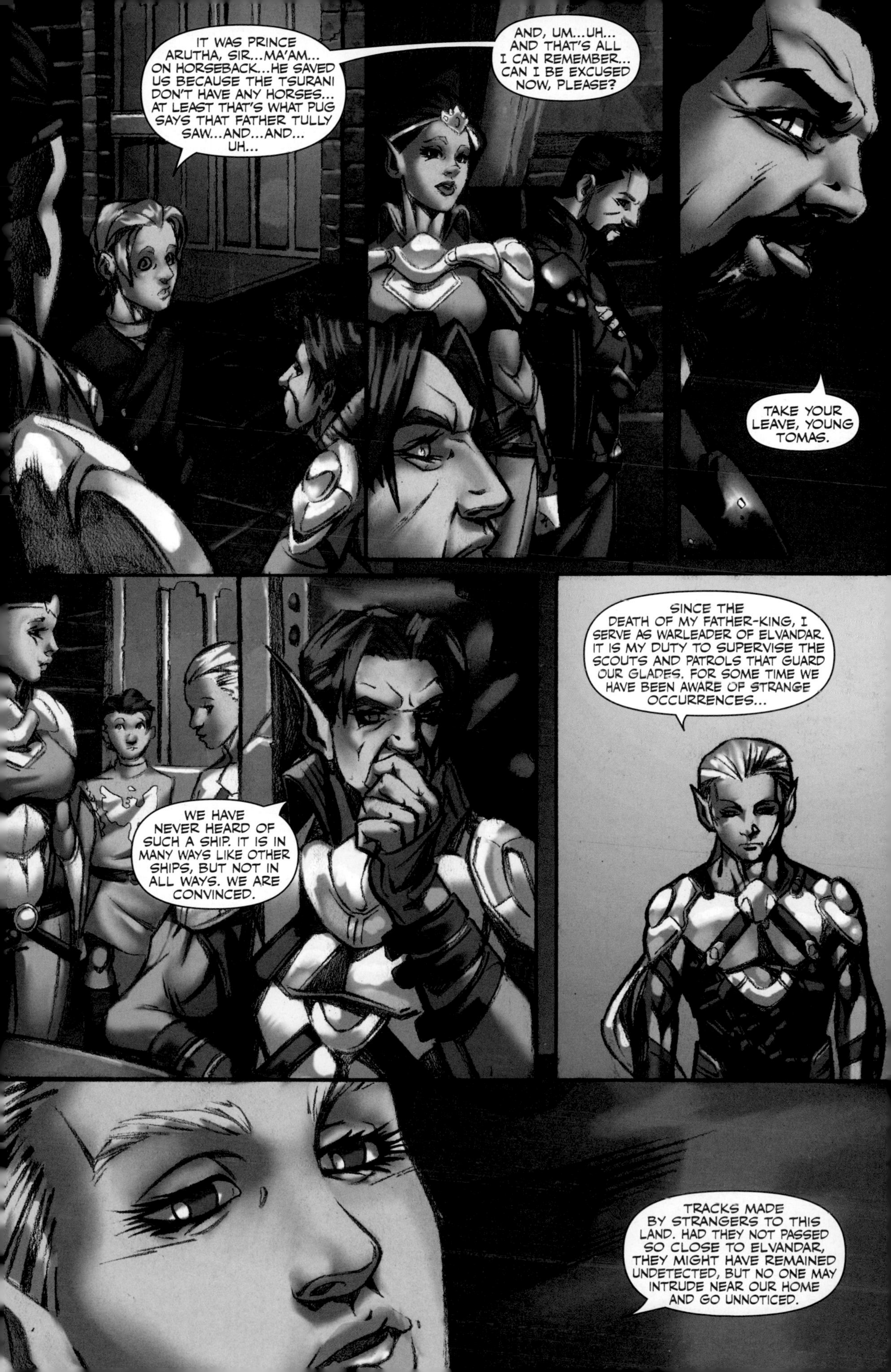
IT WAS PRINCE ARUTHA, SIR...MA'AM... ON HORSEBACK...HE SAVED US BECAUSE THE TSURANI DON'T HAVE ANY HORSES... AT LEAST THAT'S WHAT PUG SAYS THAT FATHER TULLY SAW...AND...AND... UH...
AND, UM...UH... AND THAT'S ALL I CAN REMEMBER... CAN I BE EXCUSED NOW, PLEASE?
TAKE YOUR LEAVE, YOUNG TOMAS.
WE HAVE NEVER HEARD OF SUCH A SHIP. IT IS IN MANY WAYS LIKE OTHER SHIPS, BUT NOT IN ALL WAYS. WE ARE CONVINCED.
SINCE THE DEATH OF MY FATHER-KING, I SERVE AS WARLEADER OF ELVANDAR. IT IS MY DUTY TO SUPERVISE THE SCOUTS AND PATROLS THAT GUARD OUR GLADES. FOR SOME TIME WE HAVE BEEN AWARE OF STRANGE OCCURRENCES...
TRACKS MADE BY STRANGERS TO THIS LAND. HAD THEY NOT PASSED SO CLOSE TO ELVANDAR, THEY MIGHT HAVE REMAINED UNDETECTED, BUT NO ONE MAY INTRUDE NEAR OUR HOME AND GO UNNOTICED.

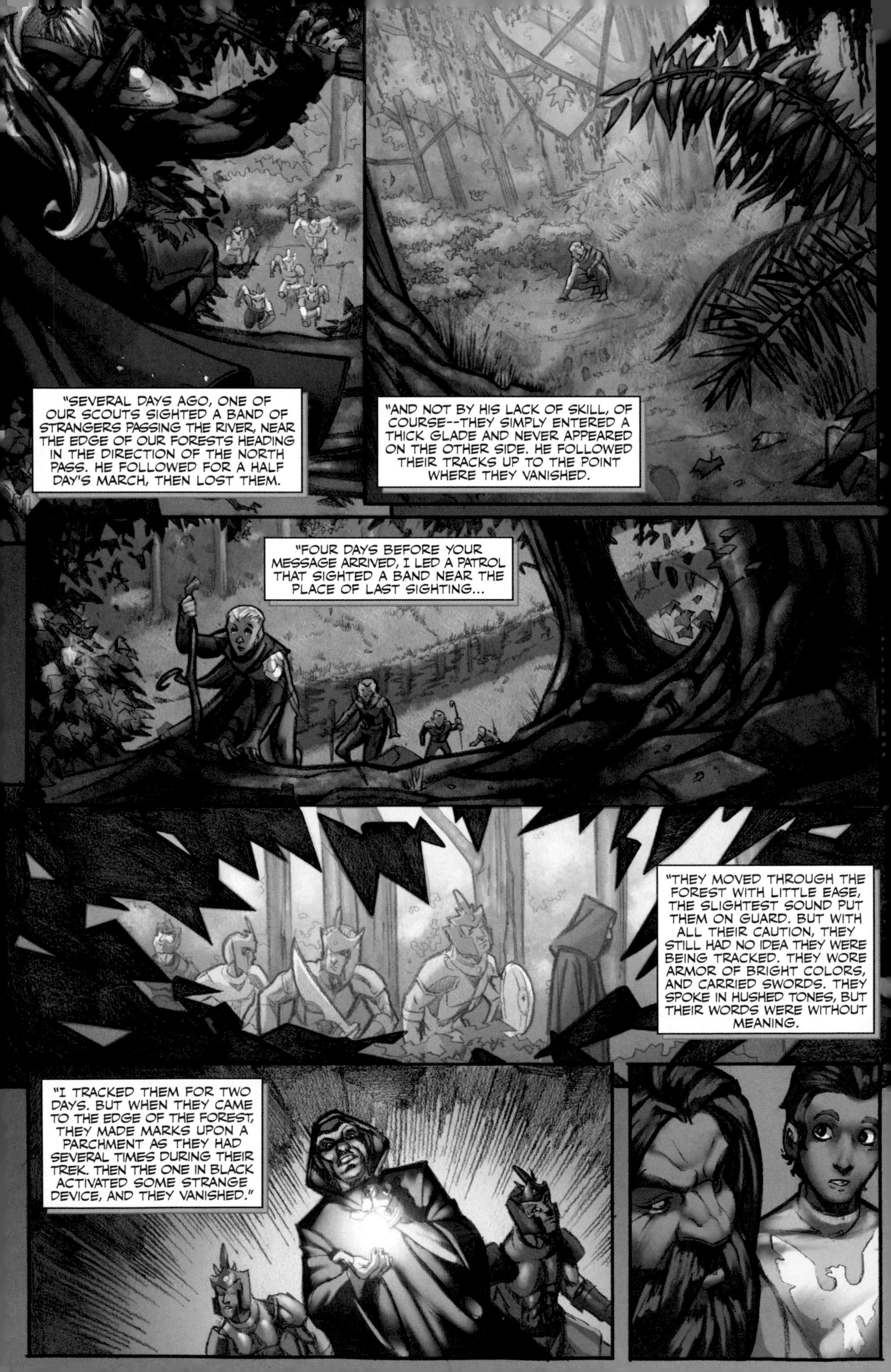
"SEVERAL DAYS AGO, ONE OF OUR SCOUTS SIGHTED A BAND OF STRANGERS PASSING THE RIVER, NEAR THE EDGE OF OUR FORESTS HEADING IN THE DIRECTION OF THE NORTH PASS. HE FOLLOWED FOR A HALF DAY'S MARCH, THEN LOST THEM.
"AND NOT BY HIS LACK OF SKILL, OF COURSE--THEY SIMPLY ENTERED A THICK GLADE AND NEVER APPEARED ON THE OTHER SIDE. HE FOLLOWED THEIR TRACKS UP TO THE POINT WHERE THEY VANISHED.
"FOUR DAYS BEFORE YOUR MESSAGE ARRIVED, I LED A PATROL THAT SIGHTED A BAND NEAR THE PLACE OF LAST SIGHTING...
"THEY MOVED THROUGH THE FOREST WITH LITTLE EASE, THE SLIGHTEST SOUND PUT THEM ON GUARD. BUT WITH ALL THEIR CAUTION, THEY STILL HAD NO IDEA THEY WERE BEING TRACKED. THEY WORE ARMOR OF BRIGHT COLORS, AND CARRIED SWORDS. THEY SPOKE IN HUSHED TONES, BUT THEIR WORDS WERE WITHOUT MEANING.
"I TRACKED THEM FOR TWO DAYS. BUT WHEN THEY CAME TO THE EDGE OF THE FOREST, THEY MADE MARKS UPON A PARCHMENT AS THEY HAD SEVERAL TIMES DURING THEIR TREK. THEN THE ONE IN BLACK ACTIVATED SOME STRANGE DEVICE, AND THEY VANISHED."

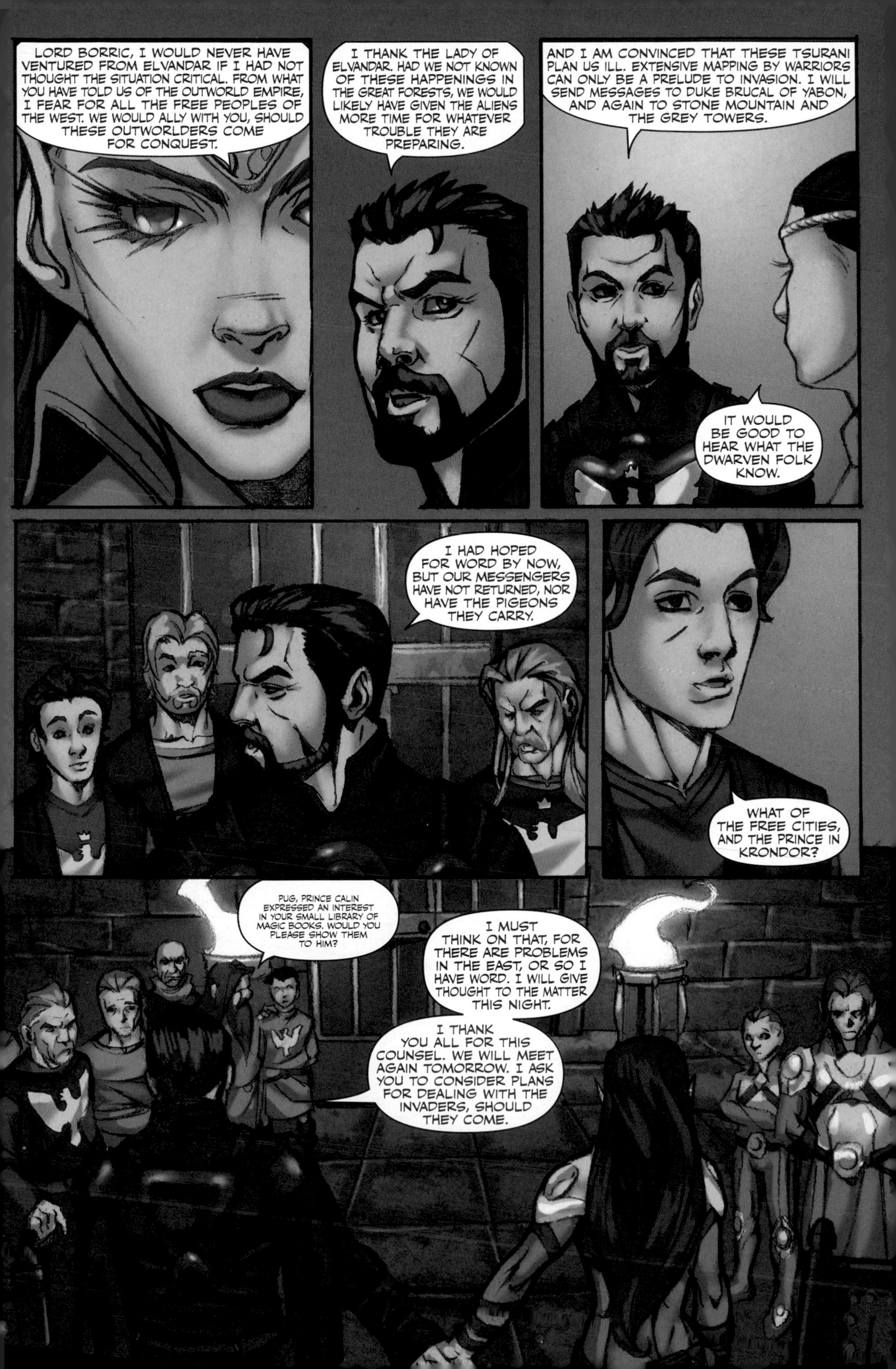
LORD BORRIC, I WOULD NEVER HAVE VENTURED FROM ELVANDAR IF I HAD NOT THOUGHT THE SITUATION CRITICAL. FROM WHAT YOU HAVE TOLD US OF THE OUTWORLD EMPIRE, I FEAR FOR ALL THE FREE PEOPLES OF THE WEST. WE WOULD ALLY WITH YOU, SHOULD THESE OUTWORLDERS COME FOR CONQUEST.
I THANK THE LADY OF ELVANDAR. HAD WE NOT KNOWN OF THESE HAPPENINGS IN THE GREAT FORESTS, WE WOULD LIKELY HAVE GIVEN THE ALIENS MORE TIME FOR WHATEVER TROUBLE THEY ARE PREPARING.
AND I AM CONVINCED THAT THESE TSURANI PLAN US ILL. EXTENSIVE MAPPING BY WARRIORS CAN ONLY BE A PRELUDE TO INVASION. I WILL SEND MESSAGES TO DUKE BRUCAL OF YABON, AND AGAIN TO STONE MOUNTAIN AND THE GREY TOWERS.
IT WOULD BE GOOD TO HEAR WHAT THE DWARVEN FOLK KNOW.
I HAD HOPED FOR WORD BY NOW, BUT OUR MESSENGERS HAVE NOT RETURNED, NOR HAVE THE PIGEONS THEY CARRY.
WHAT OF THE FREE CITIES, AND THE PRINCE IN KRONDOR?
PUG, PRINCE CALIN EXPRESSED AN INTEREST IN YOUR SMALL LIBRARY OF MAGIC BOOKS. WOULD YOU PLEASE SHOW THEM TO HIM?
I MUST THINK ON THAT, FOR THERE ARE PROBLEMS IN THE EAST, OR SO I HAVE WORD. I WILL GIVE THOUGHT TO THE MATTER THIS NIGHT.
I THANK YOU ALL FOR THIS COUNSEL. WE WILL MEET AGAIN TOMORROW. I ASK YOU TO CONSIDER PLANS FOR DEALING WITH THE INVADERS, SHOULD THEY COME.

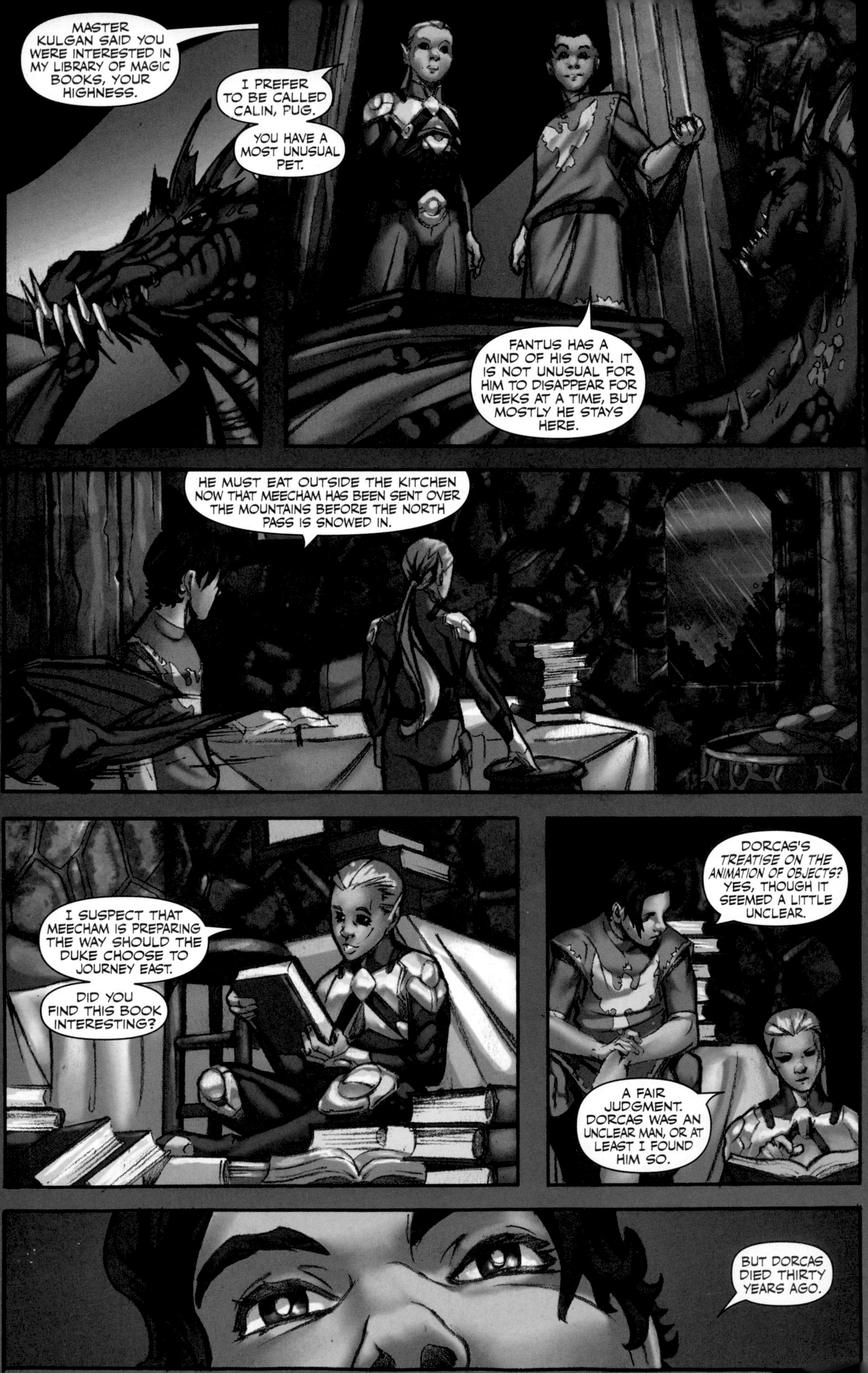
MASTER KULGAN SAID YOU WERE INTERESTED IN MY LIBRARY OF MAGIC BOOKS, YOUR HIGHNESS.
I PREFER TO BE CALLED CALIN, PUG.
YOU HAVE A MOST UNUSUAL PET.
FANTUS HAS A MIND OF HIS OWN. IT IS NOT UNUSUAL FOR HIM TO DISAPPEAR FOR WEEKS AT A TIME, BUT MOSTLY HE STAYS HERE.
HE MUST EAT OUTSIDE THE KITCHEN NOW THAT MEECHAM HAS BEEN SENT OVER THE MOUNTAINS BEFORE THE NORTH PASS IS SNOWED IN.
I SUSPECT THAT MEECHAM IS PREPARING THE WAY SHOULD THE DUKE CHOOSE TO JOURNEY EAST.
DID YOU FIND THIS BOOK INTERESTING?
DORCAS'S *TREATISE ON THE ANIMATION OF OBJECTS*? YES, THOUGH IT SEEMED A LITTLE UNCLEAR.
A FAIR JUDGMENT. DORCAS WAS AN UNCLEAR MAN, OR AT LEAST I FOUND HIM SO.
BUT DORCAS DIED THIRTY YEARS AGO.

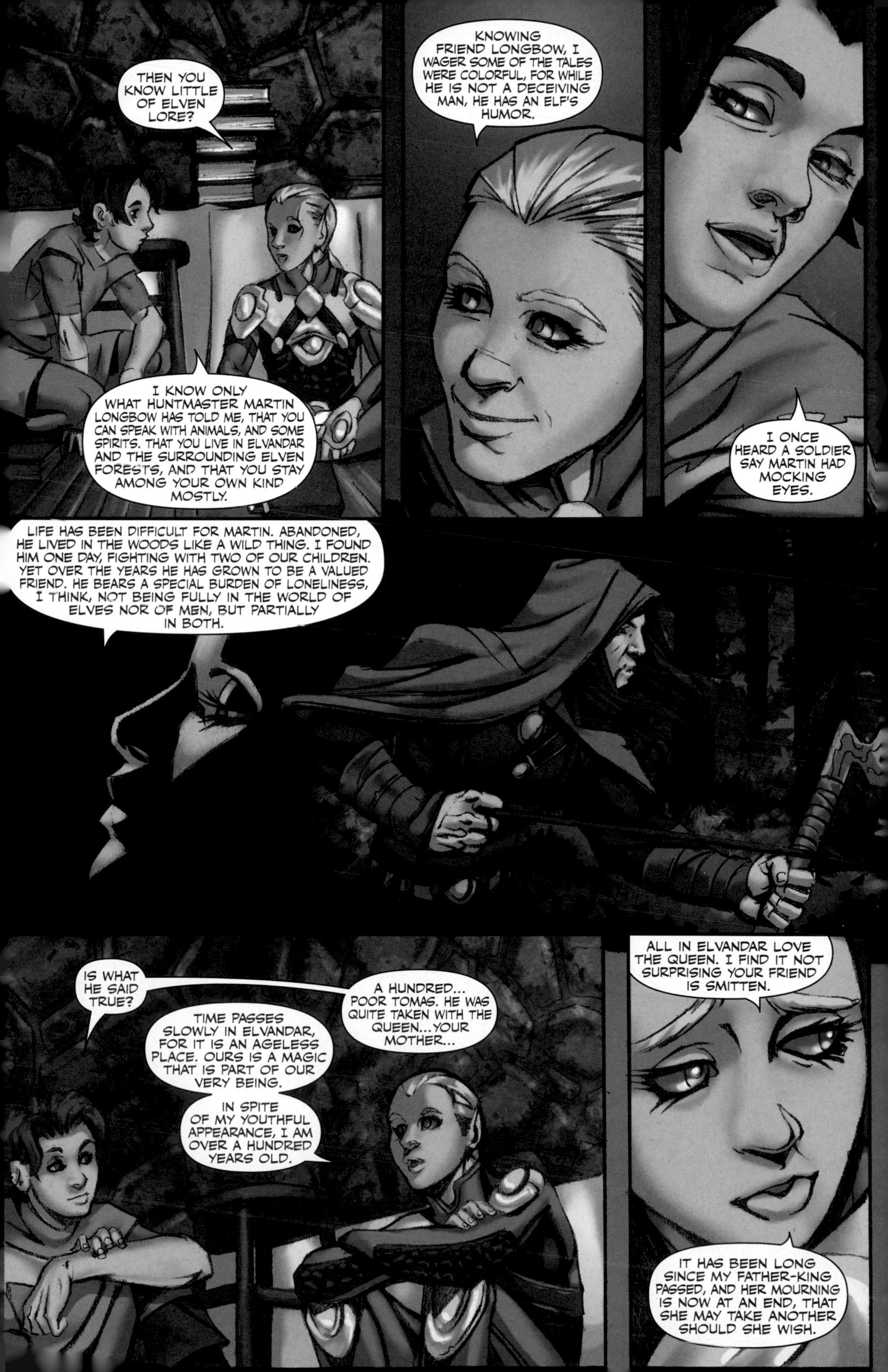
THEN YOU KNOW LITTLE OF ELVEN LORE?
I KNOW ONLY WHAT HUNTMASTER MARTIN LONGBOW HAS TOLD ME, THAT YOU CAN SPEAK WITH ANIMALS, AND SOME SPIRITS. THAT YOU LIVE IN ELVANDAR AND THE SURROUNDING ELVEN FORESTS, AND THAT YOU STAY AMONG YOUR OWN KIND MOSTLY.
KNOWING FRIEND LONGBOW, I WAGER SOME OF THE TALES WERE COLORFUL, FOR WHILE HE IS NOT A DECEIVING MAN, HE HAS AN ELF'S HUMOR.
I ONCE HEARD A SOLDIER SAY MARTIN HAD MOCKING EYES.
LIFE HAS BEEN DIFFICULT FOR MARTIN. ABANDONED, HE LIVED IN THE WOODS LIKE A WILD THING. I FOUND HIM ONE DAY, FIGHTING WITH TWO OF OUR CHILDREN. YET OVER THE YEARS HE HAS GROWN TO BE A VALUED FRIEND. HE BEARS A SPECIAL BURDEN OF LONELINESS, I THINK, NOT BEING FULLY IN THE WORLD OF ELVES NOR OF MEN, BUT PARTIALLY IN BOTH.
TIME PASSES SLOWLY IN ELVANDAR, FOR IT IS AN AGELESS PLACE. OURS IS A MAGIC THAT IS PART OF OUR VERY BEING.
IN SPITE OF MY YOUTHFUL APPEARANCE, I AM OVER A HUNDRED YEARS OLD.
IS WHAT HE SAID TRUE?
A HUNDRED... POOR TOMAS. HE WAS QUITE TAKEN WITH THE QUEEN...YOUR MOTHER...
ALL IN ELVANDAR LOVE THE QUEEN. I FIND IT NOT SURPRISING YOUR FRIEND IS SMITTEN.
IT HAS BEEN LONG SINCE MY FATHER-KING PASSED, AND HER MOURNING IS NOW AT AN END, THAT SHE MAY TAKE ANOTHER SHOULD SHE WISH.

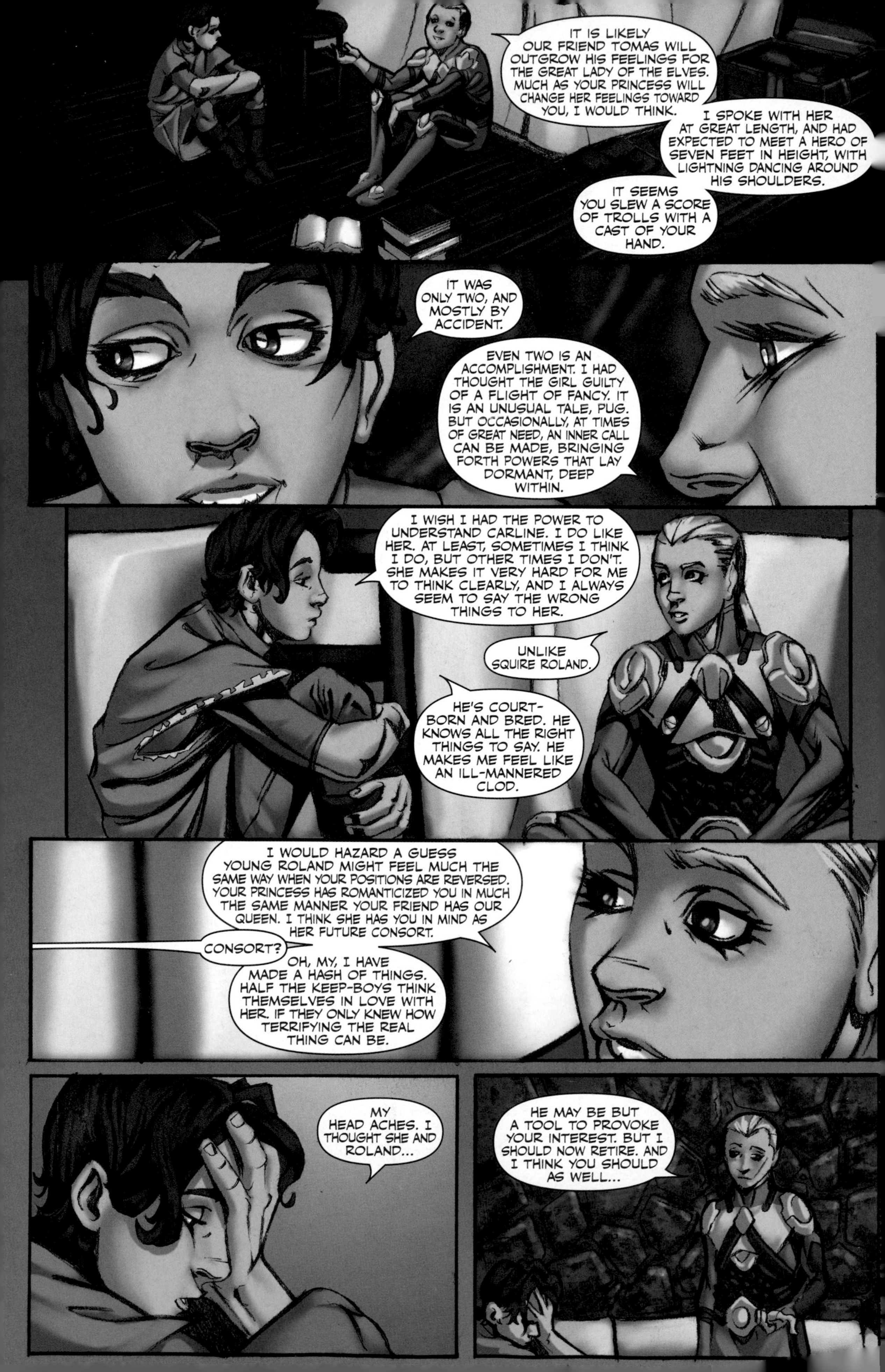
IT IS LIKELY OUR FRIEND TOMAS WILL OUTGROW HIS FEELINGS FOR THE GREAT LADY OF THE ELVES. MUCH AS YOUR PRINCESS WILL CHANGE HER FEELINGS TOWARD YOU, I WOULD THINK.
I SPOKE WITH HER AT GREAT LENGTH, AND HAD EXPECTED TO MEET A HERO OF SEVEN FEET IN HEIGHT, WITH LIGHTNING DANCING AROUND HIS SHOULDERS.
IT SEEMS YOU SLEW A SCORE OF TROLLS WITH A CAST OF YOUR HAND.
IT WAS ONLY TWO, AND MOSTLY BY ACCIDENT.
EVEN TWO IS AN ACCOMPLISHMENT. I HAD THOUGHT THE GIRL GUILTY OF A FLIGHT OF FANCY. IT IS AN UNUSUAL TALE, PUG. BUT OCCASIONALLY, AT TIMES OF GREAT NEED, AN INNER CALL CAN BE MADE, BRINGING FORTH POWERS THAT LAY DORMANT, DEEP WITHIN.
I WISH I HAD THE POWER TO UNDERSTAND CARLINE. I DO LIKE HER. AT LEAST, SOMETIMES I THINK I DO, BUT OTHER TIMES I DON'T. SHE MAKES IT VERY HARD FOR ME TO THINK CLEARLY, AND I ALWAYS SEEM TO SAY THE WRONG THINGS TO HER.
UNLIKE SQUIRE ROLAND.
HE'S COURT-BORN AND BRED. HE KNOWS ALL THE RIGHT THINGS TO SAY. HE MAKES ME FEEL LIKE AN ILL-MANNERED CLOD.
I WOULD HAZARD A GUESS YOUNG ROLAND MIGHT FEEL MUCH THE SAME WAY WHEN YOUR POSITIONS ARE REVERSED. YOUR PRINCESS HAS ROMANTICIZED YOU IN MUCH THE SAME MANNER YOUR FRIEND HAS OUR QUEEN. I THINK SHE HAS YOU IN MIND AS HER FUTURE CONSORT.
CONSORT?
OH, MY, I HAVE MADE A HASH OF THINGS. HALF THE KEEP-BOYS THINK THEMSELVES IN LOVE WITH HER. IF THEY ONLY KNEW HOW TERRIFYING THE REAL THING CAN BE.
MY HEAD ACHES. I THOUGHT SHE AND ROLAND...
HE MAY BE BUT A TOOL TO PROVOKE YOUR INTEREST. BUT I SHOULD NOW RETIRE. AND I THINK YOU SHOULD AS WELL...

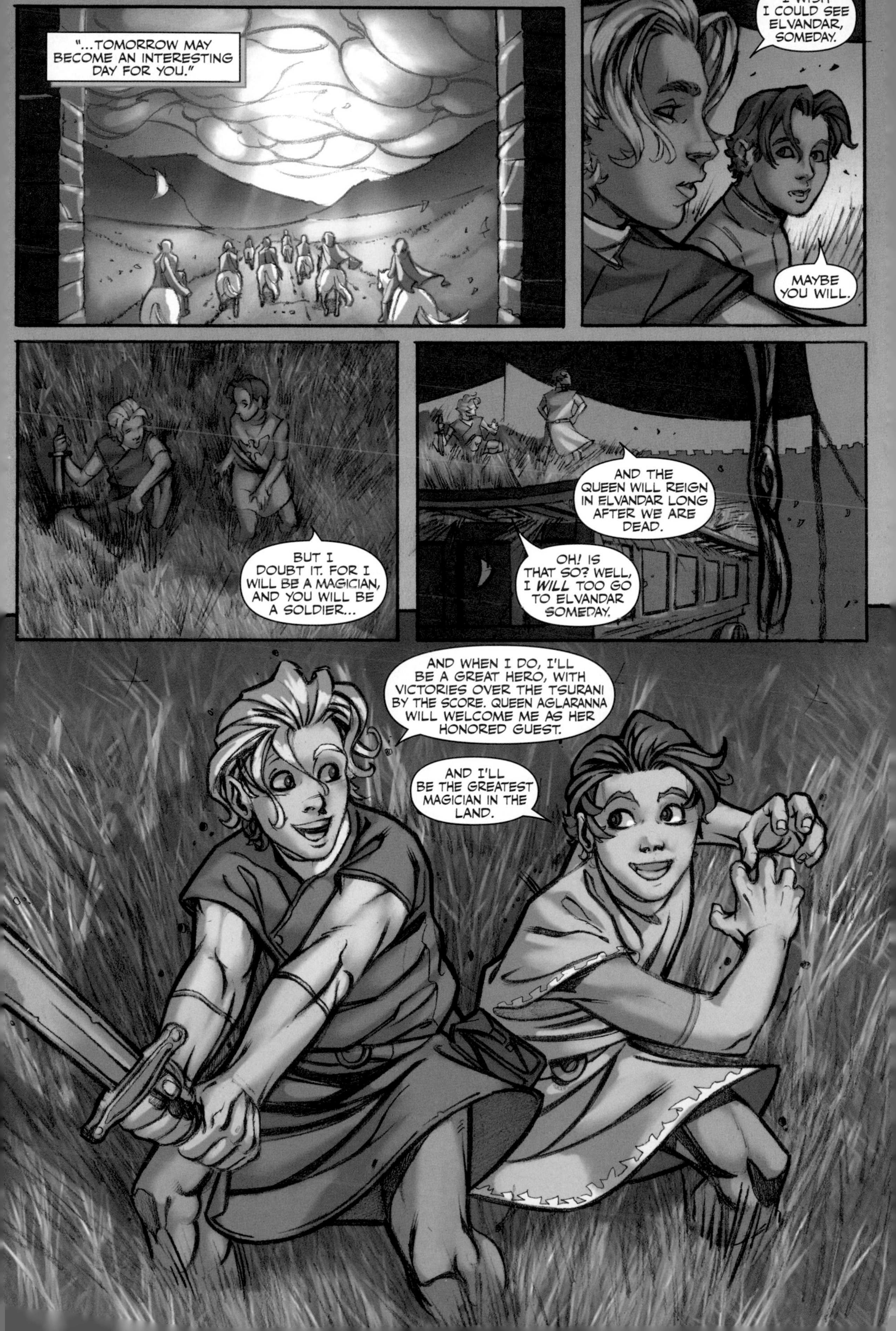
"...TOMORROW MAY BECOME AN INTERESTING DAY FOR YOU."
I WISH I COULD SEE ELVANDAR, SOMEDAY.
MAYBE YOU WILL.
BUT I DOUBT IT. FOR I WILL BE A MAGICIAN, AND YOU WILL BE A SOLDIER...
AND THE QUEEN WILL REIGN IN ELVANDAR LONG AFTER WE ARE DEAD.
OH! IS THAT SO? WELL, I *WILL* TOO GO TO ELVANDAR SOMEDAY.
AND WHEN I DO, I'LL BE A GREAT HERO, WITH VICTORIES OVER THE TSURANI BY THE SCORE. QUEEN AGLARANNA WILL WELCOME ME AS HER HONORED GUEST.
AND I'LL BE THE GREATEST MAGICIAN IN THE LAND.

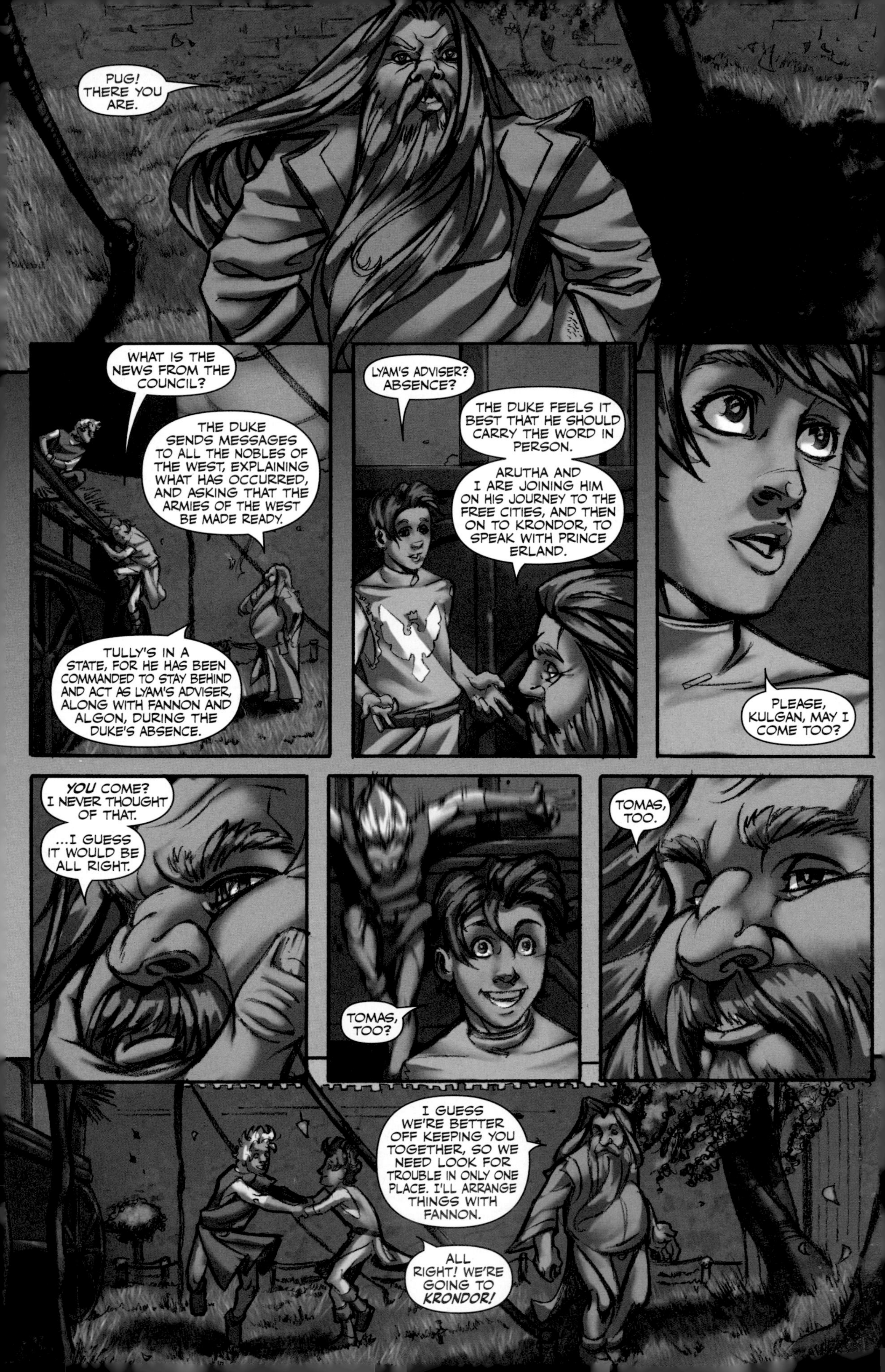
PUG! THERE YOU ARE.
WHAT IS THE NEWS FROM THE COUNCIL?
THE DUKE SENDS MESSAGES TO ALL THE NOBLES OF THE WEST, EXPLAINING WHAT HAS OCCURRED, AND ASKING THAT THE ARMIES OF THE WEST BE MADE READY.
TULLY'S IN A STATE, FOR HE HAS BEEN COMMANDED TO STAY BEHIND AND ACT AS LYAM'S ADVISER, ALONG WITH FANNON AND ALGON, DURING THE DUKE'S ABSENCE.
LYAM'S ADVISER? ABSENCE?
THE DUKE FEELS IT BEST THAT HE SHOULD CARRY THE WORD IN PERSON.
ARUTHA AND I ARE JOINING HIM ON HIS JOURNEY TO THE FREE CITIES, AND THEN ON TO KRONDOR, TO SPEAK WITH PRINCE ERLAND.
PLEASE, KULGAN, MAY I COME TOO?
YOU COME? I NEVER THOUGHT OF THAT.
...I GUESS IT WOULD BE ALL RIGHT.
TOMAS, TOO?
TOMAS, TOO.
I GUESS WE'RE BETTER OFF KEEPING YOU TOGETHER, SO WE NEED LOOK FOR TROUBLE IN ONLY ONE PLACE. I'LL ARRANGE THINGS WITH FANNON.
ALL RIGHT! WE'RE GOING TO *KRONDOR!*

CHAPTER SIX

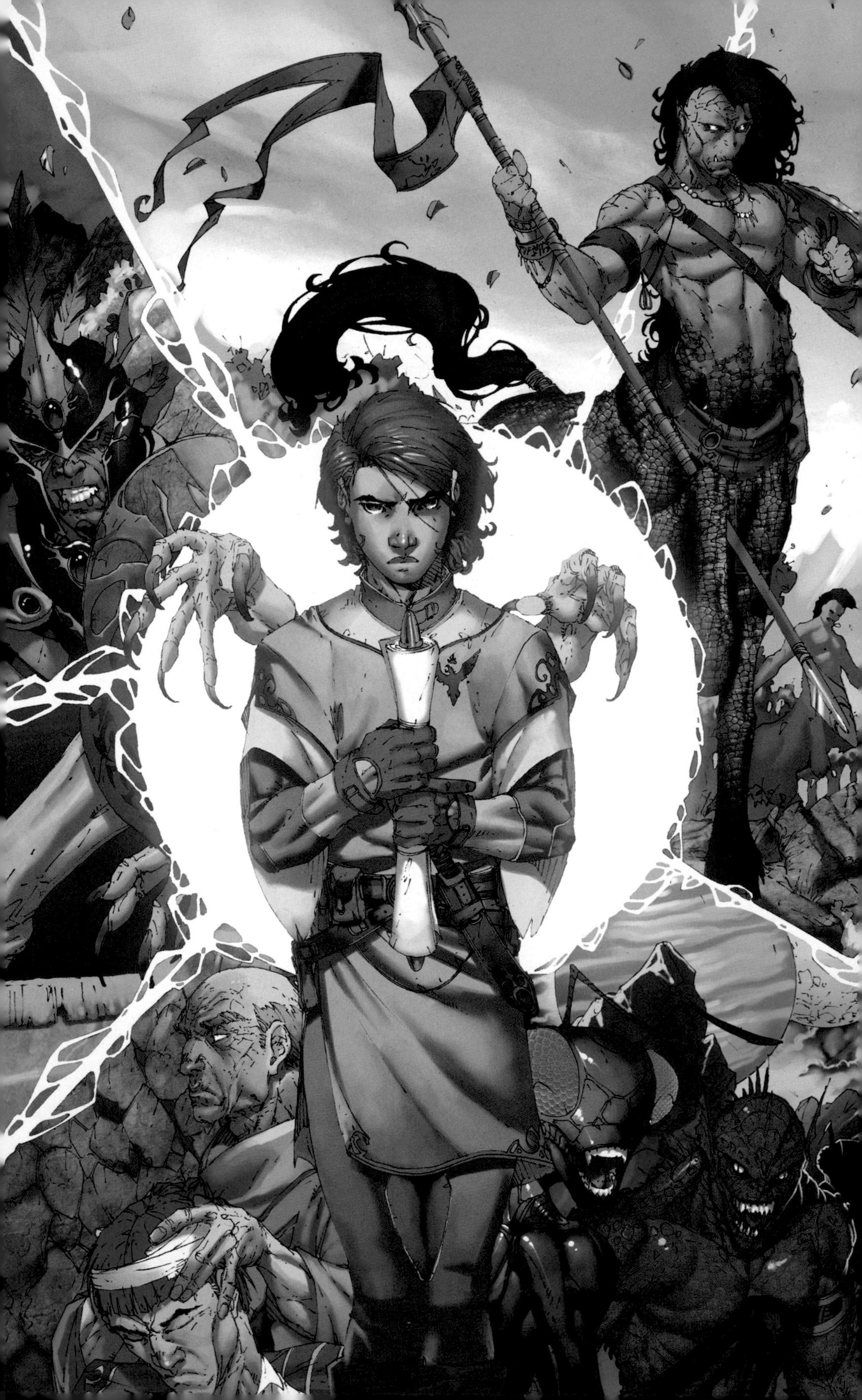

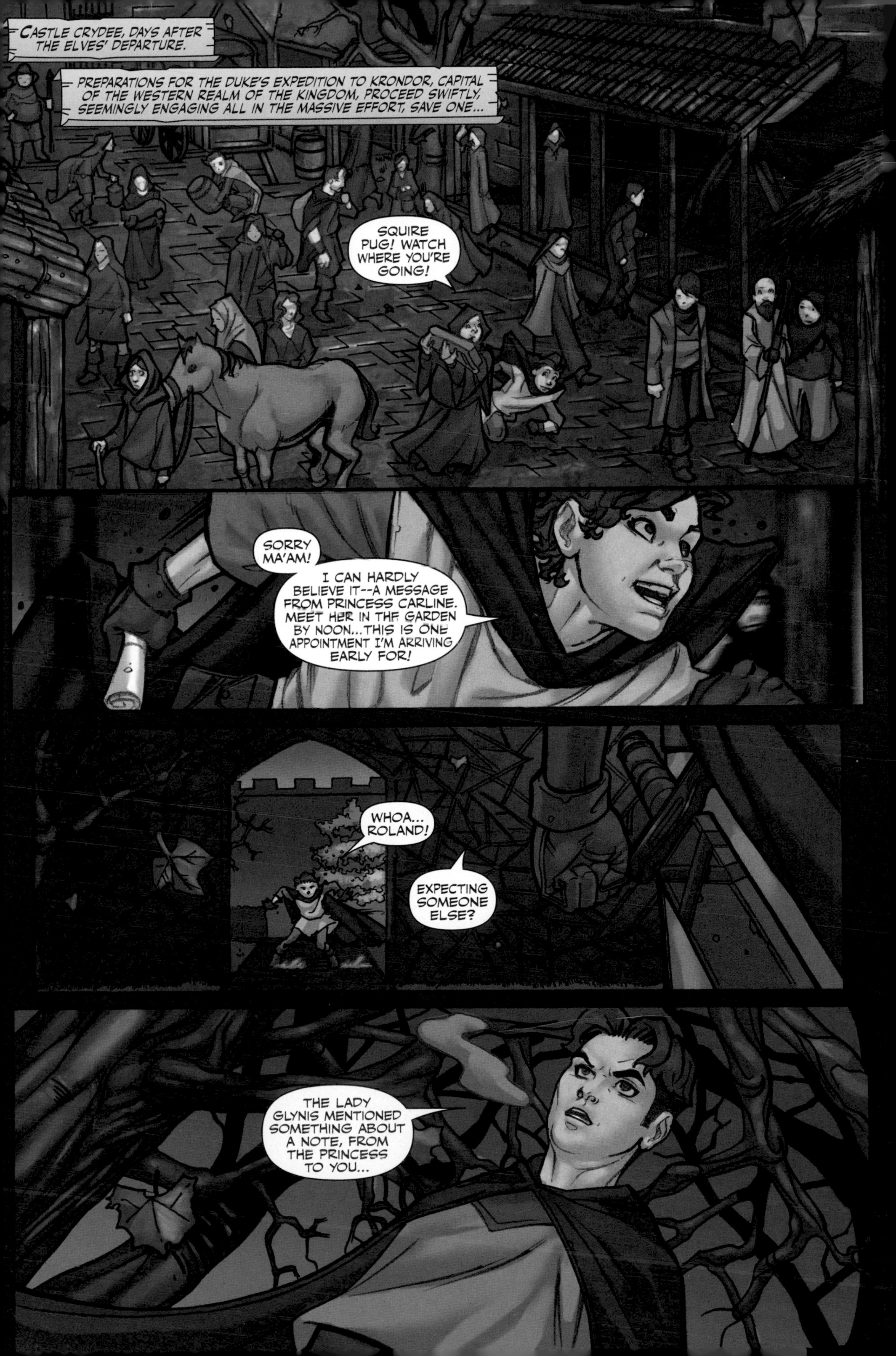
CASTLE CRYDEE, DAYS AFTER THE ELVES' DEPARTURE.
PREPARATIONS FOR THE DUKE'S EXPEDITION TO KRONDOR, CAPITAL OF THE WESTERN REALM OF THE KINGDOM, PROCEED SWIFTLY, SEEMINGLY ENGAGING ALL IN THE MASSIVE EFFORT, SAVE ONE...
SQUIRE PUG! WATCH WHERE YOU'RE GOING!
SORRY MA'AM!
I CAN HARDLY BELIEVE IT--A MESSAGE FROM PRINCESS CARLINE. MEET HER IN THE GARDEN BY NOON...THIS IS ONE APPOINTMENT I'M ARRIVING EARLY FOR!
WHOA... ROLAND!
EXPECTING SOMEONE ELSE?
THE LADY GLYNIS MENTIONED SOMETHING ABOUT A NOTE, FROM THE PRINCESS TO YOU...

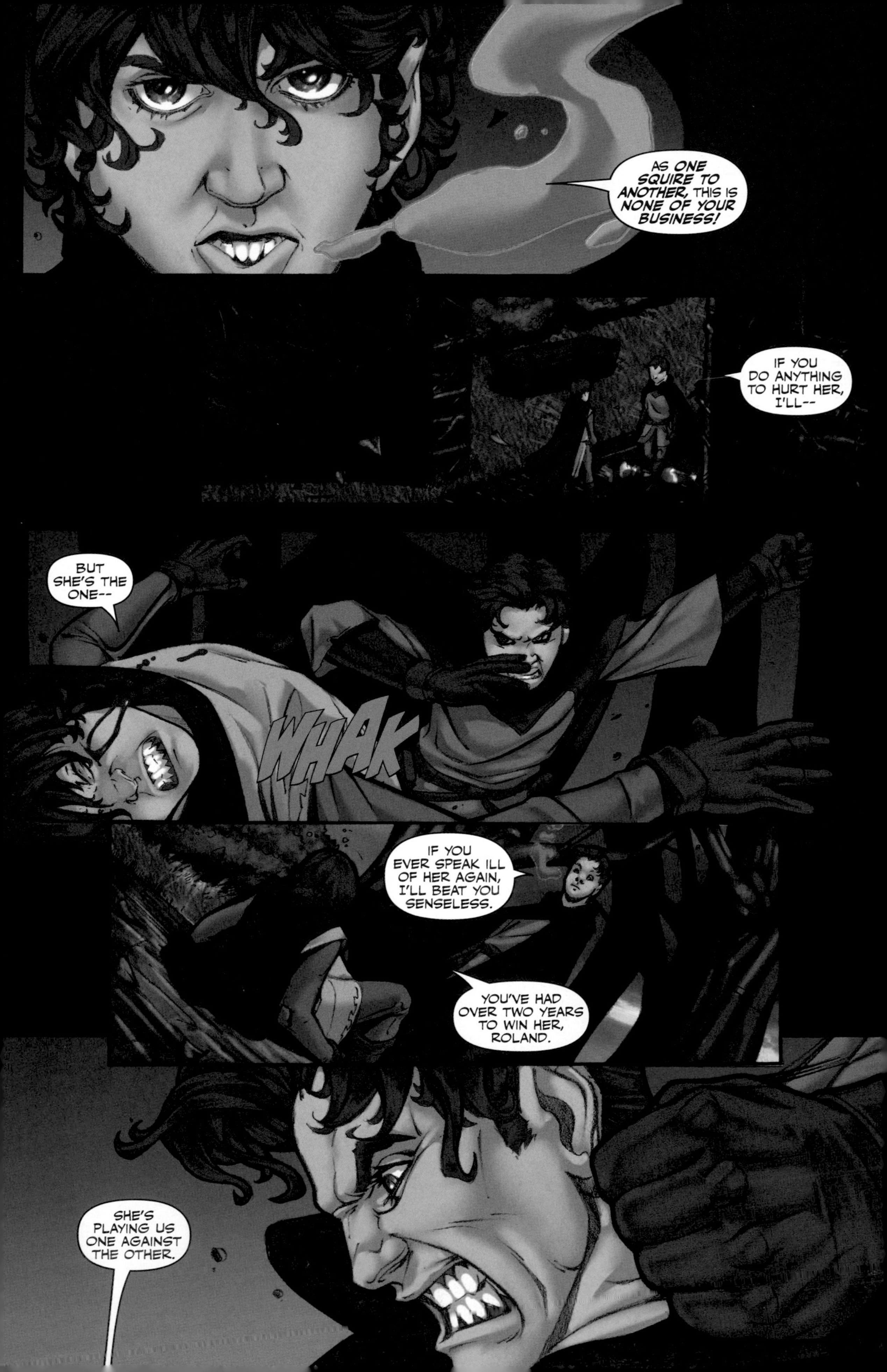
AS ONE SQUIRE TO ANOTHER, THIS IS NONE OF YOUR BUSINESS!
IF YOU DO ANYTHING TO HURT HER, I'LL--
BUT SHE'S THE ONE--
WHAK
IF YOU EVER SPEAK ILL OF HER AGAIN, I'LL BEAT YOU SENSELESS.
YOU'VE HAD OVER TWO YEARS TO WIN HER, ROLAND.
SHE'S PLAYING US ONE AGAINST THE OTHER.

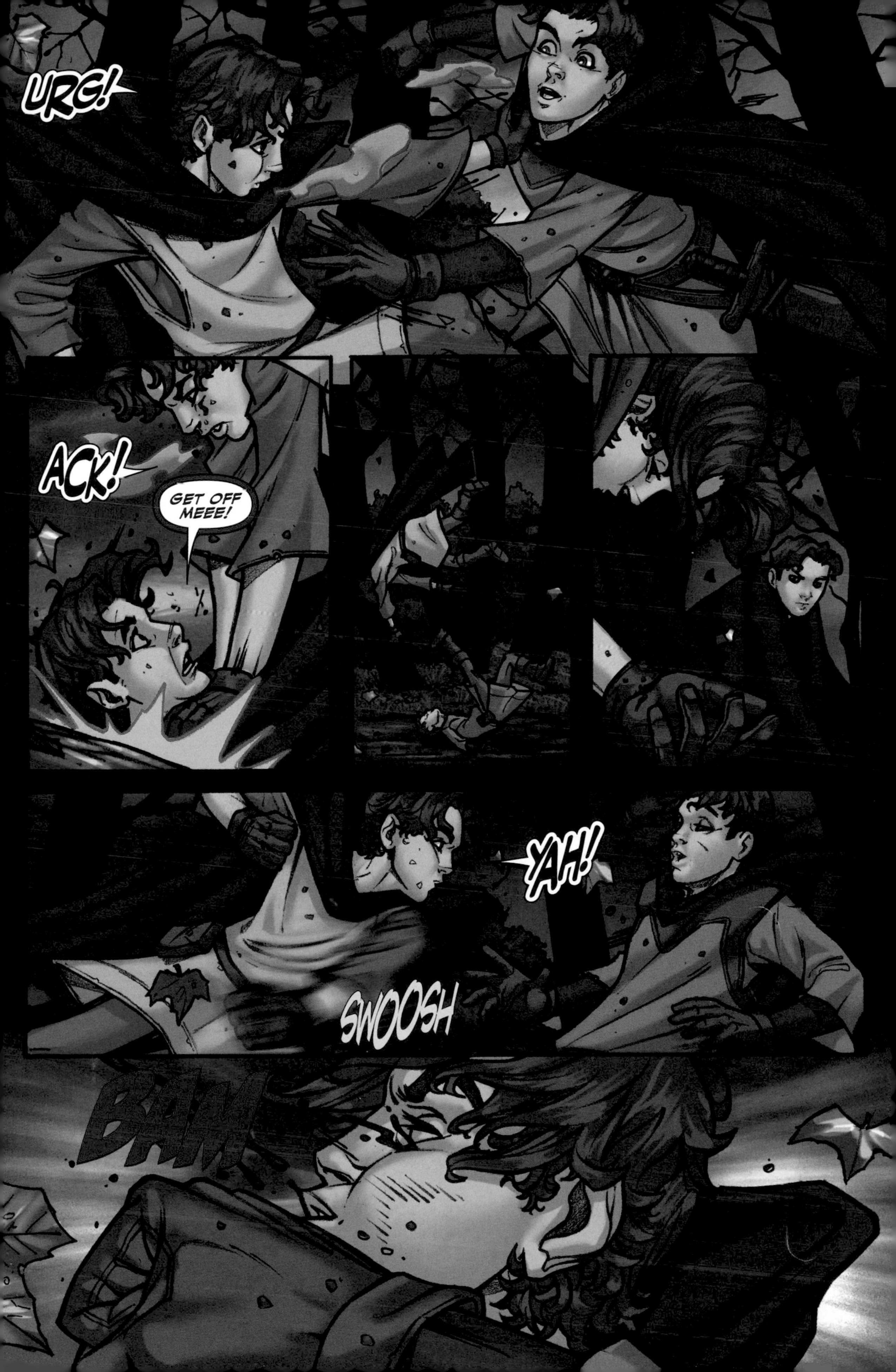
URG!
ACK!
GET OFF MEEE!
YAH!
SWOOSH
BAM!

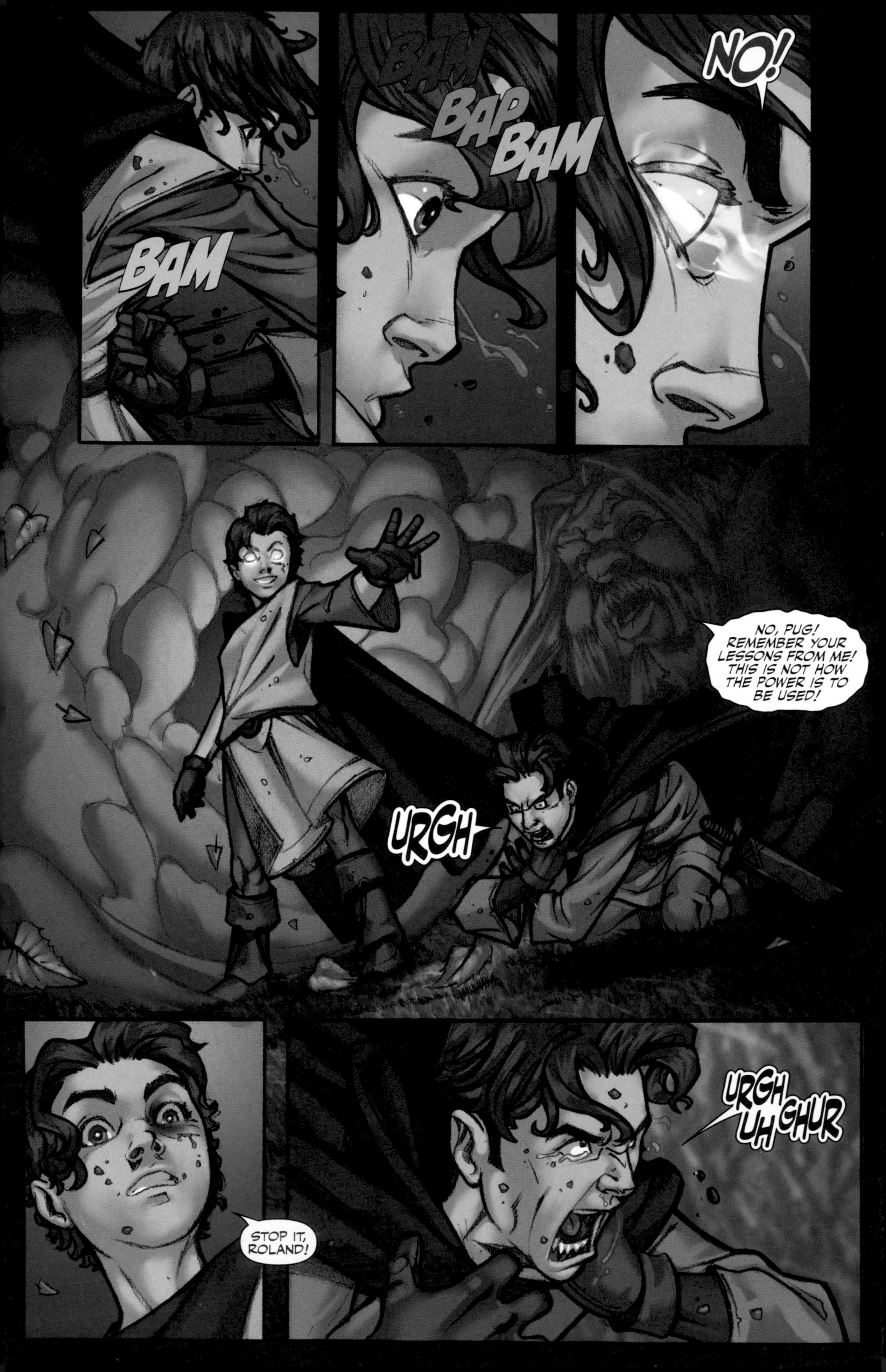
BAM
BAM
BAP BAM
NO!
NO, PUG! REMEMBER YOUR LESSONS FROM ME! THIS IS NOT HOW THE POWER IS TO BE USED!
URGH
STOP IT, ROLAND!
URGH UH GHUR

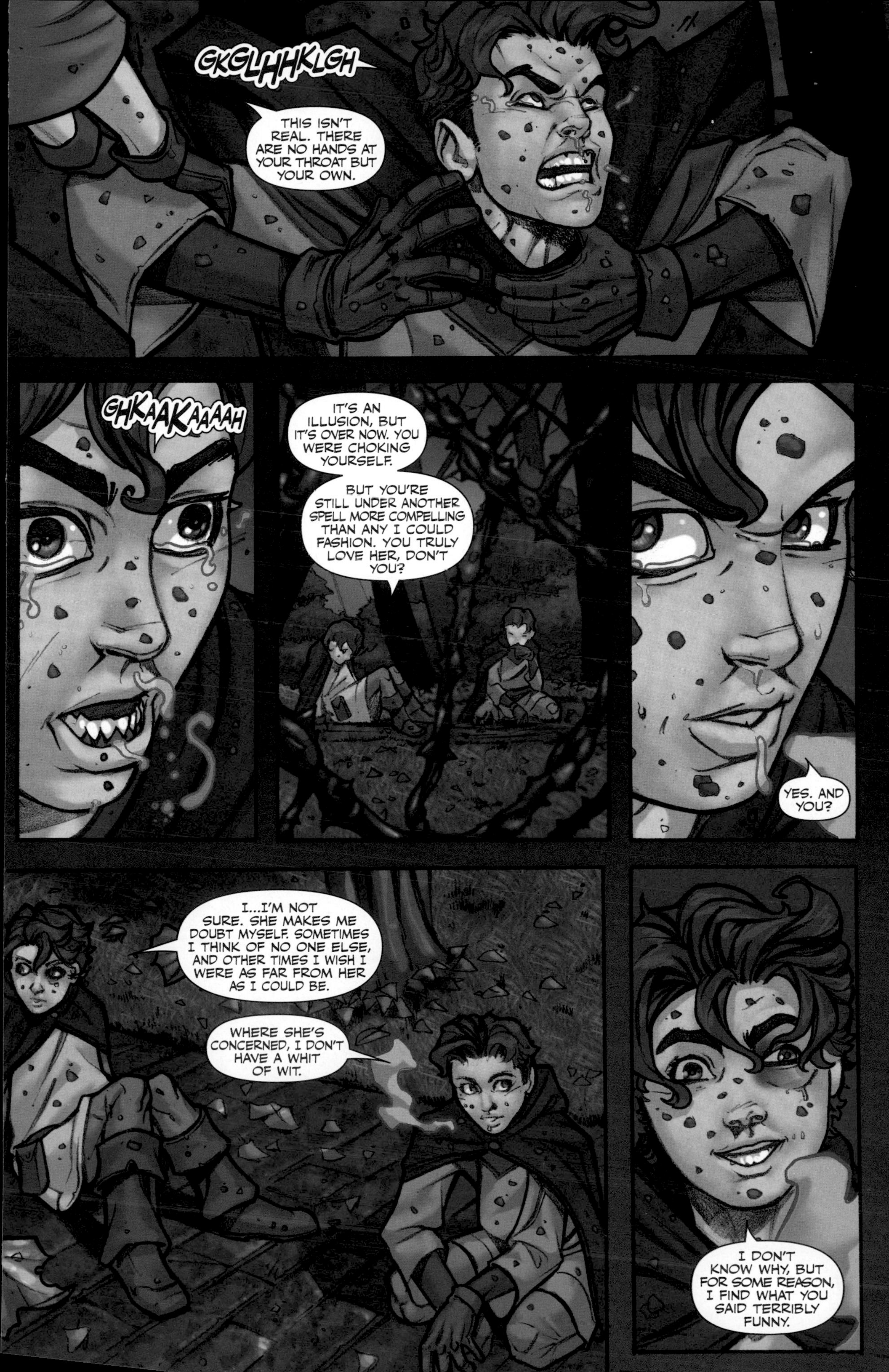
GKGLHHKLGH
THIS ISN'T REAL. THERE ARE NO HANDS AT YOUR THROAT BUT YOUR OWN.
GHKAAKAAAAH
IT'S AN ILLUSION, BUT IT'S OVER NOW. YOU WERE CHOKING YOURSELF.
BUT YOU'RE STILL UNDER ANOTHER SPELL MORE COMPELLING THAN ANY I COULD FASHION. YOU TRULY LOVE HER, DON'T YOU?
YES. AND YOU?
I...I'M NOT SURE. SHE MAKES ME DOUBT MYSELF. SOMETIMES I THINK OF NO ONE ELSE, AND OTHER TIMES I WISH I WERE AS FAR FROM HER AS I COULD BE.
WHERE SHE'S CONCERNED, I DON'T HAVE A WHIT OF WIT.
I DON'T KNOW WHY, BUT FOR SOME REASON, I FIND WHAT YOU SAID TERRIBLY FUNNY.

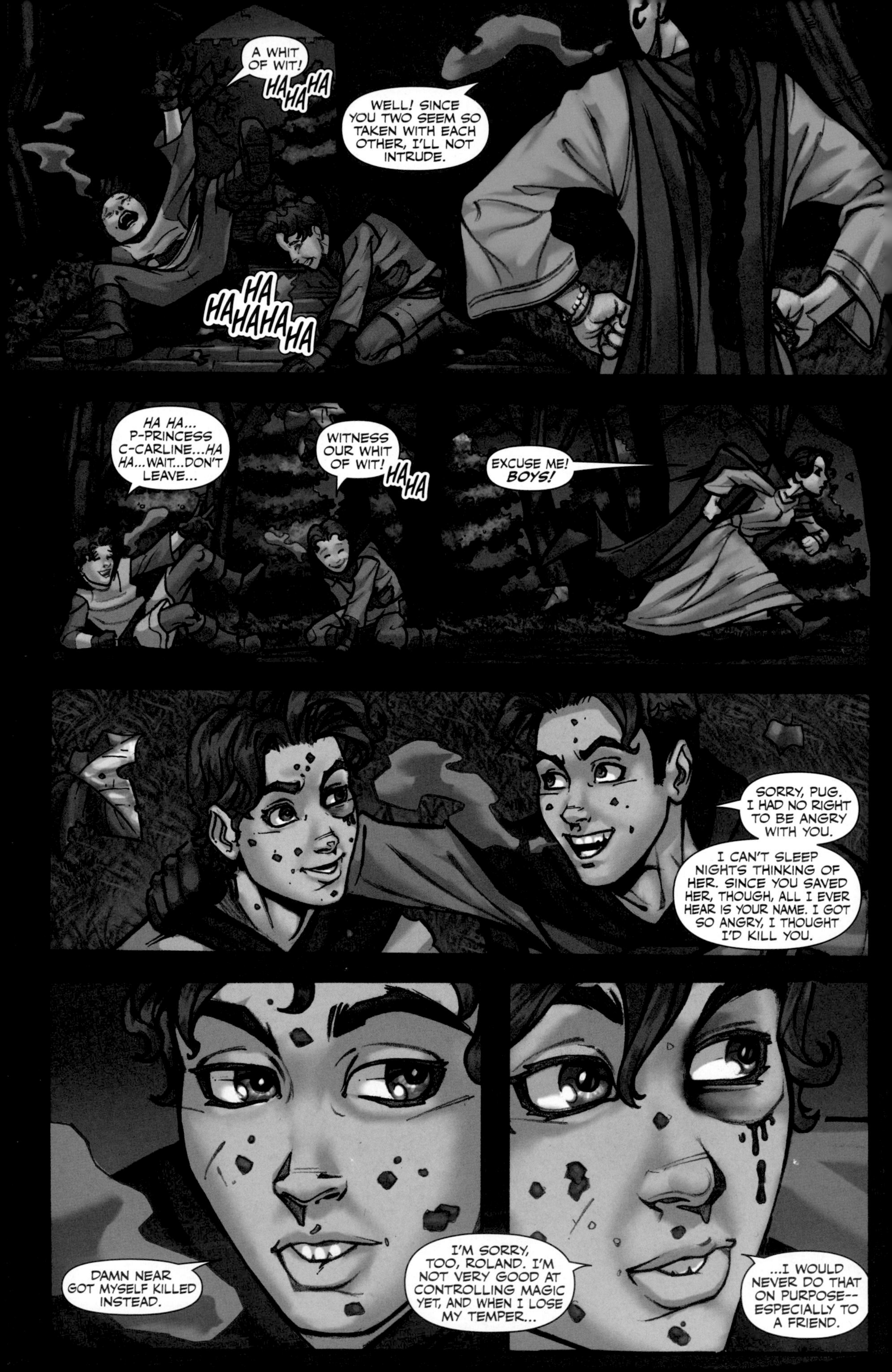
A WHIT OF WIT!
HAHAHA
WELL! SINCE YOU TWO SEEM SO TAKEN WITH EACH OTHER, I'LL NOT INTRUDE.
HA HAHAHAHAHA
HA HA... P-PRINCESS C-CARLINE...HA HA...WAIT...DON'T LEAVE...
WITNESS OUR WHIT OF WIT!
HAHA
EXCUSE ME! BOYS!
SORRY, PUG. I HAD NO RIGHT TO BE ANGRY WITH YOU.
I CAN'T SLEEP NIGHTS THINKING OF HER. SINCE YOU SAVED HER, THOUGH, ALL I EVER HEAR IS YOUR NAME. I GOT SO ANGRY, I THOUGHT I'D KILL YOU.
DAMN NEAR GOT MYSELF KILLED INSTEAD.
I'M SORRY, TOO, ROLAND. I'M NOT VERY GOOD AT CONTROLLING MAGIC YET, AND WHEN I LOSE MY TEMPER...
...I WOULD NEVER DO THAT ON PURPOSE-- ESPECIALLY TO A FRIEND.

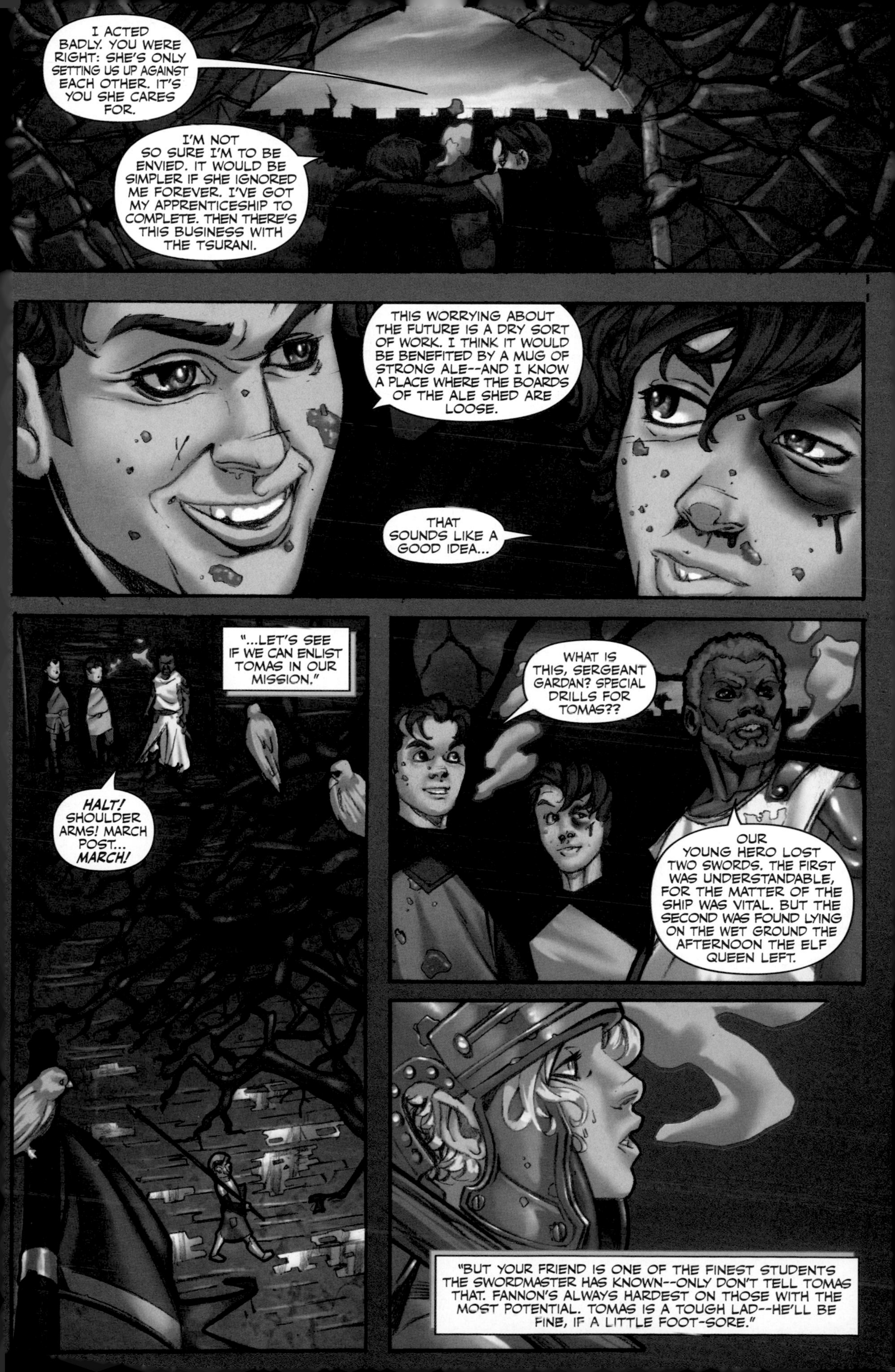

I ACTED BADLY. YOU WERE RIGHT: SHE'S ONLY SETTING US UP AGAINST EACH OTHER. IT'S YOU SHE CARES FOR.
I'M NOT SO SURE I'M TO BE ENVIED. IT WOULD BE SIMPLER IF SHE IGNORED ME FOREVER. I'VE GOT MY APPRENTICESHIP TO COMPLETE. THEN THERE'S THIS BUSINESS WITH THE TSURANI.
THIS WORRYING ABOUT THE FUTURE IS A DRY SORT OF WORK. I THINK IT WOULD BE BENEFITED BY A MUG OF STRONG ALE--AND I KNOW A PLACE WHERE THE BOARDS OF THE ALE SHED ARE LOOSE.
THAT SOUNDS LIKE A GOOD IDEA...
"...LET'S SEE IF WE CAN ENLIST TOMAS IN OUR MISSION."
HALT! SHOULDER ARMS! MARCH POST... *MARCH!*
WHAT IS THIS, SERGEANT GARDAN? SPECIAL DRILLS FOR TOMAS??
OUR YOUNG HERO LOST TWO SWORDS. THE FIRST WAS UNDERSTANDABLE, FOR THE MATTER OF THE SHIP WAS VITAL. BUT THE SECOND WAS FOUND LYING ON THE WET GROUND THE AFTERNOON THE ELF QUEEN LEFT.
"BUT YOUR FRIEND IS ONE OF THE FINEST STUDENTS THE SWORDMASTER HAS KNOWN--ONLY DON'T TELL TOMAS THAT. FANNON'S ALWAYS HARDEST ON THOSE WITH THE MOST POTENTIAL. TOMAS IS A TOUGH LAD--HE'LL BE FINE, IF A LITTLE FOOT-SORE."

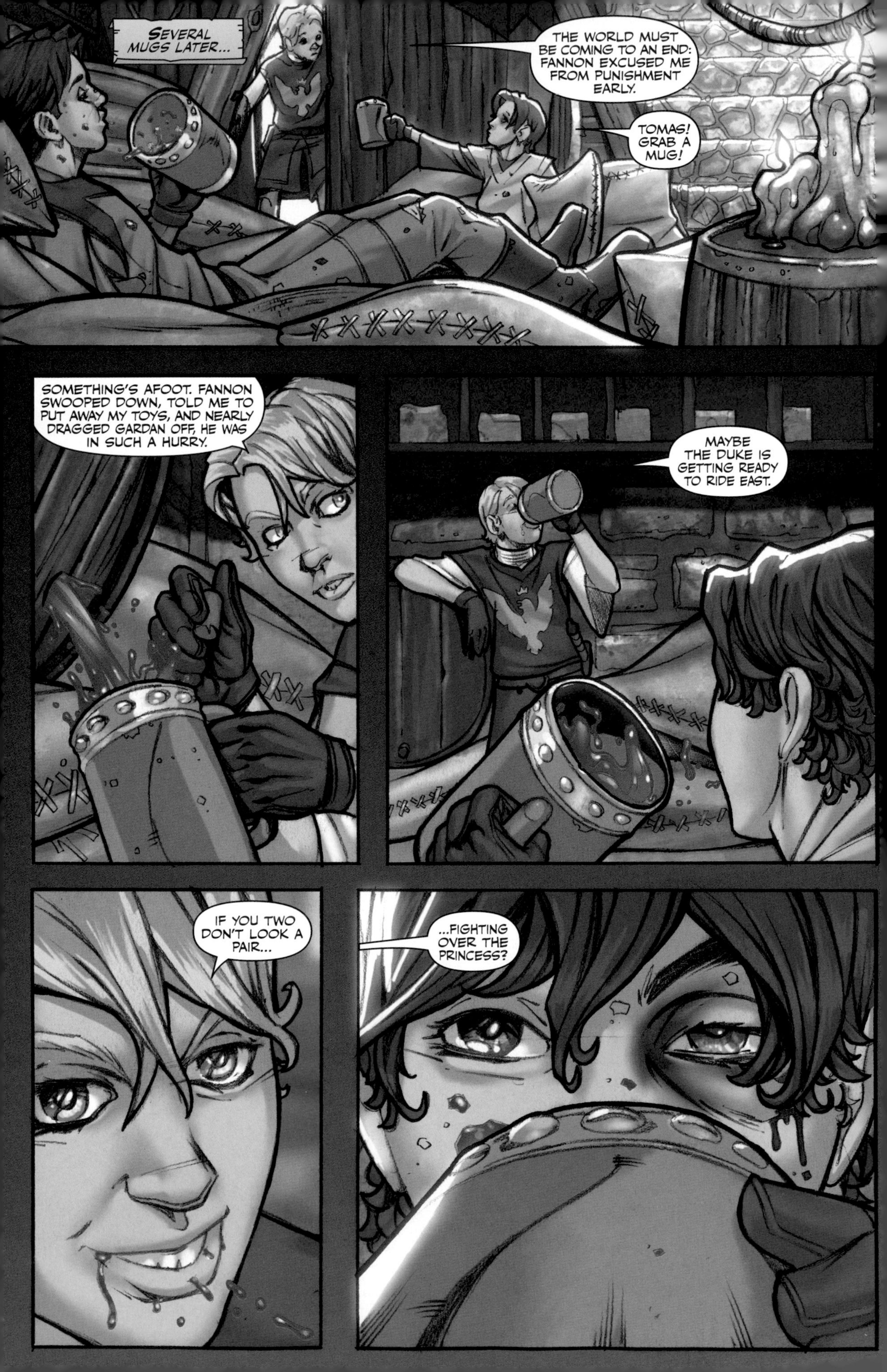
SEVERAL MUGS LATER...
THE WORLD MUST BE COMING TO AN END: FANNON EXCUSED ME FROM PUNISHMENT EARLY.
TOMAS! GRAB A MUG!
SOMETHING'S AFOOT. FANNON SWOOPED DOWN, TOLD ME TO PUT AWAY MY TOYS, AND NEARLY DRAGGED GARDAN OFF, HE WAS IN SUCH A HURRY.
MAYBE THE DUKE IS GETTING READY TO RIDE EAST.
IF YOU TWO DON'T LOOK A PAIR...
...FIGHTING OVER THE PRINCESS?

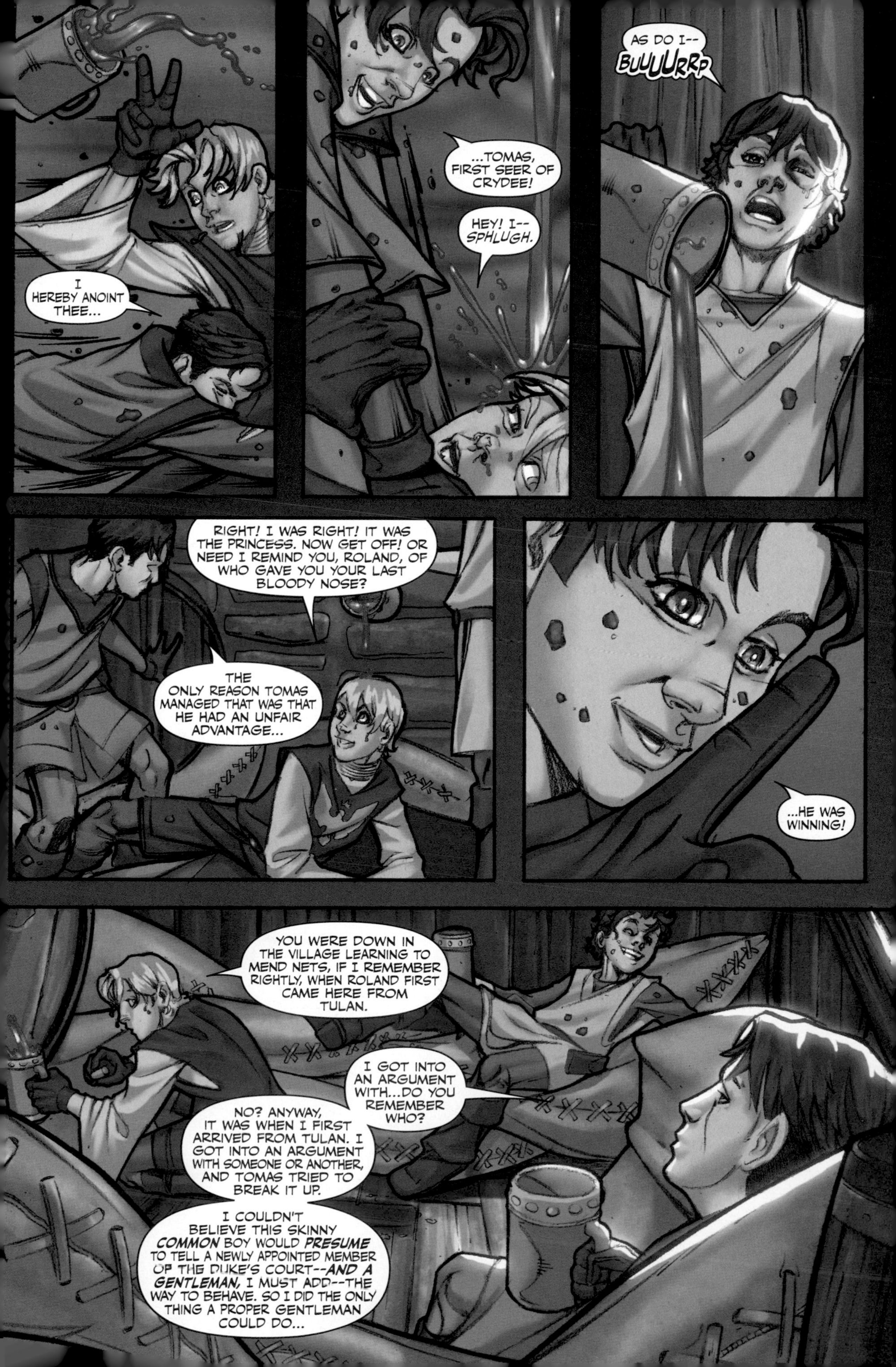
I HEREBY ANOINT THEE...
...TOMAS, FIRST SEER OF CRYDEE!
HEY! I-- SPHLUGH.
AS DO I--
BUUUURRP
RIGHT! I WAS RIGHT! IT WAS THE PRINCESS. NOW GET OFF! OR NEED I REMIND YOU, ROLAND, OF WHO GAVE YOU YOUR LAST BLOODY NOSE?
THE ONLY REASON TOMAS MANAGED THAT WAS THAT HE HAD AN UNFAIR ADVANTAGE...
...HE WAS WINNING!
YOU WERE DOWN IN THE VILLAGE LEARNING TO MEND NETS, IF I REMEMBER RIGHTLY, WHEN ROLAND FIRST CAME HERE FROM TULAN.
I GOT INTO AN ARGUMENT WITH...DO YOU REMEMBER WHO?
NO? ANYWAY, IT WAS WHEN I FIRST ARRIVED FROM TULAN. I GOT INTO AN ARGUMENT WITH SOMEONE OR ANOTHER, AND TOMAS TRIED TO BREAK IT UP.
I COULDN'T BELIEVE THIS SKINNY COMMON BOY WOULD PRESUME TO TELL A NEWLY APPOINTED MEMBER OF THE DUKE'S COURT--AND A GENTLEMAN, I MUST ADD--THE WAY TO BEHAVE. SO I DID THE ONLY THING A PROPER GENTLEMAN COULD DO...

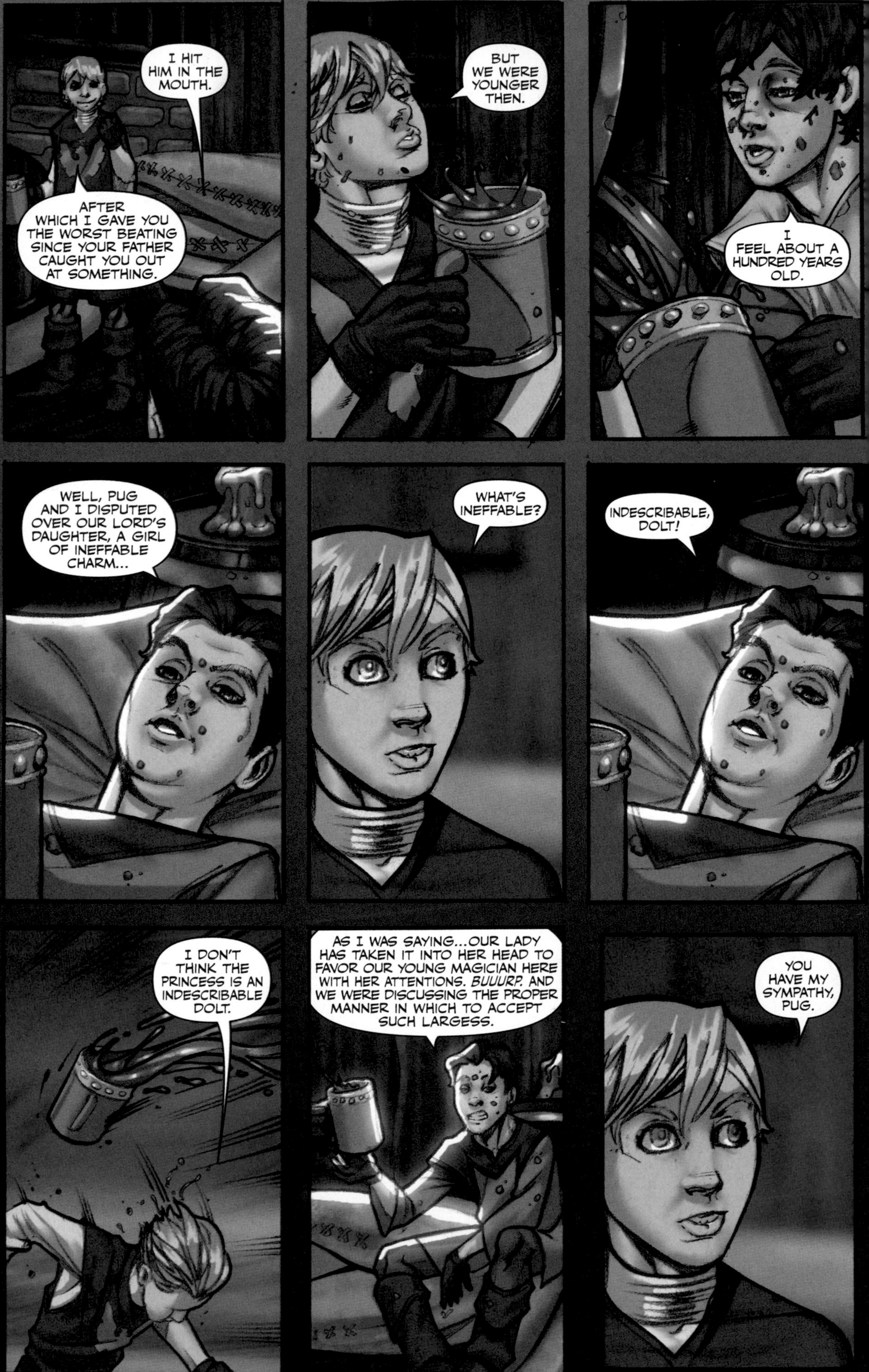
I HIT HIM IN THE MOUTH.
AFTER WHICH I GAVE YOU THE WORST BEATING SINCE YOUR FATHER CAUGHT YOU OUT AT SOMETHING.
BUT WE WERE YOUNGER THEN.
I FEEL ABOUT A HUNDRED YEARS OLD.
WELL, PUG AND I DISPUTED OVER OUR LORD'S DAUGHTER, A GIRL OF INEFFABLE CHARM...
WHAT'S INEFFABLE?
INDESCRIBABLE, DOLT!
I DON'T THINK THE PRINCESS IS AN INDESCRIBABLE DOLT.
AS I WAS SAYING...OUR LADY HAS TAKEN IT INTO HER HEAD TO FAVOR OUR YOUNG MAGICIAN HERE WITH HER ATTENTIONS. *BUUURP.* AND WE WERE DISCUSSING THE PROPER MANNER IN WHICH TO ACCEPT SUCH LARGESS.
YOU HAVE MY SYMPATHY, PUG.

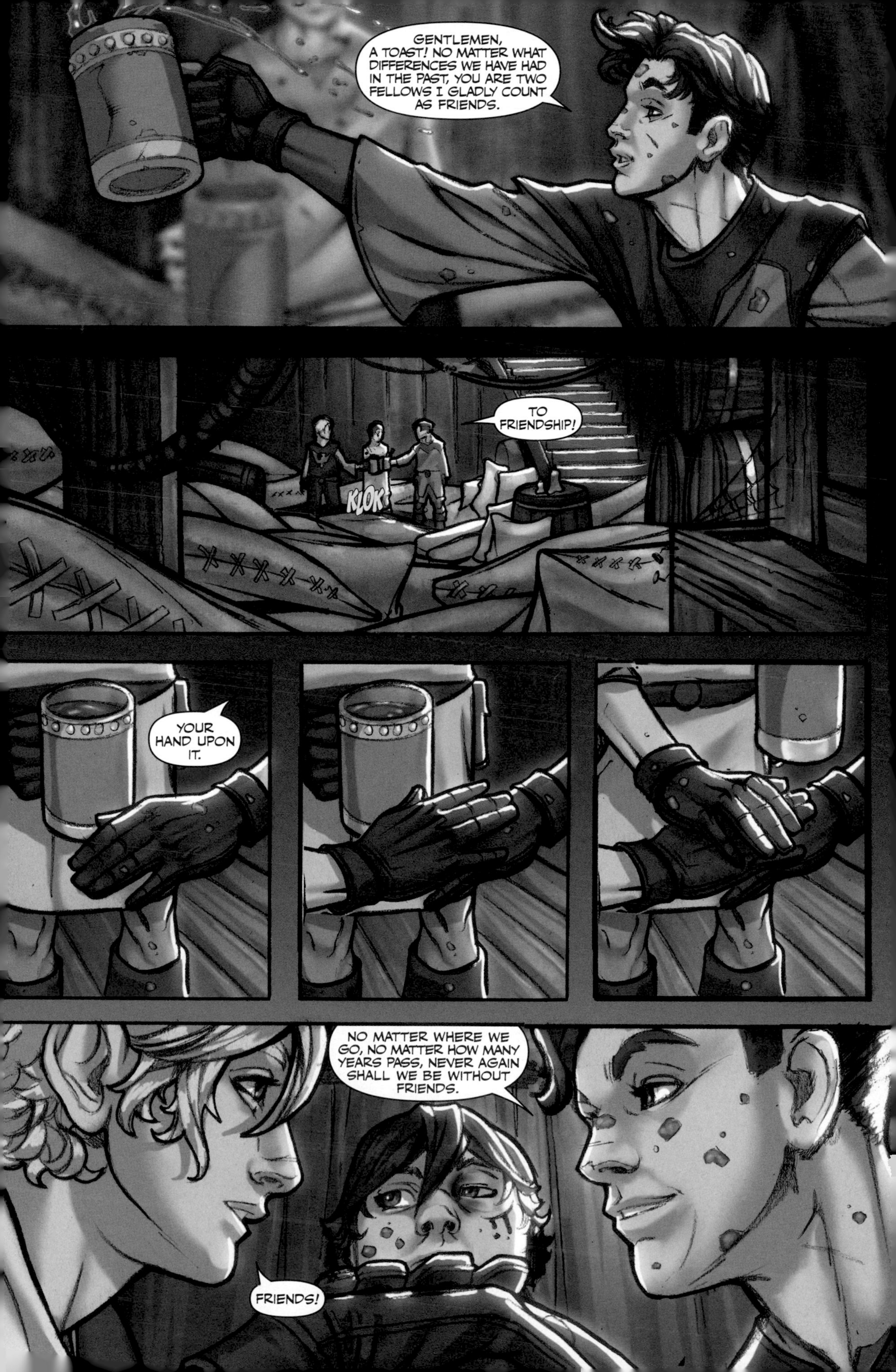
GENTLEMEN, A TOAST! NO MATTER WHAT DIFFERENCES WE HAVE HAD IN THE PAST, YOU ARE TWO FELLOWS I GLADLY COUNT AS FRIENDS.
TO FRIENDSHIP!
KLOK
YOUR HAND UPON IT.
NO MATTER WHERE WE GO, NO MATTER HOW MANY YEARS PASS, NEVER AGAIN SHALL WE BE WITHOUT FRIENDS.
FRIENDS!

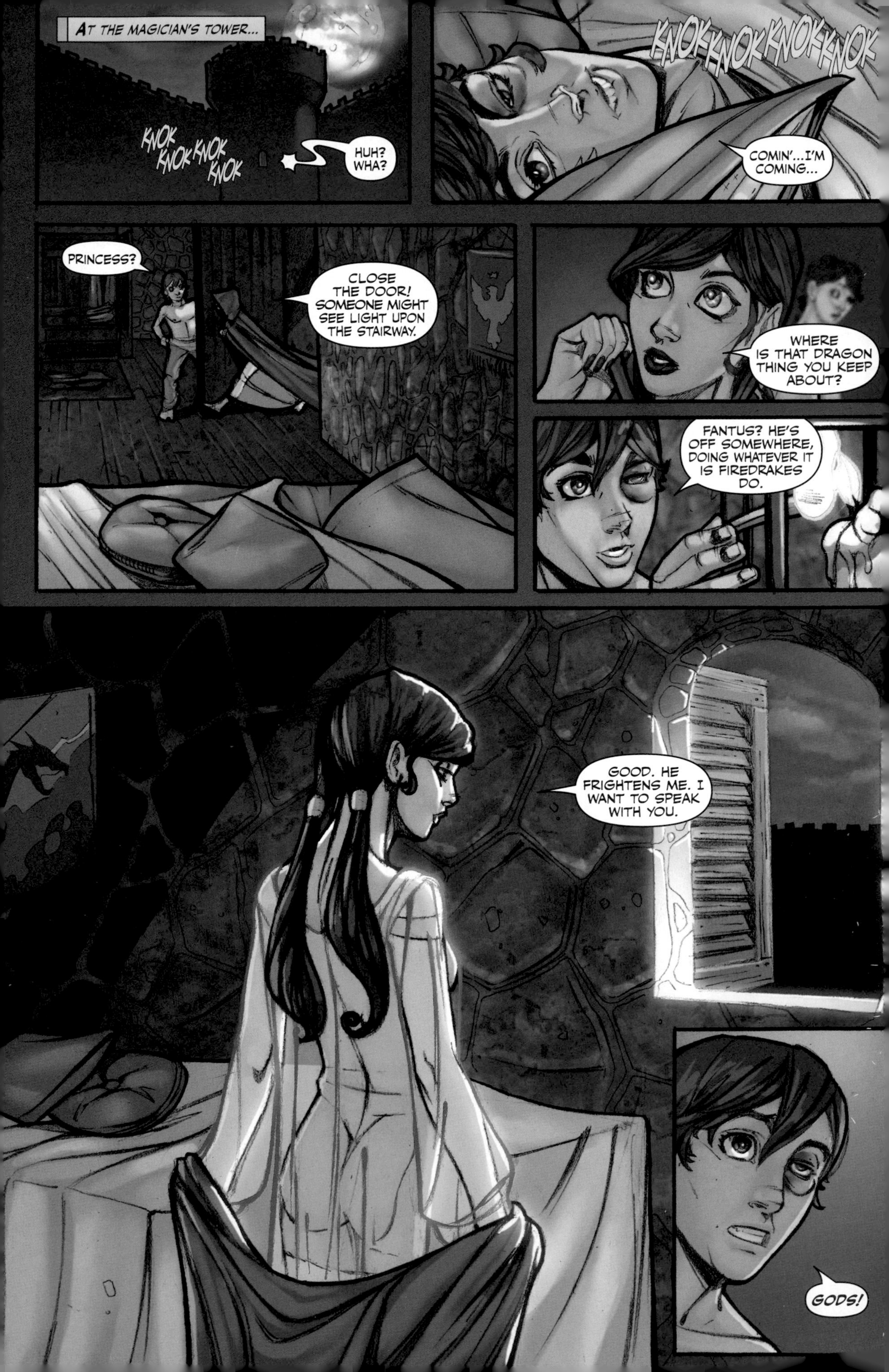
AT THE MAGICIAN'S TOWER...
KNOK KNOK KNOK KNOK
HUH? WHA?
KNOK KNOK KNOK KNOK
COMIN'...I'M COMING...
PRINCESS?
CLOSE THE DOOR! SOMEONE MIGHT SEE LIGHT UPON THE STAIRWAY.
WHERE IS THAT DRAGON THING YOU KEEP ABOUT?
FANTUS? HE'S OFF SOMEWHERE, DOING WHATEVER IT IS FIREDRAKES DO.
GOOD. HE FRIGHTENS ME. I WANT TO SPEAK WITH YOU.
GODS!

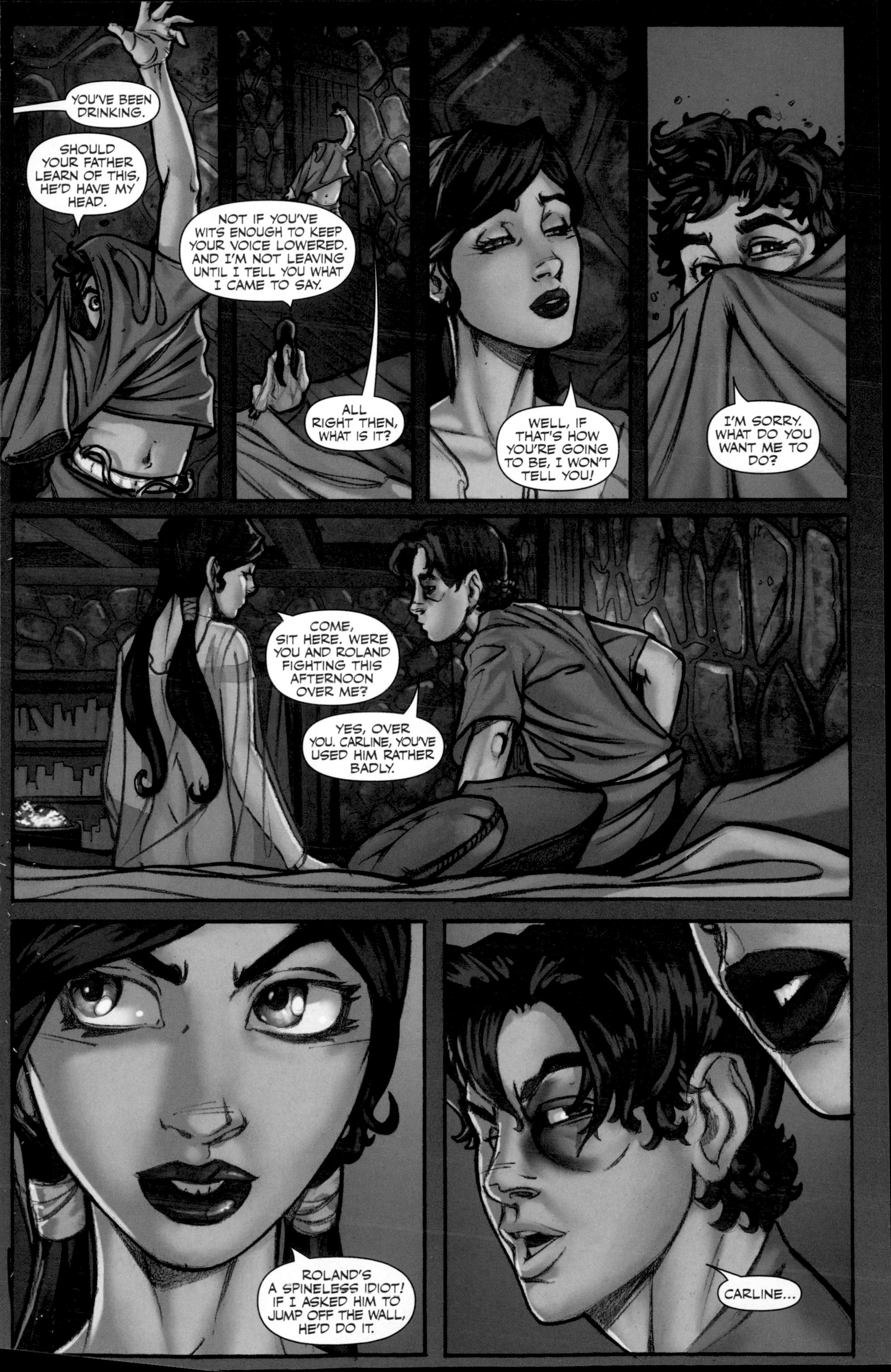
YOU'VE BEEN DRINKING.
SHOULD YOUR FATHER LEARN OF THIS, HE'D HAVE MY HEAD.
NOT IF YOU'VE WITS ENOUGH TO KEEP YOUR VOICE LOWERED. AND I'M NOT LEAVING UNTIL I TELL YOU WHAT I CAME TO SAY.
ALL RIGHT THEN, WHAT IS IT?
WELL, IF THAT'S HOW YOU'RE GOING TO BE, I WON'T TELL YOU!
I'M SORRY. WHAT DO YOU WANT ME TO DO?
COME, SIT HERE. WERE YOU AND ROLAND FIGHTING THIS AFTERNOON OVER ME?
YES, OVER YOU. CARLINE, YOU'VE USED HIM RATHER BADLY.
ROLAND'S A SPINELESS IDIOT! IF I ASKED HIM TO JUMP OFF THE WALL, HE'D DO IT.
CARLINE...

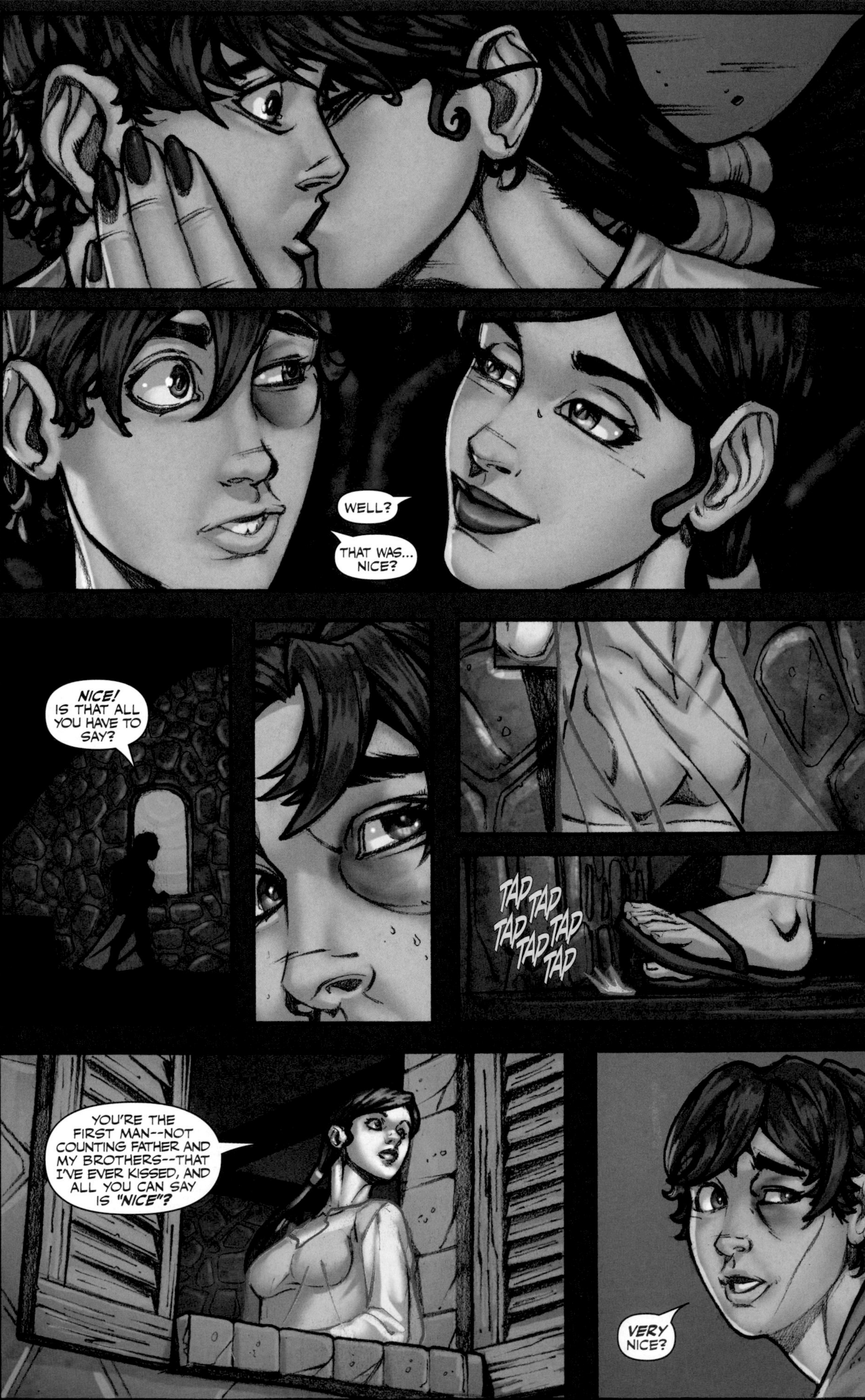
WELL?
THAT WAS... NICE?
NICE! IS THAT ALL YOU HAVE TO SAY?
TAP TAP TAP TAP TAP TAP TAP
YOU'RE THE FIRST MAN--NOT COUNTING FATHER AND MY BROTHERS--THAT I'VE EVER KISSED, AND ALL YOU CAN SAY IS "NICE"?
VERY NICE?

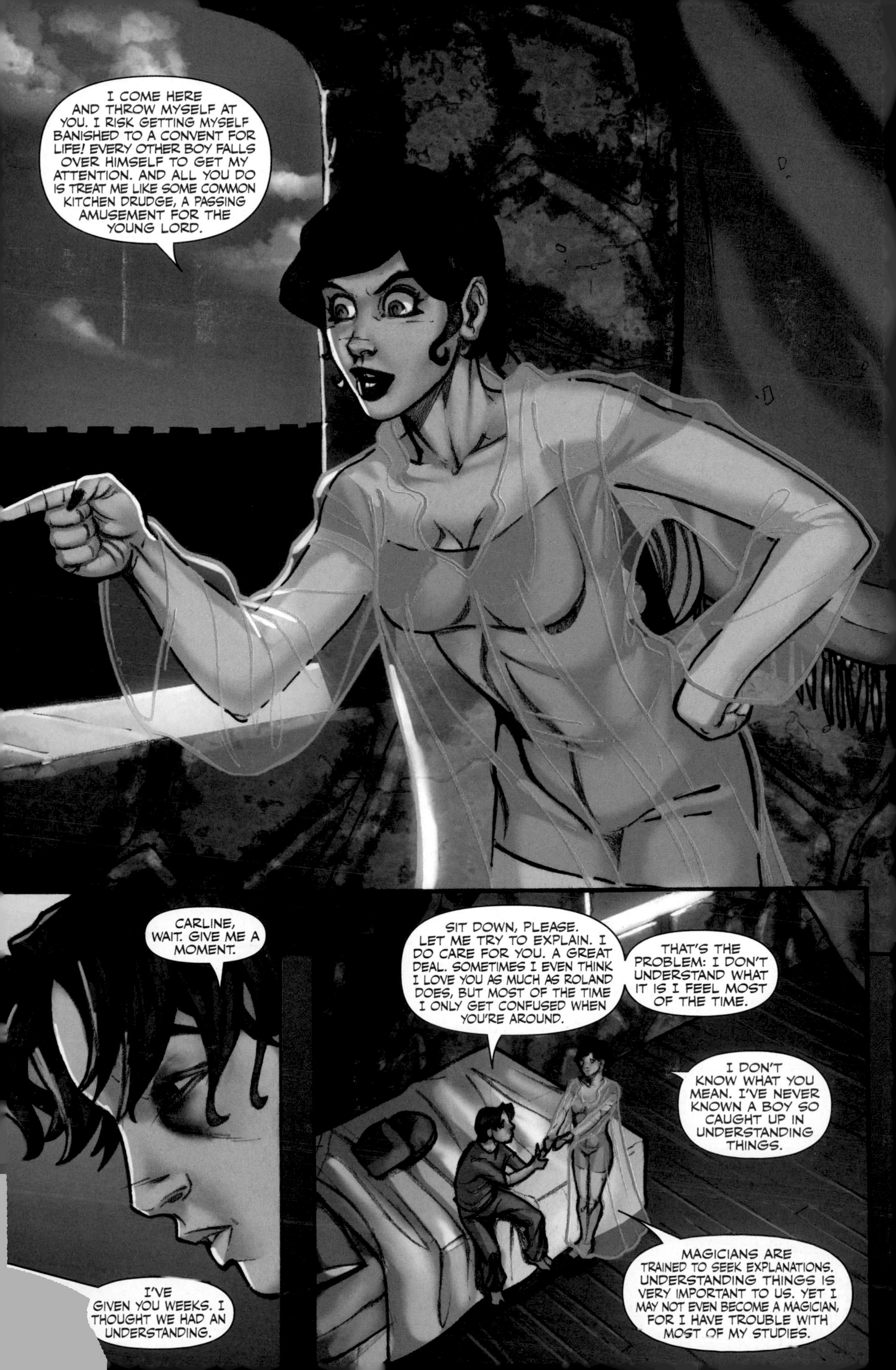
I COME HERE AND THROW MYSELF AT YOU. I RISK GETTING MYSELF BANISHED TO A CONVENT FOR LIFE! EVERY OTHER BOY FALLS OVER HIMSELF TO GET MY ATTENTION. AND ALL YOU DO IS TREAT ME LIKE SOME COMMON KITCHEN DRUDGE, A PASSING AMUSEMENT FOR THE YOUNG LORD.
CARLINE, WAIT. GIVE ME A MOMENT.
I'VE GIVEN YOU WEEKS. I THOUGHT WE HAD AN UNDERSTANDING.
SIT DOWN, PLEASE. LET ME TRY TO EXPLAIN. I DO CARE FOR YOU. A GREAT DEAL. SOMETIMES I EVEN THINK I LOVE YOU AS MUCH AS ROLAND DOES, BUT MOST OF THE TIME I ONLY GET CONFUSED WHEN YOU'RE AROUND.
THAT'S THE PROBLEM: I DON'T UNDERSTAND WHAT IT IS I FEEL MOST OF THE TIME.
I DON'T KNOW WHAT YOU MEAN. I'VE NEVER KNOWN A BOY SO CAUGHT UP IN UNDERSTANDING THINGS.
MAGICIANS ARE TRAINED TO SEEK EXPLANATIONS. UNDERSTANDING THINGS IS VERY IMPORTANT TO US. YET I MAY NOT EVEN BECOME A MAGICIAN, FOR I HAVE TROUBLE WITH MOST OF MY STUDIES.

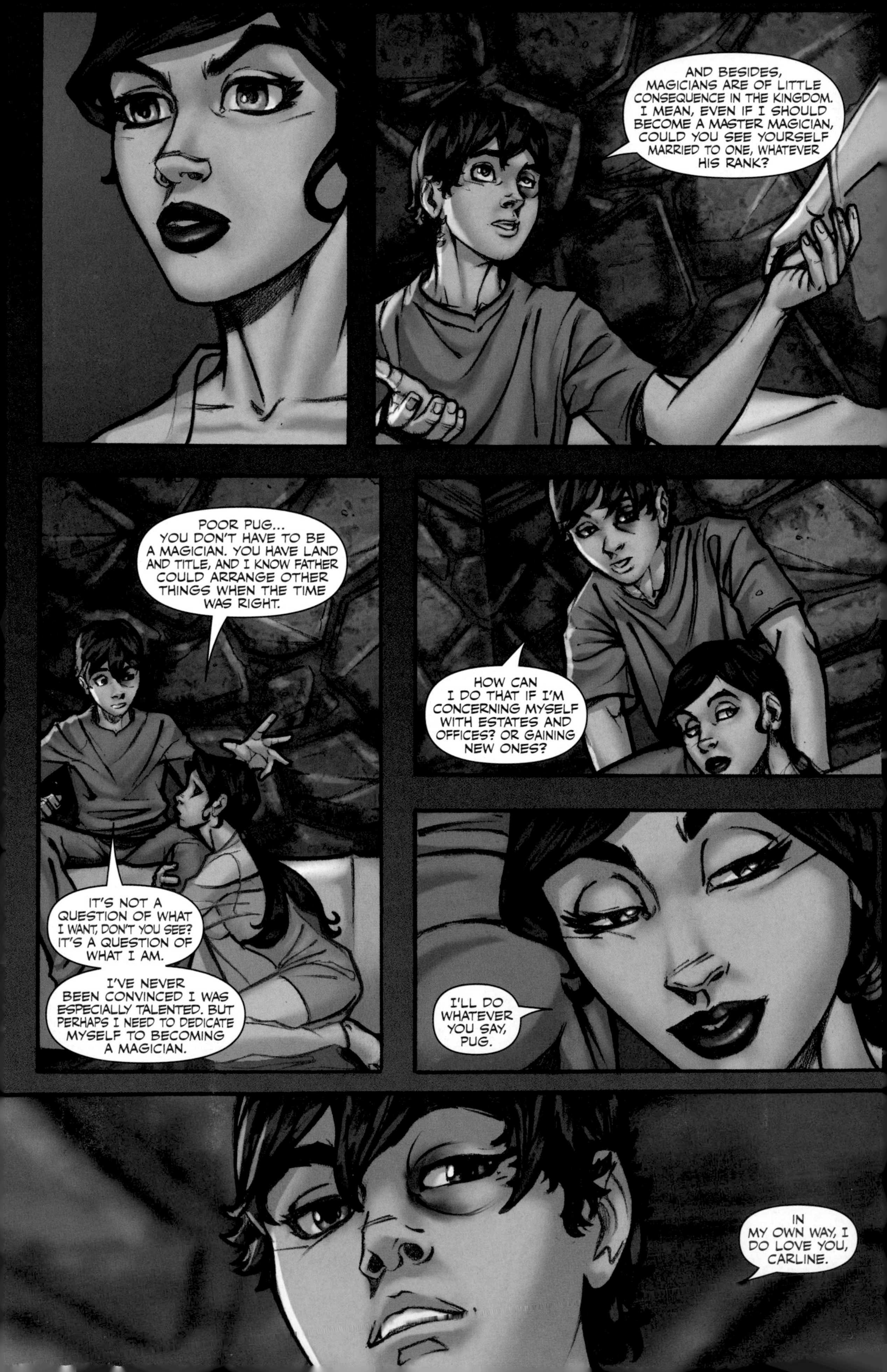
AND BESIDES, MAGICIANS ARE OF LITTLE CONSEQUENCE IN THE KINGDOM. I MEAN, EVEN IF I SHOULD BECOME A MASTER MAGICIAN, COULD YOU SEE YOURSELF MARRIED TO ONE, WHATEVER HIS RANK?
POOR PUG... YOU DON'T HAVE TO BE A MAGICIAN. YOU HAVE LAND AND TITLE, AND I KNOW FATHER COULD ARRANGE OTHER THINGS WHEN THE TIME WAS RIGHT.
IT'S NOT A QUESTION OF WHAT I WANT, DON'T YOU SEE? IT'S A QUESTION OF WHAT I AM.
I'VE NEVER BEEN CONVINCED I WAS ESPECIALLY TALENTED. BUT PERHAPS I NEED TO DEDICATE MYSELF TO BECOMING A MAGICIAN.
HOW CAN I DO THAT IF I'M CONCERNING MYSELF WITH ESTATES AND OFFICES? OR GAINING NEW ONES?
I'LL DO WHATEVER YOU SAY, PUG.
IN MY OWN WAY, I DO LOVE YOU, CARLINE.

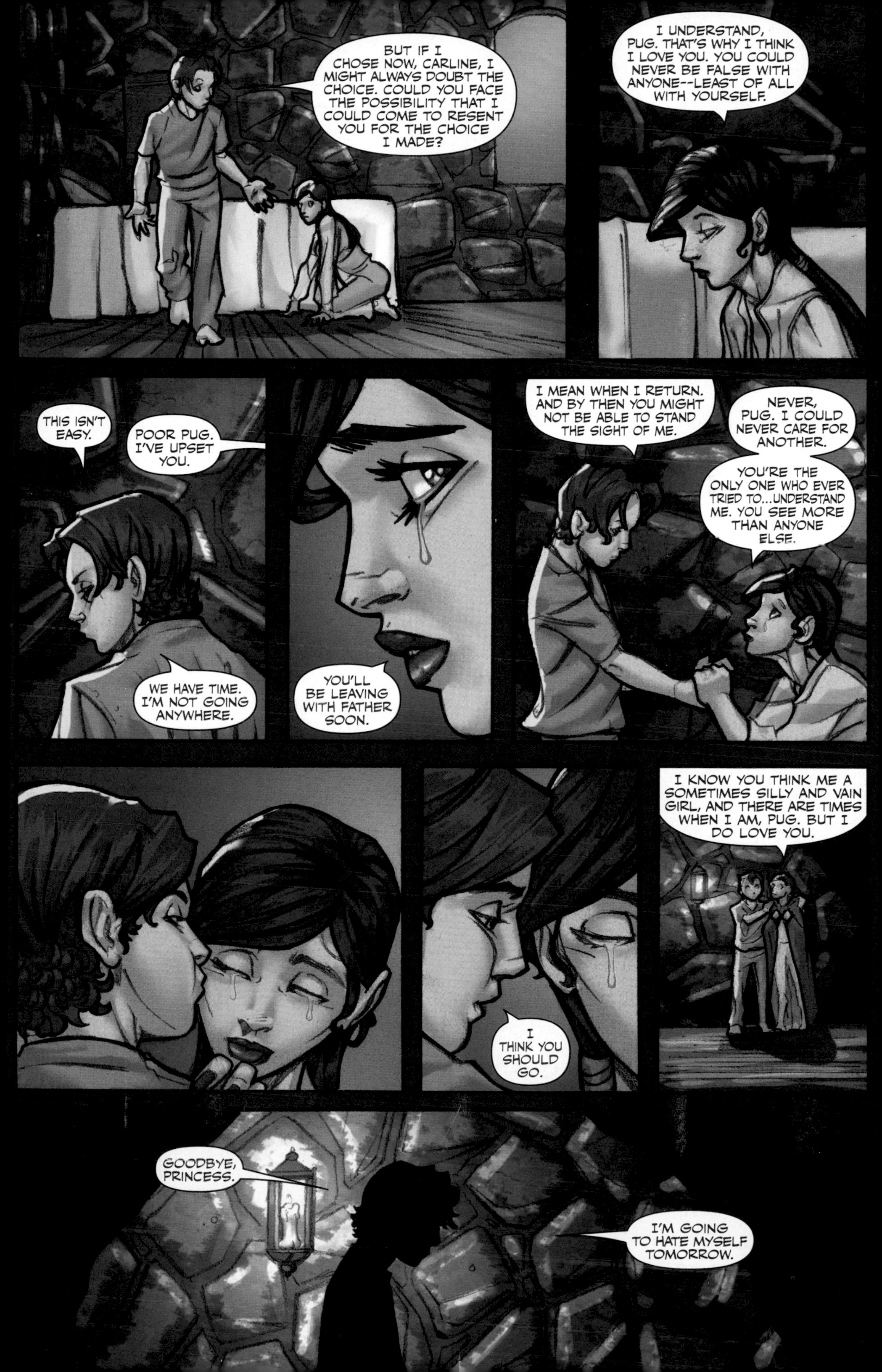
BUT IF I CHOSE NOW, CARLINE, I MIGHT ALWAYS DOUBT THE CHOICE. COULD YOU FACE THE POSSIBILITY THAT I COULD COME TO RESENT YOU FOR THE CHOICE I MADE?
I UNDERSTAND, PUG. THAT'S WHY I THINK I LOVE YOU. YOU COULD NEVER BE FALSE WITH ANYONE--LEAST OF ALL WITH YOURSELF.
THIS ISN'T EASY.
POOR PUG. I'VE UPSET YOU.
WE HAVE TIME. I'M NOT GOING ANYWHERE.
YOU'LL BE LEAVING WITH FATHER SOON.
I MEAN WHEN I RETURN. AND BY THEN YOU MIGHT NOT BE ABLE TO STAND THE SIGHT OF ME.
NEVER, PUG. I COULD NEVER CARE FOR ANOTHER.
YOU'RE THE ONLY ONE WHO EVER TRIED TO...UNDERSTAND ME. YOU SEE MORE THAN ANYONE ELSE.
I THINK YOU SHOULD GO.
I KNOW YOU THINK ME A SOMETIMES SILLY AND VAIN GIRL, AND THERE ARE TIMES WHEN I AM, PUG. BUT I DO LOVE YOU.
GOODBYE, PRINCESS.
I'M GOING TO HATE MYSELF TOMORROW.

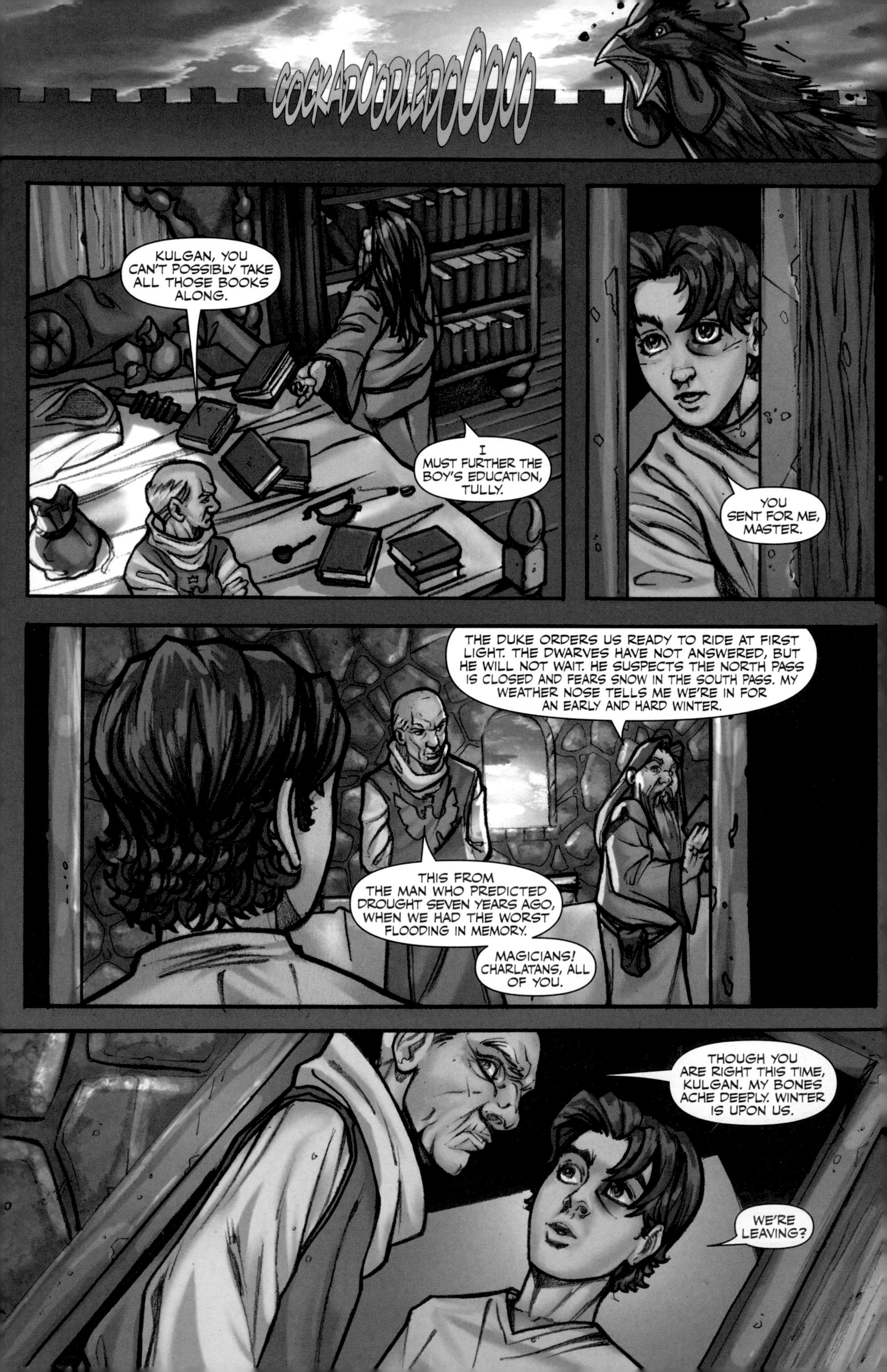
COCKADOODLEDOOOOOO
KULGAN, YOU CAN'T POSSIBLY TAKE ALL THOSE BOOKS ALONG.
I MUST FURTHER THE BOY'S EDUCATION, TULLY.
YOU SENT FOR ME, MASTER.
THE DUKE ORDERS US READY TO RIDE AT FIRST LIGHT. THE DWARVES HAVE NOT ANSWERED, BUT HE WILL NOT WAIT. HE SUSPECTS THE NORTH PASS IS CLOSED AND FEARS SNOW IN THE SOUTH PASS. MY WEATHER NOSE TELLS ME WE'RE IN FOR AN EARLY AND HARD WINTER.
THIS FROM THE MAN WHO PREDICTED DROUGHT SEVEN YEARS AGO, WHEN WE HAD THE WORST FLOODING IN MEMORY.
MAGICIANS! CHARLATANS, ALL OF YOU.
THOUGH YOU ARE RIGHT THIS TIME, KULGAN. MY BONES ACHE DEEPLY. WINTER IS UPON US.
WE'RE LEAVING?

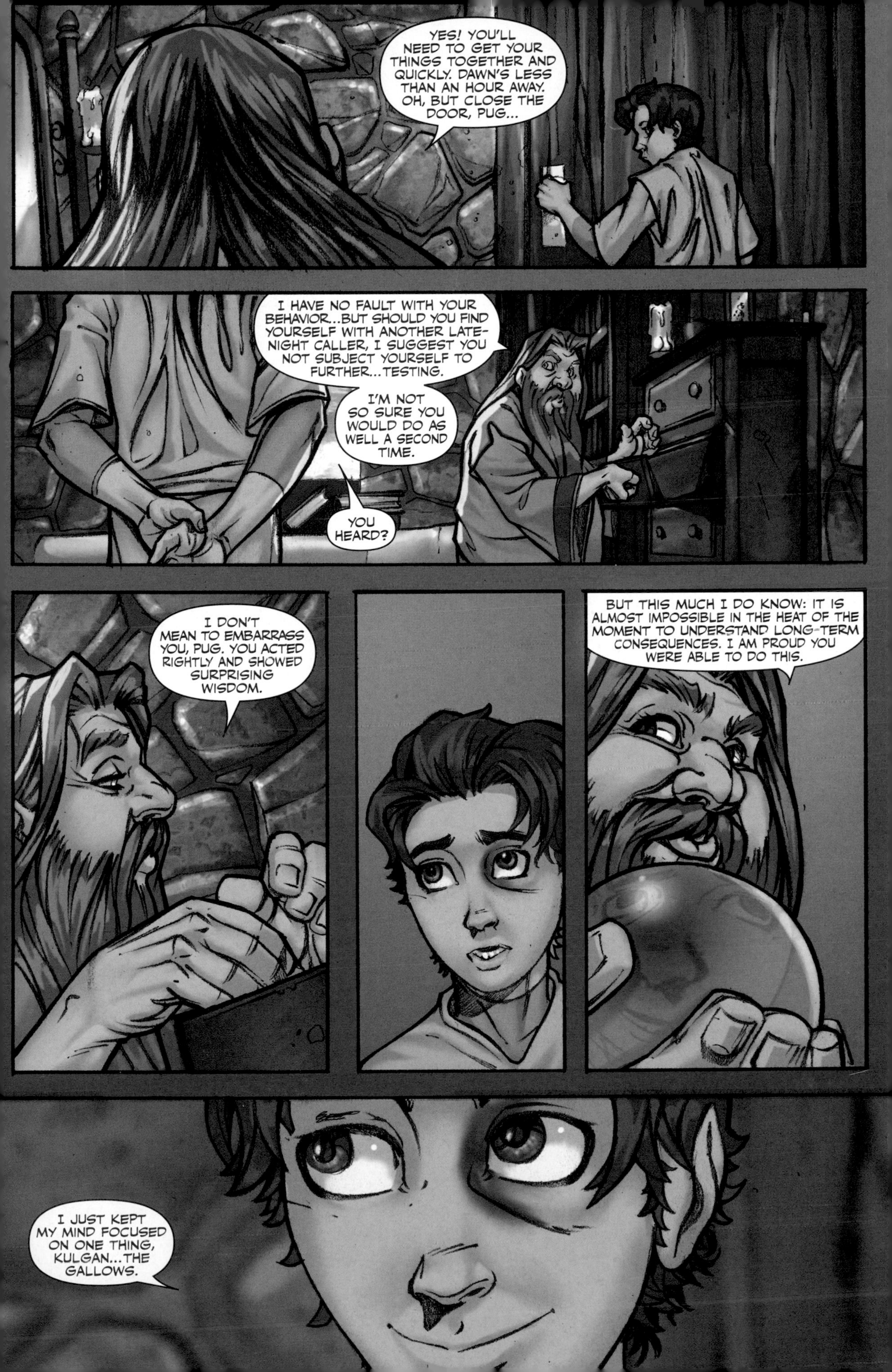
YES! YOU'LL NEED TO GET YOUR THINGS TOGETHER AND QUICKLY. DAWN'S LESS THAN AN HOUR AWAY. OH, BUT CLOSE THE DOOR, PUG...
I HAVE NO FAULT WITH YOUR BEHAVIOR...BUT SHOULD YOU FIND YOURSELF WITH ANOTHER LATE-NIGHT CALLER, I SUGGEST YOU NOT SUBJECT YOURSELF TO FURTHER...TESTING.
I'M NOT SO SURE YOU WOULD DO AS WELL A SECOND TIME.
YOU HEARD?
I DON'T MEAN TO EMBARRASS YOU, PUG. YOU ACTED RIGHTLY AND SHOWED SURPRISING WISDOM.
BUT THIS MUCH I DO KNOW: IT IS ALMOST IMPOSSIBLE IN THE HEAT OF THE MOMENT TO UNDERSTAND LONG-TERM CONSEQUENCES. I AM PROUD YOU WERE ABLE TO DO THIS.
I JUST KEPT MY MIND FOCUSED ON ONE THING, KULGAN...THE GALLOWS.

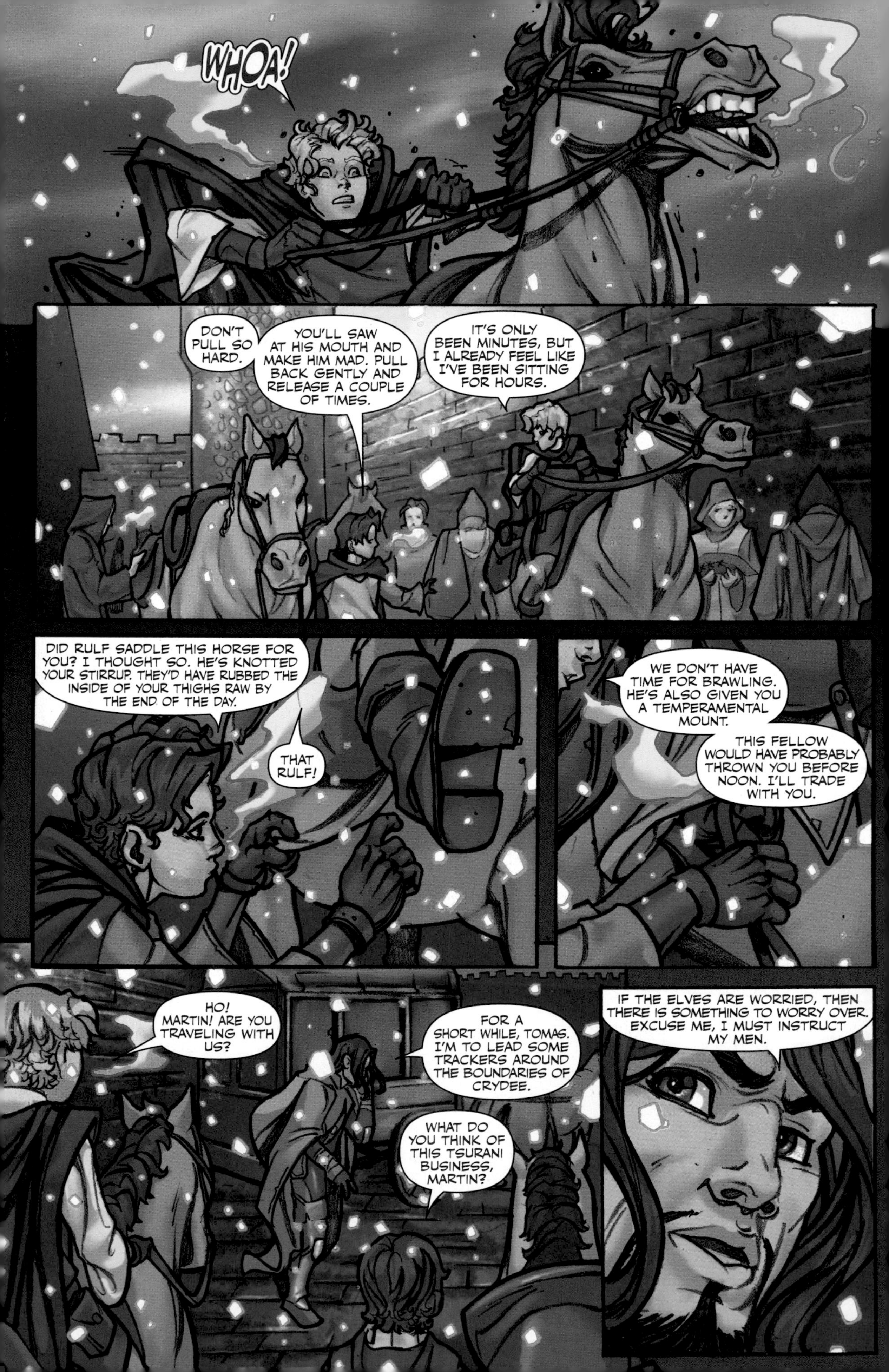
WHOA!
DON'T PULL SO HARD.
YOU'LL SAW AT HIS MOUTH AND MAKE HIM MAD. PULL BACK GENTLY AND RELEASE A COUPLE OF TIMES.
IT'S ONLY BEEN MINUTES, BUT I ALREADY FEEL LIKE I'VE BEEN SITTING FOR HOURS.
DID RULF SADDLE THIS HORSE FOR YOU? I THOUGHT SO. HE'S KNOTTED YOUR STIRRUP. THEY'D HAVE RUBBED THE INSIDE OF YOUR THIGHS RAW BY THE END OF THE DAY.
THAT RULF!
WE DON'T HAVE TIME FOR BRAWLING. HE'S ALSO GIVEN YOU A TEMPERAMENTAL MOUNT.
THIS FELLOW WOULD HAVE PROBABLY THROWN YOU BEFORE NOON. I'LL TRADE WITH YOU.
HO! MARTIN! ARE YOU TRAVELING WITH US?
FOR A SHORT WHILE, TOMAS. I'M TO LEAD SOME TRACKERS AROUND THE BOUNDARIES OF CRYDEE.
WHAT DO YOU THINK OF THIS TSURANI BUSINESS, MARTIN?
IF THE ELVES ARE WORRIED, THEN THERE IS SOMETHING TO WORRY OVER. EXCUSE ME, I MUST INSTRUCT MY MEN.

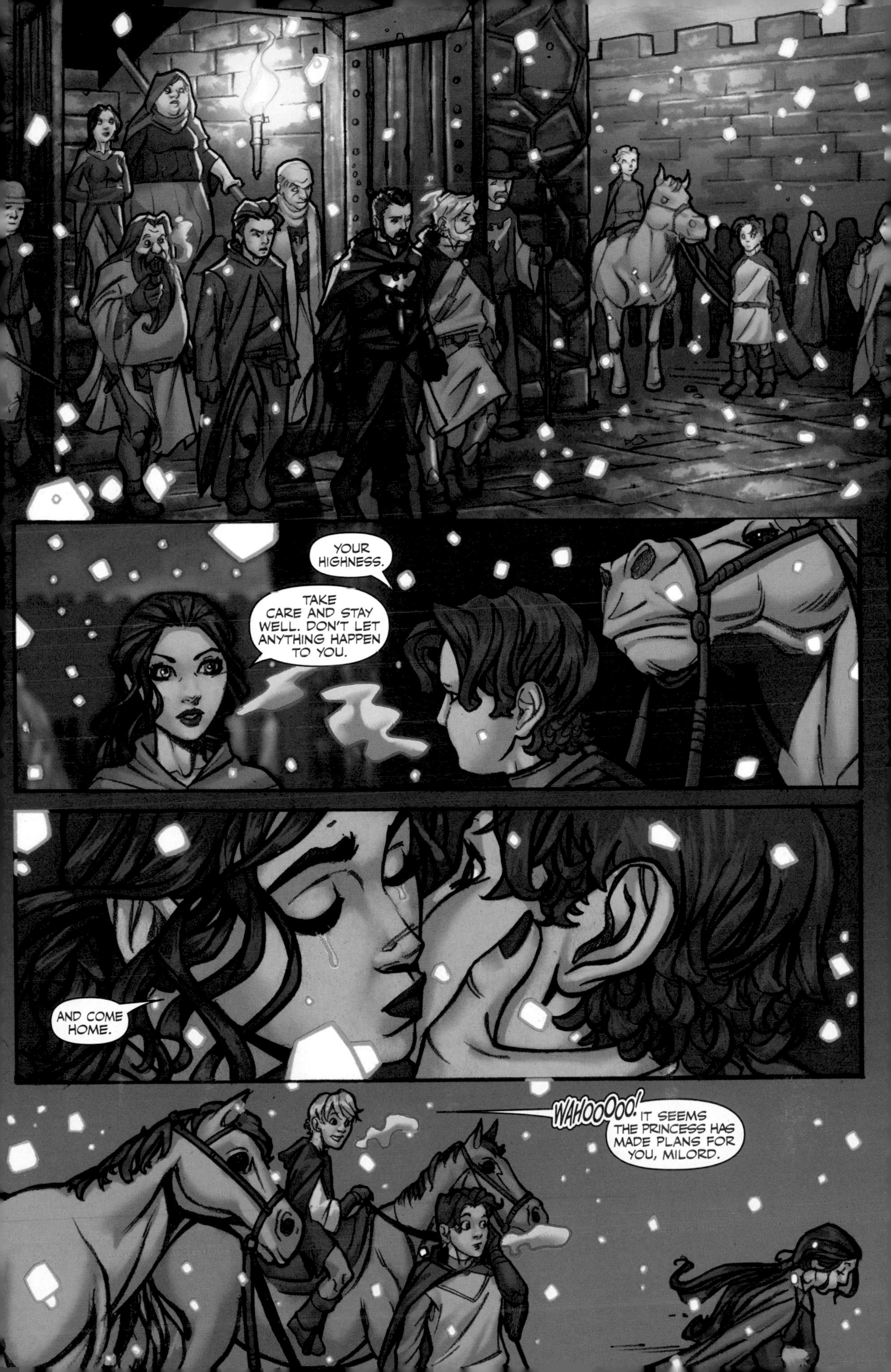
YOUR HIGHNESS.
TAKE CARE AND STAY WELL. DON'T LET ANYTHING HAPPEN TO YOU.
AND COME HOME.
WAHOOOOO!
IT SEEMS THE PRINCESS HAS MADE PLANS FOR YOU, MILORD.

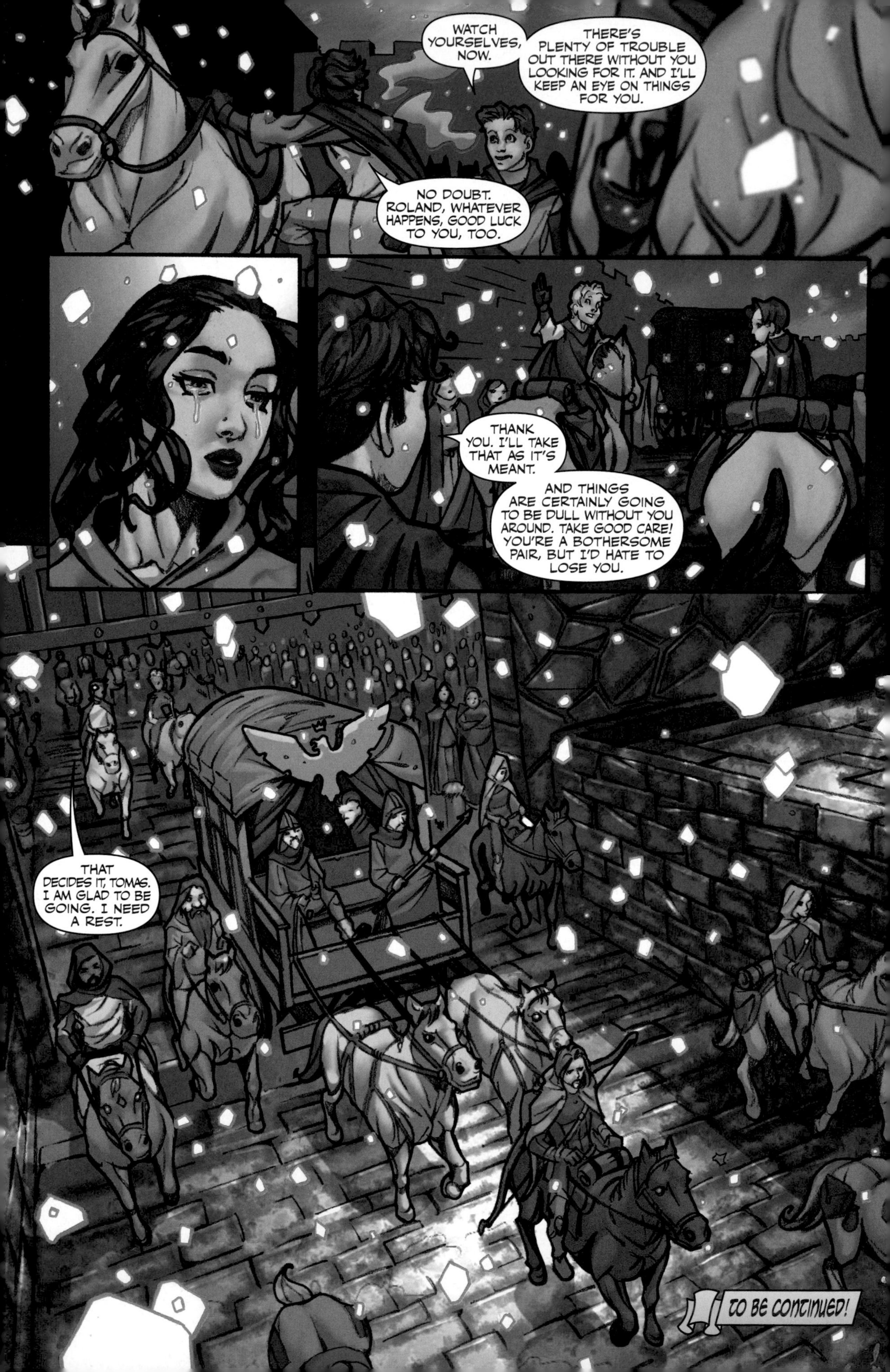
WATCH YOURSELVES, NOW.
THERE'S PLENTY OF TROUBLE OUT THERE WITHOUT YOU LOOKING FOR IT. AND I'LL KEEP AN EYE ON THINGS FOR YOU.
NO DOUBT. ROLAND, WHATEVER HAPPENS, GOOD LUCK TO YOU, TOO.
THANK YOU. I'LL TAKE THAT AS IT'S MEANT.
AND THINGS ARE CERTAINLY GOING TO BE DULL WITHOUT YOU AROUND. TAKE GOOD CARE! YOU'RE A BOTHERSOME PAIR, BUT I'D HATE TO LOSE YOU.
THAT DECIDES IT, TOMAS. I AM GLAD TO BE GOING. I NEED A REST.
TO BE CONTINUED!

THE RIFTWAR CONTINUES...

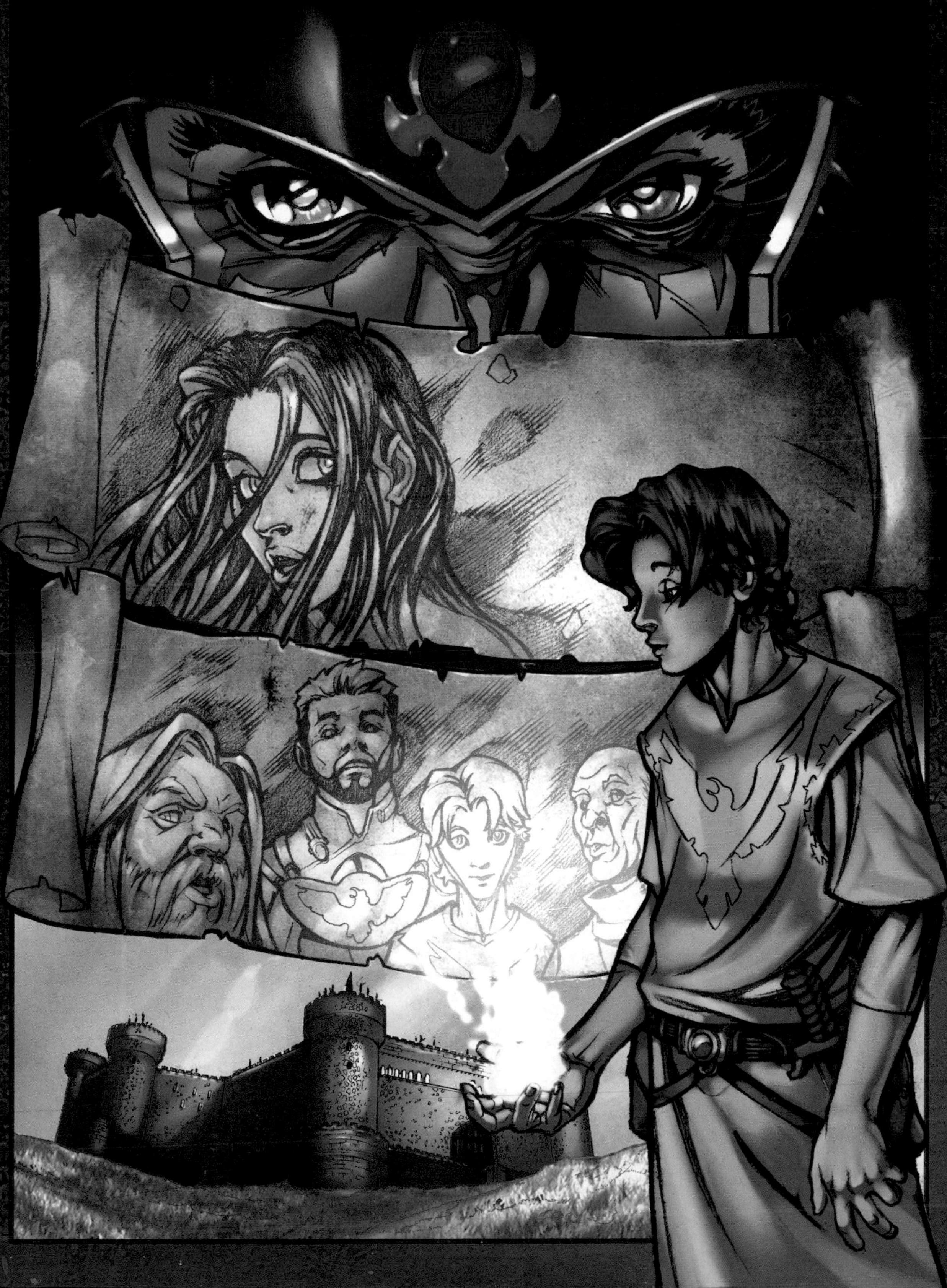

BONUS ARTWORK

UNUSED ART FROM ISSUE FOUR
AND ORIGINAL CHARACTER ART

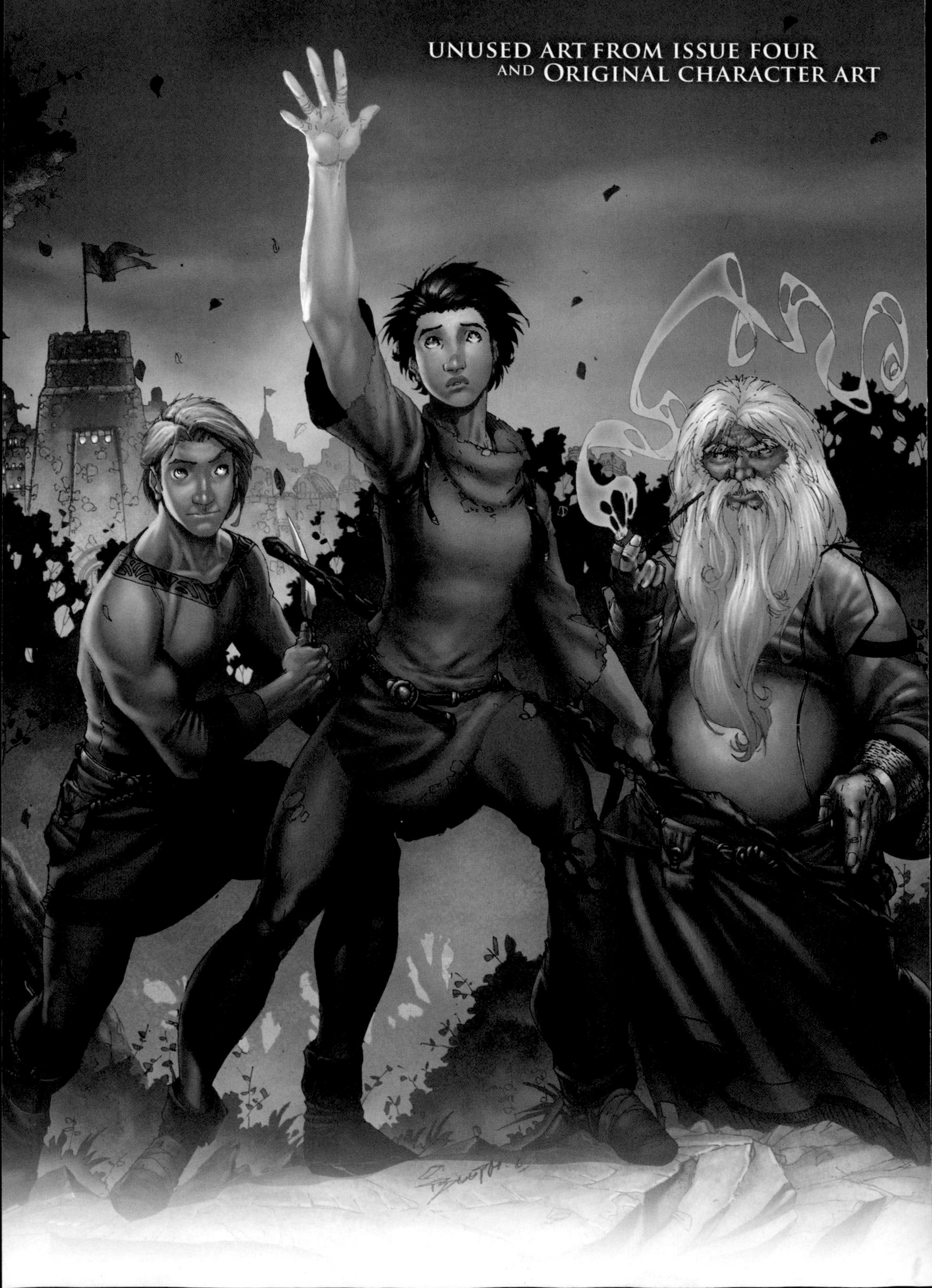

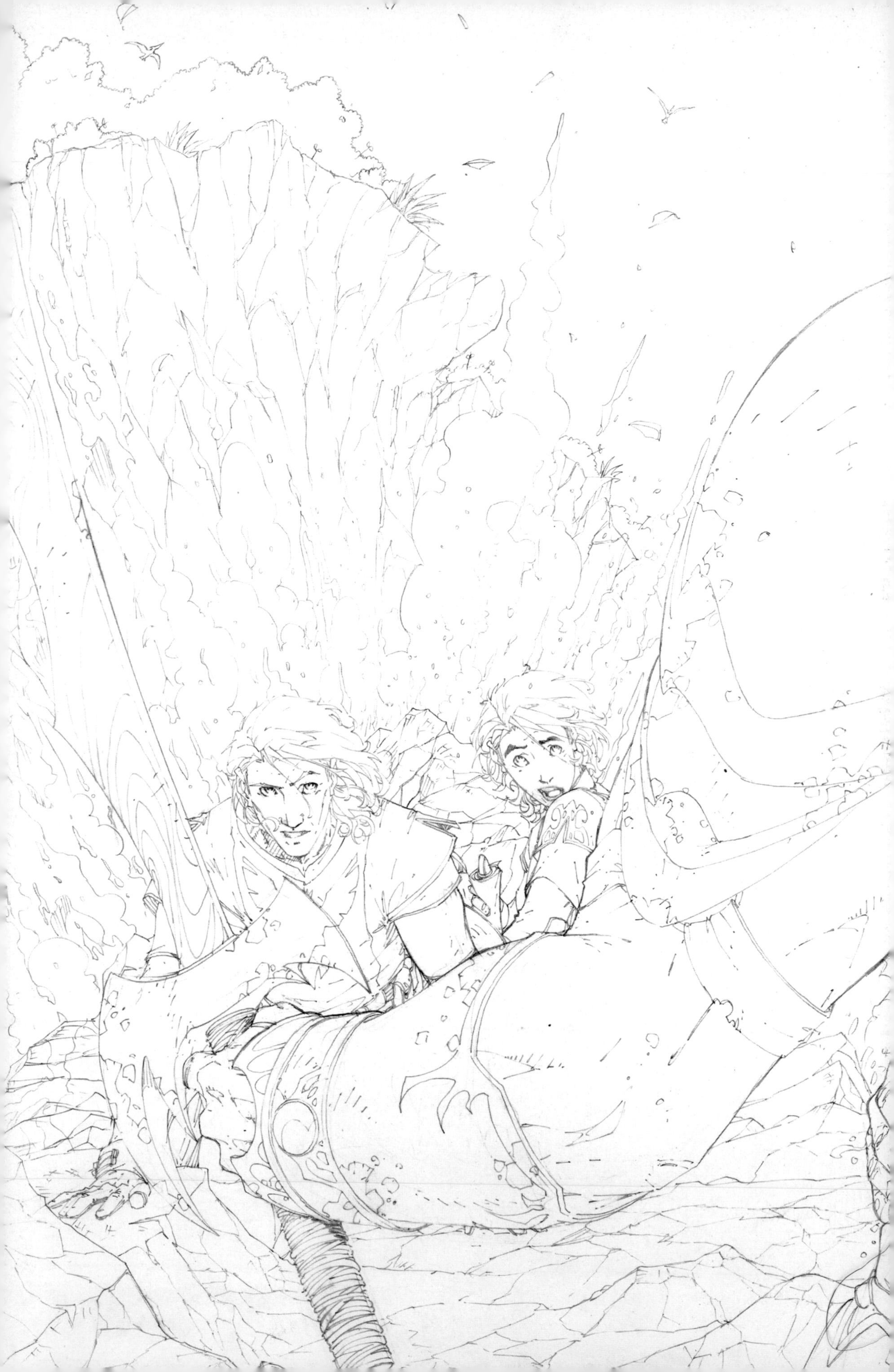

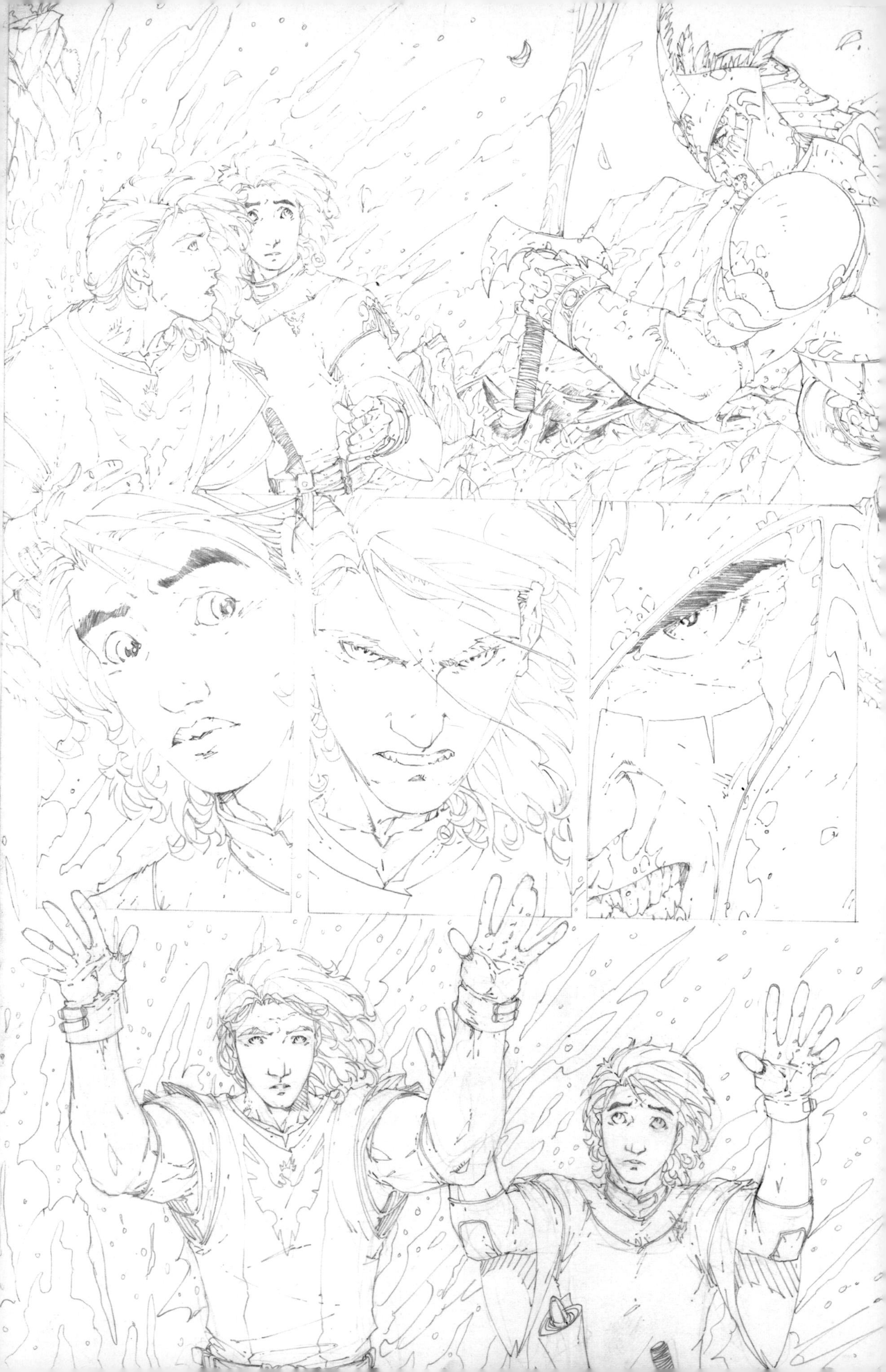

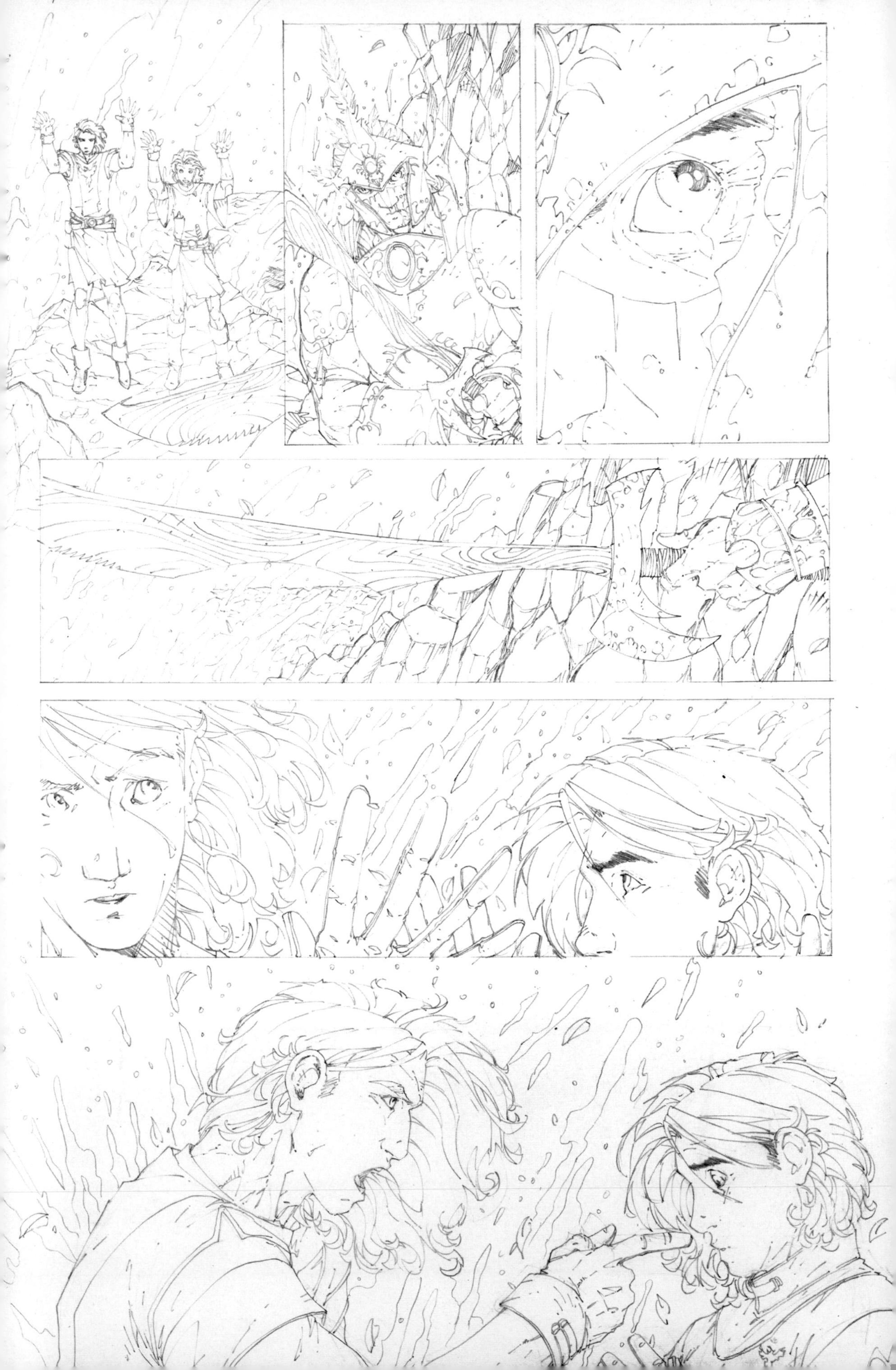

MAGICIAN APPRENTICE #4

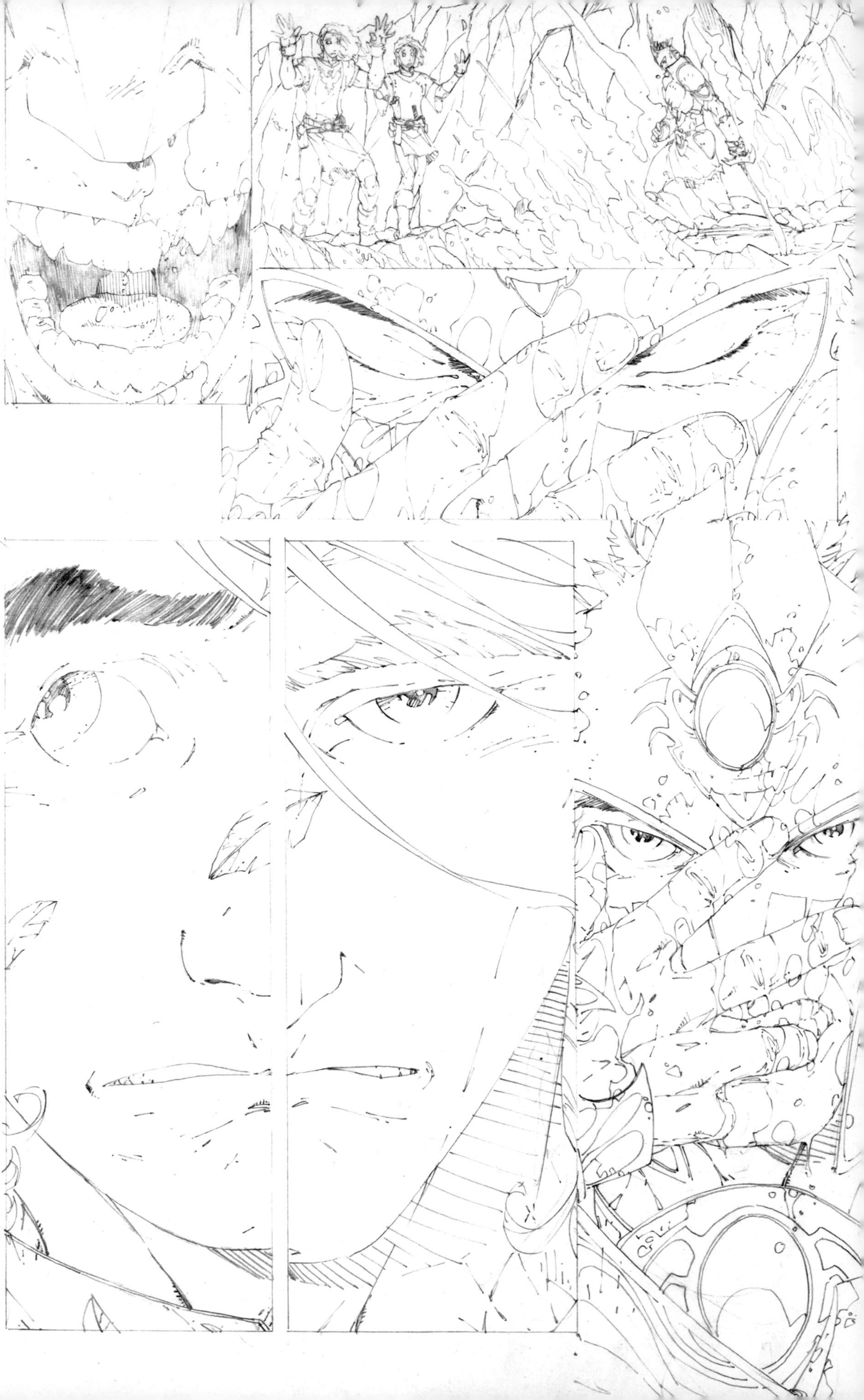

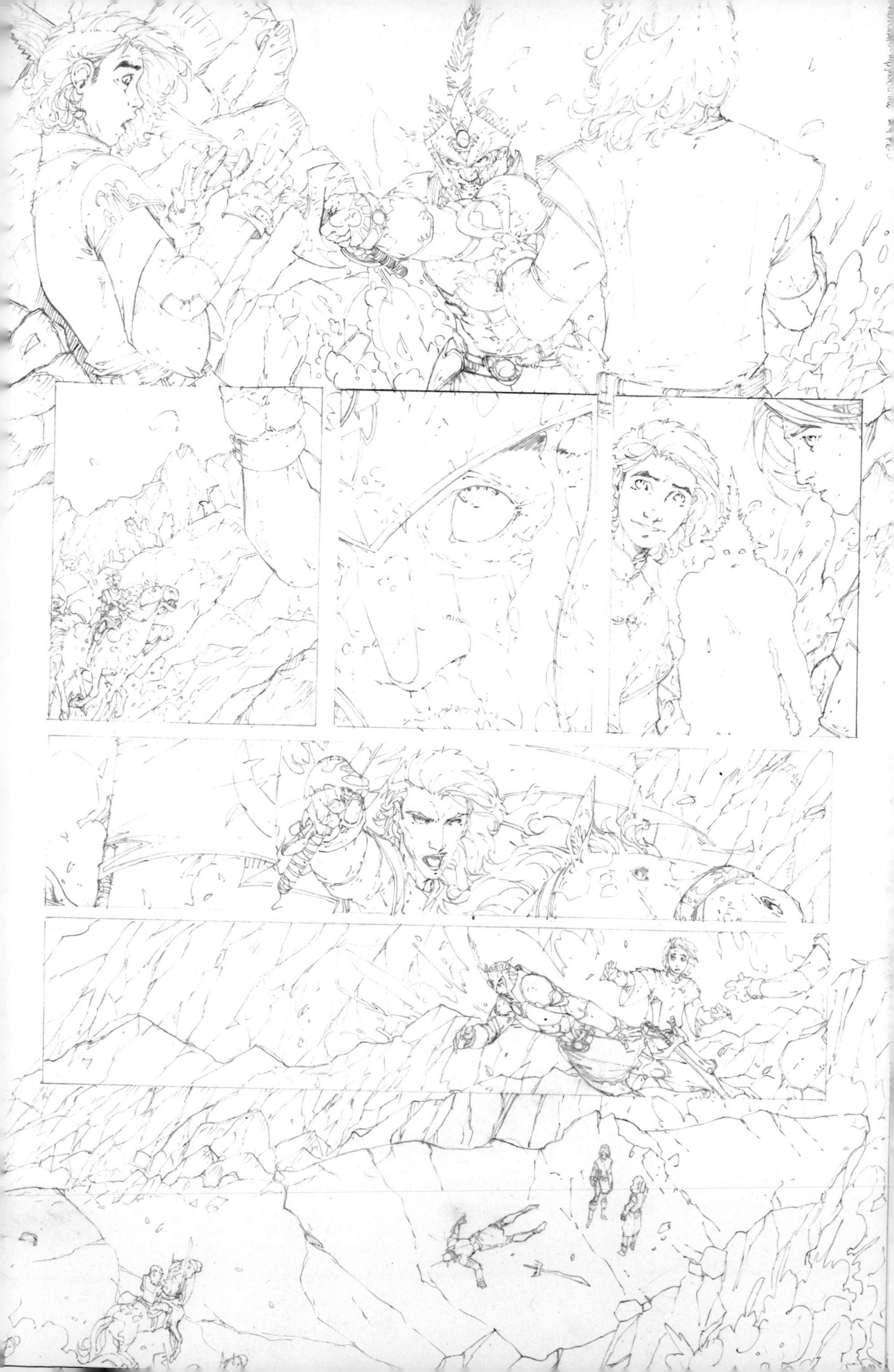

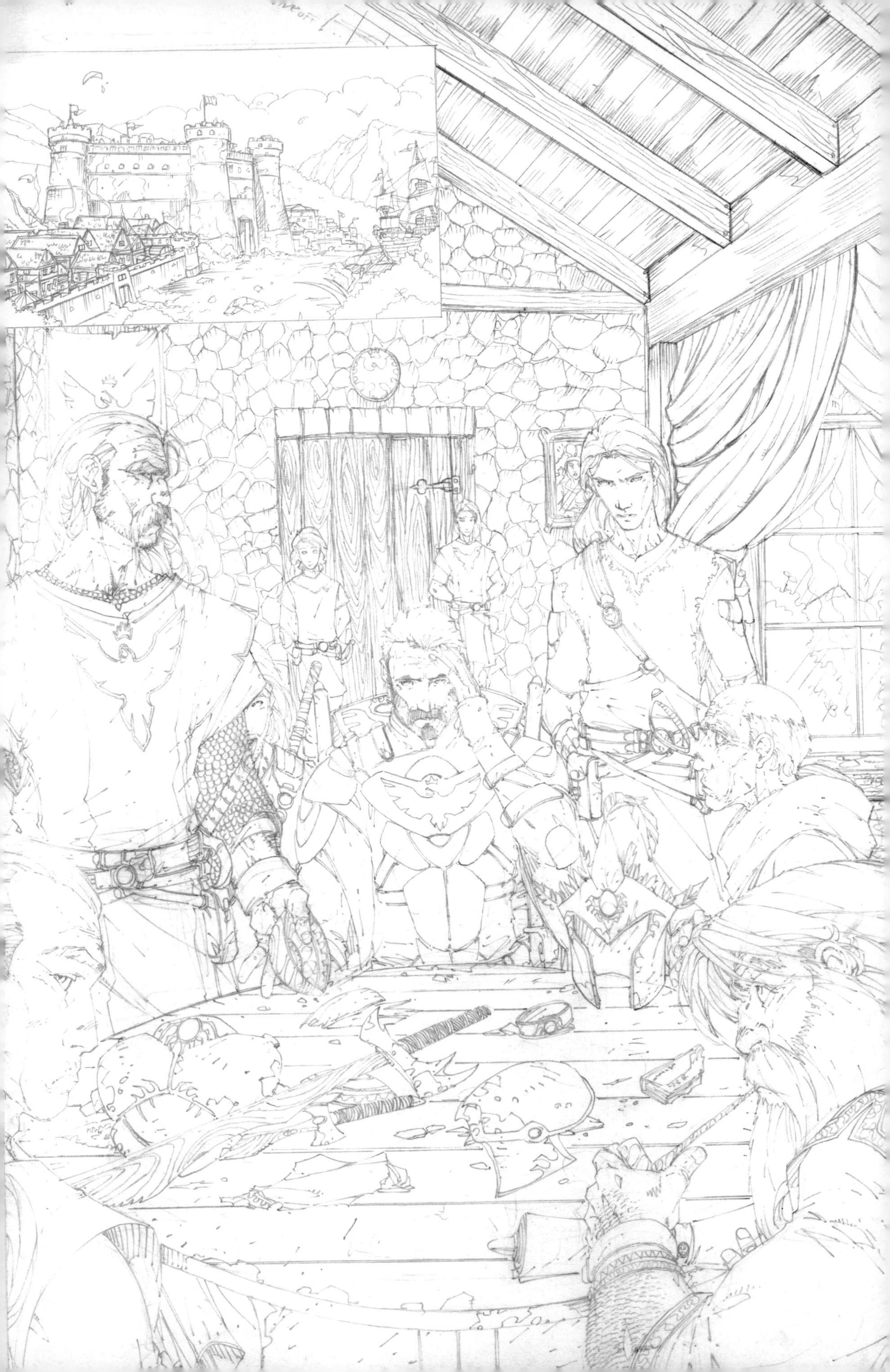

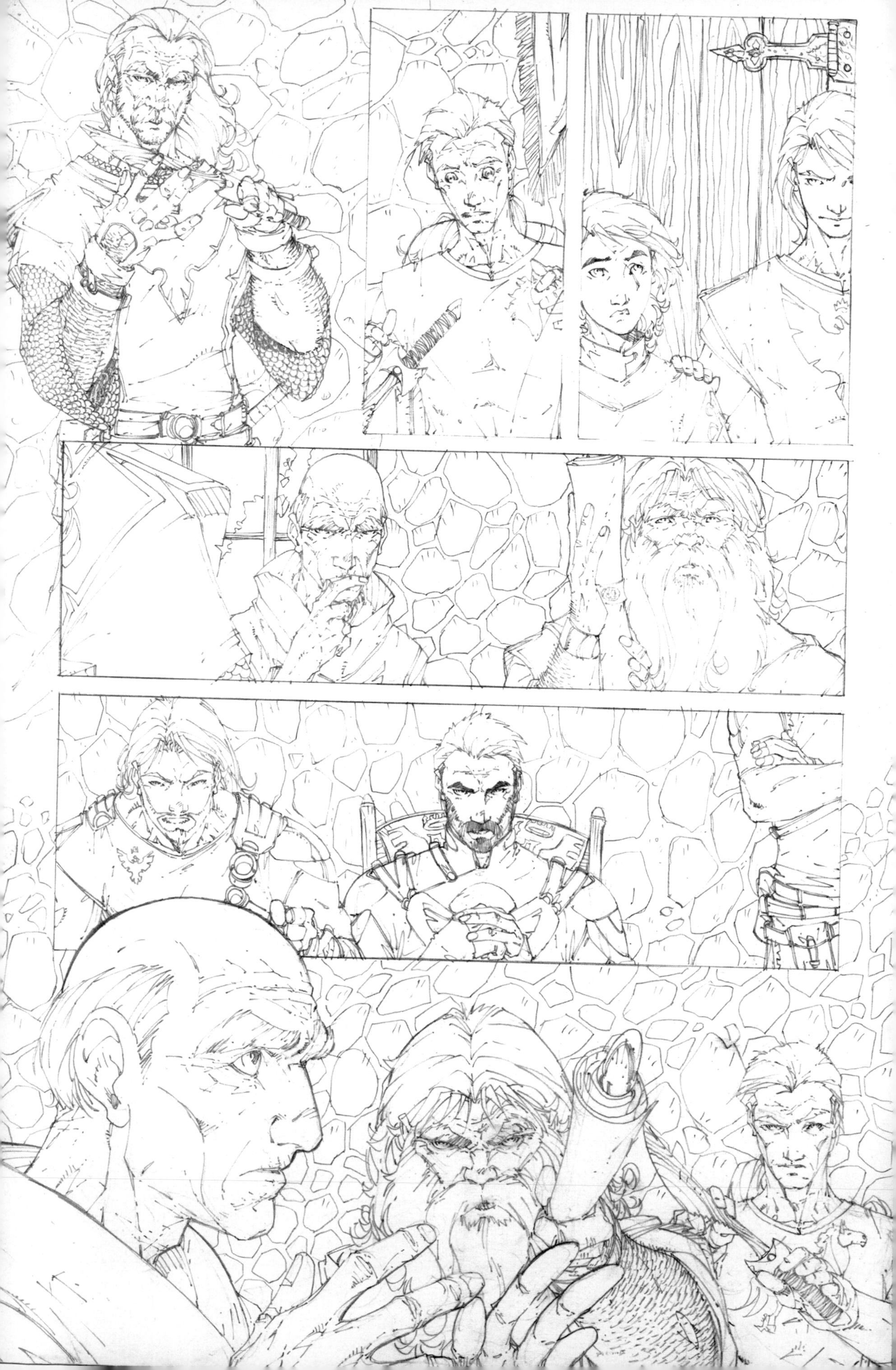

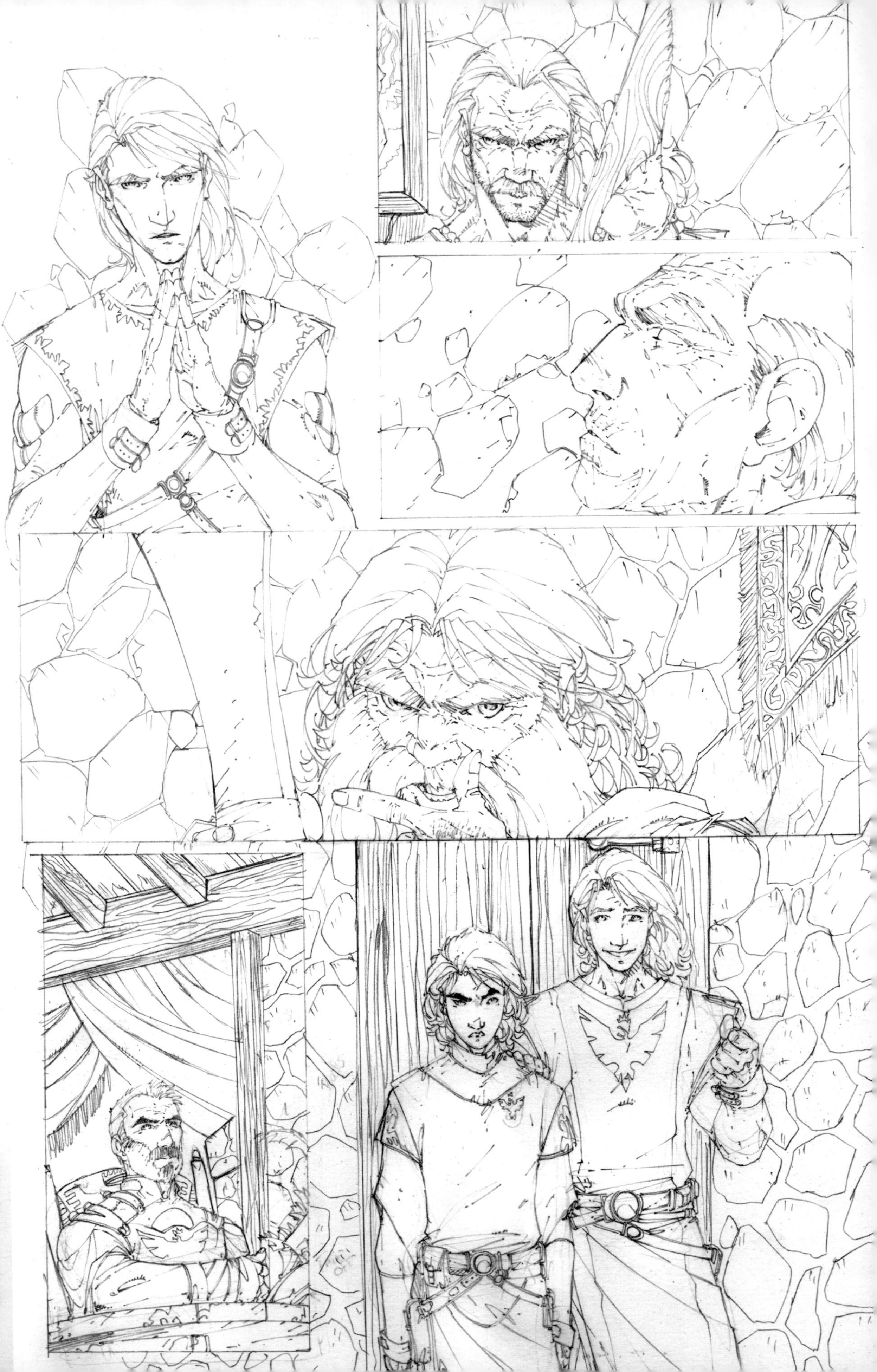

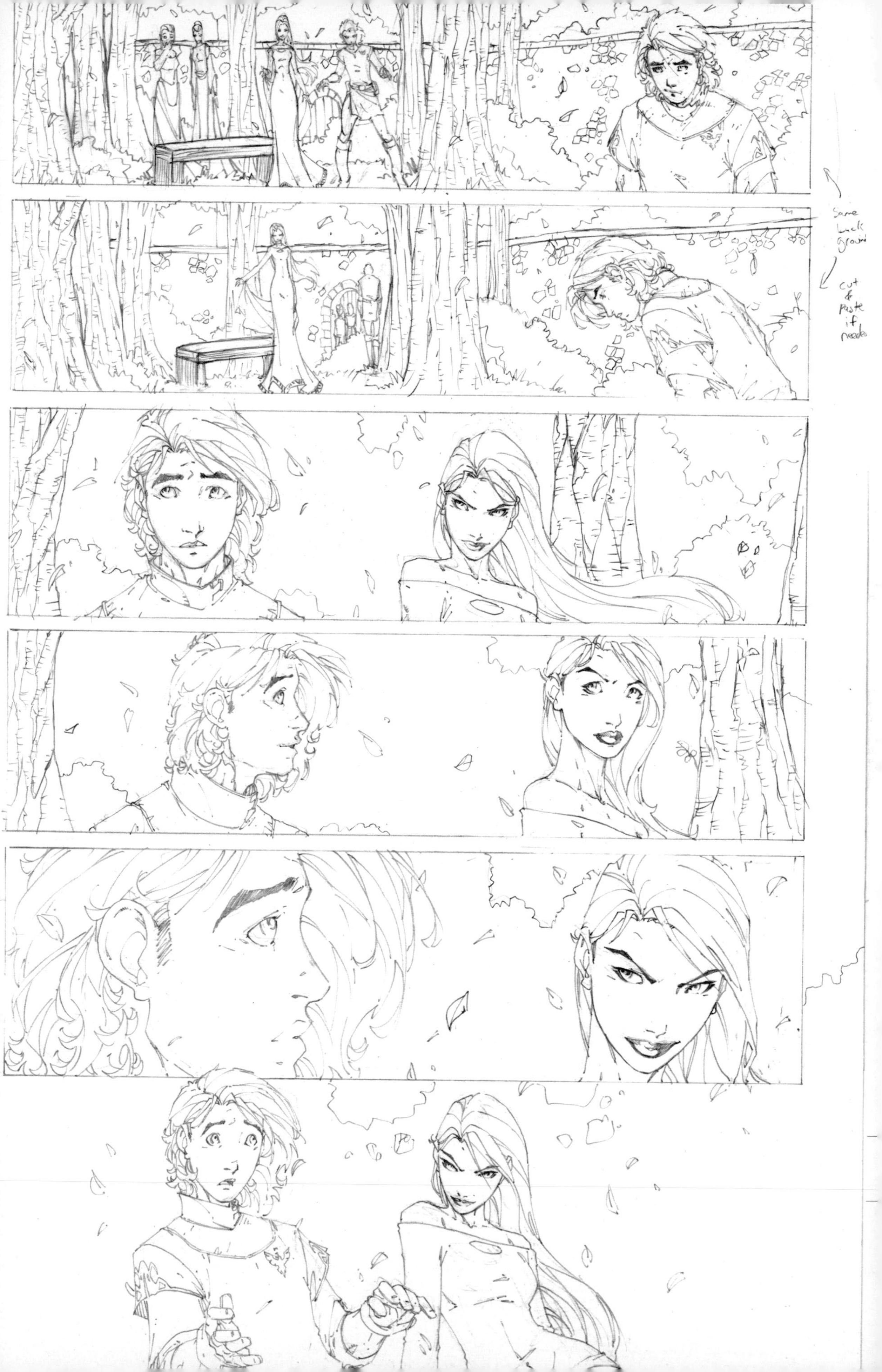
Same background
cut & paste if needed

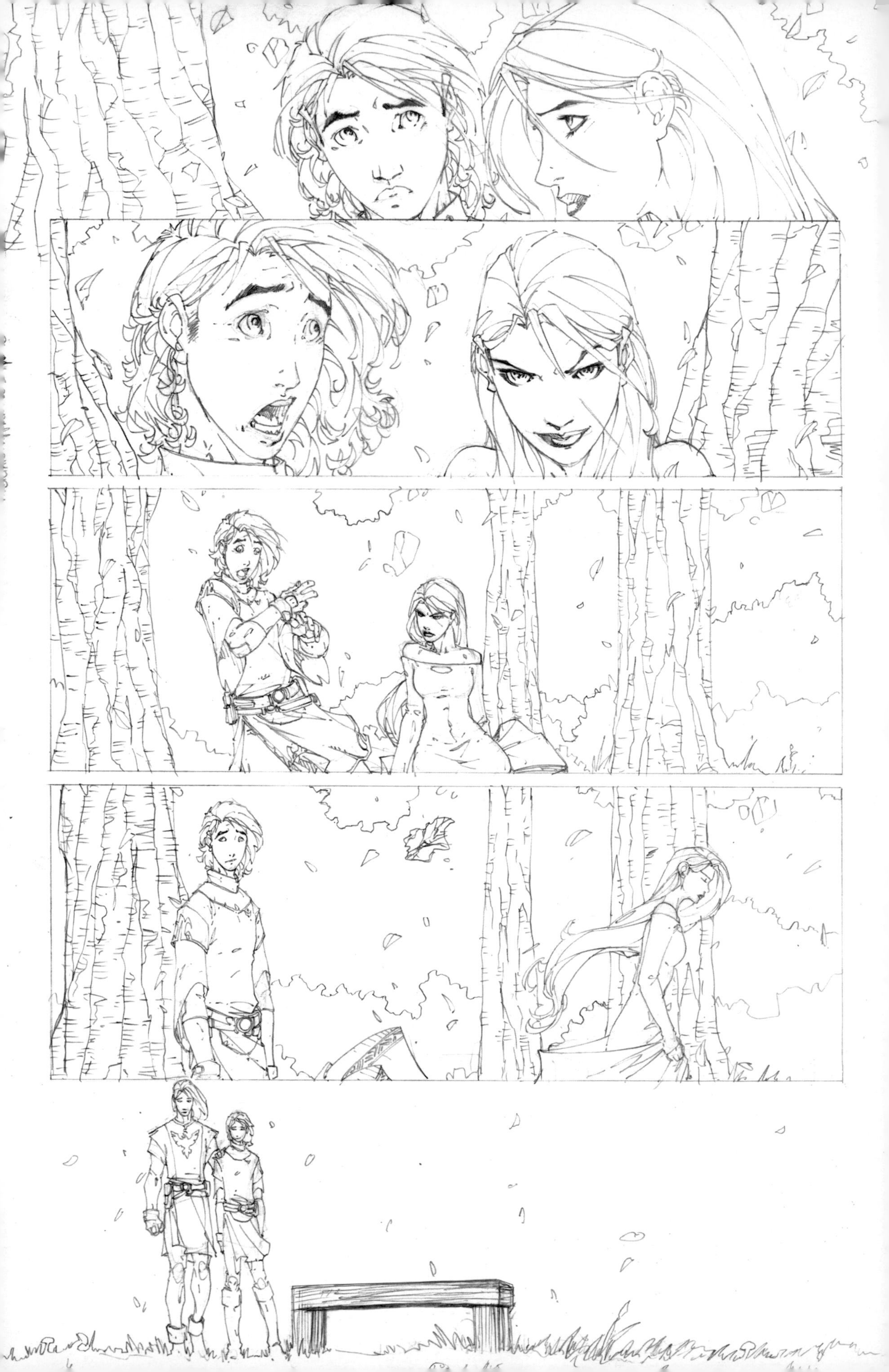

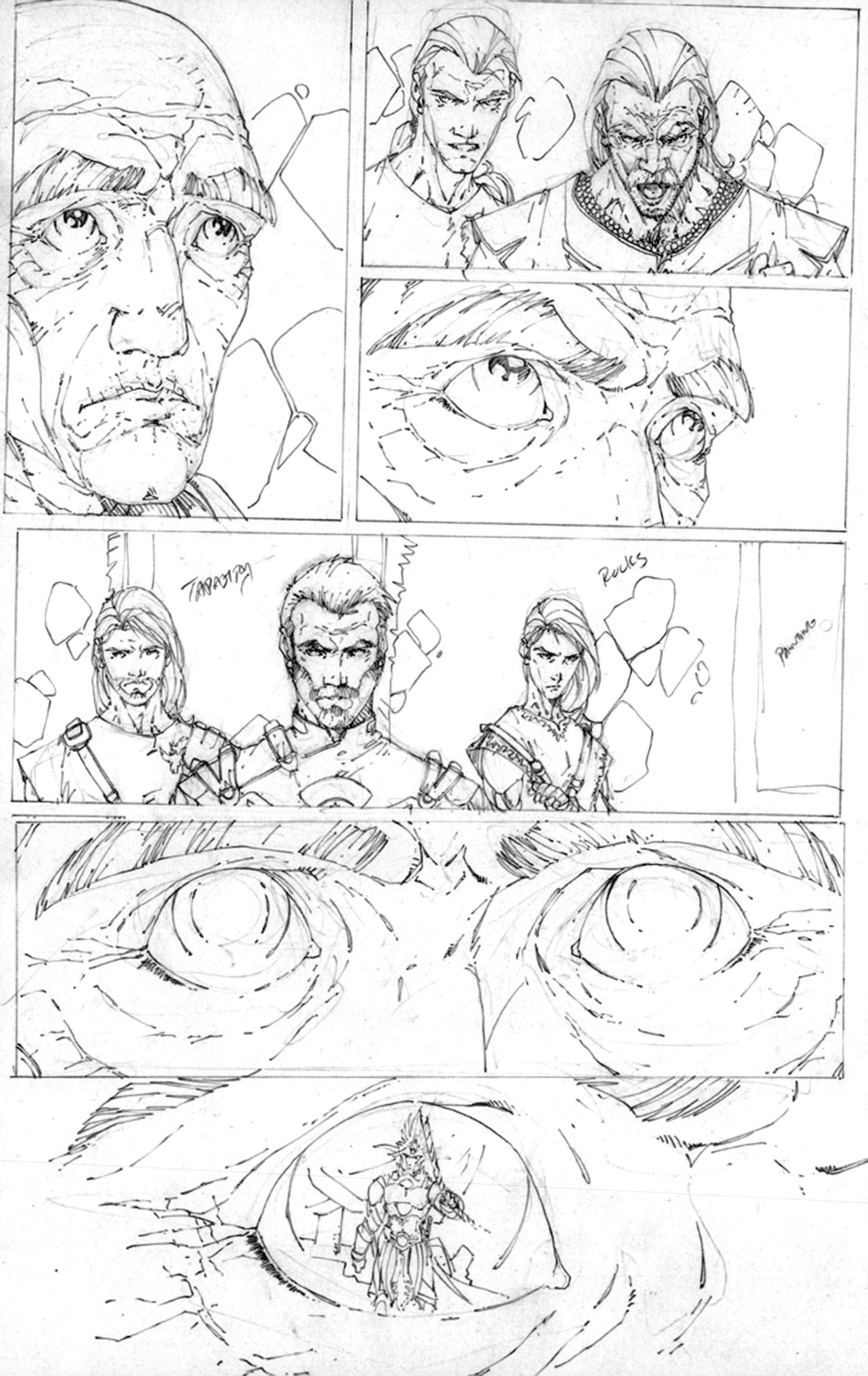
ROCKS

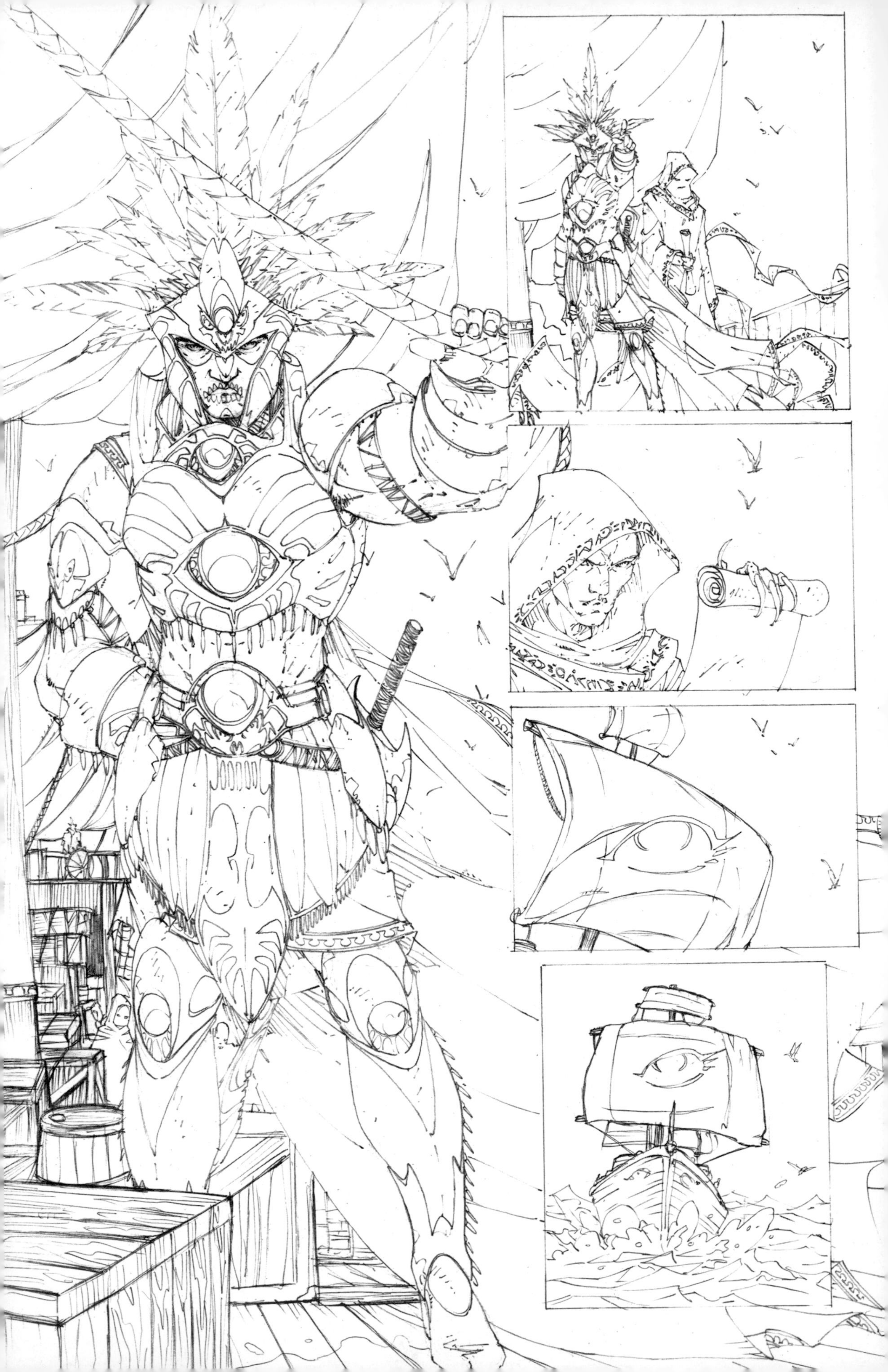

Duke Borric

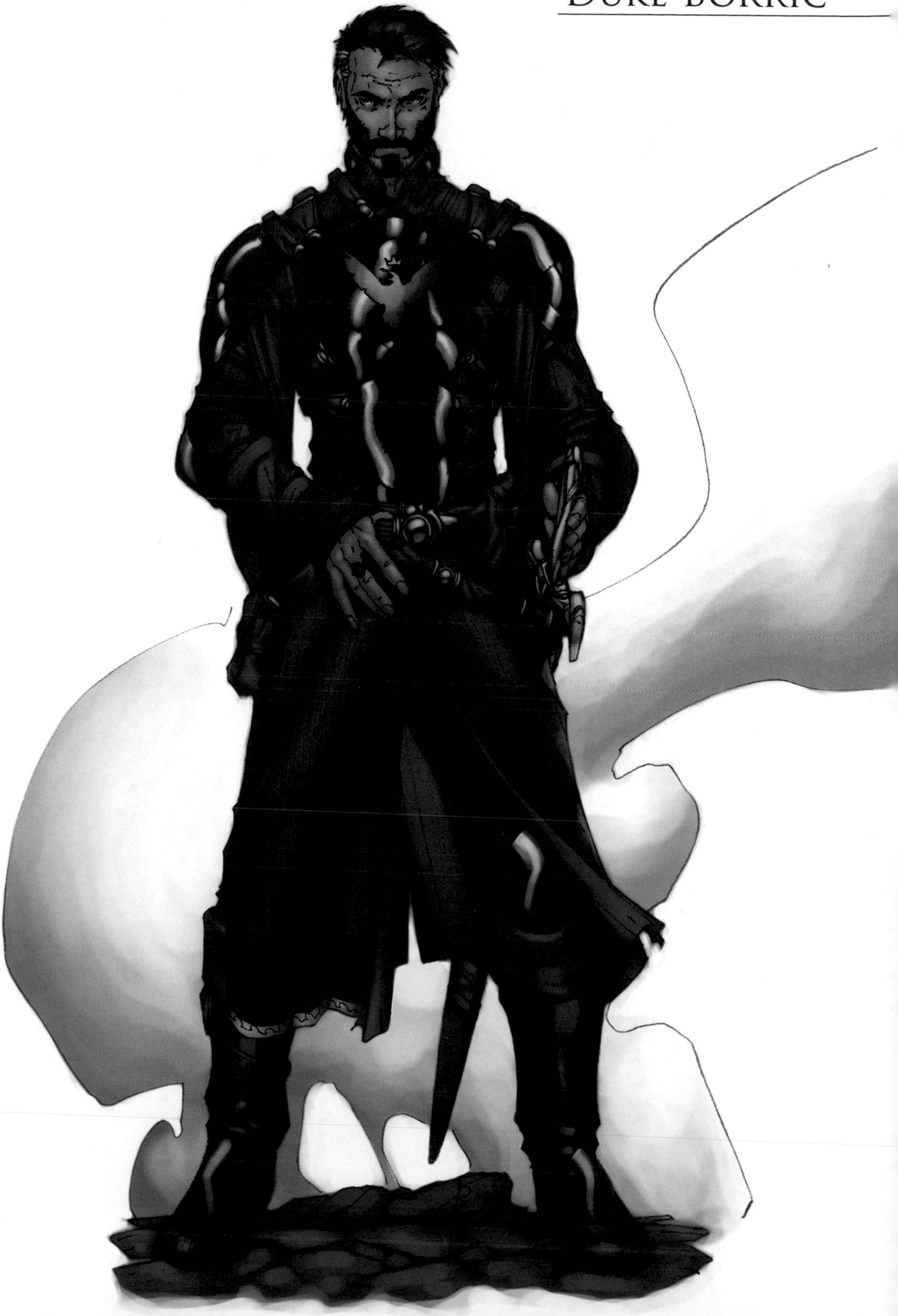

Master Kulgan

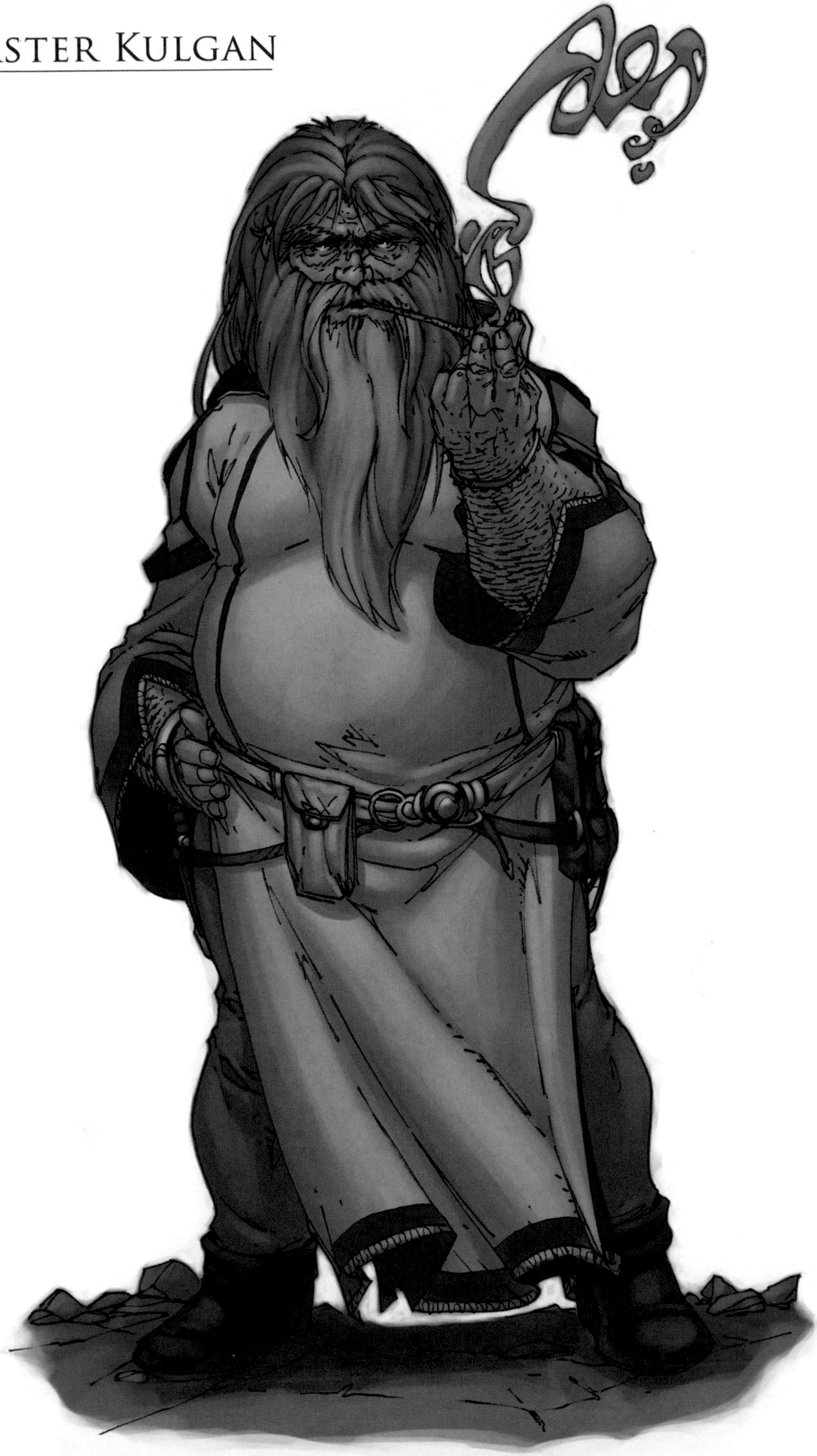

Princess Carline

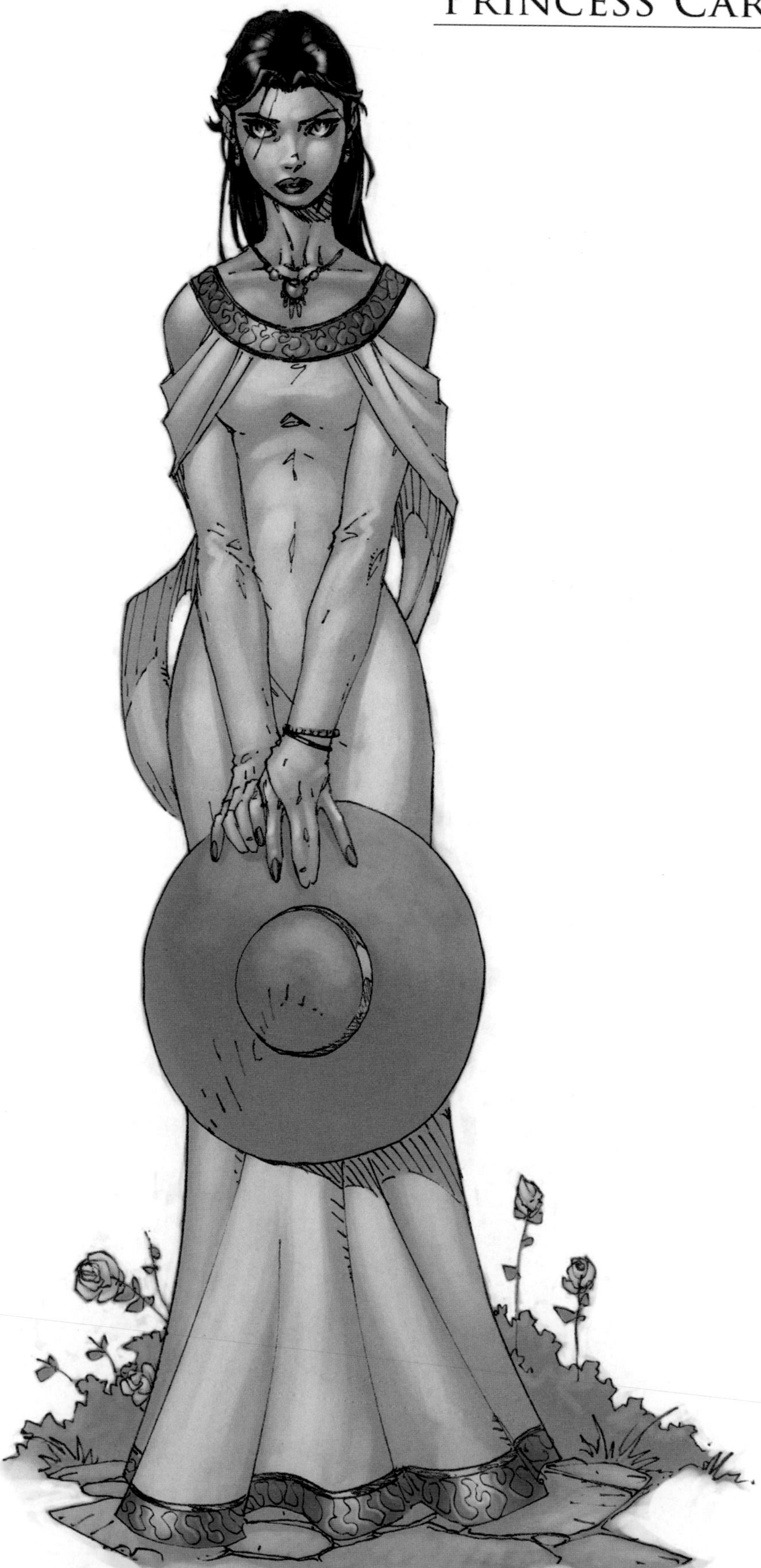

THOMAS

Pug

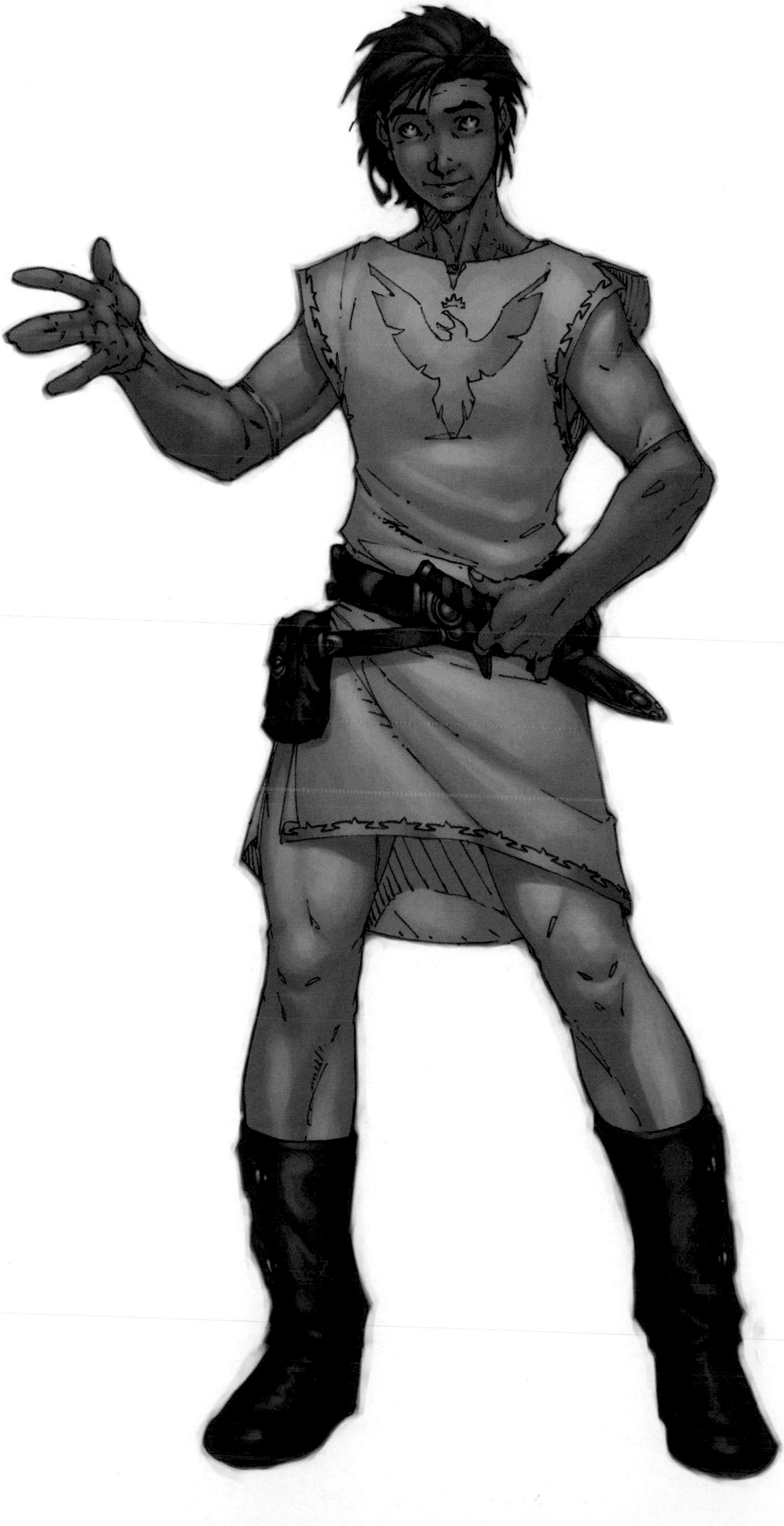

NORTHLANDS

The Great Northern Mountains

· Sar

Vale of Isban

Thunderhell
Steppes

Harlech · Plain of Isbandia

Moraelin

Stone
Mountain

Inclindel Gap

Armengar ·

Edder
Forest

Th

THE LAKE
OF THE
SKY

Yabon Hills
(Hadati Country)

Tyr-Sog ·

Elvandar

Yabon
Forest

Yabon

Caldara

LaMut ·

Loriel ·

Crydee ·

The
Green
Heart

The
Grey
Towers

· Zūn

Hawk's Hollow

Eggley ·

Dir

Walinor ·
Hūsh

Ylith

Calastius Mountains

Tannerus ·

THE GR

Carse ·
Jonril ·

Natal ·

Questor's
View ·

Sarth ·

Port
Natal ·

· Tulan

· Port
Natal

· Queg

THE FARCOAST

THE FREE CITIES

Bordon ·

Lan ·
Port

Margrave's
Port

THE
ENDLESS
SEA

SUNSET
ISLES

Palanque ·

SORCERER'S
ISLE

THE
KINGDOM
OF QUEG

Krondor ·

Port
Vykor ·

Do

Landr

· LiMeth

THE
BITTER SEA

Land's End ·

SEA OF
DREAMS

THE STRAITS OF
DARKNESS

Durbin ·

Shamala ·

VALE OF
DREAMS
(DISPUTED BORDER)

THE
SEA

Starde

Novindus

Elarial ·

· Ranom

Trollhome
Mountains

JAL-PUR
DESERT

The
Pillars
of the Stars

Caralyan ·

Rainshadow
Mnts.

THE EMP

· Nar

Eagles
Eyrie
Mnts.

Ipithi ·

DRAGON
SEA

· Draconi

Fará

· Taroom

MIDKEMIA
THE CONTINENT OF
TRIAGIA

0   100   200   300   400   500

Miles

The Official Atlas to the Worlds of Raymond E. Feist
(http://www.elvandar.com)

Map by Ralph M. Askren, DVM
Midkemia, Krondor, and all other place names, as well as the distinctive
features of this map are Trademarks of Raymond E. Feist, the Bittersea
Company, and Midkemia Press. Used by permission. Permission to
reproduce or retransmit expressly denied.

· Toowamba

· Sh

Toa

Injune ·

The
Watchmen

· Loranough

We
Gua

· Jandowae

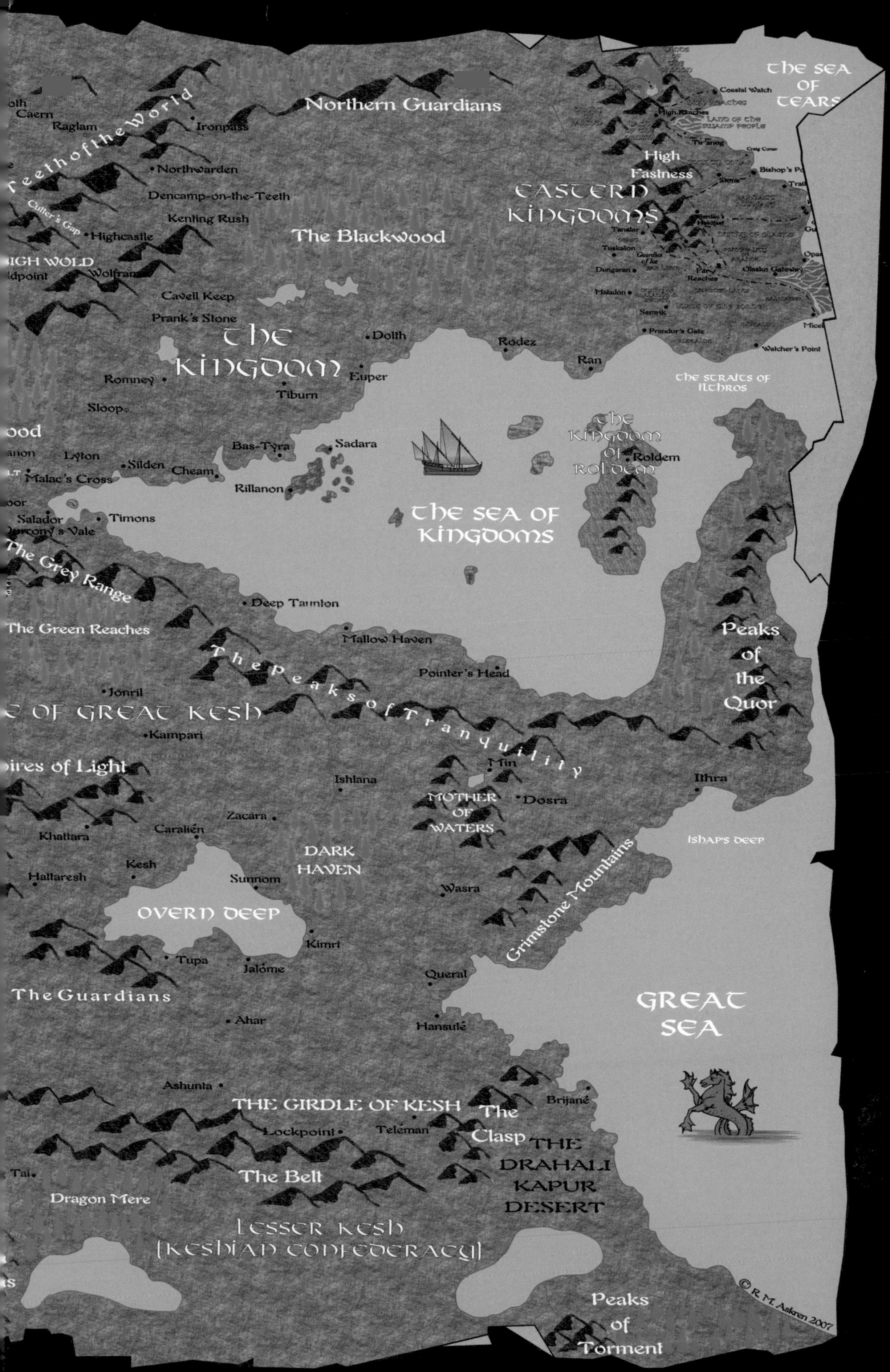
[redacted]
[redacted]
Northern Guardians
THE SEA OF TEARS
Coastal Watch
High Reaches
LAND OF THE SWAMP PEOPLE
Tir'anog
High Fastness
Bishop's Po
Caern
Raglam
Ironpass
Teeth of the World
Northwarden
Dencamp-on-the-Teeth
Cutter's Gap
Kenting Rush
Highcastle
The Blackwood
EASTERN KINGDOMS
IGH WOLD
ldpoint
Wolfram
Tanslar
Tuskalon
Dungaran
Far Reaches
Olasko Gateway
Maladon
Semrik
Prandur's Gate
Cavell Keep
Prank's Stone
THE KINGDOM
Dolth
Rodez
Ran
Watcher's Point
Romney
Euper
Tiburn
Sloop
THE STRAITS OF ELTHROS
ood
Lyton
Bas-Tyra
Sadara
THE KINGDOM OF ROLDEM
Roldem
Silden
Cheam
Malac's Cross
Rillanon
Salador
Timons
THE SEA OF KINGDOMS
The Grey Range
Deep Taunton
The Green Reaches
Mallow Haven
Peaks of the Quor
The peaks of Tranquility
Pointer's Head
Jonril
E OF GREAT KESH
Kampari
pires of Light
Ishlana
Min
Ithra
MOTHER OF WATERS
Dosra
Zacara
Khattara
Caralién
ISHAP'S DEEP
DARK HAVEN
Kesh
Hattaresh
Sunnom
Wasra
Grimstone Mountains
OVERN DEEP
Kimri
Tupa
Jalóme
Queral
The Guardians
GREAT SEA
Ahar
Hansulé
Ashunta
Brijané
THE GIRDLE OF KESH
The Clasp
Lockpoint
Teleman
THE DRAHALI KAPUR DESERT
Tai
The Belt
Dragon Mere
LESSER KESH
[KESHIAN CONFEDERACY]
© R. M. Askren 2007
Peaks of Torment

RAYMOND E. FEIST

MAGICIAN

APPRENTICE

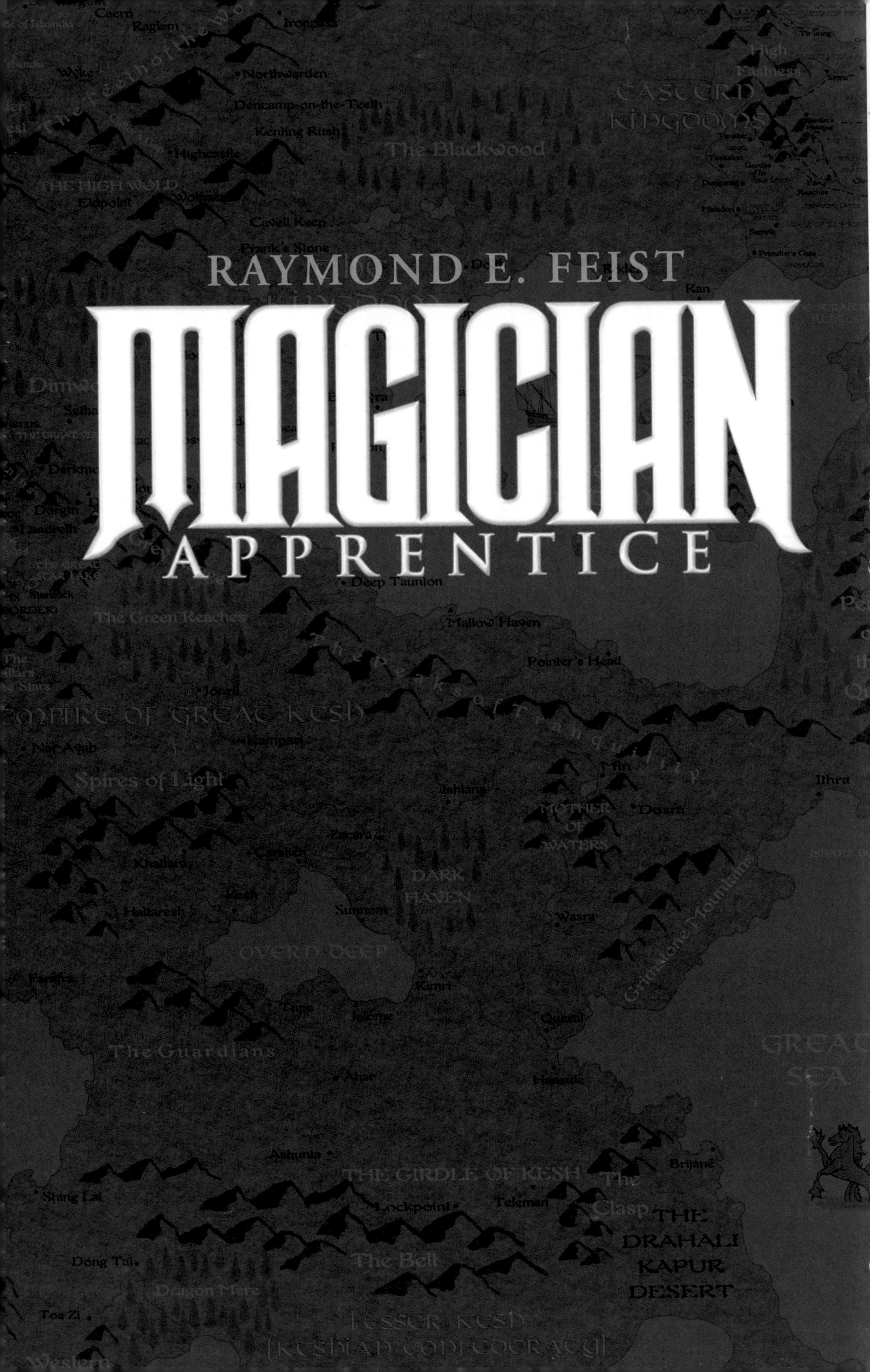
Caern
Raglam
Ironpass
Wyke
Northwarden
Dencamp-on-the-Teeth
Kenting Rush
The Blackwood
Highcastle
THE HIGH WOLD
Eldpoint
Cavell Keep
Frank's Stone
EASTERN KINGDOMS
High Fastness
Ran
Darkmoor
Dorgin
Landreth
Deep Taunton
The Green Reaches
Mallow Haven
Pointer's Head
Jonril
EMPIRE OF GREAT KESH
Nar Ayab
Spires of Light
Ishlana
Ithra
MOTHER OF WATERS
Dosra
Zacara
Khallara
DARK HAVEN
Kesh
Sunnom
Hallaresh
Wasra
OVERN DEEP
Grimstone Mountains
Kimri
The Guardians
Ahar
Hansule
GREAT SEA
Ashunta
THE GIRDLE OF KESH
Brijane
The Clasp
Shing Lai
Lockpoint
Teleman
THE DRAHALI KAPUR DESERT
Dong Tai
The Belt
Dragon Mere
Toa Zi
LESSER KESH
[KESHIAN CONFEDERACY]
Western